TOURNAMENT APPROACHES TO POLICY REFORM

TOURNAMENT APPROACHES TO POLICY REFORM

Making Development Assistance More Effective

Clifford F. Zinnes

BROOKINGS INSTITUTION PRESS
Washington, D.C.

Library of Congress Cataloging-in-Publication data

Zinnes, Clifford F.
  Tournament approaches to policy reform : making development assistance more effective /
Clifford F. Zinnes.
       p.   cm.
  Includes bibliographical references and index.
  Summary: "Assesses a new 'tournament' approach promising improvement on the performance of conventional foreign aid methods, where beneficiary groups compete to achieve
the best implementation of a particular project. Evaluates performances, sustainability, time
frames, and costs of recent applications. Discusses opportunities for improving and scaling
up the application of tournament-based projects"—Provided by publisher.
  ISBN 978-0-8157-9719-7 (pbk. : alk. paper)
  1. Economic assistance, American. 2. Technical assistance, American. 3. Letting of
contracts—United States. 4. Requests for proposals (Public contracts)—United States.
I. Title.
  HC60.Z535 2009
  338.91'73—dc22   2009009161

9 8 7 6 5 4 3 2 1

The paper used in this publication meets minimum requirements of the
American National Standard for Information Sciences—Permanence of Paper
for Printed Library Materials: ANSI Z39.48-1992.

Typeset in Adobe Garamond

Composition by Circle Graphics
Columbia, Maryland

Printed by Versa Press
East Peoria, Illinois

To my mother

Harriet

Whose books have both inspired me and set a high bar

And to my wife

Anca

Whose support on many levels has been essential

Contents

List of Figures

List of Tables

Foreword

We at Brookings regard it as a strategic priority for the institution to contribute to the search for more ambitious and effective ways of defeating the scourge of global poverty. In spite of admonitions for the rich countries to increase their aid contributions to 1 percent of GDP, however, there has been a secular decline (HIV applications aside) of donor budgets in real terms until recently. At the same time, there has been a growing frustration with the slow pace of discernable improvement in well-being in many of the least-developed countries. This has been coupled with a growing realization that poverty and such socioeconomic ills as youth unemployment are contributing to global terrorism. Parallel impatience has emerged within the developing countries themselves, leading to vocal irritation with national and local governments; blaming "globalization" is no longer acceptable.

These factors have led to an increasing demand, internationally, for aid projects to be more cost-effective and, domestically, for governments to be more responsive to their citizens. Monitoring and evaluation are being resurrected by sponsors in a more rigorous manner, with even some randomized trials being used. There has been an accelerated movement toward decentralization and devolution, some incorporating performance-based revenue transfers. Hence the creation in 2006 of our Global Economy and Development program and the Wolfensohn Center for Development, established through the generosity of our trustee, James D. Wolfensohn, the former president of the World Bank and chairman of Wolfensohn and Company. The Wolfensohn Center has already staked out high ground as a source of high-quality, high-impact, independent research on the key questions facing governments, international institutions, the private sector, and nongovernmental organizations in their common task of making globalization a more equitable phenomenon. One of the many ways in which the Center achieves its impact is through books like this one.

Among the key insights upon which *Tournament Approaches to Policy Reform* rests is that sponsor and domestic government NIE interventions, be they reform, capacity building, or investment, can only succeed and be sustainable if perceived as legitimate by stakeholders and if executed in a way consistent with local formal and *informal* institutions, such as culture and norms. Moreover, ensuring that these conditions are met requires beneficiary cooperation and participation in all aspects of the process. Building on these insights leads to the book's main thesis, namely, that it should be possible to design interventions that use strategic incentives to encourage constituent interests within each beneficiary group to form a team to work cooperatively to achieve the intervention's objectives. Such designs might actually be able to generate competition among teams, causing them to exert a higher level of effort than under a standard bilateral project agreement.

This thesis is advanced—skillfully and rigorously, and persuasively—in the context of a critique of past and current policies. As a timely contribution to this search for more effective interventions, this book assesses the effectiveness of "interjurisdictional competition" (IJC) as an incentive mechanism upon which to base government and sponsor initiatives to address socioeconomic development. Toward this end, Clifford Zinnes, senior fellow at the IRIS Center, Department of Economics, and affiliate faculty member at the Maryland School of Public Policy, both at the University of Maryland, evaluates numerous government, nongovernment, and donor applications to date. He asks how successful and sustainable the outcomes of past IJC-related applications have been across a variety of sectors, issues, and circumstances, and, therefore, whether the approach merits replication and scaling up—and under what initial conditions. He also considers the feasibility and economic efficiency of IJC as a delivery vehicle for development assistance in projects and policy reforms.

The analytic lens of the book is the "new" institutional economics (NIE). From that perspective, Zinnes interprets the incentive mechanism upon which the initiator—be it a donor, level of government, or even civil society development organization—bases the project intervention as a "game" and therefore something that explicitly or implicitly has players, rules, strategies, beliefs, and payoffs. Examples of the players are jurisdictions (such as provincial, municipal, or village local governments) and individual organizations (such as schools, hospitals, and even water companies). This NIE perspective forces the project designer to think in terms of which party has what information critical to project success, the transaction costs of collective action within the player qua team, misalignments between beneficiaries and those who bear decisionmaking risk, as well as other principal-agent problems. As corollaries Zinnes argues that NIE implies an important role, first, for pre- and postintervention strategic communication (for example, education of the target population) and participatory project design, since the need for collective action in an IJC requires that there be an initial indigenous desire for change, and, second, for the sponsor qua referee and focal point.

While he identifies several variations of incentive mechanisms used by IJCs, Zinnes argues these can be classified into just four types. In *simple certification* the sponsor "grades" players against a preestablished performance benchmark. The results of the certification process may, therefore, impact player reputation—for example, being a good place to do business, which might attract investors—or lead the player's constituency to demand changes or strengthen its support of the player. *Pecuniary certification* is the same as simple certification, and once certified, in addition to the two aforementioned results, the player is guaranteed a tangible reward, such as access to financing or technical assistance. In *pure tournaments*, while all eligible players may compete, only those with the N best performances (where N is announced in advance) win the rewards—the winning score is thus not known at the start. In a *mixed tournament*, a tournament is used to allocate rewards (for example, investment financing) and pecuniary certification is used to encourage weaker or less confident players to participate in the tournament. It does this by offering a "consolation prize" to those whose performance was inadequate to win but exceeded some minimum preset threshold. Zinnes points out that tournaments are not just certification with a continuum of "bars." Winning a tournament depends on a player's performance *relative to* others, whereas, in certification, actions of others are irrelevant. Zinnes finds that a surprising number of existing projects utilize some form of certification mechanism; tournament applications are much rarer.

The pages that follow explore various theoretical aspects of the four types of IJCs in a way that also reveals their distinguishing characteristics and how they compare to the conventional "contract" approach of aid agencies. Zinnes has developed an analytical framework marked by subtlety and breadth. In doing so, he disentangles the differences among incentive approaches. For example, of particular importance for project success is whether the project design rewards ex-ante or ex-post project performance and, independently, whether the evaluation of project performance is input or output based.

From this theoretical foundation and using a common case study framework he also develops, Zinnes then devotes a major part of the book to describing and assessing in some detail a dozen projects in Africa, Asia, Eastern Europe, and Latin America supported by the Millennium Challenge Corporation, the World

Bank, USAID, the government of Indonesia, UNIDO, and the Ford Foundation, as well as a large number of other applications in less detail. The last third of the book then synthesizes the extensive set of facts and observations developed in the case studies by identifying tentative lessons learned on how each type of IJC affects project effectiveness (including sustainability), makes idiosyncratic demands on a country's initial conditions, and contains prospects and limitations for scaling up. Zinnes calls these lessons learned "tentative" because the challenges he faced in collecting unbiased data for their analysis—plus the small sample size amassed due to tournament approaches being a recent phenomenon—limited the scope for rigorous statistical analysis. Still, the richness of his tentative findings should encourage others to pin them down more precisely. Of particular interest is that no single incentive mechanism appears to dominate the others. The choice of the most effective mechanism appears to depend on initial conditions, the number of recipients, and sponsor objectives.

Zinnes identifies some rules of thumb regarding the choice of project incentive design mechanisms. The *conventional approach* (standard bilateral contract) may be best where there are one or few recipients, where recipients require substantial technical or financial help, where objectives require limited idiosyncratic local information, and where rigorous evaluation is not desired. A *certification-type approach* may be best where adequate performance is more important than achieving highest feasible performance, where sponsors have a clear idea of what feasible performance levels are, where there are potentially many recipient-players, and, in the case of pecuniary rewards, where sponsors have a flexible budget or clear idea of the number of likely certifications. Finally, *tournament-type approaches* come into their own when a scarce resource needs to be allocated to the best performers, systemic exogenous shocks are a concern, there are potentially many recipient-players, and the donor has a poor idea of what level of performance is achievable.

Concerning the effectiveness of *certification* approaches, Zinnes finds that projects that were able to build on strong social or cultural norms within the target region and that were successful in communicating the meaning of the certification were more successful than those that weren't successfully communicating, even if the project itself offered no specific pecuniary rewards. On the other hand, projects that were not able to enforce strict quality control on their certification were less successful than those that were. Likewise, poor dissemination of the certification scores weakened their incentive effects, contributing further to lost project impacts. Instituting multilevel certifications was seen to be more economically efficient, where feasible, than having a single certification level since it increased participation.

Concerning the effectiveness of *tournament* approaches, Zinnes argues that projects that offered salient rewards and adequate technical assistance during the competition performed better than those that did not. IJC projects whose programs maintained the quality of their reputation, which winning conferred, were able to have both a demonstration effect as well as a participation effect. Moreover, in general, incentive-compatible mechanisms as a class required less sponsor monitoring than conventional projects. On the other hand, a tournament where competition was based on indicators of *past* performance had a much weaker incentive effect than those based on performance *during* the competition. Likewise, where rewards were insufficiently specific, their incentive impact was not commensurate with their implementation costs (for example, USAID's R4).

Finally, Zinnes examines whether IJCs take more time to design and to implement. He finds the answer is not always clear cut, since conventional, bilateral donor negotiation is also time consuming and typically serves just one site, while IJCs serve many and typically impose a credible deadline for project results.

Zinnes also provocatively makes the case for a number of advantages to IJCs, which he challenges future practice and scholarship to examine further. First, he believes that tournament applications have the potential to increase the effectiveness of policy initiatives and donor assistance by leveraging available funds. He reasons that the lure of fewer but larger rewards from a fixed budget should stimulate reform efforts across a larger number of players, compared to the standard practice where the same budget would be divided in advance across just a few players. Second, he finds evidence that IJCs with rewards based on ex-post performance appear to avoid adverse selection and other perverse incentives often caused by more conventional delivery vehicles, since only successful outcomes count toward rewards; thus recipients only interested in the funds but not reforms are discouraged from playing. Third, he also finds evidence that IJC-based projects, given they involve "teamwork" within the jurisdiction to win, are likely to generate *more* cooperation and collective action than one based on a noncompetitive approach. Moreover, he speculates that once disparate interests within a community observe the power of cooperation, they will learn the merits of collective action for other joint endeavors. Finally, Zinnes provides examples that suggest that when IJCs use performance-based rewards, they create incentives for recipients to apply their own idiosyncratic private information in the interest of the intervention, increasing the chances of success and reducing the need for sponsor monitoring.

Turning to the role of *initial conditions*, Zinnes observes that since many IJC applications were to encourage de facto local level implementation of de jure laws, an important prerequisite for an IJC application is that an adequate legislative and regulatory framework already be in place to be exercised. Likewise, he points out that local public finance laws need to be sufficiently decentralized to accept the pecuniary distributions proposed by these mechanisms. Surprisingly, Zinnes did not find that a lower level of development was per se an obstacle to tournament-based incentives (and he even proposes it for co-opting warlords in fragile states like Afghanistan). Rather, he finds that the devil is in the details of crafting and calibrating the incentive structure to fit local cultural and business norms. Due diligence, focus groups, and pretesting are, therefore, essential, he stresses. While he finds that it is simpler to implement an IJC based on homogeneous players, which permits competition design to be based on *levels* of performance, Zinnes argues that IJCs are still feasible where there is not a level playing field by using a metric based on *changes* in performance (incremental improvements). Of course, the ambitiousness of reforms to tackle must be commensurate with the institutional capabilities of those segments of society and government agencies whose collaboration is required. Regardless, Zinnes finds no evidence of collusion, even in smaller tournaments. Finally, Zinnes argues that one should also be cognizant that initial conditions *within* the government or sponsor should be suitable for IJC success, such as a willingness to accept decentralized solutions, to commit for an extended period, and to subject interventions to quantitative measurement.

Concerning *sustainability*, Zinnes prompts us to distinguish between the sustainability of the institution running the assistance distribution mechanism and the sustainability of the projects thereby implemented. For example, the Ford Foundation set up a nongovernmental organization in the Philippines called Galing Pook (the "process"), with the goal of identifying scalable demonstration projects (the "product"). Regarding the former, Zinnes finds that mechanism sustainability depends on the organizer's ability and commitment to the continued quality of its reputation and that this requires the long-term credibility of the referee. He finds this is easier if a foreign sponsor stays engaged. With only a local referee, he warns that care must be taken to avoid loss of mechanism reputation from creeping corruption, especially if there is a pecuniary prize at stake. Second, he finds that mechanism sustainability was more likely where the structure of rewards, whether directly offered or indirectly generated, led to both private *and* public capture of benefits and where the mechanism had strong ties to a government agency. Third, Zinnes finds no evidence for "loser regret" in IJCs, a result for which he provides several explanations. Finally, given the concern that people eventually lose interest in games, be they children or staff offered recognition awards, Zinnes examines whether there were cases where boredom set in and jeopardized IJC sustainability. He finds limited evidence for this outcome and only on the donor side (USAID's R4 and UNIDO's Morocco IJCs) in projects with longer-duration setup time, but no evidence for this among IJC players. In fact, Zinnes offers several counterexamples where IJCs have been long-lasting, and in diverse applications. Zinnes provides arguments as to why this is so.

What about the sustainability of the projects themselves awarded through IJCs? Motivations (aside from corruption) for sole sourcing have often been speed and cheapness of contracting. Zinnes provides evidence that what is more important for sustainability, however, is the local legitimacy of the initiative and, in particular, whether there has been local ownership in project design and whether there are long-term gains that can be captured locally. He argues that the sustainability of projects funded through a tournament tend to be higher since participation is often voluntary and initial project goals are aligned to existing preferences in the target population. On the other hand, he finds that sustainability was *more* likely in projects resulting from tournaments using output-based rather than input-based performance rewards and *less* likely in tournaments based on a pretournament (yes, many donors do this!) rather than posttournament performance to select winners. Finally, he found that project sustainability was helped by using intermediate rewards for achieving concrete project milestones since this encouraged greater participation and a broader base for improvements in the case of weaker players.

Zinnes also examines the potential *scalability* of the IJCs he reviews. As in the case of sustainability, he makes a distinction between the process scalability and the product scalability of the funded activity. For each he provides guidelines to help determine the scalability of an IJC mechanism, as well as examples. In general, he argues that the nature of IJCs makes them intrinsically amenable to both vertical and horizontal scaling up. He then goes on to identify factors that eventually may limit this expandability.

The book concludes by identifying some of the remaining uncertainties regarding the application of tournaments and where further research is required. On the policy front, among the issues requiring further thought is the extent to which IJCs can or should be used as a substitute mechanism for allocating government goods, services, or funds. Do IJCs create a "crutch" for or act as a facilitator of local government institutions? At the same time, Zinnes raises several concerns regarding government and sponsor reticence to use IJC. While some may be due to its novelty and some, the author admits, due to decision variables hidden from him, he argues that politicians and aid agency staff alike are reluctant to engage in a process in which they give up their dictatorial and discretionary control, just as twenty years ago they were wary of markets and prices for resource allocation. Likewise, many government agencies and donors themselves face de facto institutional disincentives to engage in the sort of quantitative measurement IJC entails. Next, on the technical side, the areas Zinnes identifies for further work include empirical methods for setting the size and structure of pecuniary rewards and the application of advances in strategic communications to improve the use of pretournament public relations and posttournament dissemination of player scores.

Zinnes has provided a great service by collecting a diverse set of cases on a new and potentially important class of policy tool and by developing a number of useful frameworks with which to evaluate the applicability of the tool and how to put it into practice. His goal is oriented toward promoting the use of what he calls more "incentive-compatible" policy vehicles—that is, interventions where the interest of the recipient and sponsor are aligned. Beyond that important task, however, he has helped the donor community and government policymakers think—and act—more broadly and more effectively, thereby contributing substantially to the goal that Brookings and the Wolfensohn Center have set themselves.

STROBE TALBOTT
President
Brookings Institution

Washington, D.C.
March 2009

Acknowledgments

This work builds on several years of fruition and discussion with my colleagues, especially Stefano Giovannelli (UNIDO), Patrick Meagher (the IRIS Center) and Jonathan Alevy (University of Nevada, Reno). Chapters 3 through 5 benefited from research assistance as well as some preliminary drafting by Mauricio Palacios.

I would also like to acknowledge the generous financial support of the Wolfensohn Center for Development, funded by James Wolfensohn, and to thank Johannes Linn, the Center's director, for his field-hardened feedback, willingness to pursue innovation, and continued enthusiasm, without which this book would have never seen the light of day. In leading the Wolfensohn Center's search for replicable, scalable, and cost-effective project models to apply to its core areas, I am fortunate that the Center identified the inter-jurisdictional competition (IJC) concept as a reform and project delivery vehicle meriting consideration. It launched a policy research initiative that subjected the IJC concept to a review of its theory and practice. The review was then evaluated, critiqued, and fine-tuned by distinguished scholars and practitioners in series of workshops. This volume and its associated Brookings Policy Brief are the result. The hope is that the publication of this book will lead donors and other development actors to organize and rigorously test specific pilot applications.

I would also like to express my gratitude for comments on previous versions of related work from Shaqk Afsah, Roy Bahl, Chas Cadwell, Bruno Frey, Avner Greif, Kai Kaiser, Stuti Khemani, Steve Knack, Peter Murrell, Doug North, Wally Oates, Sanjay Pradhan, Frank Sader, and Paul Smoke, as well as by seminar participants at the annual meeting of the International Society of New Institutional Economics (2004); the USAID Economic Growth, Agriculture, and Trade workshop on international development (2004); and "brown bag" meetings at the IRIS Center, Department of Economics at the University of Maryland (2005), the World Bank Public Sector Governance seminar (2007), the Lincoln Institute for Land Policy (2007), and the Urban Economics, Finance, and Management Thematic Group (World Bank) conference (2007), Incentive-Based Considerations for Designing Decentralized Infrastructure Programs. Thanks also go to Lael Brainard and other participants at Brookings Institution presentations (2006 and 2007). Written comments from an anonymous referee on the penultimate draft of this manuscript were especially invaluable. I also appreciate the useful factual information, materials, and feedback from those associated with some of the projects described in this report, including Talib Esmail, Scott Guggenheim, Milwida Guevara, José Larios, Bjorn Nordthueit, Ranjula Bali Swain, and Lynnette Wood. Finally, I would like to thank Starr Belsky for her superb editing and Azad Amir-Ghassemi for introducing me to Johannes Linn. All errors and omissions, however, are my own.

Abbreviations and Conventions

All values stated in the text are nominal in the year of the project unless otherwise specified. The term "dollar" refers to the U.S. dollar.

AGETIP	*Agence d'Exécution des Travaux d'Intérêt Public*
BDS	business development services
CBO	community-based organization
CDD	community-driven development
CNOAS	*Coordination Nationale des Opérateurs en Alphabétisation du Sénégal*
CRC	citizens' report card
CRI	Center for Regional Investment (Morocco)
DPL	development policy loans (the World Bank)
EBRD	European Bank for Reconstruction and Development
ERR	economic rate of return
FDI	foreign direct investment
FPSU	Federal Project Support Unit (Nigeria)
GEF	Global Environmental Facility
GOI	Government of Indonesia
IDA	International Development Association, the World Bank's grant window for the poorest countries

IFI	international financial institution
IJC	interjurisdictional competition
ILO	International Labor Organization (United Nations)
IRIS	Center for Institutional Reform and the Informal Sector, Department of Economics, University of Maryland
KDP	Kecamatan Development Program (Indonesia)
LEEMP	Local Empowerment and Environmental Management Program (World Bank, Nigeria)
LDC	less developed country
LGA	local government area
LGU	local government unit
M&E	monitoring and evaluation
MCA	Millennium Challenge Account
MCC	Millennium Challenge Corporation
MENA	the Middle East and North Africa region
MEPI	Middle East Partnership Initiative (U.S. Department of State)
MFI	microfinance institution
NGO	nongovernmental organization
NIE	new institutional economics
OECD	Organization for Economic Cooperation and Development
O&M	operations and maintenance
PAPF	*Projet d'Alphabétisation Priorité Femme*
PBG	performance-based grant
PIJC	prospective interjurisdictional competition
PPP	public-private partnership
PROPER	Program for Pollution Control, Evaluation, and Rating (Indonesia)
R4	Results, Review, and Resource Request (USAID)
RFRF	World Bank Regional Fiscal Reform Fund (for Russia)
SPSU	State Project Support Unit (Nigeria)
SNG	subnational government unit
SME	small- or medium-scale enterprise
TA	technical assistance
UNIDO	United Nations Industrial Development Organization

1

Introduction

Why is it that there is almost universal agreement that foreign aid—sometimes called donor aid or development assistance—has not been particularly effective (Collier 2002; Espina and Zinnes 2003; Easterly 2006a and 2006b; World Bank 1998)?[1] Slowly the donor community has come to realize that the problem is not primarily one of insufficient funding.[2] Rather, it appears to be related to the incentives created by the relations among donor country voters, donor organizations, technical assistance implementers, intermediary recipient governments, and final aid beneficiaries, among others (Murrell 2002). Clearly, some of these relationships are horizontal and some are vertical. In some there may be "teamwork" or competition; in others there is hierarchy, which may be well or poorly managed (or supervised).

In short, the root of the problem of aid effectiveness is *institutional.* By institutions I mean the set of rules, strategies, payoffs, and players, as well as player beliefs about all of these.[3] Thus "institution" may refer to culture, norms, markets, firms, government, organizations, and legislation. It also includes donor-recipient assistance contracts. Associated with this insight is the ever greater attention paid to governance, monitoring and evaluation, indicator design,

---

1. See also William Easterly, "Dismal Science," *Wall Street Journal,* November 15, 2006, p. A18; "The U.N. Millennium Project for Ending World Poverty," *Wall Street Journal,* December 5, p. A19.

2. There are those (Sachs 2005) who nevertheless believe that a significant increase in funding is a central part of the solution. I revisit this view in section 6.5.3.

3. See Weingast (1995) and Williamson (2003) for discussions of the role of institutions in economic development.

public participation, and participatory development (Williams and Kushnarova 2004). Likewise, these are not issues limited to donor aid but are also applicable to local-level government services and regulation as well as private sponsors of diverse initiatives. Part of the reason for the emerging deeper understanding of these challenges comes from advances made over the last two decades in what is now called the new institutional economics (NIE).[4]

1.1 Challenges to Effecting Change

Consider briefly the sponsors' conundrum.[5] They wish to provide development assistance to recipients (or, in the case of a central government, revenues to decentralized local governments) in an environment foreign to the sponsors and in such a way that the sponsors' explicit and implicit objectives are met.[6] These tend to be highly multidimensional (Alesina and Dollar 2000) and include a desire for the consequences of sponsor intervention to be sustainable in the long run.[7] Likewise and at least officially, sponsors would like their funds to be applied in a cost-effective fashion. Unfortunately, this is more of a challenge than first meets the eye.

To understand why one must examine the path or steps through which this process might typically pass.[8] First, the sponsor must manage and empower its own staff to identify an appropriate area for recipient country improvement and then determine the requisite intervention to address the problem. It must then find and contract an implementer, which it must monitor. The implementer will generally have to interact with agencies of the recipient government, which may in turn need to delegate to their subordinate territorial units. When presented this way, the opportunities for mistakes as well as malfeasance or shirking are formidable. Given the limited local knowledge as well as operative control the sponsor has in a typical situation, it is no wonder things do not always go the sponsor's way, ignoring whether its own objectives were appropriate in the first place.

4. See Furubotn and Richter (1999) for an extensive treatment or Azfar (2003) for a review of NIE.

5. The word "sponsor" rather than "donor" has been chosen to underscore that the mechanisms upon which the present work focuses apply to most non-market initiatives organized by an outsider.

6. "Foreign" here is in the sense of "unfamiliar," for example, a given municipality's environment is generally foreign to its central government. With regard to objectives, the U.S. Agency for International Development (USAID), for example, in spite of having an explicit Results Review and Resource Request (R4) framework (see section 3.1.4), also wants to promote trade and business with the United States, American air carriers, U.S. small business, and U.S. female entrepreneurs, not to mention having a case-specific political agenda. The question of the suitability of the donors' objectives—both in terms of their appropriateness and their number—is dealt with later.

7. The issue of sustainability is discussed later. Unfortunately, many donor initiatives tend to peter out once donor funding ends.

8. In a similar spirit, Martens and others (2002, pp. 14–28) refer to this as the "disruption in the feedback loop between donor country taxpayers and recipient beneficiaries."

These issues of control and monitoring are aspects of what economists refer to as principal-agent problems.[9] They encompass some of the central challenges for the provision of development assistance (Murrell 2002) and thus are dealt with repeatedly in this discussion. Principal-agent issues often may manifest themselves hierarchically in a "chain of command." Clearly, the longer the chain, the more susceptible an intervention is to unanticipated breakdowns or even failure. Such considerations should encourage a modicum of modesty in application designs.[10]

But there are still further challenges. Sponsor interventions such as reform activities, capacity building, or other local improvements generally require that local stakeholders coordinate—or at least cooperate—among themselves. Lack of trust and a "zero-sum" attitude lead to reluctance to work together across political groups, economic sectors, and jurisdictions.[11] Likewise, how can a sponsor separate serious from frivolous local requests for assistance?[12] In other words, how can a potential aid recipient signal to a sponsor its seriousness to engage in high-level efforts, that is, prove that its incentives are aligned with sponsor objectives? What credible commitment mechanism can the recipients employ?[13]

Sponsors have historically, albeit unintentionally, responded to these dilemmas in several ways.[14] One is to assess their own impact by measuring project inputs, for example, the number of entrepreneurs trained, the value of loans placed, amount of seed distributed, or whether an environmental law was promulgated.[15] This is easier to document to donor constituencies back home (and less risky to staff member careers) than proving outcome effectiveness associated with each of these aforementioned inputs, namely, an increase (due to training) in small- or medium-scale enterprise (SME) value added, the sustainable impact of the project loan, the impact on rural household caloric intake, or the degree of firm compliance, respectively.

Donors have also engaged in "conditionality." A country promises to do X in the future and the donor promises to give Y in the present. A more sophisticated version of this is for the donor to require the recipient to "go first," though this is often difficult because Y is often an input to X. There has been a growing

---

9. A set of problems associated with an arrangement in which a principal hires agents to represent her, promote her interests, or carry out actions in her stead. Examples are shareholders and their firm's managers, voters and their elected representatives, and ministers and their bureaucracies. See Azfar (2003).

10. I thank Johannes Linn for raising this concern.

11. This can also lead to what economists call coordination failure.

12. Economists call this a risk of adverse selection.

13. Note how credible commitment is related to monitoring. When precommitment is credible, a donor may use its funds more effectively since monitoring costs would be lower.

14. It is outside the scope of this book to provide a full review of aid mechanisms and aid effectiveness. See World Bank (1998), Zinnes and Bolaky (2002), Svensson (2003), Collier and others (1997), and Martens and others (2002) for treatments of these issues.

15. In its R4 framework, USAID euphemistically calls these intermediate results.

literature as to why conditionality often fails.[16] This makes the so-called merit good (X) appear to the recipient (or rather the "agent" of the recipient or principal) as a "price" it must pay to get what it wants (Y). It is hardly likely that the recipient will implement Y with much enthusiasm under such an arrangement. Moreover, where the government is not fully accountable to its population's interests, conditionality tends to be "time inconsistent," namely, once the donor has fulfilled its side of the bargain, it is not in the donor's interest to penalize the country if the government defaults on its side—especially if the government changes over the course of the agreement period. Kenya and the donor community have played this game so many times that *The Economist* in 1995 called it a "ritual" (as quoted in Svensson 2003). Why would donors tolerate this behavior? Svensson (2003) and others point out that part of the reason is the way in which donors allocate assistance. First, the donor's country teams that develop the projects rarely experience much of an opportunity cost to the funds they program. They operate under the implicit rule of "use it or lose it." Second, within departments of the donor organization, there tend to be positive bureaucratic incentives to maximize their budget size rather than their program effectiveness, an observation made many years ago by Niskanen (1971) in conjunction with government in general.

Now sponsors have come full circle and are beginning to focus on meeting their own objectives more effectively. For example, participants at the 2005 Paris High-Level Forum issued the Paris Declaration on Aid Effectiveness, in which they "committed their institutions and countries to continuing and increasing efforts in harmonization, alignment, and managing for results, and listed a set of monitorable actions and indicators to accelerate progress in these areas."[17] Likewise, Martens (2005) observes that in the 1980s and 1990s, emphasis was on donor agenda and thus conditionality, whereas more recently it is on ownership and donor alignment, the brokering of which is the role of an aid agency. He therefore concludes that the job of aid agencies is "to mediate between diverging preferences of donors and recipients and package aid flows in a contract that reduces ex post uncertainties for donors" (p. 20).

It is natural to ask, therefore, whether there might be a way to design sponsor interventions so as to minimize the consequences of the sponsor's operational and informational inadequacies.[18] Research suggests that the answer may lie in harnessing the power of incentives rather than in trying to fight them (Brook and Petrie 2001; Zinnes and Bolaky 2002; Kremer 2003; Collier 2002).[19] Such incen-

16. See, for example, Collier (2002) and Svensson (2003).

17. Aid Harmonization and Alignment, "Paris High-Level Forum (2005)" (www.aidharmoniza tion.org/secondary-pages/Paris2005).

18. There is also the important complementary approach of better designing institutional incentives *within* a donor to make development effectiveness a principal objective of its bureaucracy. This is the approach taken by Ostrom and others (2002), Collier (2002), Zinnes and Bolaky (2002), and Svensson (2003).

19. An online version of Brook and Petrie (2001) is available at www.gpoba.org/docs/05intro.pdf.

tives would be simple, "bright," transparent, easily and objectively assessable, and necessarily focus on outcomes, not inputs. They would encourage the "players in the aid game" to use their asymmetric local knowledge in a way aligned to the sponsor's objectives. As a likely corollary, it would probably require that the recipient have a predominant role in the identification of both problems as well as solutions. Based on these insights, one might speculate that the preferred mechanism to deliver aid would also encourage recipient country stakeholders to collaborate rather than fight each other for a "piece of the action."[20]

This may seem to be a tall order for aid delivery. However, based on my own field experience as well as a careful reading of the innovation and experimentation literature spawned by the failure of aid effectiveness (Espina and Zinnes 2003), I have proposed elsewhere an approach that appears to hold promise.[21] The approach is called prospective interjurisdictional competition (PIJC) and brings together several desirable, tried-and-true, incentive-compatible mechanisms found in existing projects. A principal goal of this book is to assess the broader applicability of PIJC toward improving the effectiveness of development assistance.

The Brookings Institution's Wolfensohn Center for Development, with its mandate to explore and assess emerging new solutions to development problems with an eye to sustainability and scalability, has identified the PIJC mechanism as a potentially powerful technology for its mission.[22] Given the lack of a comprehensive written assessment of this mechanism, it has solicited the present book to fill the lacuna.

1.2 The PIJC Concept

As understood in the public finance literature (for example, Oates 2002) interjurisdictional competition (IJC) often occurs naturally as states, municipalities, and even countries compete in a tacit, decentralized way to attract business investment and new citizens with high human or financial capital. In this "game" jurisdictions use tax holidays, regulatory and immigration exemptions, publicly paid-for amenities and infrastructure, and even direct subsidies. The push toward devolution and decentralization worldwide may also be considered as utilizing IJC principles. And many more creative applications have been implemented: overlapping public utility jurisdictions (Frey and Eichenberger 1999), environmental certification (Afsah and Vincent 1997), local government report cards

---

20. Harford and Klein (2005a, 2005b) argue that it is this competition to redistribute donor funds rather than produce value added that leads countries that receive substantial donor aid to appear like countries with rich natural resource endowments.

21. See Zinnes (2004), Meagher and Zinnes (2004), and Zinnes, Meagher, and Giovannelli (2006).

22. See www.brookings.edu/wolfensohn/about-us.aspx.

(Public Affairs Foundation 2004), and allocation of bilateral donor assistance.[23] However, the power of IJC is potentially much broader. It is also a fundamental component of adaptive evolutionary processes in which entities continually test their survival mettle in an ever changing environment of competing alternatives (Young 1998). Thus IJC can be thought to apply to any set of alternative institutions, which could refer to cultural manifestations (such as religions); intragovernmental ministries, departments, or agencies; intergovernmental organizations (for example, across donors), and of course private volunteer organizations (nongovernmental organizations [NGOs]).[24]

While experience is growing with these innovative applications, the writings describing them and their lessons learned are scattered across several disciplines. This makes it hard to identify underlying factors responsible for their performance. In fact, a comprehensive assessment of their performance in the public policy sphere does not appear to exist.[25] However, some of the theory developed in a series of articles in the 1980s (Lazear and Rosen 1981; Nalebuff and Stiglitz 1983; Green and Stokey 1983) does investigate the efficiency issues considered here in regard to tournaments, certification, and direct contracts.[26] Those articles, as well as the present discussion, underscore the importance of uncertainty and who bears the risk of the tasks (though, in fact, this book goes further by considering the issue from the perspective of both the team player itself as well as the decisionmaker *within* the player team).

Green and Stokey (1983), for example, start by identifying two sources of (additive) risk, the idiosyncratic efforts of the player and the common shock affecting all players. Briefly, they find that when the common shock "is sufficiently diffuse, then the optimal tournament dominates using independent contracts," and if the number of players is sufficiently large, then a player's rank is sufficient information for the tournament's sponsors to know the player's output level of effort net of the common shock. I will draw on these insights in later chapters. One difference in the present application, however, is that the jurisdictions in principle *want* the reforms but face, in part, a collective action problem whereas these authors have in mind employment contracts in which effort by definition causes "disutility." Nonetheless, these results pose a challenge to the tournament designer since they presuppose that it is easier to quantitatively measure the player's input performance over output performance.

Meanwhile development of new uses of IJC based on the new institutional economics proceeds apace. Examples of potential applications for technical assist-

---

23. See the Millennium Challenge Corporation website at www.mcc.gov.

24. With regard to IJCs and donors, see William Easterly, "Tired Old Mantras at Monterey," op-ed., *Wall Street Journal,* March 18, 2002.

25. One that comes close is Mookhergee (2006).

26. A *tournament* can be defined as a contest in which "reward structures [are] based on rank order" rather than achieving a particular performance (Green and Stokey 1983, p. 350).

ance, which are summarized below, include women's entrepreneurship and youth employment in Morocco, the dairy sector in Uzbekistan, human trafficking in Bangladesh, higher education in Nigeria, and human rights in China (Druchel, Russell-Einhorn, and Zinnes 2005). Of particular interest are applications under development that harness interjurisdictional competition *prospectively* as a mechanism to guide public policy and allocate development assistance so as to create substantially more effective and sustainable outcomes (Meagher and Zinnes 2004). Prospective here means that the players—whether local government jurisdictions, agencies within a central government, or NGOs—explicitly agree in advance to compete in a game with predefined explicit rules and rewards, which may be in the form of goods, services, financing, or recognition and publicity.

Activities in a PIJC Application

As described in detail in section 2.1, a generic, tournament-based PIJC comprises a number of activities or steps, some of which can be simplified or even skipped, depending on initial conditions and objectives. Say the sponsor wants subnational governments (SNGs) to implement a reform (for example, improving the budgeting process) in a target region. First, the sponsor must make the objective explicit to stakeholders (for instance, more efficient use of existing fiscal resources through better management and transparency of the budget) and identify a list of tasks, each of which either fulfills or contributes to the objective (for example, conformity of SNG budget to budget code or consolidation of extrabudgetary funds). The task list should derive from stakeholder consultation. Next the sponsor assigns a quantifiable, actionable indicator and aggregation weight to each task (such as the degree to which the budget is standardized or the percent of off-budget funding reduced).[27] The weights reflect the sponsor's view of the task's importance to the objective and may be thought of as game points. Then rule brochures are prepared, and the sponsor convenes a conference with representatives of all prospective teams (SNGs) to explain the game. During the actual tournament period, the SNGs would compete to amass as many points as possible. They do this by allocating their efforts across a subset of tasks (or reforms) of their choosing on the aforementioned list, subject to time, budget, collective action constraints within the community, and based on their collective preferences. During the tournament the sponsor offers technical assistance, generally in the form of multiplayer workshops and not one-on-one site visits. Note how this demand-driven approach is also allocatively efficient: only the communities can know their own cost functions and preferences, and only the sponsor can know its own (marginal) valuations of the proposed tasks. Likewise, since participation is voluntary, reforms only occur with the complete cooperation of

27. Indicators may be dichotomous (for example, all extrabudgetary funds have been converted, yes or no) or continuous, and may contain thresholds (for instance, no points given unless certain parts of the budget meet the standards).

representatives of the population of potential "players"—in short, the tournament has great legitimacy.

Sustainability and Scalability

Sponsors have rightfully recognized that their effectiveness must be measured not just by whether a development initiative is successful but whether it is likely to remain so, especially once the sponsor has departed—a project characteristic referred to as sustainability. Often sponsors also want to know how portable a successful project is (replicability) and whether it might work at different sizes of implementation (scalability). Portability refers to the potential for implementing the initiative among different groups of similarly characterized players, for example, a set of jurisdictions in a different region of the same country or even in a different country.[28] Furthermore, scalability and scale are not the same thing. Scale refers to the size required for a successful application, which will be discussed during examination of the initial conditions required for utilizing a particular incentive mechanism. Finally, to a lesser extent, project scope is considered, that is, the diversity of applications or sectors for which use of an incentive mechanism may be suitable. This book, therefore, not only evaluates the effectiveness but also the sustainability and scalability of the PIJC concept in general and application experience in particular.[29]

Need for Assessment

Clearly, the PIJC concept sounds good in theory, but does it work in practice? Fortunately, as shown in chapters 3 and 4, there are many public policy initiatives in the developing and transition countries that are based on full or partial prospective interjurisdictional competitions. Likewise, I shall argue that the development community has considerable experience with each of the components of a PIJC, so the feasibility of implementing these components as part of a single application would appear reasonable to explore. For example, governance indicators have been used extensively by such donors as the U.S. Agency for International Development (USAID), the World Bank, the European Bank for Reconstruction and Development (EBRD), and the Millennium Challenge Corporation (MCC).[30] The Organization for Economic Cooperation and Development (OECD) also promotes governance indicators as a tool in government effectiveness (OECD

28. In fact, scalability also comes into play during the testing of a PIJC in a new location, since the preferred protocol would usually entail administering a small pilot program first, especially if the intervention is planned for a relatively large geographic area or is likely to be costly in financial or political terms.

29. The reader may refer to Hartmann and Linn (2008) for a recent review of the literature on and sponsor experience with scalability.

30. Popular sources for governance indicators include Freedom House, Transparency International, International Country Risk Guide, Polity IV, and the Heritage Foundation.

2004).[31] In addition, development assistance applications are turning more and more to performance- or output-based contracting (OECD 1999).[32] Finally, donors already use competition to better target assistance, such as in their grant programs for SMEs, for civil society organizations (Polishchuk and Brown 2002), and even for their own sources of innovation (Wood and Hamel 2002). Hence, to help evaluate the suitability of PIJC in terms of its potential for sustainable success as well as scalability, section 2.5 lays out a simple assessment framework. Then in chapters 3 and 4 this framework is used to examine a series of selected past and present sponsor applications.

1.3 Overview of PIJC in Developing and Transition Countries

To provide the reader with a clearer picture of PIJC use, a number of extant PIJC applications are summarized according to several policy categories; many of these applications are then described in more detail in chapters 3 and 4. Likewise, to illustrate the potential of the PIJC approach, the final category describes several applications that have so far only made it to the solicited proposal stage.

What is *not* included is the largest category of interjurisdictional competitions, namely, those that are *not* prospective—that is, where the rules are not agreed to by the players in advance. In those cases the rules of the game are unwritten and amorphous. Examples of such would be investment promotion games among competing countries in the form of export promotion zones or sites for foot-loose foreign factories, and tax competitions across states within a federation (such as the United States or the European Union). Many of these nonprospective tournaments are clearly a "race to the bottom" in that they encourage players to compete by offering exemptions on some fiscal, social, or regulatory requirements rather than by strengthening them.[33]

Local Government Reform Initiatives

These are cases where a sponsor has used a local government tournament as a means for both encouraging local reform efforts as well as allocating its aid. In Russia, for example, as a major component of a fiscal reform loan, the World Bank has run a tournament in which eighty-nine regions compete for budget support

31. As is the case with any powerful tool, the scope for misuse is also ubiquitous (Arndt and Oman 2006).

32. See also Brook and Petrie (2001).

33. While it is usual for competition to whittle down the economic rents of parties to a transaction, the aforementioned exemptions typically carry hidden redistributional consequences in that the parties who benefit from winning are not the ones who bear the costs of the exemptions. The latter parties may be sectorally, geographically, or even temporally distinct from the winning parties. Such decisionmaking is often the result of principal-agent failures. Ironically, since such exemptions are typically given to foreign investors, it is the weaker domestic firms that are forced to compete against the foreign direct investment under the stricter fiscal or regulatory regime.

of $6–9 million apiece by implementing a range of reforms and administrative improvements on extending budget coverage, making local tax law more transparent and consistent with federal legislation, improving expenditure management, strengthening information and audit functions, and improving debt management (see chapter 4). Quantitative targets (indicators) are used to ensure transparency and objectivity. So far fifteen regions have won, and the Russian government has been so impressed with the results that it has committed its own budget funds through 2008 to run three more tournaments.

USAID has funded the Center for Institutional Reform and the Informal Sector (IRIS Center) at the University of Maryland to design and run a quasi-tournament to encourage further deregulation of administrative barriers degrading the business environment in Romania (chapter 3). Simple indicators were used to focus local efforts to address five specific impediments. Most efforts required effective private-public partnerships for success. Out of the eighty municipalities in the country, twenty-nine actively took part and four cities "won." Here, rather than pecuniary rewards or extra donor technical assistance, winners received unprecedented publicity and acknowledgement, which they viewed as a valuable signal to outside investors of their business friendliness (and mayors appreciated as political capital).[34]

In Honduras USAID funded the design and implementation of a competition among municipalities to carry out reform tasks in the areas of good governance, sustainability and commitment to maintain and attract investment, and absorptive capacity for future technical assistance (chapter 4). Out of all the municipalities in the country, thirty-five were deemed eligible to compete. Then their past performance was measured against seven indicators. Municipalities that scored the highest on the aggregation of these indicators—what USAID called the sustainability quotient—won a rich array of technical assistance. Here again the mayors specifically pointed to the political capital they believed winning would confer.

The World Bank is also running a project in nine Nigerian states to strengthen local government use of federation transfers (Esmail and others 2004; Terfa 2005a and 2005b) by including local government areas (LGAs) as beneficiaries in the other components of the International Development Association (IDA) and Global Environmental Facility (GEF) grant-funded technical assistance program (see chapter 3).[35] This project component grades participating LGAs according to a "scorecard," with eight indicators and their subindicators, to assess LGA commitment to effective service delivery (looking at administrative efficiency, budget and financial appraisal, and overall financial integrity) and responsiveness to rural

34. USAID recently ran a procurement to implement a PIJC to address governance issues in Bolivia (USAID 2006).

35. The World Bank program is called the Local Empowerment and Environmental Management Project (LEEMP).

communities (Terfa 2005a, p. 4-1). This initiative is especially interesting because it focuses on *poverty reduction* and on *scaling up* (Terfa 2005a, p. 1-7).

The UN Industrial Development Organization (UNIDO) Investment Promotion Office, in recognizing its frustration with finding bankable cofinancing opportunities for its programs in the Maghreb, teamed up with the IRIS Center to design a PIJC to stimulate local government initiatives to improve the business and investment environment in Morocco (chapter 4). Morocco was chosen because it had recently enacted sweeping legislative reforms to devolve spending and regulatory authority down to various levels of SNG. Since these reforms were de jure, the provincial governors, communal councils, and business leaders showed great interest in exercising these new powers. A pilot tournament was designed in collaboration with local stakeholders to encourage communes to undertake tasks that would require the de facto application of the new laws. Pre- and posttournament quantitative benchmarks would be taken, and the top-ranked communes would receive both substantial technical assistance and computer hardware while their local firms would be offered trade missions in Europe and access to cofinancing.

Revenue Sharing

The trend in fiscal federalism and decentralization in general has brought to the fore the question of how national and lower-level revenue sources are to be shared. While this is not the place to review such an important literature, among its conclusions are that "successful decentralization cannot be achieved in the absence of a well-designed fiscal transfers program" and that "the role of [such] transfers in enhancing competition for the supply of public goods should not be overlooked" (Shah 1997, p. 32).[36] For example, "in Mexico, South Africa and Pakistan, federal revenue sharing transfers finance up to 99 percent of expenditures in some provinces" (Shah 1997, p. 31).

Several of these cases of revenue sharing or intragovernmental transfers may be viewed as a type of PIJC.[37] In these cases jurisdictions are aware that their transfers will depend on recent or expected performance. For example, in South Africa "the central government has implemented a conditional grant aimed at providing incentives for reform of urban services for large cities after having devolved powers to city governments" (Ahmad and others 2005, p. 21). Moreover, the role of the donor in the PIJC is taken up by oversight committees (Bolivia), provincial

36. See also Smoke (2008), Bahl and Linn (1992), and Oates (2002) as well as Shah (1997) for a review and assessment.

37. On the other hand, the literature on the design of equalization grants (see, for example, Martinez-Vazquez and Boex 1999) does not seem explicitly to advocate using revenue sharing to stimulate expenditure effectiveness competition among recipients. Of course, no such ambiguity exists on the raising of revenues, for which competition among subnational government units should be avoided at all cost.

finance commissions (Pakistan), or grant commissions (for instance, in Australia, India, and Nigeria).[38]

Steffensen (2007) provides an in-depth operational analysis of performance-based grants to SNGs. He surveys many known developing country examples in which "performance-based grants (PBGs) provide incentives for [local governments] to improve their performance by linking the access to and size of the release of grants with their performance in predetermined areas" (p. 10; emphases omitted).[39] PBG objectives include improving administrative performance, organizational learning, and accountability; bringing funds on-budget; and streamlining and coordinating donor support (Steffensen 2007, p. 11). This implies that such grants *supplement* the objectives of other grants; they are *not* used to fund core services or recurrent costs.[40] According to Steffensen, the purpose of PBGs depends on the level of development: they start with process-oriented goals (institution building) and later focus on sector output targets (such as service delivery).[41] He classifies these into single and multisector grants, where the latter offer greater latitude to SNGs to choose how to invest. Like Zinnes (2006), Steffensen notes that PBGs allow "spending where performance is good and absorption capacity is available, and where funds are not misused" (p. 12, emphases omitted), and can be used to create "a balance between adherence to national targets and ensuring local autonomy/efficiency" (p. 15).

At the same time, efforts to improve accountability and governance, especially at the subnational level of government, have led to the expanded adoption of performance-based budgeting, "the allocation of fiscal resources based on the achievement of specific, measurable outcomes" (Fielding Smith 1999; Moynihan 2003). They are similar to the PIJC in that they involve expenditure allocation decisions upon which lower levels compete (the budget lines, so to speak), strategic planning in which core tasks and government goals are identified, and performance information that is used to manage and measure performance. Moreover, the last is often explicitly made available to the general public: "some U.S. states, such as Missouri and Virginia, provide extensive performance data on government Web sites" to increase accountability to the public (Moynihan 2003). This kind of information is also provided by EU states (see box 1-1).

---

38. See, respectively, Faguet (2000), Ahmad and others (2005, p. 23), and Martinez-Vazquez and Boex (1999, p. 39).

39. The countries include Uganda, Kenya, Tanzania, Nepal, Bangladesh, and Sierra Leone, with projects under way in Sudan, Ghana, Philippines, Cambodia, Indonesia, and the Solomon Islands. This experience seems to belie the observation by Bahl and Linn (1992) that "the threshold level of economic development at which fiscal decentralization becomes attractive appears to be quite high."

40. This was a key concern of Afonso and Guimarães (2008).

41. The institution building found in process-oriented PBGs associated with lower levels of development would, for example, focus on good governance, accountability, and financial management; participatory development planning and budgeting; resource mobilization; expenditure management; audit reports; and transparency.

Box 1-1. *Linking Budget Support to Performance*

The European Commission is explicitly linking part of its budget support to performance. The amount to be disbursed is based on progress in social service delivery, notably health and education, and in public expenditure management. Progress is measured by a small number of performance indicators agreed to by the recipient and the European Commission. Indicators are typically drawn from the recipient's poverty reduction strategy. For the first set of countries, the most frequently used indicators are

—planned and actual expenditures in the social sectors,
—differences in unit costs of key inputs between the public sector and the market,
—use of primary and antenatal health care services,
—immunization rates,
—enrollment rates for boys and girls,
—births assisted by medical personnel, and
—cost of primary education (private and public).

After a joint evaluation by government and donors, a score is calculated for each indicator: one point if the agreed objective is attained, half a point if there is evidence of "considerable positive development," and zero if there is no progress. The budget support provided is the maximum amount available multiplied by the (unweighted) average performance score (ranging from zero to one). The approach is not mechanical and also takes into account external factors.

The performance-based system highlights the quality of data. According to the European Commission, the system is not an end but a means: getting policymakers and the public in developing countries to pay more attention to results than to declarations of intentions and conditions set by donors.

So far, 30 percent of the European Commission's budget support is linked to performance indicators. This is deliberate, motivated by the desire to introduce a new approach gradually and to balance performance rewards and the recipient's need for predictable budget finance.

Source: World Bank (2005b, box 11.7).

Dissemination and Signaling

Perhaps the second most prevalent use of PIJC (after donor grant programs) is jurisdictional recognition awards, for example, "blue-ribbon" city competitions.[42] The example analyzed here is the Ford Foundation's promotion of the Galing Pook Foundation in the Philippines (see chapter 4). This program was established in 1993 with the hope of stimulating a response to the then new local governance code. Galing Pook runs a tournament with the goal of "building the capacities of local government units by disseminating, popularizing, and replicating" best practices of awardees (Galing Pook Foundation 2005). The winners of the tournament are determined through a multilevel screening process. The only reward to winning is national recognition and publicity, which apparently municipal politicians covet. Over its history to date almost 3,000 local governance programs have competed, 175 of which have won some category of recognition.

The Indonesian environmental authorities developed a simple yet astonishingly effective disclosure program concerning large enterprise environmental performance based on a signaling model (chapter 3). These firms were color coded to reflect the degree to which they were meeting national standards, world standards, and state-of-the-art performance. The simple color codes, which were advertised and which the firms displayed, were easy for the person on the street to understand, unlike more precise statistics, and social pressures among elites led owners and managers to improve their environmental performance to avoid negative peer and social stigmas.

Donor Country Allocations

At least two multilateral aid agencies use a quasi-PIJC approach to allocate their financial resources at the country level. The IDA uses a complex set of sixteen public expenditure management indicators to evaluate the progress of heavily indebted poor countries (HIPCs) and to set country allotments.[43] The MCC conducts a veritable tournament by only offering to work with countries that score above the median for their group on sixteen governance-related indicators (chapter 4). The hope is that the lure of substantial funds—for example, $300 million in the case of Mongolia's proposed compact—will create a consensus of special interests within a country to focus on good governance. Many and from many quarters (Thiel 2004; Boone and Faguet 2002; Collier 2002; Svensson 2003) are essentially calling for donor aid to be disbursed in a more competitive fashion with greater recognition of opportunity costs and based on effectiveness.[44] Ironically, with the two

---

42. Even China has gotten into the act (see Dollar and others 2004). Appendix A includes a description of ten of these.

43. See IDA and International Monetary Fund, "Update on the Assessments and Implementation of Action Plans to Strengthen Capacity of HIPCs to Track Poverty-Reducing Public Spending," April 12, 2005 (www.imf.org/external/np/pp/eng/2005/041205a.pdf).

44. See also Easterly, "Tired Old Mantras."

exceptions just noted, most of the competition in the market for aid is among the donors fighting for the attention of recipient country governments. Finally, some donors have been looking retroactively at how they have been allocating assistance (World Bank 1998), and some have even scrutinized their own programs. A particularly revealing example is found in box 1-2 concerning the International Labor Organization (ILO), which ran an internal assessment activity requiring that employment generation performance exceed the mean for projects in the program, thus giving this evaluation activity a tournament structure.

Donor Grant Programs

Many donors run grant programs, too numerous to list, aimed at every development sector imaginable. These are structured as tournaments and often aim at encouraging experimentation. Some encourage civil society to engage in service provision or public participation in oversight of local government. Others aim to encourage technology transfer and collaboration between recipient and donor countries. Still others seek to discover new approaches to perennial problems, such as the World Bank's Development Marketplace in which outside proposals compete for a reward based on a subjective appraisal of innovativeness, relevance, and feasibility (Wood and Hamel 2002). Likewise with globalgiving.com, in which proposals vetted for effectiveness compete for funding over the Internet like goods sold on eBay, only that contributors may participate by investing less than the full amount.[45]

On a larger scale, there is the World Bank's *kecamatan* (district with many villages) development program (KDP; chapter 4) in Indonesia that seeks to address the ineffectiveness of top-down aid programs in reducing local-level poverty. In this project participating kecamatans receive a block grant budget of $50,000–150,000. An intervillage meeting is then held to decide collectively which of the projects proposed by its villages should be funded. Villages can develop reputations for good project outcomes during the five competitive replenishment rounds of the overall project, which has disbursed over $1 billion to the poorest 34,233 villages in the country. The overall project appears to be successful since the government took over funding it once the World Bank's financing was exhausted.

Management Control

To improve its effectiveness and ability to respond to an often hostile Congress, USAID in 1995 developed a monitoring system that "required managers to: (1) establish performance indicators, (2) prepare performance monitoring plans, (3) set performance baselines, (4) collect performance data, and (5) periodically assess data quality" (see Williams, Adley and Company 2002). One component

45. Of course, the project is only executed once enough investors contribute to reach the full investment amount.

Box 1-2. *ILO Program for Small Enterprise Development*

Like most programs, Small Enterprise Development (SEED) had been feeling the pressure within the Employment Sector of the International Labor Organization to demonstrate an impact on employment generation and determine the cost-effectiveness of its various programs. Moreover, senior management was genuinely eager to learn more about the employment impact and efficiency of their business development service (BDS) programs. Over the period 2001–2004, the ILO's InFocus Program on Boosting Employment through Small Enterprise Development did a small impact assessment of the effect of SEED BDS programs on employment and income generation, covering over sixty countries in Asia, Africa, Latin America, and eastern Europe.

These impact assessments were then used to channel SEED funds to the program that was most efficient in terms of cost and employment generation. Program leaders within the main BDS activities, therefore, paid considerable attention to the results of the impact studies, regardless of the country hosting the activity. They were told that additional funding would be contingent on their activities having an employment impact greater than or equal to the average of the other BDS activities.

While the intention was clearly to encourage greater project effectiveness, it did not easily translate into action. This was not necessarily due to staff laxity or corruption but rather to the large size of the ILO bureaucracy, where organizational changes are regularly made and staff is transferred internationally. The result was a loss of knowledge, dilution of original efforts (like evaluations), and less effective implementation. Apparently the outcome of this attempt to evaluate aid effectiveness was never published in a working paper, which makes one question how much interest there truly was in redressing the findings of the assessments. It seems that almost none of the BDS programs did especially well. Within a couple of years, the director of SEED was transferred, and the program was restructured so that the team was absorbed by various other subsectors of the employment sector. Some team members were transferred internationally to other ILO offices; others left ILO and moved on. So, in the end, SEED did get an idea about what worked and what did not; however, it is likely that this information was not used as effectively as it might have been. Moreover, the current ILO website confirms that several of the same old programs have continued with or without the old managers.

Source: Former SEED staff member, confidential communication, 2006.

of the system was the annual Results Review and Resource Request (R4) reports (chapter 3). USAID's individual country missions would send these to Washington as a management device "to link resource allocations and performance" (General Accounting Office 1996, p. 13). The system was also expected to generate some "race-to-the-top" competition among project officers, missions, and even bureaus within the agency.

Public Service Provision

Prospective contests have been used to raise the quality of public services such as education, health, parks, solid waste, and water infrastructure management, to name a few. France and Britain use competitive concessions to manage the waterworks across their river basins. Such "yardstick competition"—in which each concessionaire's performance may be judged by the average performance of concessionaires in the other basins—allows the water ministries to overcome the monopoly nature of water provision.

Poor or inadequate public services are a way of life in most developing countries, though these services are an important input to poverty alleviation. In Jharkhand, India, the Citizen Report Card (CRC) initiative (see chapter 3) "is a simple but powerful tool to provide public agencies with systematic feedback from users of public services . . . [by eliciting] feedback through sample surveys on aspects of service quality that users know best, and enabl[ing] public agencies to identify strengths and weakness in their work" (Public Affairs Foundation 2004). The CRC provides a benchmark on the initial quality of public services (in rural credit, forestry, health, education, and drinking water), as perceived by the intended beneficiaries, through "a comparison with other services, so that a strategic set of actions can be initiated" (Public Affairs Foundation 2004).

To achieve a substantial reduction in illiteracy, especially among females in order to ensure an immediate social and economic impact on the country, the government of Senegal launched a literacy education program using public-private partnerships (PPP) to exploit the private sector competencies (chapter 3). Literacy course development and instruction were outsourced to private entities by utilizing competitive bidding based on *quality,* not price, which was fixed per enrolled beneficiary. Funding proposals were generally developed between groups of villages and a community-based organization (CBO), and then scored by a special government selection committee. Over five years, the program funded 99 proposals (out of 368) and trained 200,000 women.

Charter Schools

These are intended to revitalize and improve the effectiveness of public schools (O'Reilly and Bosetti 2000, p. 19) by using market mechanisms such as school choice plans. Though they receive public funding, each school is autonomous and has a unique charter (O'Reilly and Bosetti 2000, p. 20). The license of charter schools must be renewed every five years and requires that the charter school exceed (typically) the average score of the regular public schools in standardized testing. Chile permits Catholic schools access to public education financing to compete against public schools; Canadian provinces allow choosing among public and private schools for the receipt of their property tax dollars (Shah 1997, p. 32).

Potential Proposal Stage Applications

By now it should be clear that the potential range of applications of the PIJC concept is rather broad. Yet the richness of the approach continues to be tested, as proposals submitted to sponsors (and their reactions) attest.

The Foreign Agricultural Service of the U.S. Department of Agriculture considered a proposal to organize a series of agricultural subsector competitions among counties (*rayons*) in Uzbekistan (Zinnes, Hansen, and Miller 2005).[46] The purpose was to improve the local institutional and technical support environment along the consumption-production chain. A tournament mechanism would encourage stakeholders within each competing rayon to engage in both collective action and individual efficiency improvements to increase the quantity and quality of their output *actually consumed*. The project would also involve local university partners who would not only provide the requisite local knowledge but also experience increased human and institutional capacity. Winning rayons would then receive rewards (such as further agricultural technical assistance, regional promotion of their agricultural products, access to international trade shows, or improvements in local infrastructure).

Together with the Bangladesh National Women Lawyers' Association, the IRIS Center formally proposed to the U.S. Department of State to introduce a set of tasks, focused on the problems of trafficking in persons, to encourage local officials and NGOs to improve local provision of law enforcement and social services.[47] Key elements included measurable, actionable benchmarks; a competition among localities based on the benchmarks; and publicity and extra technical assistance to the local governments of the most improved localities as rewards for success. Public discussion and transparent reporting on local progress would have an advantage over government-led programs in that it would not be susceptible to accusations of political motivation, not be hostage to ministry inaction or inattention, and not be held back by the slowest or worst performers.

Those with great expectations for Nigeria were greatly dismayed that no Nigerian university placed among the top 1,000 in a 2004 ranking of universities world-

---

46. Also unusual in this proposal was its plan to cover the project's costs in Uzbekistan with the local currency generated from sales of PL-40 wheat (bought from U.S. farmers with USDA aid funding).

47. This description has been paraphrased from Cadwell (2005).

wide conducted by *The Times*.[48] The minister of education of the Federal Republic of Nigeria requested I draft a preproposal for running a "tournament" among higher education institutions in Nigeria to encourage and empower local collaborative efforts to overcome "local obstacles" to school performance. Tasks were to include more powerful parent-teacher associations to improve public input and an independent source of accountability, greater parent involvement in providing after school activities, better local government oversight of school officials and budgets, more effective community provision of campus and neighborhood security, creation of part-time paid work in the community for students, greater administrative transparency, and better planning. Critically, the tournament was also to stimulate links between the educational and business investment environments, making better and more jobs go together.

Why none of these proposals has yet been implemented raises interesting questions. Are the applications inappropriate, were the proposals poorly designed, was there political resistance in the recipient country, or were the donor institutions intellectually or organizationally unprepared? While these questions are revisited in the last two chapters of the book, the short answer is that I do not believe there was a single common reason for their rejection. Still, it is likely that donor tepidness was an important factor. The institutional incentives in donor agencies encourage risk aversion, in spite of an official position to the contrary, and thus donors are reluctant to innovate, especially if one cannot point to a prior implementation.

1.4 Caveats and Contents

Before proceeding, some caveats are in order. First, while the focus is on tournaments, examination of alternative incentive mechanisms based on competition—auctions, procurement, privatization, insurance, and internal agency incentive systems (such as performance bonuses)—will be strictly limited, though they may play an important role in the effectiveness of sponsor and receipt organizations.[49]

Second, for the most part attention is limited to public policy experiences in developing and transition countries rather than countries in the OECD. Within this group the focus will be on the suitability of alternative formal incentive structures for influencing policy implementation and performance, especially when the cooperative participation of multiple stakeholder groups is necessary for success.

To make this task more manageable, however, I will not devote much attention to the political and institutional dynamics between the polity, government,

48. Times Higher Education, "World University Rankings 2004" (www.timeshighereducation. co.uk/hybrid.asp?typeCode=194&pubCode=1&navcode=120).

49. See Laffont and Tirole (1993) for an extensive treatment of many of these other types of competitions.

and sponsor that led to the selection of a particular incentive structure.[50] It will be apparent, though, that most of the cases considered here involve voluntary participation, so even if an initiative is sponsor driven—and this would run counter to the demand-driven nature of the approaches examined—individual or even all jurisdictions could opt out if they were uninterested in the sponsor's program. The fact that few do suggests that beneficiaries perceive the initiatives—regardless of their genesis—as worth their efforts. Moreover, a PIJC is usually designed to overcome adverse selection, that is, its incentive structure encourages only those who truly want the reform to self-select to participate. Thus, while each case study in chapters 3 and 4 begins with the objective stated by the sponsor and stakeholder beneficiaries, the extent to which a key stakeholder—say the government—has a different "real" motivation is not likely to diminish the outcomes of the first round of the contest. (This is also why precontest calibration through field testing of the task menu and rewards is so crucial to good outcomes.) In the longer term, a misalignment between sponsor and principal stakeholder objectives could adversely influence sustainability, especially if funding for future rounds depends on that stakeholder, a point emphasized in the case study discussion.

Third, it is important to stress that very few careful evaluations of tournaments have been done due to their newness. Without the availability of such data, the present research could not engage in the level of statistical rigor necessary to come to the definitive conclusions one would have liked. Therefore, both judgments about success or failure as well as recommendations based on apparent lessons learned must remain tentative.

Fourth, activities in the field of public policy and development assistance are extremely disparate. Hence the selection of cases whose diversity of applications and conditions reflects and illustrates the variety of public policy purposes for which PIJC might add productive performance incentives. Moreover, satisfactory outcomes under such diverse situations should increase confidence in the robustness of the approach.

On the other hand, this locational and substantive variation makes it difficult to keep up with the latest applications since, by their very nature, they are carried out in places of the world where communication is not always the best.[51] Likewise, no one country or organization has a monopoly on good ideas. This is especially true since advances in aid effectiveness are often one and the same as advances in government effectiveness, for which there are many microlevel, local initiatives under way around the world. Thus this book does not purport to be a compendium of *all* relevant projects under way or concluded.

---

50. I thank an anonymous referee for suggesting that this focus be made explicit. For an analysis of the political economy of policy reforms, see Brinkerhoff (2002).

51. There are donor efforts to improve communication, such as the World Bank's Development Gateway and USAID's microLINKS, which are clearly making laudable progress by using the Internet to close this information gap.

This incompleteness may not be as serious as one might think. Take the case of grant programs: once one understands the incentive mechanisms underlying the various types of grants encountered, cataloging them all would probably provide limited additional public policy information. On the other hand, this approach requires that the examples included in this book capture the range of relevant experience to date. Still, as discussed in section 2.6, there are limitations to relying on a small number of cases, even if statistical analysis is not contemplated. These include the risk associated with information from secondary or even potentially biased sources. I have tried to reduce these pitfalls by basing assessments on multiple sources, including unpublished expert opinion.

Finally, I should explicitly acknowledge the challenges of pursuing the idealized assessment models described in chapter 2.[52] One of these is to avoid the potential problems that could arise from defining the PIJC approach too narrowly. For example, as indicated above, manageability will require skirting the political and institutional dynamics that led to the choice of incentive mechanism. Another challenge relates to time: it might take a long time for some benefits of a PIJC to reach fruition; likewise, a PIJC's sustainability can only be judged in the long term, yet most of the cases examined here have not been in operation for a sufficient duration. In these instances the merits of the application are judged by the shorter-term benefits actually observed; thus I can only speculate on the application's prognosis for sustainability.

The next chapter continues the introduction of the concepts required to understand the PIJC and its component mechanisms, as well as the review of the literature begun above. It also presents the classification and evaluation frameworks used to assess experience to date with PIJC practice. In chapters 3 and 4, these frameworks are applied to a dozen PIJC examples, and additional experiences are briefly considered in chapter 5. In chapter 6 the application-specific conclusions are synthesized to analyze why some have been successful while others have not. Of particular interest is the source of an application's sustainability as well as the relevance of initial conditions. Chapter 7 concludes by weighing the pros and cons of PIJC as a development assistance delivery vehicle and identifies the institutional and other conditions under which the various types of PIJC might be most effective. Given all the caveats above, I must end on a cautionary note by underscoring that any "conclusions" reached will need to be taken as only suggestive, awaiting further study, either by more detailed research for a specific case or by identifying a larger number of similar applications.

---

52. I thank an anonymous referee for pointing out this concern.

2

The PIJC Approach

This chapter examines the PIJC concept and approach in more detail, decomposing it into analyzable incentive components to facilitate an assessment of past experience, especially in terms of sustainability, scalability, and the role of initial conditions. It begins with the canonical steps in a PIJC application and proceeds with an explanation of the concepts that underpin the analysis.[1] With this as a foundation, section 2.2 decomposes the PIJC into its constituent incentive components, which then leads to a discussion in section 2.3 of the typology of PIJC mechanisms. Subsequently section 2.4 makes a small detour to show how PIJC approaches are ideally suited for rigorous evaluation, an up-and-coming area of major emphasis among sponsors. Next, section 2.5 presents the evaluation framework, used in chapters 3 and 4 to evaluate past and current experience with PIJC applications. The chapter ends with discussions of how the case studies in chapters 3 and 4 were selected for inclusion in this analysis and how they are organized for presentation purposes.

2.1 Canonical Steps in a PIJC Application

Just as economists study the perfect competition model to understand the impact of the inevitable real-world deviations from it, I begin by examining the stylized full-blown version of a PIJC. Then actual cases are provided where one

1. Canonical here means idealized, comprehensive, or complete as specified by the full model. Perhaps a synonym would be full-blown. As will be seen, in practice not all the canonical steps are always taken.

can observe what design characteristics are absent or additional, why, and whether it matters.

Any sponsor (for example, central government) must explicitly or implicitly address several steps in the design of a PIJC. In practice the complexity of these steps depends on initial conditions and objectives.[2] Still, in principle a PIJC comprises the following steps, each with a number of tasks.

State the Problem

A successful intervention needs to begin with a correct assessment of what is "broken." Such an assessment may be done by the sponsor or by the recipients or their representatives (for example, the government). All incentive designs are amenable to being driven by beneficiary demand and collective action in particular. This assessment consists of two parts: identifying the symptoms and identifying the causes.

Recipients may not be aware of causal symptoms since they have lived under them for so long. Thus symptom identification can benefit from the observations of an outside authority. However, a recipient may not agree that the symptoms are a problem, so that any further intervention by a sponsor may encounter resistance. It is even less likely that recipients will be aware of the true causes of the symptoms under which they suffer. It is not surprising, therefore, that identification of causes is typically the purview of the sponsor or initiating NGO.

Set Objectives

The sponsor makes the objective(s) explicit. For concreteness in illustrating the remaining steps, consider two alternative cases for a target region containing municipalities. In the first the central government desires to reduce corruption; in the second it desires to increase youth employment.

Set Tasks

The sponsor identifies a list of tasks to certify or reward, each of which either fulfills or contributes to the objectives. In the case of corruption, these might include a reduction in time and effort to acquire start-up, construction, and operating permits; public declaration of senior officials' assets; presumptive permitting; an independent oversight office; an anonymous telephone hotline; and transparent dissemination of new regulations and budget allocations. In the case of increasing youth employment, these might include improving government investment-related rules and administrative procedures, support for job skills training,

2. *Initial conditions* refers to any country characteristics present at the initiation of the project that might influence outcomes. Such characteristics may be institutional (cultural, religious, legislative, organizational or governmental), economic, demographic, climatic, political, social, geographic, historical, or financial, among others.

placement centers, civic action, and business initiatives, and better oversight of governance at the communal level. Appendixes B and C provide additional examples of tasks appropriate for the case of local government reforms.

Ideally, the objectives and tasks should derive from focus groups of key stakeholders and small-scale surveys of the targeted population and their decision-makers, as well as a sponsor's independent assessments. A youth employment PIJC application would likely require collaboration with and canvassing of youth organizations, business associations, local government agencies, religious schools, and the like. Once this initial due diligence has identified a draft superset of potential tournament tasks, these then should be subject to further scrutiny, for example, by experts and possibly via town meetings.

One cannot overstress the importance of beneficiary involvement in task identification. Such participation ensures that a sponsor has chosen an issue that is of specific use to the jurisdiction and has tailored it to the jurisdiction's idiosyncratic initial conditions. Beneficiary input also creates buy-in during implementation; it gives beneficiaries a stake in the outcome, and they feel they are in charge of their own efforts instead of simply being dictated to from above. These effects have been shown to lead to much more effective impacts (Platteau 2005). Still, as corroborated by the experience of the World Bank with development policy lending (DPL), when an objective of PIJC is policy change, the underlying mechanism "should focus on [changes] that are state-initiated (and not civil society–initiated), as the government cannot assume responsibility for actions that are not within its realm of control" (World Bank 2005a).[3]

It is important to make a clear distinction between the task menu, which is established in advance of PIJC play, and the activities a player may select to achieve each task. Unlike the standard approach of sponsors where they use their extensive knowledge and experience to dictate which, how, and when tasks are to be done, PIJC is ideally suited to take advantage of the more recent community-driven approach (Platteau 2005). Hence, while the sponsor sets final objectives, tasks, and the methodology to measure outcomes (indicators), the sponsor need *not* dictate how players are to achieve their own outcomes. Moreover, in the case of a tournament, since the mechanism design already motivates players do their best, the idea is that players will draw optimally on their own idiosyncratic local knowledge and sponsor recommendations in their efforts to win.

Establish Outcome Indicators

The requirement that the indicators be objective, viewed as legitimate, and free of (measurement) discretion implies that they must comprise measurable characteristics. Thus the construction of quantitative measures is crucial to generating

---

3. Also available online at ftp://ftp.worldbank.org/pub/asyed/PrintVersions/DPL07.02.07.pdf. See the end of chapter 5 for more lessons from the World Bank's experience with DPLs in connection with PIJC.

effective competition. Indicators may be dichotomous, discrete, or continuous. Data may come from pre- and postgame surveys as well as from statistics already being collected by the government or other agencies. Critically, each task indicator must be actionable, ungameable, and highly correlated to the task it purports to measure.[4] These last two characteristics are particularly insidious. For example, using the number of students graduated as a measure of school performance could lead school administrators to graduate students who have not achieved the academic standards. Whether or not a baseline and an endline measurement are required before and after game play, respectively, depends on whether the rating system is based on the level of performance or the degree of improvement and on whether there is to be quantitative, prospective, and impact evaluation. Finally, in addition to ensuring the critical characteristics above, tests of appropriate indicators should also confirm that potential players will easily understand the indicator and accept its methodology as legitimate.[5] The Indonesian Program for Pollution Control, Evaluation, and Rating (PROPER) and the Moroccan Business Investment Environment (BIE, pronounced "buy") indicator program, discussed in detail in section 3.1.3 and section 4.2.3, respectively, are exemplary in this regard.

While this is not the place to review the literature on indicator design, it is useful to briefly mention several types typically used in a PIJC.[6] The first uses certification indicators to confirm whether (typically intermediate) tasks in the competition have indeed been completed. An example would be the issuance of a regulation, an intermediate outcome. The second uses a procedure to compute a measurable score for each task of each player (for example, the degree to which firms are in compliance with a regulation, which might be considered a final outcome for a competition). The third type of indicator design for a PIJC involves constructing aggregate indicators that summarize overall performance in a way that citizens can easily understand. For example, Glewwe, Ilias, and Kremer (2003) use a school ranking indicator, Meagher and Zinnes (2004) propose the BIE Star rating (analogous to the Michelin guides), and the Global Competitiveness Report uses a country ranking indicator.

It is important that all potential jurisdictions know that *regardless of their decision to participate,* their jurisdiction will be benchmarked (rated) so as to avoid creating an incentive for risk-averse decisionmakers to opt out. Note that while the aggregate indicators reflecting each PIJC objective are usually themselves not directly actionable, their constituent task subindicators should be. In any case, the

---

4. For an indicator to be *actionable,* it should be clear to the player what actions it can take to directly affect the indicator. Hence an indicator of generalized corruption in a country (such as a corruption perception index) would not be actionable, whereas an indicator of the number of officials indicted for bribe taking at the department of taxation would be. For an indicator to be *ungameable,* it should be difficult for players to undertake actions that would raise their indicator score without simultaneously making progress on the associated task.

5. This distinction is discussed further in section 2.3.

6. See Arndt and Oman (2006) and Zinnes, Eilat, and Sachs (2001) for details.

exact indicators as well as their methodologies must be transparent and made available to the players before the start of the game to achieve maximum incentive response.

The use of an objective measurement tool creates several advantages.[7] First, it motivates competition since it translates diffuse goals of effectiveness into "bright" performance measures. Second, it allows the sponsor or the higher-level government overseers to identify more successful outcomes—an often noted benefit of innovation resulting from decentralization. Third, it allows players or sponsors to monitor outcomes and to introduce midgame corrections when a particular implementation appears not to be bearing fruit.

Set Priorities

The sponsor should assign points to each task or activity to reflect its importance in achieving the specified objective.[8] *Importance* refers here to the sponsor's valuation—paternalistic or otherwise—of the benefits of the particular task, not the degree of implementation difficulty for the player. In other words, one may think of the point system as weights or "shadow prices" reflecting the sponsor's priorities. Finally, since the method of indicator aggregation will generally carry implications for the implicit weights the tasks receive, the point scheme should also be explicitly described in the game manual.

In setting priorities, the sponsor may establish minimum thresholds of acceptable performance for each task (indicator) so that no points are received below the threshold and so that consolation prize credit is given above it.[9] The sponsor must also decide whether, in the case of tournament designs, there will be a fixed set of tasks, whose thresholds a winner must exceed, or a menu of task categories from which players may pick and choose.[10]

For simplicity, the set of predefined tasks, the outcome indicator for each, and the aggregation methodology (with the weights reflecting sponsor preferences) are referred to as the *rating system*. To be maximally motivating, the indicators and methodology should be simple enough so that all stakeholders and players can fully understand them and view them as feasible and legitimate. It should be stressed

7. Of course, inadequately aligned indicators can lead to player gaming of the indicators and even perverse outcomes (for example, graduation of failing students where school performance is based on graduation rates). See Arndt and Oman (2006).

8. When a tournament has multiple objectives, priorities (and weights) must also be assigned to the objectives. This gives the municipality more latitude to choose the objectives to pursue, with the weights reflecting the sponsor's preferences.

9. Of course, if the player wins or places, then it presumably would not receive a consolation prize. As I argue further on, the consolation prize is important for ensuring maximal participation of jurisdictions whose self-assessment of potential performance is low relative to their beliefs about that of potential competitors.

10. Recall from section 1.2 that a tournament is a contest in which "reward structures [are] based on rank order" rather than on achieving a particular performance (Green and Stokey 1983, p. 350).

that the level of complexity of the rating system is an important decision parameter in tournament design and must be commensurate with the players' capacity to understand and internalize the ensuing incentives. This may lead, for example, to a system with no aggregation (no subindicators) and equal task weights.

Establish a Commitment Mechanism

Since an important aspect of the PIJC is to overcome impediments to collective action and coordination failure, it is helpful for the PIJC design to include a sequence of incremental actions that the players must take to signal their growing commitment to the PIJC and its objectives. For example, a prospective player would need to send a representative to attend the initial, convened conference to explain the PIJC. Players may need to form committees or elect game representatives or leaders (such as the president of the communal council or mayor of the municipality). Additional requirements may include the holding of public hearings, a letter to the king (in the case of Morocco), the passage of a local order or a letter to the overseeing ministry committing the SNG to the undertaking, or advertisements in the local media by the local administration stating their commitment. In a common configuration, for example, such signaling would then allow the player access to basic technical assistance during the early months of game play. As play progresses and the serious players continue to reveal themselves by beginning to generate concrete intermediate results, they gain access to additional, more valuable (and expensive to the sponsor) technical assistance and perhaps milestone "prizes."

Offer Technical Assistance

Players exhibiting evidence of striving to implement PIJC tasks may be offered assistance on a graduated scale throughout the game period, though it should be concentrated during the first half. The technical assistance is an input to the improvements sought, not an end in itself. Given the large number of players (for example, municipalities) the PIJC motivates, assistance may be provided in two complementary ways to reduce transaction costs. First, assistance at the start of play should be provided through workshops attended by representatives of each player group. These group sessions get smaller over time since continued participation in them is contingent upon players demonstrating their seriousness *through reform action* during the early stages of the competition. The workshops allow players to share challenges, experiences, and even confusions about PIJC play. Second, where feasible, the Internet may be used to offer an easy way for hundreds of project stakeholders to stay informed and receive technical information updates on PIJC activities.[11] The Internet may also be used to *receive*

---

11. This is a natural extension of present proposals for the introduction of "e-government" (Bhatnagar and Deane 2004).

information from players, such as self-reported performance updates.[12] Furthermore, Internet forums can facilitate inter- and intracommunal sharing of reform experience. Finally, technical assistance questions and clarifications of PIJC procedures can be answered via the Internet, with responses quickly distributed to all.

Plan Strategic Communications

Such planning is extremely important for the success of the enterprise. First, it must create public awareness—and, ideally, interest—in the PIJC, both before and during game play. Second, since one of the PIJC's most powerful rewards is the "PR" it generates for the locality and its politicians, it is critical that credible and effective means are provided for broad dissemination of who the winners, placers, also-rans, and laggards are—and that the participating public know *in advance* that this will be done. Hence in many PIJCs results are disseminated by a dedicated website. However disseminated, in the more successful applications, task indicators are easily interpretable by the audience whose behavior is targeted. Third, the task selection process should involve special communications and public participation protocols to ensure legitimacy, precommitment, and stakeholder ownership. It is not surprising, therefore, that several of the case studies examined in chapters 3 and 4 include pre-, mid-, and post-PIJC plenary meetings with representatives of all player teams. Finally, while not strictly part of strategic communications, the PIJC manual should be carefully tested, perhaps in a focus group milieu, to ensure it supports the incentives underlying the game.

Design and Select Incentive Mechanisms

PIJC in principle can create a different kind of motivation than is typical for government transfers or development assistance. Rather than merely serving as a conduit of funding, training, or information, the heart of the PIJC approach is to create cooperation by fielding a competition in which the players are generally jurisdictions. The competition becomes a temporary albeit credible and neutral "institution" that acts to bring otherwise suspicious and uncooperative local interests together to pursue common goals.

In a typical application, a PIJC harnesses the incentives of competition *across* jurisdictions (the "players") in a prescribed geographic area to stimulate cooperation and collective action of groups *within* each jurisdiction to improve targeted aspects of local government performance. The players, for example, may be the individual municipalities, counties, or communities; specific public agencies within each of these; or teams comprising both. A good PIJC design seeks to exploit links among stakeholders within teams. For example, to address youth unemployment in Morocco, the PIJC aligned incentives to link communal officials with private business—encouraging value-added enhancing reform, not cor-

---

12. Likewise, civil society will be able to track activity and report on compliance over the Internet.

ruption. Likewise, in the proposed Nigerian education PIJC described in section 1.3, links were created between the school administration, stakeholders in the broader educational environment, and those offering job opportunities.

To design a PIJC, the sponsor first needs to identify explicitly the target group and the eligibility criteria, create the rules of the game on how players may compete, and set the length of play and when events should occur (for instance, the baseline and follow-up surveys). The design must also indicate how to amass "points" on the rating system as well as whether it is the *level* achieved or the degree of *improvement* made in performance that counts. This generally depends on the task and range of player starting conditions.[13] Scoring of *improvements* along a task is used when it is necessary to prevent the most "advanced" players at the start of the game from having an unfair advantage and, worse, discouraging other players from competing. These features of the game help establish the necessary incentives for the overall project to function.

Still, several countervailing factors enter in the design of scoring. On the one hand, it may seem obvious that the award should go to the highest-performing player. However, such a basis for awards might send confusing signals. For example, if a jurisdiction goes from zero "stars" to three stars on a business environment rating, it is still not likely to be as good a place to do business as one that begins and ends with four stars. On the other hand, it may seem silly to give an award to a jurisdiction that did nothing but just happened to have high scores on the requisite indicators before the start of the PIJC. However, a sponsor might not know this before running the baseline. Such a situation occurred during a PIJC in Romania, where one of the winners (Timisoara) began the competition being practically in compliance with all the tasks (see section 3.1.1). This is a particular danger for the absolutist or certification approaches. If the certification bar is placed too low, then those jurisdictions that find themselves above it need not exert any additional effort. If the bar is placed too high, too many jurisdictions will feel intimidated and not try at all. Yet, as the examples in this book illustrate, this approach is essentially the predominant one used, even though it places relatively heavy informational burdens on the sponsor.

During the actual period of play, the PIJC players—for example, municipalities—compete to amass as many points as possible. Players will take care to select only those tasks *they* believe would receive the strongest support within their constituency and which their jurisdiction might collectively be capable of implementing. (This need for teamwork is one reason why local public hearings should be held as part of the commitment process.) They then allocate their efforts across some or all of the tasks (or reforms) of their choosing from the PIJC task menu, subject to time, budget, and collective action constraints of the player (for

13. From an econometric perspective, this is analogous to the issue of when to use a difference-in-differences approach (see Bertrand, Duflo, and Mullainathan 2004).

example, community), and based on their collective preferences. As a consequence, different players will generally pursue different combinations of tasks. It is the role of the weights to signal, as would prices in the marketplace, the relative values the seller (that is, the sponsor) places on each task.

As discussed in detail in section 6.2, this demand-driven approach tends toward allocative efficiency: only players can know their own cost functions and preferences, and only the sponsor can know its own (marginal) valuations of the proposed tasks. Likewise, where player teams have a role in the identification of activities and where participation is voluntary, reforms only occur with the complete cooperation of representatives of the population of potential players—in short, the PIJC can have great legitimacy. From the sponsor's perspective, since most jurisdictions engage in the reforms but only winners receive significant sponsor rewards in a tournament PIJC, this format also leverages the sponsor's funds, limited local knowledge, and monitoring effort.

Determine Rewards

While the main benefit of competing is surely the fruits of reform, there are still a number of other reasons for outside support. First, where a recipient is serious about exerting the requisite efforts, additional resources—and not necessarily of the financial sort—can provide inputs unavailable locally, speed outcomes, and increase its chances of success. Second, experience suggests that additional targeted incentives are often required to overcome principal-agent and coordination problems, as well as to compensate decisionmakers bearing unspreadable risk. Thus, while the nature of the prizes will depend on the specific reform objectives, the types of prizes should be selected to maximize player (stakeholder) interest—that is, from those groups in government, the private sector, and civil society whose actions and cooperation are needed to effect change.[14]

The reward schedule should cover winning and placing players as well as those meriting a consolation prize for exceeding a task threshold score. In the case of youth employment, these rewards may be, for example, in the form of access to more substantial technical assistance, cofinancing for firms in the municipality, and free investment and trade promotion (including foreign travel for some municipal officials). In the case of anticorruption efforts, these rewards might be technical assistance in procurement and even infrastructure financing. In this way, aid

14. On a given application, a donor should elicit information about costs (effort) and benefits to player principals and agents in order to design a strategy to stimulate high levels of effort (performance). Consider the example of municipalities. To get the decisionmaker on board so that the individual assumes the risks of failure, a guaranteed reward must be offered. Next, to ensure that the decisionmaker does more than "go through the motions" (does not shirk), he or she needs a contingent reward. To get the polity on board, credible insurance must be offered against switching and retooling costs (from pretournament objectives to tournament objectives). Likewise, to get the polity to focus on doing well and to exert pressure on their decisionmakers, a contingent reward may be required.

is given to those who are serious about the sponsor's agenda and show through their own performance that they can take advantage of the aid.

To elicit high effort among differentially capable competitors (a point returned to later), prizes or awards may also be tiered. In the case of Galing Pook in the Philippines, discussed below, there are municipality innovation prizes for the winners of the annual event as well as prizes for municipalities that have won prizes in several of the annual tournaments (Galing Pook Foundation 2005). In a tournament run by International Child Support in Kenya, a two-tiered award system was used, one for top-scoring schools and one for most-improved schools (Glewwe, Ilias, and Kremer 2003). At the extreme, the prize can be a continuous function of performance, an example being the trainer bonus used in a USAID SME marketing training initiative (Azfar and Zinnes 2003).

In tournaments where tasks are either more complicated or require an extended time for implementation or to observe results, the PIJC designer should consider offering intermediate result prizes. As suggested above, at a minimum this would include a schedule of technical assistance accessible by degree of progress. In the case of the Moroccan PIJC, communes that had met the milestone of implementing the de jure parts of a task were offered a computer workstation.

Integrate Evaluation (Optional)

A monitoring and evaluation (M&E) plan is now becoming a part of donor projects (Kusek and Rist 2004), as epitomized by MCC and Gates Foundation practices.[15] Due to the requirement that the PIJC have rigorous and nonmanipulable performance measures and that there be a relatively large number of players, the additional design effort for a prospective, rigorous M&E plan in a PIJC application is relatively straightforward.[16] To be effective, however, the M&E plan must be clear to all stakeholders, implementers, and their supervising agency. M&E has several benefits, which are discussed below.[17]

It is interesting to compare just how similar the steps in this framework are to those proposed by Klitgaard, MacLean-Abaroa, and Parris (1998) to address municipal corruption, including

—participatory diagnosis (including those involved in corruption),

—setting rewards and penalties and collecting information that is then linked to them,

—using publicity to raise awareness of efforts and the problem,

15. See the MCC website at www.mcc.gov.

16. As discussed further on, the main challenges are to identify a control group that is free of contamination and to ensure that the control group includes some players who wanted to "play" but were not allowed to. The latter is required to avoid false positives, that is, the confounding of positive performance effects on players of the tournament with self-selection effects (where only better performers would enter the tournament and weaker ones would stay out).

17. See Picciotto (2005) for a discussion of how to use evaluation to improve aid effectiveness.

—using measures to allow civil servants tangible recognition so that positive efforts are seen to pay off, and

—increasing the use of information collection.

2.2 Decomposition of the PIJC Mechanism

As pointed out in chapter 1, the concept of IJC is well known in the literature of public finance economics (Oates 2002). In its usual form, localities and even countries compete against each other, typically for business investment. For example, Singapore has successfully competed against Hong Kong and other countries with good port access and quick cargo transit. Cities compete on the quality of their infrastructure to host the Olympic Games. Here competition has led to a "race to the top" in which jurisdictions claim to offer more highly educated workers and better amenities. In a different manifestation, U.S. states have used tax holidays to lure Japanese car manufacturers to set up plants in their jurisdiction, while at the same time some in the United States assert that developing countries have (unfairly) competed against them by offering less stringent regulation (such as via so-called "pollution havens" and lack of child labor prohibitions). These are examples of where competition can lead to a "race to the bottom."

With a PIJC-based delivery vehicle, there are several ways to ensure that the race is to the top. A principal reason this is possible is because the competition is *prospective,* namely, the jurisdictions commit in advance to a set of preestablished ground rules on what to achieve, how to do so, and what the reward structure will be. Thus the competition is not tacit but explicit. Moreover, sponsors and players are able to agree on tasks that are not immiserating. Such competition draws out the most efficient effort from participants—efficient in that a player's effort is endogenously determined by the size of the rewards (both indirect benefits, due to the reform per se, and direct rewards from the sponsor) and the privately valued costliness (degree) of effort expended by the player.

Tournament incentives can be harnessed in powerful ways. Incentives of this type have become prevalent in a large number of economic settings because of their ability to generate high performance across all contestants even when organizers have limited information on the capabilities of participants or do not want to set bounds on possible performance levels.[18] Executive compensation, research and development (patent races), college admissions, the Olympics, and agricultural production contracts all have incentive structures that can be classified as tournaments. In 2007 the X Prize Foundation and the software giant Google announced a tournament with a top prize of $20 million in which the winner is the team that first puts an unmanned rover on the moon, drives it for 500 meters,

---

18. The tournament nature of many economic transactions is extensively analyzed in the experimental economics and mechanism design literatures (see Kagel and Roth 1995).

and beams back high-quality videos.[19] PIJC takes advantage of the incentive properties of the tournament by tailoring tasks and rewards to activities that strengthen local political institutions and civil society with the aim of fostering economic development.

Since only a few PIJC tournaments have actually been implemented—not to mention evaluated—there is limited experience with their performance and necessary conditions for success. As discussed in section 1.4, this fact substantially weakens the confidence in any conclusions one may reach. This book attempts to address the limited opportunity for practical assessment by first disaggregating a generic tournament application into its constituent incentive components in this section and then considering in the next two chapters the experience with the much greater number of applications that do exist containing subsets of PIJC components. As will be seen, there is conceptual overlap among the groupings used here to organize the PIJC components.

Before these components are examined, an important design issue must be clarified, namely, the possibility that project performance may be concerned with either an *input* or an *output*. Here, input refers to an intermediate result whose occurrence is necessary for achieving a downstream objective; output refers to a final result that *is* the ultimate objective. In other words, an input is part of the means to the output. For example, the PIJC approach may reward inputs (law passed, entrepreneurs trained) or outputs (degree of compliance with the law, increased production or profits of trained entrepreneurs). The terms inputs and outputs, however, only make sense relative to a *process*. In the above example, the reform process is to improve regulation or to generate economic growth. At the same time, a PIJC is itself a process and consists of a "before" and "after." One must be careful, therefore, to make a substantive distinction between the inputs and outputs of the reform process and of the PIJC process.

This may seem obvious, but there is much ambiguity in the literature, where a player's pre-PIJC baseline performance is called an input measure and player's post-PIJC endline performance is called an output measure. Yet there are PIJCs where the postcontest outcome is the passage of a law or training of entrepreneurs, which I have just argued is an input, and PIJCs where the winner has the smallest budget deficit at the start of a certification process, which refers to a *pre*contest *output*. In what follows, baseline and endline measures will refer to pre- and postcontest *performance,* respectively, and input and output will refer to the different stages in the governmental reform process. This book argues that the most successful PIJCs are those in which winning performance is based on postcontest *outputs*, not *inputs*.

There is a growing applied literature on output-based approaches to economic development, perhaps initiated by the work on procurement (for example, Laffont

---

19. There is also a prize for second place. As of this writing, twelve teams are in the running. See X Prize Foundation, "Google Lunar X Prize" (www.googlelunarxprize.org) for the latest details.

and Tirole 1993), and such approaches are becoming more common in a raft of applications. The OECD has now recognized the importance of this design element for public sector modernization—what it calls "governing for performance" (OECD 1999). A host of examples exists for infrastructure provision and operation (such as ports, rail, and highways) and service provision (such as water provision and rubbish collection).[20] This means that winning and placing in a PIJC should be based on de facto performance, not de jure intent. For example, passing stroke-of-pen reforms, while perhaps necessary to effect change, should not be sufficient to generate PIJC "points"; only measurable results pursuant to the stated objective should be.[21] This orientation has the added benefit of allowing one to exploit evaluation technologies to assess rigorously the extent that the tournament had an impact, a feature covered later in section 2.3 and one that is useful, for example, when a ministry is to consider scaling up a local PIJC application to the national level.

Competition Mechanism

PIJC components contain a mechanism that works toward increasing the *allocative efficiency* and cost-effectiveness of the intervention. A principal reason for this is that the tournament mechanism possesses all the properties—good and bad—that economists have discovered in competition. For example, the tournament mechanism can encourage maximal efforts from participants. Its use of competition means that what counts is *relative* performance, and as discussed in section 2.1, this helps to overcome the informational problem for the donor (and often for the recipient, too) of knowing how much achievement (effort) a recipient is capable of. Likewise, a tournament mechanism per se ensures a tremendous leveraging of donor funds. For example, in the case of Galing Pook in the Philippines, the cost of providing financial and nonpecuniary incentives to between 5 and 10 recipient jurisdictions motivated over 200 jurisdictions to carry out reforms. Furthermore, the technical assistance is targeted: it is "laddered" so that the amount and type of technical assistance a jurisdiction receives depends on how far along a predefined schedule of milestones the jurisdiction has gone, and it is provided only to those jurisdictions that meet reform-dependent thresholds of performance. In addition, the effect of this results-based technical assistance is enhanced by being demand driven.[22]

---

20. For many additional examples, see Penelope Brook and Murray Petrie, "Output-Based Aid: Precedents, Promises and Challenges" (www.gpoba.org/docs/05intro.pdf).

21. In the Morocco example, while stroke-of-pen "reforms" are sufficient to signal commitment and thereby trigger receipt of sponsor technical assistance *during* the tournament, points are only awarded for changes on the ground as a result of reform implementation.

22. Note that unlike most output-based aid, which focuses on efficient delivery through linking payment to performance (see, for example, Smith 2001), PIJC applications additionally contain mechanisms that ensure that beneficiary preferences will guide the nature of the services actually provided—that is, PIJCs also include a demand side.

Incentive Alignment Mechanisms

Another set of mechanisms within PIJC ensures the *incentive compatibility* of the PIJC. This refers to the property that the incentives facing the players (jurisdictions) and created by PIJC are such that they align player objectives (and therefore efforts) to those of the sponsor. As will be shown, this is possible by giving the beneficiary a real role in the selection of project goals, tasks to achieve them, and assistance they would require; strengthening institutional governance; and explicitly providing in-kind, pecuniary, or reputational rewards for those who would otherwise bear net costs from the intervention, either because as decisionmakers they assume direct political risks or because the project produces positive externalities.[23]

A major benefit of this PIJC feature is that in principle much less onsite monitoring of reform efforts by the sponsor is necessary than is normally the case. First, the players themselves have an interest in the success of the activity. Second, since performance is relative, all players have an active interest in detecting and reporting any "cheating" or corruption that other players might engage in. Third, performance is generally determined by quantitative measurement (baselines or endlines or both). This is in stark contrast to the conventional situation where donors spend considerable resources, both in money and time, monitoring recipient actions. Due to the explicit steps typically taken in a PIJC to involve the potential beneficiary in task identification and to have participation voluntary through self-selection, the tournament design effectively harnesses rather than fights recipient incentives.

Incentive compatibility has yet another consequence. It helps to overcome the tremendous information asymmetry between donors (and their foreign consultants) and the local recipients—that is, critical project know-how is impacted with the recipient. As in the sense of Williamson (1975, p. 31) *impacted* here means that the know-how cannot be transferred to others (such as the donor or its foreign implementers) and only can be drawn upon indirectly through the execution of its (local) owner's skills—for example, how to introduce microfinance skills to women in rural Indian households or how to navigate humanitarian assistance through a corrupt port or guerilla-controlled territory. Under the incentive-compatible design of a PIJC, the sponsor recognizes that the players have their interests broadly aligned to those of the sponsor and therefore is less dependent on extracting the players' local know-how or on micromanaging local implementers with such know-how.[24]

---

23. Economics explains that when a service generates positive externalities, those bearing the costs will underprovide for (underinvest in) its provision. From a public policy perspective, this is often considered a valid reason to subsidize it.

24. Notice how know-how and preferences over service provision are not the same thing; the former is very hard to transfer while the latter is not (though their revelation can be subject to strategic responses).

Harnessing Socially Based Incentives for Change

A PIJC should strive to harness as many incentives as possible while keeping its overall design as simple as possible. There are certain components of change, often overlooked, that are instrumental to the PIJC approach and, especially, to increasing the *legitimacy* of the reforms it stimulates. One is the power of public participation and public feedback mechanisms.[25] To ensure that all stakeholders are on board and form a team focused on placing in a tournament, a PIJC should require that commitment devices be used to engage them. Thus the PIJC approach advocates requiring that public hearings (or their analogous equivalent, depending on the application) be held as a condition for a tournament task to be registered. For a PIJC in Morocco, Meagher and Zinnes (2004) required that municipality mayors sign public statements of their decision to participate after holding such town meetings.

Likewise, in a PIJC the jurisdictions themselves should participate in creating the menu of reforms from which they may then choose a subset of individual reforms to implement. The technical assistance a jurisdiction receives during the tournament should also be demand driven. On the one hand, it is left to the jurisdiction to decide whether to participate in particular technical assistance workshops; on the other hand, the sponsor requires the jurisdiction to fulfill certain performance conditions (discussed below) to be eligible for the technical assistance.

A second underutilized mechanism is the power of collective action, either through public-private partnerships or with adjacent municipalities. Such devices are particularly useful for small municipalities that cannot achieve economies of scale. Examples include joint purchasing (for instance, fire equipment), joint concessions (trash removal), and joint industrial park creation (in the Moroccan PIJC) and road building (in the Kecamatan Development Program [KDP] in Indonesia). A PIJC may take advantage of this mechanism by requiring that a collaborative interjurisdictional task be included in the tournament, either as an item on the menu of eligible tasks or as a required task.

While collective action and competition-inducing cooperation can be viewed as positive incentive forces, the PIJC should also make use of a third socially based component of change: peer and social pressure, sometimes referred to as the "blame and shame" mechanism. This is especially effective when jurisdictions differentiate themselves ethnically, religiously, politically, or even just jurisdictionally (as in "our hometown football team is better than their hometown team"). In other words, a jurisdiction-based tournament tends to harness social capital, leading to collective action and using the power of peer pressure to mit-

---

25. This is also referred to as empowerment. See World Bank (2001c, part 3) and Narayan (2002) for a further discussion on the power of these forces to improve institutional performance.

igate free riding.[26] This is another example of the point underscored throughout this book, that *inter*jurisdictional competition has the power to encourage *intra*-jurisdictional cooperation.

From this perspective, it is critical that *all* jurisdictions within the target population be measured—and their baseline and benchmark results be widely disseminated—for maximum incentive effect. Otherwise, potential participants will simply opt out of playing for fear of being compared to other jurisdictions. Moreover, members of a jurisdiction frequently will not otherwise even be aware of their relative standing. For example, in the PROPER tournament in Indonesia (see section 3.1.3), players—in this case large industrial plant owners—were not previously aware of how bad their own environmental profiles were.[27]

Benchmarking Mechanism

Perhaps the most concrete as well as commonly employed mechanism in a PIJC application is the use of actionable indicators and benchmarking. To repeat, during a PIJC application, a set of indicator readings are taken before and after the tournament. Roughly, changes between the two measurements are then attributed to differential efforts of the player during the PIJC.[28] The adjective "actionable" must be stressed: it is important that players can act upon the benchmarks generated *and* also trust that the benchmarks are correct, which would be less likely if they were purely conceptual. It is also important to stress that readings are taken of all potential players within the population targeted, whether they agree to play or not. This incentive design essentially leads to (almost) voluntary disclosure, shaming of poor performance, and greater transparency and freedom of information at the level of the players' constituencies.[29]

Several applications described in chapters 3 and 4 use benchmarks to identify good business environments. This provides a way for citizens in each locality to judge just how their own institutions are faring relative to those of their

26. See Dasgupta and Serageldin (2000) or Grootaert and Bastelaer (2002) for multifaceted reviews of social capital's role in economic development. For a plethora of insights on collective action problems for development, see Ostrom (2000).

27. According to one story, owners were especially irked when their wives complained of embarrassment in front of other wives of the elite when the poor environmental scores of their husbands' factories were publicized! Personal communication from a minister, 2005.

28. That is, while there will be other factors influencing outcomes, these factors are likely to have affected all players symmetrically and therefore need not be accounted for in establishing a ranking. (Of course, such factors would need to be considered in a proper statistical impact evaluation, as discussed in section 2.4 on M&E.)

29. See Mendel (2004) for the trends and standards under way to place freedom of information on a more solid legal standing in developing countries.

neighbors.[30] Similarly, an international website can be set up and promoted so that not just domestic parties but also foreign investors and sponsors are able to see which localities are serious about improving their business and investment environment.[31]

Finally, due to the use of benchmarking with quantifiable outcome indicators, the relatively large number of jurisdictions (or players, as the case may be) participating in a PIJC means that it is ideally suited to prospective randomized evaluation. This ensures that the effectiveness of the outcomes of the donor's intervention can be known with statistical precision.

Decentralization Mechanism

A PIJC applied to local jurisdictions (as opposed to other types of players as described elsewhere in this book) may be seen as an application of decentralization. For example, in the cases described in chapter 1 regarding human rights and local governance, PIJC applications were designed to encourage local governments to exercise statutory rights already legislated but not implemented. This is akin to what physical therapy does: restore lost function by exercising atrophied or unused muscles. The PIJC performs the same way in that it encourages the players to play the game of implementing laws that hitherto had existed only in on paper ("unused muscles"). Winners of the PIJC generate innovative solutions to problems that are likely being faced by most of the other players, just like a good decentralization typically leads to some jurisdictions demonstrating solutions to local government problems ubiquitous among the other jurisdictions. While in theory this could occur with any donor intervention, in a PIJC, as in decentralization, there are large numbers of applications of the same intervention, thereby generating much more variation in experience and greater likelihood for replicable lessons.

Signaling Mechanism

The structure of a well-designed PIJC uses the mechanism of what economists call a separating equilibrium, which minimizes adverse selection. This means that the incentive design of the PIJC splits jurisdictions in two: one group of jurisdictions serious about carrying out reform that will be encouraged to self-select to participate in the PIJC (and draw upon sponsor resources) and another group not interested in reform (but *still* desirous of sponsor resources) that will opt out of tournament participation. Participation in the tournament allows members of the former group to signal to outsiders, donors, and investors alike

---

30. This innovation highlights an often neglected aspect of indicators: they are only effective if those who need to act on the information both can easily interpret them *and* have legal avenues to pursue action.

31. As was done, for instance, in Romania (Clement and Ashbrook 2001) and Morocco (Meagher and Zinnes 2004).

that they are serious about improving the environment related to the sectors targeted by the PIJC.[32]

Outside Coordinator Mechanism

A final aspect of PIJC is its use of the outside coordinator or referee or some organization that all players can trust to enforce the rules of the game, objectively assess the winners, and deliver the promised rewards. For example, eastern European countries at the start of transition *trusted* the European Union to deliver the goods promised, that is, EU accession. This had the effect of focusing minds and leading disparate interests to cooperate (for example, in Poland). However, as the reliability of the EU's promise of accession has recently been called into question, so too has its role as a focal point and outside coordinator of reform effort. As another example, any foreign "expert" will explain that half the benefit of his or her presence in the host country is as an objective referee among the competing ideas of local (real) experts.

2.3 Types of PIJC Incentive Mechanisms

The discussion above suggests that the success of a project intervention depends on how all of its components work together and not just on the effectiveness of one component or the other. For example, the degree a reward or certification might influence behavior modification, reform, or investment may depend on how the project implements the dissemination component. The reason for a conjoint effect is that a project can be seen as a game, with its set of rules, players, beliefs, and payoffs. In short, the project creates an incentive environment to influence player behavior.

Not only is the game analogy appropriate regarding strategic behavior arising from player interaction, but one can also view the project designer as "moving first" by establishing the rules of the game, whereupon the players then act. The success of the project, therefore, requires that the designers anticipate the behaviors their intervention engenders.

The case studies presented in chapters 3 and 4 offer a rich set of observations that can be used to assess sponsor experience with alternative incentive environments and mechanism design. At the simplest level, one can distinguish two types of play, each predicated on a different degree of information asymmetry between

---

32. More generally, this jurisdictional splitting PIJC can be thought of as a way to reduce "type I" (rejection of the truth) and "type II" (acceptance of what is false) errors—what economists refer to as adverse selection. In the former case, the PIJC does not want to discourage suitable reform candidates from participating because the tasks or the tournament design appear too daunting. In the latter case, the PIJC does not want the lure of rewards to encourage those not interested in reform to either game the system or cheat. Of course, many players will fall in the middle: they will not have extremely strong beliefs about their chances of placing in the tournament. I thank Johannes Linn for this set of observations.

the sponsor and recipient.[33] The "absolutist" or contract type, which is easier to understand, is by far the most prevalent and, strictly speaking, should not be confused with the PIJC approach. Under the absolutist type of incentive, the sponsor examines each player (such as a municipality) on a case-by-case basis and determines—with or without local participation—what interventions might be feasible to achieve and then sets those as goals. The jurisdiction is rewarded if the goals are *certified* as achieved. Note that this essentially mirrors conditionality in technical assistance (development loans). This approach reduces to writing a contract or memorandum of understanding between the sponsor and the jurisdiction. Under this system *each* municipality that fulfills the contract *must* be compensated: *one package of sponsor funding stimulates one instance of reform in one jurisdiction.* Similarly, the chance of a jurisdiction "winning" depends only on *its own efforts* and does not depend on actions undertaken by other jurisdictions.[34]

Under the "relativist" type of incentive, the sponsor acknowledges not knowing what jurisdictions are capable of achieving and lets a tournament among them set the standards.[35] This approach builds on two ideas. The first is that with enough players, they will reflect the gamut of possibility, given the resources and skill sets available.[36] The second idea is that competition encourages excellence. Thus those who do the best provide an indication of what was ex ante feasible, that is, trace out the production possibility frontier.[37] A variant of the pure relativist approach—a mixed tournament (see below)—combines the absolutist approach, by insisting that participants meet certain thresholds on key indicators as a necessary condition to win, and the relativist approach, by using a tournament to sort out potential winners, placers, and others.

These observations can be formalized via an incentive mechanism typology. This multilayered classification scheme is summarized in table 2-1 and will be helpful in characterizing the underlying incentive designs found in the case studies. On the one hand, there are certification and tournament mechanisms reflecting absolutist and relativist designs, as described above. On the other hand, there are input- and output-based performance measures. In the latter instance, if the task or activity whose performance is the basis for winning is an input to the outcome desired by the application's objectives, then the ensuing incentive is classi-

---

33. This distinction comes from Meagher and Zinnes (2004).

34. A variation of this approach is to set the benchmark by examining past performance of a cohort of jurisdictions, together with an assessment of current idiosyncratic local conditions. If the certification bar is anticipated to shift over time using such an updating process, then the certification takes on some tournament characteristics.

35. Benchmark ("yardstick") competition is an example of the relativist approach (Shleifer 1985).

36. In the same way, economists illustrate the production possibility frontier by tracing out the feasible combinations of outputs a jurisdiction can produce from all efficient and inefficient combinations of its inputs.

37. This is not just an information asymmetry between the sponsors and the players. Generally speaking, the players themselves will not have a good idea of what performance is possible by their group.

Table 2-1. *Typology and Examples of PIJC Incentive Designs*[a]

Performance assessed on	Mechanism			
	Certifications		Tournaments[b]	
	Simple	Pecuniary	Pure	Mixed
Inputs				
Before PIJC	Jharkhand scorecard	Mancomunidades, Honduras[c] Nigeria LEEMP Senegal literacy initiative	Mancomunidades[c]	Eligible at MCC start-up[d]
Due to PIJC			KDP, Indonesia	Current MCC eligibility[d]
Outputs				
Before PIJC		MCC compact execution[d]	Galing Pook, Philippines	
Due to PIJC	Romania "Simple and Fast" USAID R4	Indonesia PROPER[e]		Russian fiscal reform Morocco MEPI

Source: See chapters 3 and 4 in this volume for a detailed description of these applications.

a. See the Abbreviations and Conventions list for acronyms shown here.

b. In principle, one could also make the distinction between pecuniary and nonpecuniary tournaments, whether pure or mixed.

c. The Honduras application in fact comprised two separate exercises, a tournament at the level of the municipality and a certification at the level of the *mancomunidad* (a voluntary association of municipalities; see chapter 4).

d. The incentives created by the MCC were different during the first years of its operation when countries would not yet have had time to respond to the attraction of an MCC compact; once a country has a compact, the tournament incentives end and a noncompetitive certification begins.

e. This is pecuniary in that lower-level ratings would oblige the firm to engage in environmental investments.

fied as input based; if it is the outcome desired by the objective, then the ensuing incentive is classified as output based. Hence, if a project's objective is improving primary education, the number of primary school teachers trained is an input-based performance incentive whereas increasing the number of primary school students exceeding a preestablished score on a standardized exam would be an output-based performance incentive.

Finally, PIJCs can be based on performance that has occurred before or will occur after the PIJC incentives are operative.

Simple Certification

Under this approach the project provides a referee (either a committee, statutory agency, or even the sponsor itself) who performs some sort of evaluative function against an absolute, preset, and announced bar for participant performance. Simple certification may be a dichotomous distinction like a pass-fail, one with many "grades" (as in the PROPER case), or even multidimensional (as in the Jharkhand Citizen Report Card). The players (for example, jurisdictions) here are all those decisionmaking units falling under the grading program. In theory, certification may or may not include a tangible reward, such as a cash prize or access to particular goods or services. For the present purposes, it is helpful to use the term simple certification when there is *no* tangible reward and the term pecuniary certification when there *is* a tangible reward directly linked to certification. The greater the respect for the certification, the more powerful an incentive mechanism it is. Hence the more objective the referees and judges are and the better the publicity or dissemination is, the more effective the certification incentive mechanism can be. This suggests that, in terms of motivating jurisdictional behavior, there may be a sponsor trade-off between putting its PIJC resources into the pecuniary reward, on the one hand, and into a well-designed publicity campaign and steps to ensure that the certification program is regarded as legitimate and objective in the long run, on the other.[38] Finally, a certification can be very valuable when the state makes it a requirement, such as regulatory agency approval for a pharmaceutical company to sell a new drug.[39]

Pecuniary Certification

Pecuniary certification is slightly more powerful than the simple certification described above. This design entails a prize or some form of remuneration that accompanies the certification. The set of players is the same as for simple certification. As presented in chapter 3, the pecuniary certification mechanism is used in the Senegal literacy initiative as well as the Nigeria project. While listed in table 2-1 under simple certification, USAID's R4 internal project evaluation system, also presented in chapter 3, can be thought of as a pecuniary certification, but one where the reward is interpreted as the absence of a penalty (a point further developed below). Note that pecuniary certification so defined is not a tournament (see below) because any and all who fulfill the certification criteria receive the prize.

As an aside, it is also possible to view aid conditionality as a form of pecuniary certification: the recipient (reluctantly) carries out a series of agreed-upon reforms, which the donor then certifies are undertaken, and as a quid pro quo, the donor provides the recipient with funding for something the recipient wants.[40] This

---

38. Consider how unimportant the cash reward is to the reputation and desirability of winning the Nobel Prize.

39. Note that the state need not issue the certification itself for it to make certification a requirement for entry into a sector.

40. Of course, in practice the donor often does not wait for the condition to be fulfilled or operational for an extended period before providing the quid pro quo. Naturally, this has led to recipient backsliding on condition fulfillment.

interpretation raises the following question: if the primary purpose of a project is to carry out, say, village-level investment and not (necessarily) to improve governance, might governance preconditions required for the village local government's eligibility to submit an investment proposal be potentially counterproductive? This example simply illustrates the importance of a sponsor being clear about the objective of its intervention and, in turn, demonstrates how the multiple (and sometimes conflicting) goals that sponsors often incorporate into their projects can hinder aid effectiveness.[41]

Pure Tournament

The fundamental idea behind the interjurisdictional competition approach is that of a tournament. In a tournament players are compensated based on the rank order of performance among a group of "players" rather than the actual performance that each achieves. Thus a tournament is based on relative and not absolute performance so that two players with nearly identical productivity may get very unequal compensation from tournament incentives. Likewise and contrary to certification, a tournament winner may exhibit substandard performance since coming in first does not imply exceeding any standard.

Tournament incentives may be of interest to sponsors who want to elicit reform efforts from agents such as municipalities. They are useful, with some caveats, when there is asymmetric information between the sponsor and municipalities regarding their ability to participate in reform activities. In particular, unlike the contractual promise, which donors have utilized for most of their history, a tournament does not require that the donor know what the municipality is capable of achieving. Under the right reward structure, players strive to achieve the best they can, even when they themselves are uncertain of just how much that is.[42] Moreover, as shown in appendix D, under the right reward structure, a relatively small reward budget can motivate a large number of participants. Finally, tournaments with many agents can be implemented for a fixed budget that is known in advance. Hence, whereas in theory the Senegal literacy initiative and Nigerian scorecard implied an open-ended budget commitment, the budgets for the Russian fiscal reform project and the Indonesian KDP could be set in advance.[43] Tournament incentives are also useful for maintaining player efforts when play occurs in an environment subject to unpredictable, common, exogenous shocks, such as macroeconomic conditions, a point revisited often in this book.

41. The MCC's approach provides a happy counterexample, where the funding conditions are viewed as required inputs that are likely to increase the chances of successful project implementation, not as tangential quid pro quo conditionality.

42. Recall that the reward structure entails a menu of rewards by rank of winner in the tournament plus the simple subjective probabilities of attaining each rank.

43. As shown in chapter 4, the KDP activity was a tournament since only the best grant proposals made by the villages were funded.

Mixed Tournament-Certification

There is an additional option for PIJC incentive design beyond the certification mechanism on one hand and the tournament mechanism on the other.[44] Some tournaments include an implied certification, for instance, those of Galing Pook, the Russian fiscal reform, the Morocco project, and the MCC. In these examples part of the reward is an implicit or explicit certification of performance.

There is a more sophisticated way in which certification and tournament mechanisms can be combined and, in so doing, reduce two concerns some policymakers have voiced relating to the tournament approach. The first concern relates to the effects on and remedies for those jurisdictions left behind by a tournament approach. The second concern relates to the implications of withholding "treatment" from those in need. Therefore, before this alternative way of combining a certification and a tournament is explored, it is necessary to examine briefly these concerns.

There are two ways to be "left behind": either the jurisdiction competes but does not place in the tournament, or it is excluded as part of the experimental design (randomization protocol), which is addressed in section 2.4. (The case where the jurisdiction chooses not to compete is not included here.)

To run a tournament in which only the placers receive the reward means that a policy decision has implicitly been made that only the winners merit receiving a reward. For example, the MCC's philosophy is that only countries with "good" policy environments can make efficient use of aid. Here the underlying decision is that the MCC values efficiency in aid delivery more than helping those countries who are sufficiently badly off that their policy environment prevents them from making effective use of aid. There is a similar concept behind the allocation of the investment grants in the KDP project as well. Of course, the argument these donors make is that they have limited resources, so they would like the funds to go to their most productive uses.

What about the case where a jurisdictional tournament is held to raise youth employment by offering grants to SMEs as rewards in those municipalities that generate the most SME jobs for workers under the age of twenty-four? If the winning municipality increases youth employment by 10 percent and another municipality by "only" 8 percent, surely it is unfair to provide a reward to the former and nothing to the latter?[45] And if the latter municipality receives assistance, what about the one scoring 6 percent, and so on? While this can be handled to some

44. While not explicitly treated in the text, an additional subclassification for pure and mixed tournaments would be whether the rewards are pecuniary or nonpecuniary, as is the case for certification.

45. In fact, an identical problem exists for certification as well. For example, in the Senegal literacy initiative, training proposals just one point under the requisite score were not funded while those just above that threshold were.

degree by providing rewards for first, second, and third place, and so on, until the prize budget is exhausted or a politically comfortable lower score can be agreed upon, there is another solution.

The design mechanism can include both a tournament and a certification component. In the present example, there could be first, second, and third prizes as part of the tournament component, as well as consolation prizes for the certification component. The latter would acknowledge the efforts made by the lower achievers. The threshold for the certification component can be set so that the reward does not degenerate into an automatic bribe for participation. In the Morocco proposal, the consolation prizes were for the successful completion of at least one reform (whereas winners were anticipated to complete several reforms). Alternatively, the stroke-of-pen reform component can garner a consolation prize while only complete implementation of the reform would put a player in the running for the full reward.

Unfortunately, it is not always possible to apply such a design mechanism. For example, in choosing the site for the Olympics or the World Cup, the selection committees want the best sites for their events, so it is not possible to give a second prize in this instance (though it is possible to give preference to the runner-up in the next round, where the distance between first and second place was small). What about when the objective is maximum coverage, as in the case of the Senegal literary initiative, or is to highlight *all* the good performers, as in the case of Romania? If those are the goals, then again, the tournament approach alone is not likely to be the best mechanism.

Finally, note that the very fact that rewards are given out conditionally means that some jurisdictions are excluded from a sponsor's goods and services (treatment). If the sponsor is a government, then this may seem antithetical to equity considerations and may even be unconstitutional. This point is addressed in section 2.4.

2.4 Monitoring and Evaluation in the PIJC Approach

For a PIJC to be effective, players must believe that the process to identify winners is fair and not subject to manipulation, discretion, or corruption. This imposes two necessary conditions on the design of the approach: first, the criteria for winning (placing) must be crystal clear before the start of the game, and second, the means for assessing winners should be transparent and, in principle, verifiable by all players. One instrument that satisfies these conditions is the use of quantitative indicators to take post- (and often pre-) contest measurements of player performance, where the methodology and data requirements are clear and the sources acceptable to all ex ante.

From an implementation point of view, it is a small step from running quantitative baselines and endlines to using the same instruments to perform rigorous project evaluation. Of course, from a project design standpoint, evaluation often requires a rather thorough modification to the design of a proposed intervention. As explained below, this is especially true if the approach uses randomization.[46] Fortunately, some farsighted sponsors are coming to realize the benefits of such an extension (Gariba 2005, World Bank 2006c).[47] They see that such an approach bears three additional benefits. First, not only can the sponsor identify more successful outcomes, but it can determine whether the funded project was actually responsible for the result. In this way, the policy community effectively "learns by doing" in the best sense of the phrase. Second, armed with such rigorous information, sponsors and governments alike are able to defend themselves both politically and economically from their overseeing constituencies. Third, the awareness (threat) of rigorous evaluation greatly sharpens the minds of implementers, both the foreign experts and their local recipients, which also encourages improved outcomes.

Ideally, a PIJC is repeated many times. This eventuality further strengthens its incentive properties as well as spreads the fixed costs of development across more reform. Impact evaluation ensures the improvement of later PIJC rounds. Likewise, since sponsors are often interested in the scalability, replicability, and sustainability of their interventions, prospective impact evaluation ensures them that a reliable assessment of the PIJC is possible. Finally, since PIJC success depends on the quality of calibration (of task selection, scoring methodology, reward structure, and so forth), in-tournament monitoring—especially during a pilot—allows the PIJC to be adjusted (for example, by offering additional technical assistance, increasing rewards, or extending play time) if necessary.

Properly evaluating the success of a PIJC requires that comparison of contest outcomes with an appropriate counterfactual, namely, how the jurisdictions would perform on the selected tasks in the absence of the PIJC incentives and other contaminating factors. The gold standard for evaluations of this type involves statistical methods based on prospective, randomized evaluation procedures (PREP).[48] The critical element of prospective evaluation (Greenberg and Shroder 2004) is the creation of two groups of participants—treatments and controls—with the assignment of each potential jurisdiction to one of the groups through a random process. The main challenges are to identify a control group that is free of contamination and to ensure that the control group includes some players who wanted to "play" but were not allowed to. The latter group is

46. This is because eligible players would need to be randomly assigned to a control or treatment group.

47. These include the Gates Foundation and the MCC. In 2007 the Spanish government created a $16 million trust fund at the World Bank (the bank's largest) specifically to spend on project evaluation. "The fund's first criterion calls for randomized trials." See "Economic Focus: Control Freaks," *The Economist,* June 14, 2008, p. 90.

48. See Azfar and Zinnes (2003).

required to avoid confounding positive performance effects of the tournament with self-selection effects (where only better performers would enter the tournament and weaker ones would stay out).[49]

The PREP methodology is analogous to that of a medical clinical trial, in which the efficacy of a treatment can be determined relative to that of a placebo, even if one does not know all the mechanics underlying the healing process. Such is the power of M&E that today several sponsor organizations such as the World Bank, the MCC, the Gates Foundation, and others are proactively assessing country readiness for results-based monitoring and evaluation systems (Kusek and Rist 2004).

Despite these significant benefits to evaluation and randomized trials, there is still resistance from sponsor recipients. They typically see evaluation in general and randomized trials in particular as an unnecessary cost, a source of delay, and an increase in implementation complexity (which could risk reducing the size of the benefits stream). This is an ironic consequence of how sponsors, in their quest for full cost pricing and transparency, include the cost of M&E in the project budget, passing the cost on to the beneficiary. Especially in the case of a loan, recipients simply want to have programming access to all funds rather than pay for the sponsor's M&E requirements. This may be based on a belief that they know how to get the best results, making M&E superfluous; principal-agent problems in which they wish to hide low effectiveness resulting from inappropriate allocation decisions; lack of appreciation for the constructive role of M&E; or an appreciation for M&E but an unwillingness to subsidize project design improvements that a different recipient, and not they themselves, will benefit from.[50]

Consider now the case where exclusion comes from the experimental design.[51] How can a publicly sponsored activity exclude part of the public? This seems at first rather impolitic, but with some reflection, it is easy to see how most people would benefit from such an exercise. The main reason a sponsor would attempt reforms as an experiment would be that it has made some educated guesses that they might work but has no specific knowledge of their likely effectiveness. If by some chance there are municipalities where it seems likely that the reform would work so that it would be immoral to deny them the opportunity, then the sponsor can implement the reforms in those municipalities and select them out of the "study sample." The same holds for municipalities where it is likely that the reforms will not work. Among the remaining, participating municipalities, the

49. The political problems this may create are considered in section 7.2.

50. With regard to inappropriate allocation decisions, there may also be recipient risk aversion related to making investment and expenditure decisions in the context of the volatile developing-country environment. Here rigorous measurement is a no-win situation since politicians do not need rigor to claim success to a poorly informed public and, anyway, are themselves rewarded for diverting funds to favored groups.

51. This discussion draws on Azfar and Zinnes (2003).

sponsor can randomly assign and run alternative versions of the reform. Since there are a large number of local government units with meaningful responsibilities, a large enough sample can be selected so that if the effects of some versions of the reforms were of reasonable magnitude, they would be detected.

Two arguments can be used to make randomization politically feasible. First, since randomization, if explicitly done, is almost by definition fair, the government or donor cannot be accused of playing favorites. Of course, such a study should be "sold" before the random selection is made to increase political support for it. Second, those municipalities not selected in the first wave of reforms will benefit from the accumulated experience and receive for their patience more effective reforms when they participate in the second wave. Thus a prospective, randomized implementation of a youth employment reform—say, reducing the legal obstacles to firing workers—can be sold politically with some thought and packaging. Nonetheless, it is not clear why there would be concern about randomized implementation being impolitic since sponsors conduct individual pilot projects—not to mention major implementations in a single location—all the time, only that they are just not done in enough places or with enough care about collecting data on the counterfactual to be generalizable.

Regardless, it should be obvious that *interjurisdictional competition and randomized evaluation are not the same thing, nor does one require the other.* It is perfectly feasible to run an interjurisdictional competition without considering randomized evaluation—as most of the PIJC examples in chapters 3 and 4 corroborate. Conversely, it is also possible—and even likely, as the plethora of examples illustrates—to conduct randomized trials without the presence of a PIJC.[52] As will be seen, each of these methodologies carries with it its own logistical and political challenges, which the literature has sometimes conflated.

Finally, note that the type of metric used in the impact evaluation is generally dictated by the PIJC design and especially by whether performance is based on the post-PIJC level or the net change over the PIJC period, as discussed earlier in section 2.1.[53]

2.5 A Framework to Assess PIJC Experience to Date

So far this discussion has introduced several dimensions used to describe the type of PIJC a sponsor might use to implement a project. First, there are the steps a designer must address. Among these and most important is the choice of incentive design, for which four principal types have been identified. These four types

---

52. See, for example, Duflo (2005), though her intent was not to illustrate PIJC but rather the use of randomized evaluation to assess development microlevel interventions by NGOs.
53. This corresponds to the distinction in monitoring and evaluation between approaches based on performance differences and those based on differences-in-differences.

Table 2-2. *Desirable Incentive Characteristics Available to Alternative PIJC Designs*

No.	Desirable design characteristics	Type of incentive design[a]			
		C	P	T	M
1	Ex-post output-based performance focus	√	√	√	√
2	Leveraging of technical assistance	√	√	√	√
3	Game participation voluntary	√	√	√	√
4	Actionable indicators and use of benchmarking	√	√	√	√
5	Recipient selects tasks to implement (participatory development)	√	√	√	√
6	Leveraging of sponsor project funds			√	√
7	Tangible reward (beyond reputation and reform)		√	√	√
8	Social capital (power of peer pressure)	√	√	√	√
9	Collective action	√	√	√	√
10	Demand-driven targeting of technical assistance	√	√	√	√
11	Encourages maximal effort			√	√
12	Ensures minimum performance threshold is met	√	√		√
13	Use of local know-how to overcome asymmetric information	√	√	√	√
14	Use of outside coordinator or referees	√	√	√	√
15	Minimal need for sponsor onsite monitoring			√	√

a. Certification (C), pecuniary certification (P), tournament (T), tournament with minimum (threshold) score (M).

of designs may embody underlying operating mechanisms, which have also been described.

In addition, many possible positive incentive characteristics available to PIJC designers have been described. For convenience, these are summarized in table 2-2. Interestingly, this table reveals that *in principle* most of the desirable characteristics of a PIJC are independent of which incentive design one chooses. Yet in actual projects, regardless of the type of incentive design used, sponsors often do not take advantage of the full gamut of these desirable incentive characteristics.

To evaluate the suitability of PIJC in terms of its potential for sustainable success as well as scalability, chapters 3 and 4 examine a series of selected past and present sponsor applications and evaluate how the presence or absence of the desirable PIJC characteristics listed in table 2-2 might influence observed or predicted performance. This evaluation also assesses how the presence or absence of these incentive characteristics may have depended on a locality's initial conditions. An effort was made to base assessments on the objectives *the sponsor* stated for the application and not on other objectives that the evaluator might have had or that hindsight suggests should have been the goals.[54]

54. I thank Charles Cadwell for raising this concern.

Table 2-3. *Topics for Evaluating Full and Partial PIJC Applications*

Topic	Explanation
Statement of the problem	What is the issue that the sponsor wishes to address or resolve?
Objectives	What does the sponsor wish to achieve?
Sponsor and implementer	Who are the sponsors, and who have they engaged to provide the technical assistance or make the changes?
Players	Who are the participants in the PIJC tournament?
Cost	What is the size of the sponsor's contribution? Of the jurisdictions' contributions?
Rules of the game	How do you "win," and what do the players need to do to play?
Rewards	What is the schedule of benefits for participating?
PIJC components	Which PIJC components are used in the application?
Stated results	What were the outcomes claimed by the sponsor of the initiative?
Initial conditions	What preexisting local conditions most influenced the quality of the tournament's outcome?
Assessment	An appraisal of how and why the results were what they were. Was lack of a PIJC component an impediment given the sponsor's objectives?
Sustainability	To what degree are project results likely to remain, especially once the sponsor has departed or its funds have expired?
Scalability	To what extent might the initiative be applied to other locations at the same scale (replicability) or at a larger scale?

Chapters 3 and 4 focus on a representative set of existing applications that exemplify each of the types of PIJC classified in the typology shown in table 2-1.[55] For completeness and to facilitate later comparisons, a common framework is used to examine each application, employing the topics listed in table 2-3. This type of assessment also allows one to imagine how the application might perform by "filling in" the gaps for the particular situation (that is, had the missing design characteristics as per table 2-2 been included *and* been feasible). It also allows one to consider whether the *lack* or the *inclusion* of a particular PIJC characteristic led to any negative consequences for project success.

Chapter 5 takes a different tack by examining existing *non*-PIJC applications in the sectors listed in table 2-4 that contain some PIJC component techniques or mechanisms. These applications will be instructive for what they do and do not achieve. This type of assessment approximates how a full PIJC might perform by "aggregating" the experience sponsors have had across the various PIJC components.

However, given the sectoral, organizational, and geographic breadth of activities that might utilize a PIJC approach, the present study makes no attempt or

---

55. See section 2.6 for details on exactly how these applications were selected and the caveats thereby engendered.

Table 2-4. *Substantive Areas of Potential Interest for Investigation*

Agriculture	Labor issues
Aid effectiveness	Public administration
Business	Public finance
Education	Public participation; participatory development
Environment	Regulation not included elsewhere
Finance and banking	Research and development
Health	SME and employment promotion
Infrastructure and service delivery	Sports

claim to have caught all the relevant applications. In fact, hardly a week goes by without hearing of a new clever initiative in the private or nonprofit sectors.[56]

2.6 Selection and Organization of Case Studies

With the assessment framework in hand, the next steps are to select a series of existing applications for assessment and then organize them in a way that facilitates comparative analysis. The following provides the rationale for how this was done.

Case Study Selection

It would be ideal to select randomly a large number of applications incorporating simple certification, pecuniary certification, a pure tournament, and a mixed tournament. Then, by examining performance, we could analyze both the efficacy of each mechanism across the various sectors and the appropriateness of each mechanism for a given sector or class of application of each mechanism in the sector or class. Unfortunately, we were not able to find a large enough sample of applications to permit this preferred methodological approach, at least for bona fide tournaments. This left us two alternatives.[57]

First, we could select one completed application per mechanism that we believed to be representative and present it in a detailed case study. This approach would have the virtue of illustrating how the application was tailored to the specific institutional and other initial conditions of the host environment, and of allowing us to provide a detailed and evidence-based critique of what worked and why. On the other hand, it would be hard to generalize any conclusions or convince the reader that such generalizations were merited.

---

56. At the time I wrote these lines, the Nobel Prize in economics was awarded to Leonid Hurwicz, Eric Maskin, and Roger Meyerson for their work in mechanism design!

57. My thanks to an anonymous referee for raising the issue of case study representativeness and for suggesting these two options.

Second, we could identify as large a number of diverse past applications as possible, where the primary selection criterion would be that the case was sufficiently documented and disseminated so that it could be found with due diligence. The greater number and diversity of cases might then provide the reader with greater confidence of the potential robustness of the mechanisms to place, initial conditions, sector, and sponsor. On the other hand, the number of cases would still be too small for proper statistical hypothesis testing, and their diversity would likely further complicate comparisons, since by design many of the particulars regarding objectives, time frame, implementation, and initial conditions would vary across each application.

Ultimately, the second alternative was chosen since it had the merit of illustrating the diversity of public policy purposes for which PIJC mechanisms were available to add productive performance incentives. The onus would then be on the researcher to avoid selection bias, underscore why each chosen application was sufficiently representative, and stress the tentativeness of conclusions.

The research team scoured literature sources within the major donors as well as on the Internet.[58] It also conducted numerous discussions with experts working in the field of local government reform, aid effectiveness, and competitiveness. In each case we searched for examples of certifications, tournaments, or some combination thereof. Many certification-based examples were found, and those not included in chapter 3 are summarized in appendix A. The selection criteria were that the application had to be fielded in a non-OECD country, be well along in implementation so that its performance could be unambiguously assessed, and have sufficient information to enable a clear understanding of the project's design, implementation, and outcomes.[59] While there is no pretension of random sampling, it is important for the record to make clear that the cases were marked for selection *before* knowing whether they were considered "successful."

In the case of tournaments, we discovered so few bona fide applications that all the ones we found are included in chapter 4. Hence any selection bias would be due to whether there was a correlation between tournament performance and the fact that the tournament was neither written up nor made known to experts in the field. This is, unfortunately, a distinct possibility since it is precisely those poorly designed or ill-suited tournaments that would fail or abort before completion and thus not be written up. The reader should keep in mind, therefore, that our sample of tournaments has been drawn from fielded projects whose implementation was sufficiently far along that their existence would at least be known to experts.

---

58. This involved the efforts of Mauricio Palacios, in particular.
59. Only the *mancomunidades* project in Honduras came close to falling short of these criteria.

Table 2-5. *Organization of PIJC Application Vignettes*[a]

Chapter	Mechanism	Case study
3: Certifications	Simple certification	Romania "Simple and Fast"
		Jharkhand, India, scorecard
		PROPER, Indonesia
		USAID R4
	Pecuniary certification	Nigeria LEEMP
		Senegal literacy initiative
4: Tournaments	Pure tournaments	Galing Pook, Philippines
		Mancomunidades, Honduras
		KDP, Indonesia
	Mixed tournaments	Russian fiscal reform
		MCC
		Morocco MEPI
5: Other relevant experience	PIJC components	None

a. See the Abbreviations and Conventions list for acronyms shown here.

Organization of Presentation

To facilitate comparisons, the dozen selected applications are organized into two chapters of six vignettes each, as shown in table 2-5. Chapter 3 covers simple and pecuniary certifications; chapter 4, pure and mixed tournaments.

Chapter 5 presents some additional examples of related mechanisms in a greater variety of sectors. These examples further underscore both the range of applications as well as the distinguished track record of PIJC components.

3

Review of Certification Experience

The novelty of a tournament for government transfers, reforms, or as an aid delivery vehicle means that the number of PIJC applications is limited. Therefore, in section 2.5, we proposed a two-tiered approach that would enable past experience to be used to its fullest for assessing PIJC. This chapter and the next one constitute the first tier of this approach, which applies the selection process discussed in section 2.6 and assessment framework explained in section 2.5 to representative PIJC applications. Real-world cases of certification are evaluated here; real-world tournaments are evaluated in chapter 4. In both instances the operative mechanism is a competition. And to reiterate the caution in section 1.4, because few careful evaluations of tournaments exist, the present research could not engage in the statistical rigor necessary for definitive judgments about success or failure; any lessons learned, therefore, are tentative.

Chapter 5 presents the second tier of the approach, briefly examining some of the experience sponsors and reformers have had on a sectoral basis when using the constituent components of the PIJC approach in their project designs. The idea of this review is to augment the limited track record of PIJC by examining the experience with its constituent components and from that determine how much confidence to put in the PIJC process.

In all cases the discussion endeavors to make a clear distinction between judgments on the appropriateness of the PIJC design selected for the application and on what actually happened. Furthermore, after considering what *might* have happened under a different mechanism or condition, the discussion then examines the feasibility of the alternative under the actual conditions the sponsor-designer faced at the time. (Section 6.5 reveals that one can often gain insights into the sponsor's situation through such thought experiments.)

3.1 Simple Certification

Simple certification is the most common type of competition. Four examples were selected from Romania, India, Indonesia, and USAID and examined according to the assessment framework described in section 2.5. Recall that a simple certification is where a player must satisfactorily complete a preestablished set of tasks or achieve a preset level of performance. In addition to meeting the criteria set forth in section 2.6, these examples were selected because they permit particularly good comparisons within and across mechanisms. For example, the certification in Romania (below) and the tournaments in Russia and Morocco (chapter 4) are applications with similar objectives and players, but there is no pecuniary reward or pressure to excel in the former. The USAID certification (below) and the MCC tournament (chapter 4) have similar objectives, but their respective incentives target different stakeholders. The Indian and Indonesian certifications illustrate different designs to achieve similar regulatory ends.

3.1.1 Romania: "Simple and Fast" Deregulation Competition

This example from Romania is very interesting because it follows quite closely the ideal construction of what we called a complete PIJC in chapter 1, but with two exceptions: lack of pecuniary reward and use of certification instead of tournament design. As a result, this application illustrates, on the one hand, how much one can achieve with a simplified PIJC design and, on the other hand, the potential limitations of using nonpecuniary rewards.

STATEMENT OF THE PROBLEM

Registering and operating an SME in Romania has been fraught with bureaucratic and regulatory obstacles throughout the period of transition.[1] The results of prior efforts by the donors to address these problems have been spotty, perhaps due to the centralized nature of government or to arbitrary reform efforts "from above."

OBJECTIVE

Begun on July 25, 2000, the five-step deregulation competition entitled "Simple and Fast" had the goal of building an effective private-public partnership of funding, implementing, and participating parties who would then work together

---

1. The description of the objectives, methods, and results of this application draws on Clement and Ashbrook (2001).

to reduce the time and effort necessary to obtain approvals and other related site development authorizations needed to operate and register SMEs in Romania.

SPONSOR AND IMPLEMENTERS

The IRIS Center of the University of Maryland conceived and launched the program in collaboration with the Research Triangle Institute in North Carolina and with the financial support of USAID and of the U.S. Embassy in Bucharest, Romania.

PLAYERS

Eighty cities were invited to participate in the program, of which twenty-nine were interested and actively took part. The project team worked with personnel from city halls, chambers of commerce, and business associations to implement the project.

COST AND TIME FRAME

Since the initiative was added to IRIS's existing USAID program, which already had a resident office in Romania, it is difficult to specify what its total cost would have been as a stand-alone project. The direct incremental cost to the donor was probably about $150,000.[2] From the local government side, each municipality had to send a representative to several meetings, and one supposes that many meetings were held among stakeholders within each municipality that attempted to implement any of the contest tasks. These out-of-pocket expenses for a municipality can be considered part of its precommitment cost. Finally, the contest took place over a one-year period.

RULES OF THE GAME

To win, each participating municipality had to complete five tasks (enumerated below) in six months. For a flavor of the application, consider how the city of Giurgiu, the first to complete the five steps of the program, responded to the challenge of each of the five tasks to reduce bureaucracy at the local level. Its actions showed the local public administration's political will to cooperate with the private sector in order to improve the business environment.

Task 1: Eliminate operating authorization. This step was aimed at eliminating the final approval issued by the mayor for a firm's registration, which duplicated the business registration approval.

Task 2: Reduce time in local approvals process. This step was aimed at reducing the time spent by businesses during the approval process for utilities contracts.

---

2. An estimate provided to me by the IRIS backstopper at the time. No doubt the cost would have been higher had IRIS not already had an office in Romania set up for a different project and financed by the same donor.

Paperwork for these approvals was not processed simultaneously, but rather one approval had to be submitted and obtained, and then the next one was worked on. Thus businesses had to wait up to 120 days for local utilities contracts, as the project team discovered through its red tape analysis.

Task 3: Increase transparency in local approvals process. Increasing transparency in the public-private sector relationship was aimed at improving communication to the benefit of both the local administration and the business community.

Task 4: Reduce time to process building construction permits. Known to be very time consuming, this procedure needed to be shortened by improving coopera-tion among local regulatory agencies.

Task 5: Simultaneous request of the fiscal code and registration certificate. In order to register, firms previously had to apply to two different institutions: the Trade Registry (for the registration code) and the Fiscal Authority (for the fiscal code). Firms had to file duplicate documents, waiting doubly long, and also manage two different codes to identify one single company. Through this step, the number of codes and amount of documentation and time would be reduced, helping com-panies start up their activity sooner.

For each task accomplished, the city received a "star," which could be seen as a rating and something the city could use to advertise itself and investors could use to assess the business friendliness of the city. Project implementers worked with the coalition of city participants by helping them to identify how to address the competition's tasks and by providing limited technical assistance toward the tasks themselves.

COMPETITION REWARDS

It is clear from a discussion with participants that the main reward was the direct benefits of the very substantial list of deregulatory achievements of this pro-gram. Winners were congratulated in press conferences and received honorific nonpecuniary awards from the then U.S. ambassador in Romania. These cities also benefited from publicity on the web pages of IRIS and the U.S. Embassy and were invited to a reception with American business leaders in January 2001. Win-ning cities received regular invitations to embassy and American Chamber of Commerce monthly networking events. All four winning cities continued to receive technical assistance from IRIS aimed at strengthening the business climate, including study tours abroad to observe local economic development models.

STATED OUTCOMES

As of December 31, 2000, when the program reached its completion, four cities had completed all five steps of the program (Giurgiu, Timisoara, Cluj-Napoca, and Iasi). In participating cities the competition's implementers claimed that "the cost of compliance with business regulation—both in terms of fees and time—was reduced through the elimination of some approvals, the reduction of the paperwork involved in processing others, and the creation of mechanisms for increased communication and transparency between officials and the business community" (Clement and Ashbrook 2001).[3] At least half of the twenty-nine participating cities engaged in some amount of reform. It appears that eight cities completed task 1, possibly nine cities came close to completing task 2, twelve cities completed task 3, five cities completed task 4, and perhaps eleven cities completed task 5. That seems to be quite a lot of reform for the money (see costs, above).

The competition's implementers also claim that "all successful cities in the deregulation competition report substantial investor interest in their cities, directly resulting from the competition."[4] Aside from foreign investor interest (and the reported upsurge in foreign and local investment, though hard to directly link to the project), the competition did foster a sense of collaboration between local administration and the business community that Clement and Ashbrook (2001) claim was still observable a year after the competition had ended. The competition demonstrated to certain cities that they could make decisions—either procedural or legislative through local council—that would have a positive impact on their business environments. In addition to encouraging a deregulation movement and attention to future regulation creation, the competition demonstrated to cities that they had the need and ability to market themselves separately from Bucharest and even from Romania as a whole.

For example, Timisoara, one of the winning cities, described the competition's success as follows: "Ambassadors from many countries visited . . . and . . . acknowledged . . . the real success Timisoara . . . had in reducing red tape and catching the attention of the foreign investors. On February 16, 2001, 400 Italian firms and 15 TV stations had their attention focused on Timisoara. They visited the city and noticed the results of the 'Simple and Fast' Program that visibly reduced red tape" (Clement and Ashbrook 2001).

PICJ COMPONENTS

As argued below, though the Romanian competition was not a tournament, it contained several components of a full-fledged PIJC. These included a rating system, a set of predefined rewards, the use of public relations to generate rewards, local participation through required public hearings, voluntary and demand-driven implementation of preset tasks, and allocation of technical assistance only to those whose costly actions revealed that they were serious about reform.

ASSESSMENT

First, this case is not a tournament but a certification program since any and all cities that completed the five tasks would win. However, the fact that not all

---

3. However, as pointed out by an anonymous referee, one needs to be skeptical of any claims made by a project's designer and implementer.

4. Clement and Ashbrook (2001).

would or could do so meant that the fewer that did, the more winning would translate into a relative badge of distinction. This case involved no rigorous measurement or evaluation criteria (other than a dichotomous pass-fail) so that while the outcomes surely occurred, it is not possible to determine what aspect of the project design or initial conditions led to the outcomes or how effective the program was. Similarly, no field evaluation was done to determine what effect the lack of pecuniary reward, the brevity of the competition, or the difficulty of the tasks had on participation rates (twenty-nine out of eighty-nine succeeded in accomplishing at least one task, with just five cities completing all the tasks). Still, considering the voluntary nature of the initiative, the participation of one-third of the cities seems impressive.

While the number of municipalities successfully completing all the tasks was rather limited, Clement and Ashbrook (2001) claim that this was due in part to the very short project horizon of just six months. Another reason may have been the need for additional inducements to concentrate minds and stimulate collective action. The only reward other than the eventual benefits of the reforms (which in principle should dwarf the value of any rewards a donor could offer) derived from the reputational benefits of being an award winner. In receiving a reward, the municipality signals to investors its seriousness about creating a business-friendly environment.

Finally, the performance of the other two-thirds of municipalities, which either did not participate or participated but were unable to complete even one task, was not to be publicized, and this fact was known to the players in advance. This probably weakened the participation incentive for some players since it meant that there was little cost, political or otherwise, to not playing given that no one would be able to know if a nonparticipant was performing worse than its neighbors.

As essentially a certification activity, the program suffers from the pluses and minuses of such an approach. On the plus side, it was relatively simple to implement and explain to participants. The program was also implemented over a very short period, suggesting that competitions need not take an inordinate amount of time. Finally, the implementer (IRIS) already had an office in Romania and experience working in the country, so the total cost of the program appears to have been very low: less than $3,000 per reform.

On the minus side, a certification mechanism does not generally lead to maximum effort by participants—neither by the strongest nor the weakest players. This seems true in the present case. It did not stimulate the more advanced cities to do their best but only to accomplish the five tasks. Timisoara, for example, started the PIJC with essentially all tasks completed. Likewise, those cities that expected to accomplish few if any tasks opted out of the competition and thereby escaped any rating (Clement and Ashbrook 2001), a loss to investors since nonparticipation would be a noisy signal for a low-quality business environment.

IMPACT OF INITIAL CONDITIONS

An important precondition for the cost-effectiveness and quick implementation of this program was that all the national level framework legislation and regulatory statutes were already in existence. This allowed municipalities to fully focus on reforms, which were all within their own power. The project was also able to tap into several social forces. First, there were some municipalities that truly had a latent desire for change and only required a focal point, which the project created. Second, where local consensus was weaker, project design included the creation of multiparty stakeholder groups that were able to develop a consensus on what to change and, with the advice of the foreign technical experts, how. In some cases results depended on the serendipitous existence of one or two reform "champions," who then helped to lead the charge, a factor that clearly cannot always be counted on elsewhere. Finally, the donor probably was willing to fund the pilot activity only because it already had a resident technical assistance team in Romania (IRIS).

SUSTAINABILITY AND SCALABILITY

With regard to the sustainability of the reforms implemented, these do appear to be long-lasting. The admittedly modest evidence for this is the voluntary consensual manner in which they were realized and the reports of a positive investor response. However, as for the sustainability of the project itself, sadly, in spite of the good press it generated for the donor (USAID) and the winning municipalities themselves, the exercise was not repeated in Romania or elsewhere by the donor. It is doubtful that this reflects the project's lack of scalability; more likely it reflects the donor's preoccupation with other matters. Part of the problem may be that, at least until recently, the sectoral and country "stovepipe" structure of USAID's programs inhibits replication of innovation since it is very difficult for good ideas to move across such bureaucratic boundaries.[5] Likewise, within USAID the personal (private) incentives for project developers to experiment are weak. Private sector consultants, on the other hand, are generally asked only to offer specific services to USAID and not to design programs. While admittedly speculative, from a design point of view, it is likely that more municipalities would have participated if pecuniary and larger in-kind awards (including better pre- and postcompetition public relations) had been offered and more reform would have occurred if nonproject administrative factors

5. Stovepiping refers to an administrative process in which programming and funding occur within narrow bureaucratic purviews, be they by sector (such as health) or country (for instance, Romania). As an example from my own experience, USAID's privatization program was not interested in funding an activity to minimize the environmental liabilities being spun off by the state entity being sold, even where low-cost, highly efficient opportunities presented themselves. At the same time, USAID's environmental program was discouraged from providing the assistance since the process fell under the purview of the privatization program.

(between USAID and IRIS) had not limited the duration of the reform period to six months. It is also interesting to speculate whether there would have been more replication by USAID in other contexts had prospective impact evaluation been part of the activity.

3.1.2 Jharkhand, India: Public Services Report Cards

The Jharkhand report card is an example of an interjurisdictional competition that focuses on reporting and not on follow-up successful implementation. It is also interesting in that the competitive element is across agencies (the "jurisdictions") within a single local government. The ensuing discussion examines the effectiveness of such an approach.

STATEMENT OF THE PROBLEM

Poor or inadequate public services are a way of life in most developing countries, though these services are an important input to poverty alleviation. Part of the reason for this situation is the lack of accountability of elected officials as well as service providers. This is, in turn, related to a lack of stakeholder responsiveness due to an absence of effective channels for stakeholders both to voice their preferences as well as to learn what is happening.

OBJECTIVE

According to the Public Affairs Foundation (PAF 2004, p. 4), the Citizen Report Card (CRC) initiative "is a simple but powerful tool to provide public agencies with systematic feedback from users of public services . . . [by eliciting] feedback through sample surveys on aspects of service quality that users know best, and enabl[ing] public agencies to identify strengths and weakness in their work." The CRC endeavors to provide a realistic benchmark on the initial quality of public services (in rural credit, forestry, health, education, and drinking water), as perceived by the intended beneficiaries, through "a comparison with other services, so that a strategic set of actions can be initiated." The project designers chose the state of Jharkhand "because the absolute numbers of poor are high and increasing." The rationale was that since sixty percent of the state's population lives in forest fringe communities, strengthening community control over forest assets through empowerment and transparency would make significant contributions to poverty alleviation.

SPONSOR AND IMPLEMENTERS

As best inferred from written materials (PAF 2004, p. 10), the project "was carried out by the Public Affairs Foundation (PAF), a sister nonprofit company promoted by the Public Affairs Centre, which pioneered the concept of Citizen Report Cards." ORG Center for Social Research (a division of ORG-MARG Research Private Limited), a local social research agency, carried out the field operations, and PAF provided all methodological and technical input and analysis.

COST AND TIME FRAME

The cost was not reported.[6] The three phases of the project appear to have required about eighteen months and were completed by late 2004.

PLAYERS

In essence, the players were the government agencies and organizations being rated, namely, those involved in providing and regulating rural credit, forestry, health, education, and drinking water at the local level. These included local, regional, and even national government elected officials, among whose responsibilities was to ensure that citizens' interests were promoted in the public services sector. In reality, there was probably little scope for the players to have engaged in any competitive behaviors before the baseline survey measurement (first benchmark). This would not be the case in a follow-up assessment, especially if these organizations knew it was to take place and were given sufficient time to respond to pressures that resulted from the citizens' response to the first report card (baseline measurement).

RULES OF THE GAME

First, the PAF conducted focus groups of service beneficiaries to identify the critical issues and themes, to identify the contextual variables and dimensions of service provisioning, and to design the pilot survey. In addition, the PAF interviewed the service providers. Second, to assess the beneficiaries' level of service satisfaction, a survey was designed and administered in a rigorous, randomized fashion across (in this case) the forest fringe population and SNGs within Jharkhand. Third, the PAF computed detailed indicators of the levels of household satisfaction, including perceptions of the causes of performance inadequacies, for each of the five public service sectors.[7]

The indicators were designed to be simple to understand and appreciate, and allowed the PAF to rank service providers and jurisdictions along many dimensions. The PAF then disseminated the results to the various public service providers to aid them in identifying further studies and strategies for internal reforms and investment. The results were also placed in the public domain through wide distribution in the media as well as by conducting seminars and meetings with NGOs. These actions were meant to stimulate public pressure for improvements as well as public understanding of the situation, its scope, and the limitations on change.

6. Negotiations were under way to acquire this information but were not completed in time for publication.
7. The surveys also tested household receptivity to different options for reforms and investment.

REWARDS

As of this writing, there have been no prospectively offered pecuniary or in-kind rewards to the players. Rather, the idea is that the CRCs motivate players to improve their ratings and their rankings, both for bureaucratic pride and individual career advancement as well as to avoid public wrath. Given this goal, the rating reports were distributed to the related service ministries and agencies, as well as to the general public, but in a very nonconfrontational manner and in the spirit of constructive engagement.

STATED OUTCOMES

The PAF indicates that the

CRC sheds light on the degree to which pro-poor services are reaching the target groups, the extent of gaps in service delivery, and the factors that contribute to any misdirection of resources and services. They help identify issues that constrain the poor from accessing and using the services, like availability, ease of access, quality, reliability and costs. CRCs also help to identify possible ways to improve service delivery by actively seeking suggestions from citizens. Finally, CRC findings help test from the citizens' point of view some of the policy conclusions reached in other analytical studies" (2004, p. 6). The PAF also states that CRCs have earned substantial credibility.[8]

PIJC COMPONENTS

This very creative program has many of a PIJC's principal components, including initial focus groups, benchmark surveys, simple-to-understand indicators based on detailed surveys, and wide dissemination to stimulate internal reform as well as beneficiary political pressure for improvement.

One may ask whether we have correctly classified the CRC as a certification (see table 2-5). The answer is yes and no. On the one hand, since the type, costs, and conditions of each public service are so completely different and since only a one-time baseline was to be taken, the various scores for each service probably acted more to certify a level of performance than as a cross-service comparative indicator. The emphasis, in other words, was on providing an objective assessment of the quality and quantity of the different services that those living on the forest fringe were receiving. On the other hand, level-of-satisfaction subindicators for each public service were aggregated into an unweighted one-dimensional index and used to rank the public services (PAF 2004, table 30). However, because of each service's unique situation and attributes, it is unlikely that such a ranking

---

8. Of course, as the designer and implementer, the PAF cannot be viewed as a fully objective observer. On the other hand, scorecard applications have proliferated around the world.

provided any competitive pressure—hence the reluctance here to classify this application as a tournament.[9] Rather, it is a simple certification, for that is apparently how it was used.

ASSESSMENT

The CRC seems to have been very effective in initiating public pressure and stimulating debate and internal review within providers and regulators. Its use has also been a major step forward in facilitating public-private partnerships. PAF (2004) gives several examples of cooperation between the private sector and public agencies to address specific concerns in priority areas. The participatory and nonconfrontational style of the implementation no doubt contributed to these results. As another sign of the project's satisfactory outcome, the World Bank used CRC data for their projects on the public service sector (PAF 2004). While this assessment could be seen as based on self-servingly glowing appraisals by the sponsors, the fact is that this activity led to a large number of copycat projects, lending credence to the assertions made.

One particularly innovative part of the CRC design is that it compares public service provision both vertically and horizontally. In other words, not only does it compare (say) health care services across low-, medium-, and high-density forest jurisdictions but also health care service availability and satisfaction for a given jurisdiction against that of other public sectors, such as education and rural credit. While this has methodological limitations, it does allow for identification of systemic deficiencies (usually at higher levels of government or in the population as a whole) that may be outside the control of individual sectors.[10] Thampi (2007) provides additional examples of the various impacts of CRCs, which are listed in table 3-1.

However, this innovative activity has two main weaknesses. The first is the lack of a follow-up survey. While the announcement of interjurisdictional service providers and regulator rankings should stimulate change by provoking internal debate and civil society pressure, the potential impact of the CRC concept could likely be increased dramatically through one or more follow-up survey rounds, administered according to a preannounced schedule and with sufficient time allotted for players (public utilities) to undertake improvements. This would greatly help to harness competitive action. The problem is that without an expected *second* benchmark (to be taken at the end of the contest), agencies in the Jharkhand application were scored on precontest performance—that is, before they could respond to any incentives. In fact, other CRC applications seem to have recog-

---

9. In fact, the PAF report did not mention that the ranking was used nor that it had any specific effect.

10. An example of methodological limitations: how useful is it to know that one public sector has a lower satisfaction rating than another when each is faced with (at least some) unique constraints? The PAF explicitly recognizes this and tries to overcome it in several ways.

Table 3-1. *Impacts of CRCs in Different Locations*

Location	CRC impact
Cities	
Bangalore, India	Agencies discuss performance with citizens in open forums
Delhi, India	Political leadership asks for more direct feedback
Mumbai, India (slums)	Forcing political accountability in slums
	Lower-level officials cite findings to seek funds and support
Ternopil, Ukraine	Systematic citizen watchdog role in local government
Countries	
Ethiopia, Tajikistan, Zanzibar	Independent approach to monitoring pro-poor services
India, Vietnam	SNGs benchmark selves
Kenya	Regulatory bodies seek independent voices

Source: Based on Thampi (2007, slides 27 and 29).

nized this; the associated activity in Bangalore, India, comprised three survey benchmarks taken roughly four years apart (Thampi 2007).

Second, it is likely that "negative rewards"—political and social pressure on the lower-ranking participants—could be made into a stronger, more powerful incentive. This could be done by announcing a formal dissemination strategy at least a year in advance so that providers and regulators have a clear expectation as to the negative consequences of relatively poorer performance, and offering some form of positive recognition and, ideally, additional funds to the providers and regulators who show concrete efforts to effect improvements. As things stand, the implication is that additional resources will be given the worst performers. Unfortunately, knowing who the worst performers are tells little about what they would do with—or their motivation to use—additional resources in the future.

These concerns raise a subtle design challenge. On the one hand, CRC implementers touted the benefits of the cooperation they received from service providers, both during survey design and afterwards during public discussions on how to improve service provision. On the other hand, using output-based performance to encourage competition among service providers might strengthen their incentives to respond to a CRC. This suggests that designers must balance the benefits of nonconfrontation and those of greater competitive pressure. It also illustrates that a certification mechanism can be designed for stimulating distinct demand-driven or supply-driven reform action and that an application may pursue one without pursuing the other.

A worrisome consequence of the PAF's CRC is that the initiative substitutes for government action. The government, through an independent official body, should oversee and supervise the quality of public services and their responsiveness to household needs. Some countries assign part of this task to parliamentary agencies; others use independent bodies that directly report to the prime minister or president. This issue is revisited in the discussion about scalability.

Table 3-2. *Variation in Institutional Forms of CRCs*

Institutional form	Organization name, project, or location[a]
Individual civil society organizations	PAF and TIB
Civil society partnerships	People's Voice Project, PANE
Independent multistakeholder consortiums	Kenya, Tanzania
Governments	Internal (Vietnam), open (Delhi, India)

Source: Based on Thampi (2007, slide 27).

a. PAC, Public Affairs Foundation; TIB, TEMPUS Institution Building project; PANE, Poverty Action Network civil society organizations in Ethiopia.

IMPACT OF INITIAL CONDITIONS

The potential success of the CRC concept does not appear to be linked to the specific initial conditions of the forest fringe areas in Jharkhand, though of course the survey instrument and focus group protocols must necessarily be tailored to the sectors and jurisdictions in which they are administered. Likewise, the effectiveness of stakeholder follow-up action would depend on the political, social, and civil freedom a local population has to exercise its voice and the extent to which its representatives might act once subject to the light of transparency. In fact, according to Thampi (2007), CRCs are being used under many other types of implementing organizations (see table 3-2) and environments, including urban settings (Bangalore, Delhi, Mumbai, and Ternopil) and different countries (Ethiopia, India, Kenya, Tajikistan, Ukraine, and Zanzibar).

What is striking about the Jharkhand example is just how consistent the initiative's design was with the nonconfrontational style of local culture—and this in spite of having some characteristics of a tournament. The sense one gets from reading the project's documentation is that the PAF saw its role and acted as a facilitator of public-private partnership and not as an adversarial advocate with a political agenda or desire to attack officials. It crafted its dissemination materials to encourage public understanding of the constraints and challenges public service providers and their regulators face. As a consequence, it is likely that the initiative's implementation was met with less hostility—and therefore greater cooperation—than might otherwise have been the case. Clearly, then, this approach would be problematic in a country where the regulatory authorities had the power to impede such initiatives.

SUSTAINABILITY AND SCALABILITY

This project has led to a qualitative increase in the level of transparency and discourse regarding public service provision in Jharkhand, judging from the degree of media coverage and participatory interactions that followed the release of the CRC (PAF 2004). This will no doubt lead to some change. Likewise, the nonconfrontational and collaborative involvement of the service providers bodes well for sustainability. Political action and public sector reform, however, take endurance and protracted pressure to be effective. Under the project design implemented, it is not clear whether public service providers and regulators will stay the course and implement the necessary reforms and investment to fruition. The incentives to do so may be blunted due to the lack of certainty (precommitment) that the PAF (or others) will undertake a follow-up, preannounced—and funded— round of indicator and ranking surveys. As of this writing, some reforms appeared to be under way, but only time will tell whether sustainable (permanent) changes will occur and whether they are a result of the CRC.

Regarding this last point, while they laud the success of the initiatives, none of the reports describing the PAF or any of the CRC applications in other countries indicate that any prospective impact evaluation was performed. This is both odd and a lost opportunity since the applications were at pains to employ statistically rigorous sampling and survey methods. One reason for this omission may be that most of the applications were done on a shoestring. In addition, the implementers were all convinced of the effectiveness of the tool. Had it borne the added cost of rigorous evaluation, the PAF might have had an easier time raising funding for follow-up benchmarks.[11]

Scalability is another matter. While the Jharkhand application was explicitly called a pilot, the prior and subsequent existence of so many other applications, both elsewhere in India as well as in other countries (see table 3-1) lends credence to the approach's scalability, replicability, and flexibility of scope. For example, these other applications suggest that the Jharkhand CRC design is eminently applicable to larger sets of jurisdictions and diverse locations, offering greater comparative insights for providers and beneficiaries, not to mention potential sponsors. For example, some regulatory jurisdictions are overlapping (Frey and Eichenberger 1999), a situation that lends itself to an analysis of whether different quality-of-service outcomes are influenced or even due to interaction effects. Likewise, increasing the number of (in this case) regions competing would allow one to compare within-service spatial variation in provider quality. Of course, cost goes up with such approaches, though at a lower rate than the increase in the size of the targeted population (due to fixed costs in the design of focus group protocols, surveys, and dissemination).

The CRC design may also be applied at a higher level of jurisdiction, for example, at the level of the province or federal state. Still, it is an empirical question as to what level of aggregation will work well since success depends on both the degree of citizen access to channels of accountability as well as the effectiveness of public dissemination of regulatory rankings. Nonetheless, the *Global Competitiveness Report* (World Economic Forum, various years), the Corruption

---

11. This may have simply required interviewing a slightly larger number of households, randomly selected in advance, to receive a different protocol. Such a protocol might have made clear to the respondent that the results would not be made public.

Perception Index of Transparency International, the *Doing Business* series (World Bank, various years), and the *Transition Report* (European Bank for Reconstruction and Development, various years) show that one may even apply such initiatives to the international level. There is a real risk, however, that political considerations might enter the picture as the jurisdictional level rises or if the value of a better ranking increases; these forces could compromise the objectiveness of the approach.

3.1.3 Indonesia: Environmental Certifications

Indonesia has benefited greatly from industrialization. The "average Indonesian's real income has doubled since 1980 and the number of Indonesians living in poverty has fallen more than half since 1970" (Afsah and Vincent 1997, p. 1). However, industrialization also has had negative consequences for Indonesia's environment, namely, deteriorating air and water quality. This section examines one of the Indonesian government's innovations to confront such degradation: the Program for Pollution Control, Evaluation, and Rating (PROPER).[12]

STATEMENT OF THE PROBLEM

By the 1980s Indonesia's air and water quality was rapidly deteriorating due to industrialization. Indonesia established its first air-monitoring device on the island of Jakarta in 1978 and found that "airborne concentrations of suspended particulate matter already exceeded the World Health Organization's (WHO) recommended standard by 40 percent. By 1988, they were double the standard."[13] The World Bank estimated that "exposure of urban residents to airborne particulate concentrations above the WHO standard caused an additional 1,263 to 2,352 deaths, 26,609 to 71,033 emergency room visits, 184,453 to 541,618 asthma attacks, and 5.3 to 11.8 million lost work days in Jakarta in 1989." Unfortunately, Indonesia's Ministry of Population and Environment did not have the resources to enforce existing environmental regulations. Furthermore, the governors of provinces, whose main concern was to decrease unemployment and increase income for their citizens, lacked the political will to enforce environmental regulations.

SPONSOR AND IMPLEMENTER

The World Bank provided the technical assistance through foreign consultants while the Indonesian government funded the local costs of program development and implementation, the latter through the Ministry of Population and Environment.

---

12. The Clean City Program (ADIPURA) started in 1986 is another Indonesian environmental policy innovation based on voluntary participation and certification by an outside authority (see Makarim 2006).

13. The data, quotes, and conclusions from this subsection all come from Afsah and Vincent (1997, pp. 1–2).

COST AND TIME FRAME

The design and piloting cost to the sponsor was $250,000 for foreign consultants. The Indonesian government currently spends $100,000 annually to run the program, which now covers forty-three industrial sectors.

PLAYERS

There are numerous players (stakeholders) in this PIJC application. First, the industrial facilities that were being "regulated" were the important participants in the PIJC. There also was the regional development planning board (Badan Pengendalian Dampak Lingkungan [BAPEDAL]), which is the governmental agency in charge of the project and acts as information coordinator and not as a regulating body. Next there was the environmental regulatory authority, the Ministry of Population and Environment. Finally, the citizens, media outlets, NGOs, and other community-based organizations also would play a big role in the success or failure of this initiative by providing public pressure for the facilities to comply with environmental regulations.

RULES OF THE GAME

PROPER proposed a color-coded rating system for grading industrial facilities' performance on environmental regulations. The ratings were intended to elicit public pressure on the industrial facilities that were not complying with environmental regulations and to reward those that were. Therefore, the success of the program depended on a rating system that was easy for the public to understand but at the same time provided incentives for facilities to improve their ratings (Blackman, Afsah, and Ratunanda 2004, p. 237). As a result, BAPEDAL staff and World Bank consultants developed an easy-to-use rating system. A particular facility's rating was determined by a "short series of yes/no questions that covered key provisions of the regulations and made it easy to determine which color rating a specific facility deserved" (Afsah and Vincent 1997, p. 7).

The rating system worked as follows. PROPER divided facilities into two groups: those in compliance and those out of compliance with environmental regulations. Those facilities in compliance were subdivided further into blue, green, and gold ratings, where each color represented a different level of compliance. A blue rating indicated that the facility just satisfied all the provisions in applicable environmental regulations. A green rating indicated that the facility's performance was substantially better than the regulations required. Finally, the gold rating indicated that the facility's performance was exceptionally good—state of the art internationally. Similarly, the out-of-compliance industrial facilities were subdivided into two categories, red and black. A red rating indicated that the facility was "applying some environmental management effort but not enough to satisfy all the provisions, while a black rating was reserved for the worst performers, who were making no effort to control their pollution discharge" (Afsah and Vincent

1997, p. 5). These colors were chosen because they have cultural connotations in Indonesia closely related to the environmental performance that they represent.

The data for the rating system come from multiple sources, including independent inspections, a survey of prospective participants, and other environmental programs. The facilities participating in the program were also required to "monitor themselves and to report their pollution discharge on a monthly basis" (Afsah and Vincent 1997, p. 9). The participating facilities were both volunteers and also chosen by BAPEDAL, mainly based on the amount of available data.

REWARDS

The local media published the ratings of each of the facilities participating in PROPER in order to generate public pressure on those facilities that failed to comply with regulations. Initially only the facilities that earned green or gold ratings were published to give the system a positive image.[14] For the remaining facilities, BAPEDAL decided to release "just the number in each color category" to demonstrate that it was serious about identifying those facilities that were out of compliance. Furthermore, facilities that were determined to be out of compliance were given six months to improve their performance before their names and ratings were disclosed.

By publishing the ratings, the system created incentives for the facilities to comply with environmental regulations.[15] BAPEDAL felt that the ratings "could influence the facilities' reputations, and thereby use honor and shame to create reputational incentives for better environmental performance." A favorable rating would create public goodwill and positive publicity for industrial facilities, which could give the company a competitive advantage. An unfavorable rating would create public and political pressure for facilities to improve their performance.

STATED OUTCOMES

PROPER has been a huge success and has received a great deal of international attention. In the first six months of implementation, "PROPER raised the compliance rate from 36 percent to 41 percent."[16] In addition, the number of facilities that volunteered for the program more than doubled in six months, from eleven to twenty-five. There is also evidence to suggest that facilities participating in PROPER "continue to improve their performance. More than a quarter of the

---

14. The data, quotes, and conclusions from this subsection all come from Afsah and Vincent (1997, pp. 9, 11).

15. This type of instrument—voluntary disclosure—is what Tom Tietenberg (2000) calls the "third wave" of environmental regulation (after command and control regulation and economic instruments). He points out that the instrument operates by applying pressure in the capital and labor markets as well as the goods market.

16. The data, quotes, and conclusions from this subsection all come from Afsah and Vincent (1997, p. 13).

facilities rated red or black in December 1995 improved their ratings to blue or green by September 1996."

PIJC COMPONENTS

The color rating system—a key part of this program—is essentially an indicator-based system and is therefore a PIJC component. It allows the environmental regulators to take benchmarks of players to produce a monotonic rating that can be used to rank firms. This leads again to the question of whether it was correct to classify PROPER as a certification in our typology (see table 2-5). Again, the answer is both yes and no. On the one hand, as a long-standing program that produces a ranking, it clearly has some tournament properties.[17] In particular, one would have thought that the public would be more likely to judge a firm *relative to others* in its sector rather than by the absolute meaning of the firm's rating. On the other hand, in Indonesia the incentives apparently operated by drawing owners' attention to their firms' performance and thereby socially praise or shame them. Each color, after all, was like a standard within a certification scheme. For this reason the PROPER PIJC has been classified as a certification. Note, too, that as firm benchmarking occurred frequently, the certification was based on output performance; since poor performance required environmental investment, these compliance costs can be viewed as negative pecuniary rewards—another PIJC component.

The other important PIJC component found in PROPER is its use of public relations strategies to create incentives for a firm to improve its performance. By allowing the public to hold facilities accountable for polluting the environment, the public relations strategies seem to have created an indirect competitive feature in the labor and goods markets. As incredible as it may sound, many industrialists felt embarrassed—and even surprised—about their firms' poor environmental performance.[18] As a result, it seems that the program empowered the environmental officers of the firms. Also, firms began advertising their good rating and publicly attacking their competitor's bad ratings.

While no technical assistance was directly provided to rated firms as a part of the initiative, the mechanism was essentially performance based: the "rewards" (benefits or costs) to the firms depended on their own behavior. Moreover, to the extent that a bad rating was more costly to a poorly rated firm the more its competitors had good ratings, the more the rating system had a tournament orientation.

---

17. One might argue that the setting of performance standards is endogenous, and therefore PROPER is a tournament since the performance of other firms carries an externality of raising the bar in a future round of what regulators deem acceptable. While this ratchet effect is what happens under competition, this was not the case for PROPER since the standards were already limited by international norms of best practice.

18. Makarim (2006).

ASSESSMENT

There is no doubt that this instrument is to be lauded. It has created a low-cost system for improving environmental compliance in a country with weak environmental institutions. Key to its success was the existence or capacity of the Ministry of Population and Environment to collect monitoring data on the larger firms and to verify self-reporting by the other participating firms. In fact, the self-reporting element turned out to be an inspiration because the errant firm could not sue the government for biased data if the government were using information provided by the firm itself. This is an important consideration: due to severe budget constraints in environmental ministries, experience indicates that firms tend to win such cases.

This initiative also contains lessons for aid effectiveness as well as for regulatory policy. First, it indicates that a sponsor's intervention—in this case, that of the World Bank—is more likely to be successful if it is demand driven (in this case developed by the recipient itself). Second, it suggests the benefits that can be achieved when sponsor and recipient work in a synergistic and complementary fashion. Third, as discussed below, it shows the importance of the cultural context for policy success (and transplantation): the mechanism drew on social responsibility and "face," communicated at a culturally appropriate level, and used colors with local connotations. PROPER also illustrates the power of public disclosure as one (and, in this case, the only) direct reward in the pecuniary certification design. Here, though the real benefits are a less polluted environment, it is the direct impact on the player that motivates reform. Thus, since disclosure operates indirectly through commercial markets—the goods, capital, and labor markets in the case of Indonesia—environmental certification took on characteristics of a repeated game that caused PROPER also to generate tournament-like incentives.

Note that disclosure is a necessary but not sufficient condition for this mechanism to be effective. Two other requisite conditions are that the information is easily interpretable by the public (consumer, worker, and shareholder) and that the public has a means to act upon the information.

IMPACT OF INITIAL CONDITIONS

To its credit, the PROPER program can successfully operate in a country with weak environmental institutions. Nonetheless, the success of PROPER can be attributed in part to preexisting voluntary pollution control programs (Afsah and Vincent 1997). In designing and implementing the PROPER program, BAPEDAL relied heavily on previous experience from the Clean River Program or Program Kali Bersih (PROKASIH), a voluntary pollution control program aimed at reducing water pollution. In addition, PROKASIH teams collected some of the data used for rating the facilities participating in PROPER.

However, "blame and shame" campaigns do not work in all countries. It requires the existence of a family and socially conscious population, something found frequently in Asia. Therefore, not surprisingly, the majority of the copycat applications also have been in Asia. Given the use of color indicators, one would imagine that the program would also require a healthy saturation of the TV medium, which might rule out its application in some of the poorest countries. Similarly, only large firms were part of the PROPER program, but in many very poor countries, there are few such large firms, and it is small firms as a group that generate the most pollution.

Finally, any time regulatory incentives require increased enterprise investment, they will lead to backlash—both political and economic—unless the country is experiencing economic growth, something that was occurring strongly in the 1980s and 1990s in Indonesia. Hence it is no surprise that China has been experimenting with the system.

SUSTAINABILITY AND SCALABILITY

In Indonesia the long-standing record of the PROPER program is testimony to its sustainability. Still, there are specific conditions that ensure the sustainability of the PROPER system. First, the program entails very modest operation and maintenance cost to the government. Second, the regulatory authority already has a statutory obligation to collect and analyze the requisite environmental data from the participating firms, so the computation and dissemination of the color code assignations, which it also performs, is bureaucratically easy. Third, the public and the social norms are not likely to change quickly; thus Indonesian society will continue to disapprove of antisocial behaviors like not making efforts to produce relatively cleanly where possible. It is likely, however, that the regulatory authority could further strengthen the sustainability of the initiative through incremental investment to promote (advertise) the social responsibility of using cleaner production methods.

Since the PROPER system is implemented nationally but only applied to the largest industrial firms, scalability here naturally would refer to increasing the inclusiveness of the compliance population down to ever smaller firms. So far the initiative has had some success in expanding the coverage to midsize firms. Since the system requires firm-specific data, as additional smaller firms are included, the cost of data collection will grow disproportionately. One way to handle this would be to pass the obligation for monitoring onto the firms themselves and then use random enforcement with salient penalties to ensure accurate self-reporting. It is likely as well that the color code system would have to be redefined to reflect a series of meanings more appropriate to the smaller firms, which, for example, may not have the means to attain world-class standards, regardless of the efforts they would make.

Finally, perhaps the greatest barometer of success is the fact that the program is being widely imitated in other countries. China, Mexico, India, Bangladesh, and Thailand have all introduced PROPER-like programs (Blackman,

Afsah, and Ratunanda 2004, pp. 237, 242). Moreover, this is also proof of its replicability.

3.1.4 USAID: R4 Process

This case study is particularly interesting because it illustrates the pitfalls of institutionally nearsighted monitoring and evaluation by a major (bilateral) donor.

STATEMENT OF THE PROBLEM

When the private sector provides services, success is generally easy to recognize: sales soar, profitability increases, and stock prices rise. Poor service provision leads to the opposite outcomes. In public sector service provision, success is much harder to gauge, but poor service provision generally leads to immediate public outcry from the intended beneficiaries, and through the political process, elected officials take corrective action or risk losing their jobs. However, as is well known in the case of donor aid services, there is no such feedback loop between the provider and the beneficiaries since the latter are generally poor people in countries very far away—both geographically and institutionally—from taxpayers who foot the donor's bill.

This has been a perennial problem for USAID, which historically has had to face a hostile Congress whose constituencies have not had a strong interest in the poor of other countries or in the effectiveness of programs serving them. Moreover, aid effectiveness has always been considered a bit of an oxymoron. Hence, in response to the Government Performance and Results Act of 1993, which sought to improve the effectiveness and public accountability of federal programs, and to the March 1993 presidential initiative to "reinvent government," which called for a National Performance Review, USAID's administrator designated the agency a "reinvention laboratory" (General Accounting Office [GAO] 1996, p. 6) and began to develop a management plan. USAID then undertook a dramatic reorganization, including in 1995 the development of a new performance reporting system.

OBJECTIVE

This new monitoring "system required managers to (1) establish performance indicators, (2) prepare performance monitoring plans, (3) set performance baselines, (4) collect performance data, and (5) periodically assess data quality" (Williams, Adley and Company 2002).

One component of the USAID system was the preparation of annual "Results Review and Resource Request (R4)" reports. These were "the most significant performance reports that the Agency's individual operating units [that is, its country missions] [would] send to their respective bureaus" (Williams, Adley and Company 2002, p. 8). In short, it was "intended to link resource allocations and performance" (GAO 1996, p. 11). Moreover, the agency's Automated Directives

System required that the R4 reports be used for all internal and external inquiries, including for reporting requirements pursuant to the 1993 Results Act mentioned above.

Operationally, the R4 process involved the identification and development of three indicators (Center for Democracy and Governance [CDG] 1998, p. 2). First, strategic objectives were required to allow missions to "manage for results by tracking performance toward the most ambitious objective upon which it expects to have a material effect." Second, intermediate results indicators were created to track performance of lower-level objectives whose attainment developers believed was required if the higher-level strategic objectives were to be eventually achieved. Third, activity indicators were constructed to track the implementation of a specific project or program's activities.

Finally, while not particularly stressed in the system's descriptive materials, an additional impetus for the R4 process was its role in promoting learning, by both USAID staff as well as by outside development professionals, including USAID contractors.

SPONSOR AND IMPLEMENTERS

In practice, the production of R4 reports became an interactive process between USAID operating units and their contractors. Depending on the particular project or program, this was the case both for the identification of strategic objectives as well as the selection of indicators for each of the three levels.

COST AND TIME FRAME

According to GAO (1996, p. 17), as of 1996 USAID had spent $73 million on system development and deployment. In fact, while working in Romania in 1997, I was told by one of the companies involved in the system's development, installation, testing, and training that they thought USAID would end up spending $240 million over several years to get it up and functional in its seventy country missions and headquarters. This seems rather pricey, but clearly the sheer ambitiousness of the endeavor suggests it would have been very expensive.

PLAYERS

Those involved in the operation of the R4 system included program and project staff in USAID's missions around the world, as well as staff in its various bureaus in Washington. USAID's contractors were also involved as described above. In addition, as consumers of the reports, senior USAID management and ultimately congressional members and their staffs were part of the game. Finally, the Center for Development Information and Evaluation, USAID's evaluation unit, was to assist missions in setting up teams, tracking how consumers use the R4, and making recommendations on how to use the system (GAO 1996, p. 11).

RULES OF THE GAME

Mission directors, with the help of their program staff, select strategic objectives and the intermediate results and activity results to realize them. These are quantified using a series of indicators and target values (to compare to preimplementation baselines of the same indicators), and then they are approved as part of the country assessment strategy process. According to testimony by the administrator, "Activities not achieving results will be redesigned or terminated" (GAO 1996, p. 11). In principle this should have led to several competitions. Within a mission the director could compare the project performance within and across different programs. Senior management in Washington could use the R4 reports to compare program results across the many missions implementing them. Finally, contractors who did not reliably meet intermediate or activity targets would have been at higher risk of losing their funding. In parallel with the R4 process, USAID engaged in "reengineering" itself by "(1) defining and involving [its] customers, (2) empowering employees, (3) managing for results, and (4) emphasizing and rewarding teamwork" (GAO 1996, p. 11).

REWARDS

In theory, the reward for players who carried out the R4 process was the benefit they would receive from having a management-by-objectives system in place, along with its tracking system. In addition, the USAID missions as well as departments at headquarters in Washington would be in a better position to justify its activities and their budgets. The size of project impacts would also become more evident. Moreover, since in most bureaucracies bigger budgets are highly sought after (Niskanen 1971), better performance as documented by the R4 system would be seen as necessary in the quest for controlling larger budgets. The R4 system was not voluntary, however, so many participants in the system felt that the reward for submitting the information was simply the benefit of getting it over with. Likewise, there was a threat of disciplinary action if the R4 process was not followed, at least pro forma. USAID staff members do participate in a number of official and tacit incentive schemes designed to recognize higher achievement and encourage greater effort. I have not found any written documentation, however, that specifically referred to R4 indicators as being part of those schemes.

STATED OUTCOMES

After a phased-in and bumpy start, the R4 process continued on all projects for about six years, after which it only seems to have been done on a discretionary basis. Moreover, in 2001 the annual R4 reporting process was replaced by the submission of an annual report, which "relies on a more limited, standardized, and more reliable set of performance indicators than did the old R4 process" (Williams, Adley and Company2002). During this period project-specific evaluations were also no longer required of all large projects but rather allowed on a

Table 3-3. *Number of Evaluations Performed by USAID Missions, 1993–97*

Year	Number of evaluations
1993	425
1994	497
1995	342
1996	240
1997	139

Source: Greene (1999).

discretionary basis. The impact of this change is clearly illustrated in table 3-3. This connection between the R4 reports and project evaluations is revisited below.

While participants in the R4 process developed strong yet mixed feelings about the system, it definitely helped to focus attention on important questions. These included:

—Toward what greater objectives were projects being funded?

—Were projects (or particular programs or even USAID missions) achieving the impacts their proponents were claiming would occur?

—What were the costs of meeting strategic objectives and were they worth it given their impacts?

Clearly, the R4 period broke new ground for the agency, its backers, and its detractors. Moreover, it heralded the beginning of aid effectiveness as a topic and specialization in its own right—an intellectual and policy focus still very much at the forefront of donors' minds today.

PIJC COMPONENTS

The most visible PIJC component was the use of indicators to develop baselines and take benchmark readings over time. In addition to the management and learning dimensions these provided, they also may have served to attenuate principal-agent problems. Less obvious was the competitive nature of the R4 process. True, each project had explicit quantitative targets to meet, and these certainly acted as a performance certification mechanism. However, at the level of the implementing firm or USAID project officer, there was really no common metric for comparing cross-player performance other than dichotomously counting the number of targets met. Due to the low number of projects a firm or a USAID project officer would have, and due to the enormous vagaries—beyond the control of either—that influenced project outcomes, a simple cardinal comparison of such totals did not create any competitive pressure. Yet at a higher level, the R4 results were one of the decisionmaking inputs used to allocate funds across programs (and perhaps even missions). Thus, with a budget constraint at the level of

Table 3-4. *Summary of Auditor's Findings on R4 Reporting at Seven Missions, 2001*

Country	Data quality assessment not performed or documented	Performance monitoring plans not complete or updated	Data limitation not properly disclosed
India	√	√	√
Nicaragua	√	√	√
Mali		√	
Kenya		√	
Kenya/REDSO[a]		√	
Ukraine	√	√	√
Ghana	√	√	√

Source: Williams, Adley and Company (2002).
a. REDSO, Regional Economic Development Services Organization.

USAID as a whole, the R4 certification mechanism may have marginally strengthened competitive forces associated with internal fund allocation.[19]

Another PIJC component in the R4 system was the attempt to create incentives for increased cooperation among those pursuing each strategic objective. What was least visible was the incentive (reward) component of the mechanism, though on paper it existed (see above).

ASSESSMENT

While the R4 process undoubtedly brought USAID into the modern era of management, it clearly did not have the hoped-for benefits or efficiencies envisioned. USAID itself provides three stinging indictments. First, a report produced by USAID's own auditors (Williams, Adley and Company 2002), in what turned out to be the final year of the R4 process, suggests that R4 reporting was not well implemented by the missions. As shown in table 3-4, the auditors' 2001 assessment of seven USAID missions on three continents determined that almost 60 percent did not assess or document data quality, 100 percent did not complete or update their monitoring plans, and almost 60 percent did not properly disclose data limitations.

Second, a thorough study commissioned by USAID's Center for Development Information and Evaluation to look at the use and effectiveness of evaluation at USAID provided some insight into the effectiveness of the R4 process (Clapp-Wincek and Blue 2001). One of the study's many concerns was the link between

19. Of course, the budget process for an organization the size of USAID is very complex and involves both bottom-up (mission) requests as well as top-down (bureau) allocations. Moreover, it depends on exogenous federal budget forces, congressional earmarks, executive branch policy initiatives, and the implicit constraint of not deviating too much from the previous year's figure.

reporting and action. "The field-level evaluation work tends to focus on *activity* performance, especially by implementing partners. R4 monitoring systems assess progress at the strategic level. There is a disconnect between activity evaluation and SO [strategic objective] monitoring that cannot be closed by more activity monitoring. SO leaders, in the main, are not carrying out strategic evaluations at the SO level." The report provides several quotes typifying the responses on the USAID staff questionnaires. One respondent said, "I don't think USAID does a good job of analytically assessing the results of its programs on an ongoing basis" (p. 11). In analyzing their own questionnaire, the study's authors found that "there were only 7 cases cited [out of 64] where problems identified in the Results Review [R4] process prompted evaluations and 5 examples were included where evaluations were done to feed into R4 reviews."

The study also found that there was reluctance within missions to cancel an activity as a result of a poor R4 evaluation (Clapp-Wincek and Blue 2001, p. 11). This suggests that staff did not trust the results of the R4 framework or that they were not being held to task when R4 revealed poor performance or that senior management in reality saw the R4 process as pro forma. Perhaps most worrisome was the finding that the "annual three-page R4 descriptions to describe what is happening are insufficient for mission management decisions regarding where best to allocate its limited funding to achieve the most significant impact" (p. 11).

The third indictment is that USAID terminated the R4 reporting framework in 2001, just six years after making a huge investment in it. A system of this complexity requires several years to get up and running smoothly, but it seems that just as it had become fully operational, it was discontinued.

Although there are undoubtedly many reasons for this outcome, the focus here will be on those relevant to evaluating the PIJC concept. At the risk of being accused of reductionism, based on research conducted elsewhere (Espina and Zinnes 2003), it is likely that the ultimate reason for failure of the R4 system was a lack of demand within USAID *as an institution* for its output, that is, cost-effective project performance from budgetary resources was not a central concern. The reason for this is complicated. USAID is not a development agency; it is a donor aid agency.[20] Thus it has many simultaneous objectives beyond cost-effectiveness.[21] In addition, the large "distance" between the beneficiaries and the U.S. taxpayer greatly reduces the accountability of aid delivery, as does the great number of intermediaries in the process. Finally, some staff members ideologically resist boiling down socioeconomic development to a small set of numbers, given the inherent complexity of sustainably improving third world welfare.

---

20. Robert Bates made this astute observation in his comments on Espina and Zinnes (2003) at a 2003 USAID-sponsored conference on the application of the new institutional economics to improving aid effectiveness.

21. Of course, non-cost-related targets could—and were—included in the R4 process.

The complexity of the aid outcome environment also meant that it would be very hard to assign praise or blame to an impact. Too many concomitant and often unpredictable exogenous contributory forces were at work. The only really effective way to assess project or program activities in such an environment is through randomized evaluation, that is, implementing the aid "treatment" using a *prospective,* randomized design, as is done with clinical (for example, pharmaceutical) trials (Duflo 2003). Such an approach is, of course, an optional component of PIJC methodology. The problem with assessing individual staff members was that they generally did not have full control over the design and implementation of the activities they managed and therefore could not bear full responsibility for outcomes. In addition, they often would move to another position before an activity ended.

Whatever the reasons, the three "indictments" above begin to make perfect sense when one realizes that the demand for analysis and action based on quantitative performance targets was weak. Without a real demand for the information, the system had become a mechanical, pro forma exercise. As such, the requirement to feed data into the system was often simply an additional task for overobligated staff to complete, often requiring contractor assistance for development, data collection, and documentation.

Even so, there were additional holes in the mechanism design that diluted competitive pressure to produce effective aid outcomes. Consider two. First, in reality, whether due to lack of faith in the quality of the R4 indicators or to the importance of other qualitative issues, neither across-mission nor within-mission budgets were cut as a result of mediocre R4 ratings nor were staff salaries reduced for designing or managing projects with mediocre R4 ratings. This surely blunted the incentives needed for the R4 competition to generate the sort of tight management and results-oriented system its creators had envisioned. Second, those being judged were the very ones who were asked to develop the indicators and the targets. Such an institutional setup surely invited bureaucratic gaming of the system, where those who ultimately would be judged might establish indicators and targets so as to avoid failure in the eyes of the bureaucracy. For all these reasons, the mechanism produced sufficient "fatigue" for it to be abandoned—a warning to anyone contemplating the introduction of an institutionalized incentive mechanism.

While this point is revisited in chapter 6, it may be useful here to contrast the failure of the R4 process with alternative approaches used by (perhaps) more successful donors, at least from the aid effectiveness perspective. The Swedish International Development Cooperation Agency (Sida) designs projects with explicit attention to the de facto incentives they create for Sida project management staff and for their contracted implementers (Ostrom and others 2002). One consequence of this orientation is that Sida tends to focus on small, microeconomic activities. The Millennium Challenge Corporation, in many ways the second-generation U.S. aid agency, has chosen to focus on projects amenable to rigorous (and, where possible, randomized) impact evaluation.

IMPACT OF INITIAL CONDITIONS

Several initial institutional conditions made it difficult for UASID to impose a strategic management system on itself. First and foremost, such a system implied radical reform, and it is almost always the case that "self-reform" is an oxymoron. The culture of USAID was ideologically based on the premise that development is extremely complicated and cannot be measured. This culture also led only those with a similar outlook to apply to and then remain at the organization. Even the organization of activities into "stovepipes" militated against the management-by-objective approach. Any project that was sufficiently multidepartmental or implied "donor cooperation" (another oxymoron if there ever was one!) would be difficult to implement in a cost-effective way; there would be simply too many bureaucratic objectives and obstacles. In addition, Congress as well as the executive branch saw USAID as a tool for either promoting foreign policies or rewarding constituents at home. These objectives could often conflict with a "project-selection-by-the-numbers" approach. For these and other related reasons, one can see why the root of the failure of the R4 system was a lack of demand that resulted from senior management not placing a high, genuine priority on allocating budgets based on cost-effectiveness.

SUSTAINABILITY AND SCALABILITY

USAID was acutely aware that it would "face the challenge of institutionalizing the gains made to ensure the long-term sustainability of reform. The hope was that transparency in resource allocation based on results and continued training on reengineering concepts and practices [would] help capture these gains" (GAO 1996, p. 26). The cancellation by USAID of the R4 system shows that the approach as it was originally designed was not sustainable. The replacement annual report system, to the extent it is seen as a second-generation R4 methodology, may demonstrate that a less ambitious approach will be sustainable.[22]

As for scalability, USAID did run a pilot of the R4 system with some success. However, as I understood it at the time, at least some of the missions running the pilot had actually been the ones who developed the R4 idea in the first place. While this bit of organizational innovation is certainly to be commended and imitated, it is not the way to select pilot locations to ensure external validity to the results. Those who developed the idea clearly had a vested interest in its success and crafted it to fit the country and organizational conditions present at their

22. It is possible that the replacement of R4, which one may consider an institutional reform in its own right, still might not have happened had there not been a change in USAID administrator. I thank Johannes Linn of the Wolfensohn Center at Brookings for this observation.

location. An en masse institutional reform is very dependent on such initial conditions and is not for the faint of heart. It is unlikely, therefore, that an R4-type approach would be very feasible for any donor that operates under a diverse set of often conflicting objectives, where success is the result of large teams from a multitude of organizations (diffusing responsibility, blame, and praise) and where there are strong bureaucratic (legal) limits on the incentives that staff may receive.

3.2 Pecuniary Certification

Under simple certification the operative incentives are "praise and blame." Where flaws in the de facto institutional design within which decisionmakers operate do not cause the latter to internalize these intangible consequences, a reformer may add a pecuniary component to the reward. Recall that a pecuniary certification is like a simple certification except that all certified parties receive a pecuniary benefit directly from the project. Examples of pecuniary certification from Nigeria and Senegal have been selected to demonstrate how one might add pecuniary rewards to the certification incentive. In both cases a goal of the mechanism is to improve local services, though very different designs are used. These examples are also useful in illustrating the limitations of input-based versus output-based performance incentives.

3.2.1 Nigeria: Local Governance

This case study may be seen as a second-generation, significantly more sophisticated, and expensive follow-up to the Jharkhand PAF report card case presented earlier in this chapter. Despite this, in some respects the Nigerian initiative was less successful. Exploring why this is so will clarify the requisite incentive structures needed for using indicators to stimulate local government reform.

STATEMENT OF THE PROBLEM

Nigeria's modern history is fraught with military and civilian government administrations that have periodically shifted fiscal and political power toward and away from local governments (Terfa 2005a, 2005b). Nonetheless, in 1976 the country introduced a common system of local government "to empower local governments by defining their primary functions and guaranteeing them statutory transfers from the federation account and state revenues."[23] Studies conducted after the return to civilian democratic rule in May 1999 (World Bank 2002) "have shown that local governments . . . have not been able to perform satisfactorily because of inadequate finances, political and administrative constraints imposed by their state governments as well as their own failings such as poor leadership and lack of technical competence."

---

23. Quotes in this paragraph come from Terfa (2005a, chap. 1).

OBJECTIVE

This project begins with the objective of "ensuring that development planning is fundamentally anchored on the lowest tiers of governance" and the belief that successful poverty alleviation depends on community-driven development, which "treats poor people and their institutions as assets and partners, rather than simply as targets.[24] The goal of the Local Government Assessment and Capacity Building subproject of the Local Empowerment and Environmental Management Project (LEEMP) was "to identify those rural local governments in participating states whose level of commitment to effective service delivery and responsiveness to rural communities justify their inclusion in the LEEMP as beneficiaries." The "structural deficiencies and other inadequacies" (for example, nonassumption of their "appropriate responsibility for effective and efficient service delivery to the rural communities") found in the beneficiary local government administrations would be addressed "while staff at this level would be exposed to more participatory techniques in development planning."

The means to this end would involve the application of a scorecard assessment instrument to ascertain "the level of performance of the assessed local governments along key governance criteria, improvements on which will enhance their overall governance capability."[25] Focus areas included "enhanced transparency and accountability at LGAs [local government areas]; improved planning and budgeting processes; improved service delivery; improved responsiveness of LGAs to the needs of their local communities," as well as measures to "sensitize communities to demand services from their Local Governments." It was also hoped that the ensuing demonstration effects would have a positive influence on other LGAs in participating federal states.

SPONSOR AND IMPLEMENTERS

The LEEMP was funded by the International Development Association (IDA) and the Global Environment Facility. Some local contributions came from the national government and participating states, as well as from participating communities. The Canadian firm Terfa provided the international consultants to manage implementation. The mechanism design and very detailed project implementation plan was developed by Esmail and others (2004). Implementation also drew on the Federal Project Support Unit (FPSU) and the State Project Support Unit (SPSU) in each state.

COST AND TIME FRAME

According to Esmail and others (2004), the World Bank allocated $70 million in IDA resources for the nine states eligible to participate in the project. This

---

24. Quotes in this paragraph are from Terfa (2005a, p. 2).
25. All quotes in this paragraph come from Terfa (2005a, pp. 7 and 9).

project, including the development of the approach and detailed work plans, appears to have begun in 1999 and, including final analyses, ran at least until 2005.

PLAYERS

Following a set of criteria to ensure a varied but rural focus, the project selected LGAs from nine participating states out of the thirty-six in the country: Adamawa, Bauchi, Bayelsa, Benue, Enugu, Katsina, Imo, Niger, and Oyo.

RULES OF THE GAME

Between twenty and twenty-four rural LGAs were picked in each state (except for eight in small Bayelsa State) by the respective SPSU according to project guidelines, which were developed to avoid selection bias.[26] "The choice of communities for assessment interviews was completely unrelated to the subsequent selection of communities that would receive LEEMP funding. This point was emphasized to the SPSU and in project communications materials, to avoid undue attempts at influencing the choice of communities for the scorecard" (Terfa 2005b, appendix 3). This important mechanism design issue is discussed further in the assessment below. Then the FPSU and SPSUs sensitized communities and officials to the scorecard assessment initiative. Next a multidisciplinary team of local experts and stakeholders developed and administered a series of surveys and other forms of data collection, which were then analyzed by international consultants to produce scorecard assessments comprising four indicators: LGA responsiveness to communities, administrative operation, overall financial integrity, and budget and financial appraisal.[27] Appendix B2 provides a summary of the indicators and the aggregation scheme.

LGAs were then classified as "acceptable—most promising" (these are the winning LGAs), "marginal" (these LGAs may receive technical assistance to prepare themselves for a future round but no LEEMP funds for a project), and "unacceptable" (these LGAs were dropped from LEEMP consideration until future scorecard assessments). As long as an LGA passed its most recent scorecard assessment, some of its communities would receive LEEMP funds. There also was supposed to be a midproject reassessment administered, but available documentation made no mention of those results or even if it had actually been done. Finally, the project manual did not indicate what exact, aggregate, indicator score or ranking would place an LGA in one of these categories.

REWARDS

In those LGAs that pass the scorecard assessment, some unspecified number of communities directly receive (that is, without passing through their LGA's

26. Nigeria's thirty-six states have a total of 774 LGAs. In each participating LGA of the nine states selected, three communities were interviewed.

27. A detailed discussion of how these indicators were developed is found in Knack, Kugler, and Manning (2001).

account) LEEMP funds for community-driven development (CDD) projects. Available documentation did not specify the size of the CDD projects nor how many a winning LGA would or could receive. Based on the total budget for the project, one may suppose that each of the six winning states received at least $15 million in rewards, ignoring the value of technical assistance received before and during the contest. With approximately twenty-one LGAs per state and assuming three winners per state, this may have implied to participating LGAs an ex-ante expected return of $2.14 million ([3 winners/21 players] × $15 million).

LGAs that did not pass but scored a "marginal" (see above) were eligible for technical assistance funds to help them pass a future scorecard assessment.

STATED OUTCOMES

The scorecard approach demonstrated that the series of 1976 local government reforms, the 1999 return to civilian rule, and the proliferation of local governments did not have significant positive effects on citizens' participation in governance.[28] Only six of the nine states had between one and four local governments (out of an average number of twenty-one) that scored 50 percent on this index. In three states there was no record of a local government scoring at least 50 percent. In these states community outreach staff were often found to perform below average while consultation on budget issues scarcely occurred at all. Their local governments rarely responded to requests for assistance from their communities. Moreover, in many cases officers would be absent from their offices in the rural local governments, visiting these rural communities only when it was pay day. In short, the assessed LGAs exhibited limited capacity for interaction with their communities. On the other hand, the LGAs generally demonstrated that they had the required administrative machinery to carry out statutory functions. The problem seems to be that they are not oriented toward accountability to their communities and citizens and toward financial integrity. The local governments performed very poorly in budget and financial appraisal. In fact, local governments in some states were not able to provide the accounting books needed to perform this part of the assessment.

Nonetheless, it seems that as a result of scorecard assessments, local communities have begun to demand services from local governments more seriously.

At the local government council itself, the process has raised questions of accountability and created an environment of competition for projects. . . . For the first time the local governments' opportunity to get grants for development projects is based on previously exhibited transparency and accountability. The impact on the attitude of local government officials

---

28. This paragraph draws on Terfa (2005a, chaps. 1 and 4).

however varied from place to place. There are also those who did not think the project sum was attractive enough for them and so were less interested in the process" (Terfa 2005a, chap. 4.2).

PIJC COMPONENTS

It is somewhat ambiguous as to whether this activity was a tournament or a certification exercise as defined in section 2.3. The collection of data to identify jurisdictional performance is an example of certification. However, if jurisdictions believed that future benchmarks would be taken *and* that category thresholds would be based on the range of observed jurisdictional performance, then the conditions for a tournament de facto existed. Given the lack of subsequent benchmarking and the general skepticism entrenched in the country, this application has been classified as a pecuniary certification in tables 2-1 and 2-5.

Regardless, the CDD approach followed by the project to develop meaningful indicator variables and methods of collection involves the same careful participatory orientation and use of strategic communications as advocated by PIJC methodology. Similarly, as recommended by PIJC methodology, "player" participation in the scorecard assessment was voluntary, with LGAs having "the option of explicitly opting out of the assessment, and forfeiting the opportunity to participate in LEEMP" (Terfa 2005b, appendix 3). Finally, since the scorecards are essentially sets of baseline indicators, the project also included this component of PIJC methodology.

ASSESSMENT

At a basic level, the project appears to be highly successful, both in getting rigorous and meaningful data on rural communities in Nigeria as well as in breaking new ground on indicator specificity, design, and data collection. The former achievement is particularly impressive given local conditions in Nigeria.[29] The scorecards will serve as a rich source of guidance for public policy and local reform in the years to come.

This assessment, therefore, asks two questions: what insights on mechanism design does the PIJC methodology provide for assessing the scorecard initiative, and what insights on mechanism design does the scorecard initiative provide for future PIJC activities? Before these questions are addressed, it must be noted that despite the availability of two very well written, voluminous, and detailed documents, many fundamental aspects of the scorecard assessment's mechanism design remain nebulous. It is not clear whether this is because those aspects were ad hoc

29. The challenges of working in the country include getting data from state and local officials (even on a World Bank project), distances and physical accessibility of local communities, and security threats from local governments, intended to stymie the participation of both project staff and officials. See Terfa (2005a, chap. 4).

or discretionary, or whether they were inadvertently omitted from the project write-ups. Regardless, this limitation constitutes a basic caveat with regard to the following critiques.

While the scorecard assessment indeed fulfilled its goal of generating quality data on local governance, it is less clear how successful it has been in stimulating coordinated change by interested parties within each participating LGA (not to mention nonparticipating LGAs), though this appears to have been a subproject objective (see above). This is a key point that bears repeating: there appears to have been a lack of attention to the incentive environment necessary to create a *demand* at the appropriate levels of government to want the scorecard results and to act on them. Rather, the main impetus to react to the scorecard incentives was with the public, that is, the electorate. Since the effectiveness of the citizens' channels for actionable responses in Nigeria was notoriously weak, the degree that the scorecard provoked concrete changes is questionable.

Several mechanism design features of the project probably contributed to this lack of government demand. First, LGA expectations of future rounds would have been critical to stimulate postbaseline reforms. There does not appear to have been a follow-up assessment, however. Reading between the lines of project documentation, my sense is that political and bureaucratic constraints impeded progress on this ambitious project and caused its implementation to be much slower than originally hoped and may have led later assessments to be canceled. Regardless, it is unlikely that potential participants would have had the incentive to engage in between-assessment reforms in the hope of receiving future LEEMP funds. Even if some LGAs believed that there would be follow-up rounds, the scoring method, which appears to be based on a certification model (see section 2.3), would not necessarily have motivated further reforms for those LGAs that already exceeded the threshold for "acceptable" performance (see above). Note, though, that the lack of follow-up scorecard assessments means that there was no benchmarking to encourage postaward improvements. Using the terms of table 2-1, the rewards, while pecuniary, were based on inputs, not outputs.

Similarly, there was no explicit description in the project manuals regarding the amount of LEEMP funds (the actual reward) a winning LGA would receive, the exact procedure for how awarded funds would be allocated, how many communities would receive the award, or what exactly a community would have to do to get funding. Hence it is questionable whether the incentives were bright (high powered) enough to stimulate local-level cooperation to push for follow-up reforms.

At perhaps a lower level of importance, there are other incentive-compatibility concerns this project presents. First, there does not seem to have been enough attention given to motivating the LGA-level government itself. For example, what benefits did the LGA officials get besides prestige if LEEMP funds went to some of their individual rural communities? (Recall that, to avoid corruption, funds were to be disbursed directly to the local communities.) Second, once an LGA had won funding acceptance, the project sought to encourage postassessment "modest behavioral changes by mandating specific steps (related to scorecard criteria) that local governments must undertake, once accepted, in order to remain active participants" in the LEEMP (Esmail and others 2004, p. 8). This unannounced "trick" appears to be a bait-and-switch strategy and would not likely be appreciated by participants. It also would probably reduce trust in the donor as well as the operative effect of future incentives. Third, there seem to have been "limitations on LEEMP capacity to accept LGAs and thus communities—estimated at up to three LGAs per state in LEEMP's first year," though it was likely that "more [would join] in subsequent years subject to capacity." Project materials stressed that this fact "must be clearly conveyed to all parties" (Terfa 2005b, appendix 3). Again, this sort of tentativeness would likely dilute the power of incentives for LGAs to carry out desired reforms.

If, on the other hand, the scorecard assessment was *not* intended to be a competition, much less a tournament—in spite of being based on quantitative and highly developed indicators—then it would seem that project formulators missed a powerful opportunity to generate indigenously motivated change. It had all the ingredients: a scoring method, a prize, a large number of potentially interested players, and a donor agency with the wherewithal to pull off the logistically ambitious scheme.

Finally, in its desire to minimize selection bias and gaming during data collection, the project's design prevented communities who took part in data collection from receiving LEEMP funds. While this may appear sensible from a statistical standpoint, it is questionable how much sense it makes for efficient—and fair—allocation of funds. How does one know how deserving a community is if it was not measured? And why might one use an allocation mechanism that inadvertently runs the risk of freezing out high performers in the interest of poor performers? What kind of incentives does this create among communities considering responding to the project's reform incentives (such as they were)?

IMPACT OF INITIAL CONDITIONS

"After years of military dictatorship and severe politicization, Nigeria's administration—including local governments—has an entrenched culture of rent-seeking and self-interest, with little incentive to focus on serving the public. As a result, local governments are generally distrusted and held in low esteem by the public, due to past experience with service failures and mismanagement"(Terfa 2005a). Moreover, project designers had to face a lack of reliable official data due to a chronic failure of LGAs to submit records, especially audit reports, and to strategic reporting biases, since interested parties were able to influence reporting responses (Esmail and others 2004, p. 13). The scorecard instrument development and data collection sought to address these conditions and were, therefore, highly particular to the jurisdictional and legal institutions of LGAs in Nigeria; all the planning and logistical documentation for implementation would require major revision for use in a different country. Likewise, the reforms an LGA at any level can undertake, administrative or regulatory, are constrained by law and statutes set at higher-level jurisdictions. Finally, to reiterate, this certification application, as designed, would require stronger channels for the public to pressure their local officials to take the LEEMP opportunity seriously.

SUSTAINABILITY AND SCALABILITY

There are two aspects to consider with regard to sustainability: process and product. First, would the project (process) continue without further donor support? This seems unlikely unless donors made its continuation a condition for other funding. Of course, had the activity generated substantial reform, the Nigerian government itself could have easily continued to fund it and even extend its coverage to other states—much like the Russian government did after their World Bank loan.[30] On the other hand, the Niger State promised that after the World Bank LEEMP, it would go ahead to have its own local LEEMP.[31]

Second, would the reforms (product) undertaken as a result of the project remain in place after the LEEMP project ended? Likewise, will the scorecard information lead or has it led to long-term improvements in local governance? As suggested above, the project did not seem to stimulate much demand from local governments, though in about half the cases, the capacity for reform was present. Furthermore, while the concept of greater transparency and even competition for projects generated a very favorable response from the public at the community level, weak institutional channels inhibited citizens from pressuring their LGAs to make improvements. Recall that the assessment indicated that both of these conditions would be necessary for this particular design to be effective. Finally, without a follow-up scorecard assessment, it is hard to give a rigorous answer as to the longevity of the few improvements the initiative generated. Since funding was not based on postscorecard performance, the project incentives by themselves could not have provided the necessary inducements. Given the highly variable reception by local government officials to the approach, this author is not too sanguine about the sustainability of this initiative as designed.

On the other hand, I believe it would have been feasible to make this initiative sustainable, to wit,

—follow-up assessments could have been funded through higher government earmarks to the LGAs (though this would probably have required some technical assistance to regularize),

---

30. See section 4.2.

31. Statement made by the deputy governor, Alhaji Ahmed Musa Ibeto, as reported by allafrica.com on January 23, 2008.

—the nature of the "game" could have been clarified in a manual and all the actions and rewards to each party made explicit, and

—only those communities allowing themselves to be benchmarked should have been eligible to receive project funding.

This third condition would have led only those serious about engaging in reform to signal their interest in receiving funds, thereby strengthening product sustainability. If the follow-up benchmark revealed that project funds led to better (and presumably more cost-effective) outcomes, this would have encouraged the central government to continue future funding, thereby satisfying process sustainability. Again, there is every reason to presume that these conditions were feasible in the Nigerian context.

Turning to scalability within Nigeria, since all the design work (the main fixed costs) has already been done, the main sources of variable costs in expanding the project are from additional surveying and data collection in general, technical experts to evaluate project proposals, and funds to pay for proposals selected. Regarding the last item, in theory these should already be part of local government current or capital budget allocations.[32] Of course, local governments may loathe losing their discretionary authority on how and where to allocate the funds.

As for the project's suitability to other countries, I would argue that unless stronger channels are present for the public to exercise its voice, then the design's weak incentives for the government to reform itself would lead one to hesitate on proposing its application. However, if the design were modified as proposed above, then the reported enthusiasm of the Nigerian communities for the project concept would lead one to recommend that at least a pilot application be considered in other country contexts.

3.2.2 Senegal: Literacy Initiative

Public-private partnerships (PPP) take shape in a variety of forms, though at the "heart of every successful project is the concept that better value for money be achieved through the exploitation of the private sector competencies and the allocation of risk to the party best able to manage it."[33] The literacy education program in Senegal used this insight about PPP to increase its efficiency and effectiveness. Nonetheless, this example illustrates the need for rewards better tied to ex-post performance as well as how corruption can undermine project success.

STATEMENT OF THE PROBLEM

In 1997 the government of Senegal identified literacy as a national priority. The government's action plan called for the substantial reduction of illiteracy, "especially among the female population, notably the 15–39 age bracket, in order

---

32. See the discussion of performance-based grant transfers in section 1.3.
33. Nordtveit (2004a, p. 7), citing EdInvest (n.d.).

to ensure an immediate impact on the social, economic, and education indicators" (Nordtveit 2004a, p. 71).[34] In addition, the government aimed "to reduce the imbalances between regions and between urban and rural areas" (p. 71). In order to achieve its goals, the government of Senegal introduced the *Projet d'Alphabétisation Priorité Femme* (PAPF), which outsourced the most important activities of the program to private entities, utilizing a competitive bidding process described below.

OBJECTIVE

In addition to increasing literacy among the female population, the project also intended to "widen participation opportunities through strengthening civil society organizations partnership in developing sustainable literacy, numeracy, life skills and income-generating programs" (Nordtveit 2004a, p. 71). Some of the more specific goals of the program were to
—establish and test the outsourcing approach;
—enable providers, through outsourcing, to enroll 12,000 people in literacy courses;
—enable providers, through outsourcing, to enroll 8,400 people in postliteracy activities, including income-generating activities and facilitation of access to microcredit programs; and
—ensure sustainability through the development and production of literacy and postliteracy learning material in collaboration with all stakeholders.

SPONSOR AND IMPLEMENTERS

The donors who cofinanced the implementation of the public-private partnership policy strategy were the Canadian Development Agency (CIDA), the IDA, and the German Technical Cooperation. The IDA financed the PAPF project itself. Implementers were all Senegalese and included
—*Direction de l'Alphabétisation et de l'Education de Base* (DAEB), in charge of monitoring and evaluation;
—*Agence d'Exécution des Travaux d'Intérêt Public* (AGETIP), a contract-managing agency responsible for financial issues (that is, payments to providers, contract compliance); and
—civil society and community-based organizations (CBOs), responsible for subprojects covering ten to twenty courses.

COST AND TIME FRAME

In 1999 U.S. dollars, the base unit cost for this program was $50 a person for a 450-hour literacy course, with an average investment cost in human capacity

34. A slightly more up-to-date reference for a description of this Senegal initiative may now be found in Nordtveit (2008)

building and material of $12 and a beneficiary cost of $26, which includes opportunity cost plus direct costs (Nordtveit 2004b, p. 3). In 2003 dollar terms, the average price (user fee) charged to the participant over the duration of the project was $4.63 (Nordtveit 2005, p. 270).[35] The project ran from 1995 to 2001.

In addition to the implementers described above, the main stakeholders of this program were the beneficiaries. The beneficiaries were "mainly groups of illiterate and poor women living in rural areas" (Nordtveit 2004a, p. 18) who played an active role in the program. Together with private providers, the beneficiaries designed the basic skills component of the course, "decided on a course schedule, the language of instruction to be used in the course, and sometimes they helped the provider choose a course instructor" (Nordtveit 2004a, p. 18). In addition, the beneficiaries created local management committees to oversee the implementation of the project in their village (Nordtveit 2004a, p. 18).

Furthermore, the private providers responsible for the implementation of subprojects were also some of the main players in this program. They were mainly from civil society and CBOs, including grassroots organizations such as local women's groups, village associations, religious groups, and NGOs (Nordtveit 2004a, p. 19). The *Coordination Nationale des Opérateurs en Alphabétisation du Sénégal* (CNOAS), a providers' association, was created to "represent the providers' interests and to provide training to new providers in various areas including financial and human resources management" (Nordtveit 2004a, p. 20). The CNOAS was also instrumental in the dissemination of the program.

RULES OF THE GAME

In the PAPF the rules of the tournament were governed by a procedures manual developed by representatives from the different stakeholders described above. The procedures manual "explained the bidding and selection process, and the requirements of the successful bidder" (Nordtveit 2004b, p. 2). The manual required each provider, in cooperation with the beneficiaries, to prepare a literacy subproject proposal. The procedures manual "defined a standard unit price that the successful bidder received for each beneficiary enrolled in literacy classes. Hence, the bidding was not a competition for the lowest cost, but instead, for the highest quality [proposal]" (p. 2).

The subproject included ten to twenty courses in a corresponding number of villages. The courses were required to include literacy and numeracy components;

---

35. In fact, there were two types of training programs, one for basic literacy and, starting in 1999, one in which literacy and postliteracy activities were integrated into a single program. The "public" per trainee costs (in 2003 dollars) based on official enrollment were $72 and $89 for literacy and integrated programs, respectively (Nordtveit 2005, p. 268).

basic functional skills components were optional (Nordtveit 2004a, p. 18). The proposals were first submitted for accuracy checks by local-level government staff. The proposals were then sent to a "selection committee that analyzed all the proposals and decided which ones should be financed" (Nordtveit 2004b, p. 2). The following criteria were used to evaluate and rate the proposals:

—capacity of the provider (50 points);

—knowledge of the implementation sites (40 points);

—the subproject program (50 points);

—the management system, including a subproject implementation plan, an administrative and technical monitoring system, and an evaluation plan (40 points); and

—institutional issues (10 points).

To be considered for financing, the "subproject [bidder's] proposal must score at least 60% of the maximum points, i.e., it must score at least 114 out of 190 points" (Nordtveit 2004a, p. 24). The winners were then sent to the contract management agency (AGETIP), which "established contracts, paid the providers, and managed and verified the contracts" (Nordtveit 2004b, p. 2). It is especially interesting to note that there was a user fee charged ($4.63) to the individuals who participated in a course.

REWARDS

In addition to being awarded the contract for a subproject, successful bidders also enjoyed other rewards. One of the principal aims of the PAPF was to "stimulate the creation of new providers" of literacy programs (Nordtveit 2004a, p. 18). To accomplish this goal, the procedures manual included incentives for new providers to apply for funds. For example, the contract awarded to the winners included financing for "institutional support for the provider organization and human resource building" (Nordtveit 2004a, p. 19).

STATED OUTCOMES

The subprojects apparently achieved excellent results. In a five-year period, about 200,000 participants enrolled in literacy classes (Nordtveit 2004b). The dropout rate "averaged 15% (much lower than for most adult literacy programs)" (Nordtveit 2004b, p. 2).[36] Furthermore, the number of subproject proposals submitted consistently increased over a period of five years: "In 1995, with the pilot phase of the project, only 77 proposals were submitted, of which 22 were selected. . . . In 2001, a total of 368 proposals were submitted, and 95 were selected" (Nordtveit 2004b, p. 1).

36. Nordtveit (2005, p. 263) independently estimates a more realistic dropout rate of 34 percent on average.

As an interesting consequence of the way delivery services were contracted in Senegal, "the outsourcing approach led to the creation of a plethora of grass-roots associations eager to be involved in literacy activities. Also, the projects revived many language associations *(Association de Langues),* local organizations that had as their mission to preserve local languages and the local culture" (Nordtveit 2004a, p. 46). Since growth in civil society is generally considered a poverty reduction strategy (World Bank 2001a), this proliferation of civil society organizations may itself be considered an output in support of the program's objectives.

PIJC COMPONENTS

While the project was, at its core, a certification, it included many interesting innovations. The program applied principles of participatory development by requiring the provider and the beneficiary village to collaborate in identifying the training opportunities, thereby giving each a stake in putting together a good proposal. The program also was prospective in that all rules were preannounced and stipulated in a providers manual. The project design used public-private partnerships with the objective of efficiently allocating financing, service provision, and risk to the parties best able to assume them. Finally, the project design incorporated a clever circle of accountability, both among the official agencies and between government and nongovernment organizations, so that each was monitored by an outside entity.

Once awarded, though, the incentives for a successful implementation were less aligned, with the beneficiary wanting greater effort and the provider wanting to exert less. Nonetheless, in a subtle way, the project also made use of competition, since beneficiaries could, in principle, choose which provider to team with, potentially leading to a market in providers. The project also was able, in principle, to use clear metrics to assess the effectiveness (cost per trainee) of each provider's implementation, offering the opportunity to compare performance and learn from doing. The program design, however, was not really a tournament since any proposal that exceeded a preset absolute rating score was funded.[37]

37. In theory, the rating criteria could have been interpreted relatively to create a tournament. For example, the criteria, such as "quality of the subprogram" or "knowledge of the site," could have scored each application against the average value of those already received. Nordtveit (personal communication, May 5, 2008) argues that since funding was often insufficient to cover all "eligible" projects, only the best proposals were funded. This, however, was never mentioned in the rule manual nor in any other project documents, so it is not clear to which extent this happened. It is certainly unlikely that the players were aware of this unofficial policy. However, if Nordtveit is correct, then in the language of section 2.3, the overall project design functioned as an ex-post input-based tournament.

ASSESSMENT

Although this was a complex program, its institutional design was well thought out.[38] Moreover, the PAPF program appears to have been a success. The results of the PAPF program exceeded targeted levels: most of the participants of the program "achieved learning mastery levels for reading (although not for math)" (Nordtveit 2004b, p. 2). In addition, the beneficiaries had, in many cases, "direct economic benefits inasmuch as he or she learned some income-generating activities, how to keep track of income, establish a bank account, and become eligible for micro-credit programs" (Nordtveit 2004b, p. 3).

Unfortunately, several implementation flaws reduced program effectiveness. Application of the award criteria was not uniform, leading to funding of substandard proposals. Monitoring of awarded contracts was poor, and many firms received full compensation without satisfactorily completing their training obligations. There were also several imperfections in the market for providers. For example, in many cases, provider firms spontaneously emerged from the candidate village solely to take advantage of the employment opportunity, making competitor firms from outside the village less able to compete. Lack of sophistication among village decisionmakers meant that they were not able to properly assess the quality of soliciting provider firms.

There were also a few design flaws. For example, no effort was made to track past (relative or absolute) performance of provider firms in considering follow-up rewards. Hence "known bad providers [were] re-selected because they had written a good proposal (or hired someone to write [one]). . . . Sometimes the providers and/or their consultants did not even visit the community for which they proposed a literacy course."[39] While such problems could have been avoided with greater sponsor monitoring, such weaknesses are intrinsic to an input-based performance design (see section 2.3). In addition, firms with winning proposals also received institutional support, leading to firms crank out as many proposals as possible to increase the frequency of winning and receiving free capacity building.

At this point it is worth considering some of the issues that public-private partnerships—also known as outsourcing—raise for a PIJC since this feature was central to the Senegal application. Nordtveit notes that, outsourcing

> can facilitate subproject implementation that meets the demand in individual locations; in fact each intervention can be tailored to local requirements. Such program flexibility can generally make outsourcing a

---

38. The reader is again reminded that the source of the observations upon which this assessment is based is a consultant (Bjorn Nordtveit) to the World Bank, so one may rightly question his objectivity. However, there are reasons to believe that his views are unbiased. First, he did not design or implement the program. Second, his Ph.D. dissertation was a critique of the Senegal project—and some of his observations are rather negative.

39. Nordtveit, personal communication with author, May 5, 2008.

useful tool in new circumstances, for example, in post-conflict zones, or in areas with a high incidence of HIV/AIDS. Some proponents of outsourcing suggest that outsourcing avoids government obstacles with regards to setting up and financing subprojects, and may also argue that by bypassing the government, the approach also avoids the risk of public sector corruption (2004a, p. 45).

However, on the same page of his report, Nordtveit makes a different argument. First he points out that "the partnership approach . . . requires direction and strong involvement by the government . . . to ensure that a proper selection procedure is followed, and that the monitoring, evaluation, and feedback systems enhance subproject effectiveness." Hence he argues that this means that along with the obvious government policing function, there is also a capacity-building role for government that is important in performing these evaluations.

Unfortunately, my assessment above for this application remains the same. Ironically, it concurs with one of the lessons reported from the Senegal case, that "problems linked to financial management and transparency in public offices need to be addressed before setting up an outsourced program; for outsourcing is not a quick fix for mismanagement of public funds" (Nordtveit 2004a, p. 46).

IMPACT OF INITIAL CONDITIONS

This project took advantage of a particular set of institutions that may not be available in other countries. First, the AGETIP already existed as an independent agency that could write and manage contracts with the private sector. Second, the DAEB already existed as an agency that could monitor publicly issued contracts. Third, Senegal has a large and geographically dispersed group of CBOs, which were then available in principle to take advantage of the opportunity to develop training courses with their associated local communities. Likewise, Watkins (2004, p. 2) indicates that the existence of strong official support and cohesive rural communities allowed project design to take advantage of "community ownership and capacity" and to "seek official support to build trust with the local communities."

On the other hand, the country also had a tradition of corruption in the education (and other public) sectors, and the institutional design of the project was not sufficiently robust and resistant to overcome this influence.

SUSTAINABILITY AND SCALABILITY

Project sustainability can be evaluated in two ways. First, were the results long lasting? According to Nordtveit (2004b), the answer is yes, in that those who participated in the trainings were rather motivated, paid a user fee, and had follow-up opportunities to use their new knowledge. Second, is the design of the project itself sustainable? As long as the aforementioned corruption problem can be kept within "acceptable" levels, there is a good chance that the project could become sustainable in the long run. One of the factors contributing to this is that the project cleverly charged a user fee, which could be adjusted to cover the variable costs of the service delivery. This would allow the government to continue to fund the project indefinitely.[40]

Unfortunately, it seems that some experts close to the implementation concluded that "programs had weak sustainability [because] . . . when external financing ceased, most village activities ceased" (Nordtveit 2004a, p. 38). In any case, once illiteracy would be eradicated, the program would have to adjust the types of training provided.[41] One should also note that other skills in addition to literacy, such as those needed for handicrafts and business, were provided by the trainers, so future postliteracy training activities have the potential to focus successfully on those topics.

According to Nordtveit, "because of its success in providing rapidly expanding literacy services to a large population, the project became a model for literacy programs in many neighboring countries. . . . Likewise, other government sectors in Senegal [use the model] . . . for implementation of social services. Several new literacy projects in Senegal . . . continue to finance literacy courses by using outsourcing" (2004a, p. 7). For example, a similar approach has long been in use in Senegal for particular health services.[42] While this sounds like the concept has become sustainable, it does not seem that the PAPF project itself was specifically continued by the government. However, at least these latter literacy projects mentioned by Nordtveit continue to be financed by IDA and CIDA and not by the Senegalese government, though the latter has adopted an ambitious "Education for All" commitment by 2015.[43]

The project focused only on rural areas in the country in order to equalize literacy levels across urban and rural populations. Thus the question of scalability is best examined from the point of view of how to extend the project to other sectors, for example health, and whether the project would be portable to other countries, which has already been addressed in the discussion on initial conditions. As the examples in the previous paragraph suggest, there do not appear to be any inherent obstacles to applying the project's design to other sectors as long as the

40. Due to the positive externalities of education, individuals would not be willing to pay the full benefits of their education. This means that there would still be a role for public investment in education, even with efficiently priced user fees.

41. Presumably the idea is that the program's initial beneficiaries belonged to a pool of adults who missed out on primary education, but that group would diminish since the current generation of children is enrolled in public primary school programs.

42. Nordtveit, personal communication, May 5, 2008. He also suggests that in the health sector, this has led to an additional policy issue, namely, how to integrate all these individual health services to attain greater effectiveness.

43. Though it did not continue as a self-standing project, the PAPF project office, staff, and methods continued under a different funding code. Nordtveit, personal communication, May 5, 2008.

village communities show a willingness to pay for the training services offered and as long as a sufficient supply of training skills could be found. (Perhaps a "train the trainers" component could be successfully added to the project.)

The observations made here suggest that a small number of modifications to the project design could increase its sustainability.[44] First, link provider payouts to certifiable training outcomes (performance-based contracting). Second, prohibit those associated with providers who did not complete contract deliverables from being paid under future contracts within the project.[45] And last, disseminate information about the performance of contracted firms associated with their principals to help villages select the best service providers as well as know what quantity and quality performance levels to demand in the proposals developed with the providers.

44. I am happy to report that since this section was written, Nordtveit has informed me that recent reforms have led to "better control of provider selection by preidentified communities (to avoid provider monopolies), and the supervision of new providers by well-established, reputable providers with a long experience and outstanding performances in the sector." Personal communication, May 5, 2008.

45. It would not be enough to ban underperforming firms since the principals could—and did—easily reconstitute firms under other names to continue receiving project contracts.

4

Review of Tournament Experience

A s explained in chapter 2, the novelty of using a tournament for government
transfers, reforms, or as an aid delivery vehicle means that examples of such
PIJC applications are few. Therefore, a two-tiered strategy has been employed here
to enable full use of this past experience to assess PIJC. The present chapter continues with the first tier by evaluating a series of real-world tournament applications: first pure tournaments and then mixed tournaments.

4.1 Pure Tournaments

In pure tournaments winning or placing depends on one's rank, and there is no
threshold performance requirement. Our research found three examples of this,
in the Philippines, Honduras, and Indonesia.

4.1.1 The Philippines: Galing Pook Awards Program

STATEMENT OF THE PROBLEM

The Philippines consists of more than 7,100 islands, more than 100 linguistic
and ethnic groups, and a system of local government divided into a network of
provinces, cities, municipalities, and tens of thousands of tiny, close-knit units
called *barangays,* comprising 1,000 to 10,000 people. However, the development
of these local government units (LGUs) has been hindered by a long history of
centralized governance. After the regime of President Ferdinand Marcos was
deposed, the Philippines embarked on an intensive decentralization effort, which

produced the 1991 Local Governance Code.[1] The Local Governance Code gave LGUs increased power and responsibilities in an effort to encourage the development of sustainable responses to social problems.[2] Nevertheless, because many local governments in the Philippines lacked the "infrastructure and staff to handle new tasks, devolution was more of a burden than a boon."[3]

OBJECTIVE

The Galing Pook Awards program was established in 1993 in response to the Local Governance Code. The awards are meant to recognize the efforts of LGUs that have found innovative solutions to community problems. By recognizing these efforts, the Galing Pook Awards promote "innovation, sustainability, citizen empowerment, and excellence in local governance" (Galing Pook Foundation 2005).[4]

SPONSOR AND IMPLEMENTERS

In response to the new challenges faced by LGUs in the Philippines, the Department of Interior and Local Government, in partnership with the Ford Foundation, established the Galing Pook Awards—short for *Gantimpalang Panglingkod Pook,* which means "a praiseworthy local place" (Galing Pook Foundation 2005). In addition, the Galing Pook Foundation, which was established in 1998 to oversee the program, "assists in building the capacities of local government units by disseminating, popularizing and replicating" best practices of awardees (Galing Pook Foundation 2005).

PLAYERS

All provinces, cities, municipalities, and barangays across the Philippines are eligible to participate.

COST AND TIME FRAME

The Ford Foundation gave Galing Pook an endowment of $1 million in 1993 and provided it with a grant of almost $1 million annually for eleven years in support of its operations.[5] These subsidies ended recently when the Ford Foundation closed its office and ended all its programs in the Philippines. Galing Pook limits

1. See Esperanza Cabral, "Celebrating Excellence around the World," 1996 (www.fordfound. org/publications/ff_report/view_ff_report_detail.cfm?report_index=35 [July 8, 2006]).
2. See Michael Lipsky, "Globally, Good Government Goes Local," 1999 (www.fordfound.org/ publications/ff_report/view_ff_report_detail.cfm?report_index=132 [July 8, 2006]).
3. Cabral, "Celebrating Excellence around the World."
4. See also the Galing Pook website for a pdf of the 2005 report (www.galingpook.org/ download.htm).
5. The information in this section comes from Milwida Guevara, former Galing Pook director, personal communication, March 29, 2007.

its expenditures to the interest income from the original endowment and has an annual cap on its expenses of about $96,000. It still has other sources of income, including contributions from multinational and other organizations. The Department of Interior and Local Government funds the cash prize, and Galing Pook's board and the peer reviewers serve as volunteers. Since the projects submitted for consideration have already been undertaken, tournament participation costs for the players are minimal, basically involving preparation of application materials and background documentation.

RULES OF THE GAME

The Galing Pook Awards create a tournament among LGUs in which the reward incentives are recognition and publicity. The winners of the tournament are determined through a multilevel screening process (see box 4-1). The process

---

Box 4-1. *Screening Process for the Galing Pook Awards*

Eligibility Screening
Galing Pook Foundation (GPF) secretariat reviews whether the program submissions meet the eligibility criteria.

First-Level Screening
Regional Selection Committee (RSC) evaluates the program submissions and recommends programs for elevation to the next screening level.

Second-Level Screening
National Selection Committee (NSC) reviews the RSC recommendations and identifies the programs for site validation.

Site Validation
Assigned NSC members, selected RSC members, and GPF personnel validate program claims and clarify concerns raised in previous screening levels. Results of the validations serve as basis for the NSC to select the programs to be subjected to the final validation.

Panel Interview:
Local chief executives or program officers of qualified entries present and defend their programs before the NSC members and their cofinalists. Outcomes of these presentations guide the NSC in its selection of the Top 10 Outstanding Programs and the remaining Trailblazing Programs.

Source: Galing Pook Foundation (2005).

Table 4-1. *Award Criteria and Weight*
Percent

Criteria	Weight
Positive cultural, economic, environmental, gender equity, political, and social impact	35
Promotion of people's empowerment	35
Transferability and sustainability	20
Efficiency of program service delivery	10
Creative and willful use of powers provided by the Local Government Code and other national legislation on decentralization and local autonomy	Bonus

Source: Galing Pook Foundation (2005).

uses criteria based on "positive socio-economic and environmental impact, promotion of people's empowerment, transferability and sustainability, efficiency of program service delivery, and creative use of powers provided by the Local Government Code and other decentralization and local autonomy policies" (Galing Pook Foundation 2005). These criteria are shown in table 4-1.

REWARDS

The Outstanding Local Governance Program Award is given to each of the top ten programs. The next ten finalists are recognized through the Trailblazing Program Award. In addition, the Award for Continuing Excellence is given to past Outstanding Local Governance Program awardees that have sustained the program and have "improved on key impact areas of the Galing Pook selection criteria to the extent that [they have] developed a culture of excellence in their respective localities" (Galing Pook Foundation 2005). The awards are viewed as honorific since the financial component is just $250.

The Galing Pook Awards have become highly prestigious—the number of applications received more than doubled after the first year.[6] As a result, winning jurisdictional units receive a large amount of publicity as well as travel and training opportunities for their officials. This in turns seems to redirect investment toward the jurisdictional units.

STATED OUTCOMES

From 1994 through 2004, 2,339 local governance programs across the Philippines have competed.[7] Of these, 175 programs have been chosen, of which

---

6. Lipsky, "Globally, Good Government Goes Local."

7. Perhaps it is telling that the foundation's website does not use the word "competed" but rather "participated in the search for excellence." The significance of this and other public relations issues is explored in chapter 6.

90 were recognized in the "Top Ten Outstanding" category, and 85 were finalists and named as "Trailblazing" programs.

PIJC COMPONENTS

Since only ten jurisdictions a year are judged most outstanding, the awards occur within a tournament framework. However, due to the diversity of the local government programs being evaluated, there is no direct, quantitative comparability across players, adding a certain discretionary element to assessments. On the other hand, the lack of restrictions on eligible innovations does mean that program participation and implementation of innovations are voluntary and that the nature of the innovations is demand driven, with self-selection of tasks.

The program also uses public relations and strategic communication in a big way. First, the high number of applicants suggests broad dissemination of the program. Second, since the nonpecuniary rewards have meaning only to the extent that others are made aware of the winner's accomplishments, the program's design structure implicitly encourages winners to use mass media to advertise the program's existence and winners' innovations. Third, the Galing Pook Foundation has a website that explicitly disseminates "best practices" and encourages interaction of interested local governments. Finally, since more than one-third of the selection points goes to "people empowerment," it is fair to say that the program encourages local participation.

ASSESSMENT

According to Edel Guiza, a professor at the Asian Institute of Management and former director of the Galing Pook program, the success of the program can be attributed in part to local demand for good governance, which resulted from the 1986 "EDSA revolution" (the peaceful uprising that led to the overthrow of President Marcos).[8]

Since tournament tasks are not directly comparable, Galing Pook uses committees to evaluate the merit of each applicant's innovation (see box 4-1). On the plus side, such a tournament requires no baseline. On the minus side, while this opportunity for discretion does not seem to have adversely affected the incentives for participation, such inherent potential for abuse in a country well known for corruption could become problematic, especially if the initiative were to be scaled up or implemented in other countries. Why the process in the Philippines has not succumbed to corruption surely warrants further study; it may be that the corruption incentives are low given the award's lack of direct financial remuneration or the difficulty of privately capturing award rents.

---

8. Cabral, "Celebrating Excellence around the World."

Finally, lack of a rigorous framework or efforts to incorporate evaluation into the program's design means that it is hard to tell whether the lure of a Galing Pook Award has any dynamic incentive effect to stimulate *future* LGU innovations or whether it is in essence a windfall to a previously successful initiative. Yet in terms of the typology shown in table 2-2, this is an output-based mechanism, even though winning depends on actions taken *before* the start of the PIJC. This may seem counterintuitive, but in this application, awards are for the quality of the outcomes or results of the municipality's efforts (inputs), not for the efforts themselves, however noble and arduous they might be. Still, if the goal is simply to identify and disseminate best practices, rather than to motivate them, such a mechanism design is satisfactory. Given the prestige of the program, one wonders how much it might be enhanced, say, with additional strategic communications or a larger reward so as actually to stimulate new initiatives.[9] It would be interesting to study the extent to which the disseminated Galing Pook Award innovations have actually been attempted elsewhere in the country. Regardless, this tournament example illustrates the power of signaling games if the signal—in this case, the award—has been carefully cultivated, that is, had its reputation developed and been properly advertised.

IMPACT OF INITIAL CONDITIONS

A precondition for this sort of initiative is the degree of legal liberty local governments have to try out new solutions to their problems. As explained above, just before the Galing Pook project began, an intensive decentralization effort led to passage of the Local Governance Code, which gave LGUs increased power and responsibilities in an effort to encourage the development of sustainable responses to social problems. Another distinctive aspect of the Philippines context is both the relatively high level of education in the population as well as its exposure and openness to the American penchant for entrepreneurship. Furthermore, there is a very rich tradition of NGO activity within the country. These idiosyncrasies explain the population's receptivity to a major aspect of the Galing Pook award, which is its reputational value instead of cash.

While not normally considered an initial condition, it is worth noting that given the degree of LGU participation, the amount that the Ford Foundation provided annually was rather small. It is interesting to speculate whether, within reason, smaller sums get used more economically. Would a larger sum have attracted the forces of corruption, for example, or caused sloppiness or laziness in award administration?

---

9. Separately, another question for evaluation would be whether awards are really going to the innovations that would score the highest by the program's own criteria. (Whether the criteria are "optimal" is a very different issue since, by definition, the criteria *define* what is best.)

SUSTAINABILITY AND SCALABILITY

The fact that the program has operated successfully for twelve years and has continued to do so after the initial sponsor's program ended is clear proof that from the perspective of *process*, Galing Pook has been sustainable. The absence of popular "fatigue" (boredom) may be attributable to several design factors. First, the format allows a broad variety of local government activities to be eligible to "play" in the game. Second, over time locally elected officials change, and the new ones become interested in competing. Moreover, compared to typical efforts to institute a local government innovation, the cost of competing in Galing Pook is very modest and offers each cycle of elected officials the opportunity to enhance their reputations.

The Galing Pook approach appears to exhibit *product* sustainability as well. This outcome may occur for several reasons. First, awards are based on prior performance so that there is no doubt that a winner's initiative has succeeded. Second, selection, while somewhat subjective, brings to bear experts with substantial knowledge of local conditions, which further ensures that success is not illusory. Finally, the program also has the Award for Continuing Excellence, which is given to past Outstanding Local Governance Program awardees that have sustained the program and improved on its key impact areas—although without rigorous evaluation, the extent to which this award was salient is not certain.

The main sources of increasing costs related to scale are recruiting and managing the evaluation experts, who would need strong local knowledge; postaward advertising of winners; and dissemination of the innovations. The smooth growth progression of the Galing Pook program suggests that these potential impediments to scale were not obstacles, leading one to speculate that properly functioning programs are indeed scalable. The Galing Pook program is currently operating at the national level, with all LGUs eligible for participation. Hence, in the narrow sense, no further increase in scale is possible.

One could consider applying the approach to other hierarchies such as higher levels of government, for example, to Philippine states or within or across national government ministries. While success would obviously depend on the details of implementation, it is less likely that such an approach would be the best alternative at the level of the Philippine states. Here an indicator approach—such as the IRIS-UNIDO initiative for Morocco (covered later in this chapter), the World Bank's Nigerian governance project (chapter 3), or international efforts—might be more appropriate.[10] For encouraging innovation within or across ministries, the Galing Pook approach might work, though it is possible that in the across-ministries case, politics or corruption might spoil the objectivity of the award process. This is the risk whenever the stakes of an outcome become substantial.

10. With regard to international efforts, see the annual *Global Competitiveness Report* (World Economic Forum, various years) or the *Doing Business* series (World Bank, various years).

Alternatively, the PAF approach for Jharkhand (chapter 3) might be more appropriate for the within- and across-ministries cases.[11]

4.1.2 Honduras: Mancomunidades

Historically, donors have not always been known to be searching for ways to improve the impact of their funding resources.[12] However, an encouraging counterexample is found in USAID's Rating System of Municipalities and Mancomunidades project in Honduras. This project aims to increase the efficiency of resources by allocating them according to recipient performance.[13]

STATEMENT OF THE PROBLEM

The USAID mission in Honduras came to realize that many donor technical assistance projects, including its own, were less effective when paternalistically imposed from above by outsiders (whether domestic or foreign) and when the political will to use the assistance was at best tepid.[14] In a time of shrinking aid budgets, therefore, the mission decided to investigate whether it could design a project that would allocate aid more efficiently and thereby lead to more effective outcomes.

OBJECTIVES

The strategy of this project was to provide technical assistance to municipalities that had the political will to improve their economic situation and would make the best use of the assistance (ARD 2004, p. 1). To identify such municipalities, USAID had a rating system developed that allowed the agency to assess a municipality's "state of readiness" for receiving technical assistance (ARD 2004, p. 9).

SPONSOR AND IMPLEMENTERS

The local USAID mission in Honduras funded the project, the design of which was developed by the U.S. consulting firm ARD. The actual implementer, however, was a consortium of the consulting firms, Management Systems International, the Urban Institute, and Mendez England and Associates.[15]

---

11. Though the Jharkhand application was within one geographic jurisdiction, there have been others, for instance in Bangalore, that conducted certifications across states *and* ministries simultaneously.

12. Of course, there is no dearth of official donor statements lauding the importance of effectiveness. However, even the most cursory examination of the facts leads one to question whether much of a priority is placed on this objective. See Espina and Zinnes (2003) for examples.

13. This section draws heavily from ARD (2004). ARD is a project consulting and management firm based in Burlington, Vermont.

14. For a passionate argument in support of this observation, see Easterly (2006a).

15. It is not uncommon for donors to have one firm design a project and another to implement it. The motivation is to prevent the former from loading the design with expensive extras that, in the next round, the designer would get to implement.

PLAYERS

In addition to foreign experts, several parties participated in the project's field tests. The local USAID mission acted as the referee or scorekeeper for the "tournament" and provided the technical assistance. The municipalities wishing to be considered for technical assistance comprised the first group of players. The second player group was the mancomunidades, which are "voluntary associations of municipalities sharing common problems and seeking cooperative solutions" (ARD 2004, p. 13). Therefore, use of technical assistance by the mancomunidades was particularly dependent on the actions and level of commitment of its member municipalities. Finally, within each municipality there were groups of "sub-players" that may have influenced the outcome of the game, namely, the mayors and their staff, the citizens, and businesses that operated within the municipality.

COST AND TIME FRAME

Although information related to the donor cost of the initiative was unavailable, the local costs appear to have been modest and involved the completion by municipal officials of a small number of questionnaires. The four phases of the project took place over a six-month period for one round.

RULES OF THE GAME

Since the municipalities were not homogenous in their ability "to compete," and each had its own needs and limitations, they were first divided into four categories: A, B, C, and D. These were not USAID's categories but were created by the government's Honduras Social Investment Fund as a device for infrastructure development after Hurricane Mitch.[16] Then each municipality was ranked, and technical assistance was provided to those scoring the highest in their respective category. The exact formulas, which municipalities were made aware of in advance, are provided in appendix B3.

As part of the ranking process, municipalities and mancomunidades requesting technical assistance from USAID were required to complete distinct development application forms and provide supporting documentation. The form was to be completed by the mayor of the municipality or the head of the mancomunidad requesting the technical assistance. The municipalities and mancomunidades were told in advance that their responses would be used to evaluate their state of "readiness" to receive technical assistance from USAID. The form also indicated that their responses would "provide input to the first stage of [a] multiple-stage process in which USAID [would] identify the municipalities that have the best chance of successfully us[ing] USAID's technical assistance to its fullest" (ARD 2004, p. 37).

16. The exact criteria, however, were not specified in the available project documents.

The form requested information in three general areas:

—*good governance,* including transparency, civil society participation, and community development;

—*sustainability and commitment* in terms of the ability of municipalities to maintain investments already made, as well as commitment to future investments; and

—*absorptive capacity,* an indication of whether the technical assistance should be provided immediately or would be more effective at a future date.

From the municipalities' responses to the questionnaire, the project team computed a "sustainability quotient" as the weighted sum of seven ranking variables. The sustainability quotient's variables were selected to indicate the "ability of the municipality to continue to make good use of technical assistance after project completion." [17] The weights were "set so that each variable ranges from zero to 10 (giving a total possible score of 100), or [could] be based on the relative importance of each variable to the priorities and programming requirements of USAID." The winner of the tournament was the municipality that had the highest score in its respective category. In other words, municipalities were "compared among themselves, not rated against a preset threshold or cutoff point." Finally, the operational plan was for beneficiaries of project technical assistance to be retested every year and have their assistance renewed only if they maintained a high ranking, per USAID's determination.[18]

The criteria for winning in the case of the mancomunidades were a bit different from those for municipalities. In the case of mancomunidades, the intent was to use the legal and operational status of the mancomunidad and the solidarity (including commitment) of their member municipalities. Furthermore, "part of the rankings of mancomunidades is a rating of their member municipalities" (ARD 2004, p. 13). Six ranking variables were used: legal status as a mancomunidad, technical staff resources, existence of planning documents, similarities in member municipal categories, timely payment of pledges (from member municipalities to the mancomunidad), and rate of retention and participation of member municipalities in the mancomunidad.[19] However, because mancomunidades were in the early stages of their formative development at the time of the pilot, USAID decided not to compare them to each other. Rather, mancomunidades were only required to meet a preset "threshold to be selected for consideration for receiving technical assistance" (ARD 2004, p. 13).

17. All quotes in this paragraph are from ARD (2004, pp. 9, 37).
18. Lynnette Wood, ARD, personal communication, March 15, 2007.
19. Regarding the similarity criterion, recall that mancomunidades comprise multiple municipalities. Project designers determined that group homogeneity would facilitate project objectives, namely, the absorption of USAID technical assistance.

REWARDS

The benefit to the municipality for winning the tournament was the technical assistance offered from USAID. While the exact value of this assistance was not stated, from the documentation available, it appeared that the allocation of all future municipal development technical assistance would be based on the tournament outcomes (ARD 2004, p. 1). In addition, the mayors themselves gained politically. By winning the competition, a mayor was able to enhance his or her political capital by objectively signaling to constituents that he or she was not just serious about reform but also able to achieve concrete results.

STATED OUTCOMES

It appears that thirty-five municipalities were deemed winners.[20] No information was available on the number of passing mancomunidades. [21]

PIJC COMPONENTS

This project incorporated many of the components of a PIJC. First, tournament participation was demand driven and voluntary in that players agreed in advance to participate by filling out the form and providing supporting documentation. The project used indicators to identify the municipalities that were serious about reform, and the components of these indicators were selected so as to draw on observable and ungameable data to the extent possible. Moreover, all data were subject to independent verification procedures. To allocate donor resources, in the case of the municipalities, the project selected winners using a competition based on relative, within-category measurements of performance—in short, a tournament. Winners received technical assistance as a tangible reward and publicity as an additional important component. As a result, the donor was able to maximize the use of its resources by selecting only those municipalities that would make the best use of them. In addition, this project was somewhat prospective (see the assessment below) because the players knew in advance that they were going to be ranked. As chapter 6 will show, the use of a threshold for selecting the winning mancomunidades means that the incentive mechanism used by the project was a type of certification, albeit one with pecuniary benefits.[22]

20. José Larios, ARD, personal communication, 2006.
21. As a design document, the ARD (2004) source used here did not provide any assessment of the outcomes of the project. This information was also requested from the implementing consortium but has not been received in time for use in this study.
22. There is a potential caveat here. While ARD's design called for a preannounced threshold, if during implementation the threshold was not announced ex ante but determined after observing the range of mancomunidad performance, then the incentive mechanism was in fact a tournament, not a certification.

ASSESSMENT

From the point of view of creating an incentive-compatible design, there are several aspects of this project's design that might have reduced its impact compared to what might have been feasibly achievable from a canonical tournament as delineated in chapter 2. First, the project's indicators do not appear to have been salient in the first implementation of the initiative, since other than filling out a form in the most advantageous way possible, there was little incentive to improve a municipality's performance. Furthermore, there does not appear to have been any time for the players to act between the announcement that a baseline (indicator measurements) would be taken and the time they had to fill out of the forms upon which the indicators would be constructed. In other words, while the project may have succeeded in identifying good aid candidates, it did not stimulate any cooperative community action to strive toward higher levels of performance, as occurs when players compete against each other.

The simplest way to address these shortcomings would be to allow a period of time, say, twelve to twenty-four months between the announcement of the indicators and their measurement, and to have the process repeated every certain number of years.[23] Unless USAID had administrative obligations to disburse the funding quickly—and the fact that they chose to run a tournament to allocate funding suggests otherwise—the first recommendation appears to have been completely feasible. While the second recommendation also appears to have been equally feasible, USAID may not have been sufficiently confident of the approach to have made such a commitment initially. However, one presumes that a favorable outcome of this first pilot would have overcome such understandable reticence.

A second area for improvement relates to the identification of good aid recipients. First, given the probably large information asymmetry between the donor and the municipalities, it is not clear just how accurate the self-reports—which formed the basis of the indicators—were. While the indicators were selected to be verifiable in principle, time constraints and other logistical impediments would have made it hard for donors to identify inaccuracies in reporting (not to mention purposeful misrepresentation). Second, winners were selected based on "inputs" (prior good performance) and not outputs (outcomes following the support from the USAID project) since performance was predicted (inferred), not observed. In other words, identification of potential success was based on presumed (future), not actual, effort. Closely related to this is the fact that the project design did not create any incentives to encourage winners to use efficiently the technical assistance provided. Moreover, while technical assistance requests were demand driven, weaknesses in the project's design meant that its use by the winners only had to appear (to the donor) to match the municipality's needs. Since winning did not

23. While there was an intention to annually retest municipalities, it is not clear that this has actually happened.

depend on efficient use of technical assistance, the project design did not create incentives for municipalities to ensure that it did match needs—or, for that matter, that it was even implemented properly.

IMPACT OF INITIAL CONDITIONS

With regard to the mancomunidades, this project was designed to fit the jurisdictional conditions of Honduras. Nonetheless, when applied to the municipalities alone—which the project ultimately limited itself to—there do not appear to be any important initial conditions that would limit the applicability of the project to other countries nor would it appear that the initial conditions were sufficiently idiosyncratic as to have influenced the outcome in any unexpected way.

Interestingly, the most successful mancomunidades are those made up of "member municipalities with similar characteristics" (ARD 2004, p. 13). This result corroborates the findings of Olson (1965), Ostrom (2000), and others that the transaction costs impeding collective action are lower when the group is more homogenous.

SUSTAINABILITY AND SCALABILITY

The institutional design issues described in the assessment above lead one to suspect that the results of the project would not be sustainable, either from a process or product standpoint. Changing the incentives with regard to reporting, timing for action, and effective use of technical assistance could potentially overcome these weaknesses. There are no such obvious criticisms with regard to scalability, a characteristic that the project appears to possess.

4.1.3 Indonesia: Kecamatan Development Program

STATEMENT OF THE PROBLEM

Top-down aid programs have not been effective in reducing local-level poverty in Indonesia or elsewhere. There are at least two primary reasons for this. First, national level decisionmakers often do not know what is needed at the local level. Second, projects do not involve sufficient local participation or "ownership"—either in their selection or implementation—so there is little local enthusiasm for or control over oversight. The result is that funds tend to be economically and distributionally misallocated.

OBJECTIVE

As described in KDP (2005), the objective is to alleviate poverty, strengthen local government and community institutions, and improve local governance by creating a bottom-up community development program based on small block grants for activities identified by the respective communities. KDP was developed to emphasize local-level participation and inclusion, transparency, an open menu of available activities, competition for funds, decentralized decisionmaking, and simple procedures.

SPONSOR AND IMPLEMENTERS

Financing comes from the World Bank (about 40 percent of the budget), the Indonesian government (20 percent matching contributions), nearly 50 percent of Indonesia's IDA allocation (about 25 percent of the budget), and other donor trust funds (about 15 percent of the budget).[24] In the next project phase, recipient communities will also contribute some funds. The Ministry of Home Affairs oversees the KDP project, with help from the World Bank. Locals implement the project with optional technical support from project consultants.

PLAYERS

For each subdistrict (*kecamatan*), the main unit (team or player) in the competition is the village, of which there are a total of 69,956. The kecamatans selected are the poorest in the country. Other actors—but, hopefully, not players—are organizations from civil society. Local-level NGOs are competitively selected to monitor each village's compliance.[25] Figure 4-1 summarizes the other actors in the KDP project.

COST AND TIME FRAME

The total cost of the various project phases to date (1998 to October 2005) is $1.3 billion. This has come from the World Bank ($560 million), IDA ($334 million), the Indonesian government ($282 million), and donor trust funds ($145 million; KDP [2005]).

RULES OF THE GAME

Figure 4-2 summarizes the steps in the game (competition). First, workshops are held to disseminate information and popularize the program. Then each village elects a local facilitator, who organizes meetings to identify village needs and priorities and to develop the village's proposal. The KDP offers technical consultants where requested. A village can decide to collaborate on a project proposal with one or more other villages within the same kecamatan. An intervillage meeting of communities within each kecamatan is then held to decide collectively which of the village proposals to fund, and a forum is set up to select and monitor (generally local) implementers. Grants are disbursed directly to kecamatan-level accounts in three stages, assuming there are intermediate results.

---

24. Information in this paragraph is from KDP (2005).

25. What is not clear is whether the local NGO has an incentive to "rat" on a village in its own kecamatan.

Figure 4-1. *KDP Management Structure*[a]

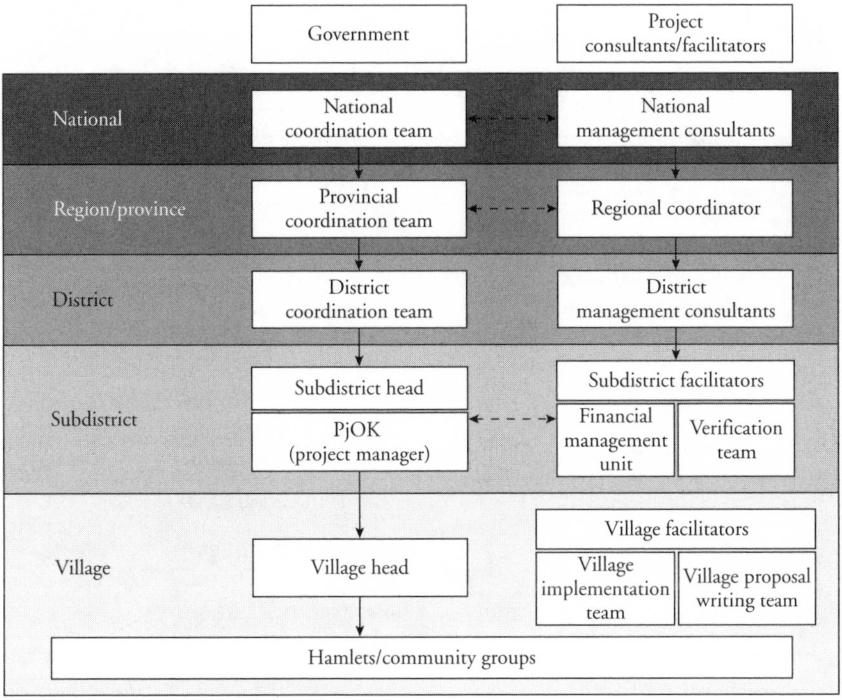

Source: KDP (2005).
a. PjOK, project managers at kecamatan level.

REWARDS

Each participating kecamatan receives a block grant budget of $50,000–150,000 to allocate among its villages according to the rules of the game laid out above (see table 4-2). A village project has a maximum size of $35,000, but villages can pool proposals. The block grant funds are replenished for the kecamatan for a minimum of five rounds of competitive bidding. Communities do develop reputations, which, according to Scott Guggenheim, has led to villages receiving awards in different rounds.[26] The value of reputation is strengthened since the government at times also provides its own rewards to star subdistricts that get an extra round of play (criteria are physical performance, audit results, and quality of participation). While communities can win as often as their proposals are deemed of sufficient merit, in practice, a previous win often acts as a "strike" in subsequent years (though this may arise from informal bargaining agreements among villages to vote for each other's projects in alternative rounds).

26. Content in this section comes from Scott Guggenheim, World Bank, personal communication, May 2006.

Figure 4-2. *The Process of Allocating Funds in the Activity Cycle (Round)*[a]

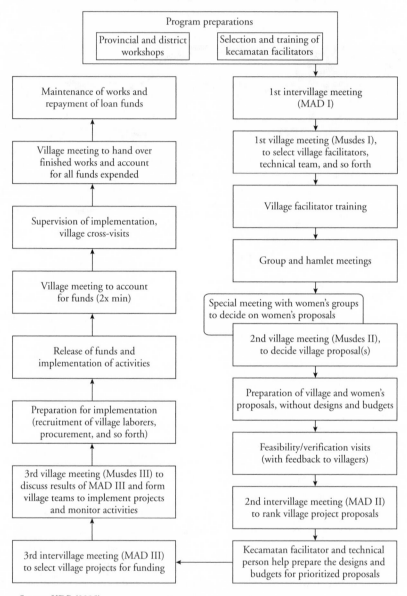

Source: KDP (2005).
a. MAD and Musdes are Indonesian acronyms for various phases of community-level management meetings, that is, at intervillage and village level, respectively.

Table 4-2. *Kecamatan Budget Limits to Distribute among Its Villages*

Amount per kecamatan (millions of rupiahs)	Kecamatan population	
	On Java	Off Java
1,000	>50,000	>25,000
750	25,000 to <50,000	15,000 to <25,000
500	15,000 to <25,000	5,000 to <15,000

Source: Scott Guggenheim, World Bank, personal communication, May 2006.

STATED OUTCOMES

While the size of the project (over $1 billion) is very large, so too are the claimed results (KDP 2005): 34,233 villages (the poorest 48 percent of the nation) given grants; 27,690 kilometers of road built or upgraded; 6,040 bridges built or reconstructed; 6,740 irrigation systems built; 6,565 clean water supply units and 2,660 sanitation units built; construction and renovation of 1,760 schools, including equipment and educational materials; 61,100 educational scholarships; and 1,450 village health units and posts.[27] Analysis of the project suggests an internal rate of return of 39 to 68 percent and implementation costs that are 56 percent less than equivalent work provided by the respective government ministry. In addition, the KDP calculates that 37 million workdays of local employment have been generated and 650,000 loans to beneficiaries have been made.

PIJC COMPONENTS

The KDP is formulated around interjurisdictional competition at the level of the village within a kecamatan. However, the project has been designed as a tournament only at the level of proposal writing (that is, to the extent that only the ex-ante "best" proposals are funded). In terms of the typology shown in table 2-1, this application uses input-based performance (since awards are for the best proposals, not the best outcomes), but the application does engender competitive proposal production. As such, no benchmark indicators are used—or need to be—to determine outcomes.[28] Moreover, the KDP design appears to engender cooperation, both within a village (so as to ensure the production of a winning

---

27. In light of the caveats at the end of chapter 1, it is important to note that these outcomes were reported by the very institution that designed and implemented the application. Although this is certainly grounds for some skepticism, given the reputation of the institution involved, I believe at least the quantity claims can be taken at face value, such as the number of grants awarded or bridges built. The same might not be said of the qualitative claims, perhaps.

28. This may not be strictly true in the sense that some intervillage community meetings may have used the guidelines suggested by the World Bank for assessing proposals, though they were not obliged to. Likewise, community drafters had guidelines for proposal preparation supplied by the World Bank, so it is probable that in some cases the indicators were implicit.

proposal) as well as occasionally across villages (since the only way to exceed the maximum funding limit is to design multivillage activities).[29]

There are direct and indirect rewards for a winning village, and these seem to be quite salient. However, while each kecamatan receives more proposals than it can fund, the fact that the funds are guaranteed available (subject to minimum feasibility and cost-benefit analysis) means that there could be room for local politics and intervillage, intertemporal bargaining to influence funding allocations. This observation is explored below.

There does not appear to be any specific project component to disseminate results, be they positive or negative. Moreover, there is no intervillage (or interkecamatan) evaluation occurring, randomized or otherwise.[30]

The KDP utilizes public participation and community demand-based development even beyond project identification. There is extensive monitoring at the community, district, province (*kabupaten*), and national levels. As described above, civil society plays an explicit oversight role. The World Bank also audits and provides oversight. Finally, there even exists an explicit grievance and complaints resolution mechanism, complete with a post office box.

Finally, a technical assistance component is available to villages, both for proposals and during implementation.

ASSESSMENT

Rate-of-return analysis suggests that the KDP initiative has been highly successful.[31] Of course, since no randomized evaluation has been performed, one can only speculate as to the value of the counterfactual use of the enormous funds dedicated to the project.[32] The enthusiasm of the government and other donors for continuing to contribute to the project suggests that this positive appraisal has fallen on receptive ears. In this context, the critical discussion that follows should be taken as a foil for evaluating the PIJC concept, not as an attack on the KDP per se.

29. "Interestingly, one result of structuring the competition such that villages compete against each other is that . . . they virtually never cooperate, with at most 2–3 villages repairing their own section of road or irrigation section. By contrast, in Afghanistan when [the World Bank] designed something similar [and] provided grants to villages . . . with no higher level competition . . . the outcome [was] quite large-scale cooperation—i.e., 50 villages pooling their entire grant to buy an energy system." Guggenheim, personal communication, May 2006.

30. In fact, to my knowledge the KDP has not yet produced any technical reports assessing the project mechanism itself, let alone generalizable assessments of individual village level outcomes.

31. Based on the World Bank's own calculations (KDP 2005). It is left to the reader to decide whether or not to believe the figures given that they are self-reported.

32. The World Bank did try a randomized pilot experiment to see whether varied forms of political representation on the kecamatan-level selection forums would affect subproject selection choice during competition. While the political composition did not have a statistical effect, the pilot did reveal that where the subproject went did vary with the degree of individual discretion allowed. Guggenheim, personal communication.

At the village level of implementation, while the project does stimulate competition, the KDP tournament initiative is input based and does not use a results-based performance incentive mechanism. There is no competitive pressure or reward for the best implementation of a *funded* activity, reputational effects for future rounds aside.[33] Rather, funds are allocated on ex-ante analysis: kecamatan forums must "pick the winners" (projects) in advance.[34] Thus there have been cases where a kecamatan forum opts for an inferior village proposal. Likewise, "strong *camats* or village heads can force a decision through and commitments to the dream of the uneconomic road that affirms ethnic identity can also triumph. But on average they don't."[35]

This also means that regardless of whether or not specific criteria for proposal selection are known in advance, some discretion must be exercised in selection. Nonetheless, because of the transparent selection process, this does not seem to have blunted the villages' incentives for competing. Still, while a project proposal's physical outputs are carefully forecast in advance, winning villages bear no cost (other than lower direct benefits from the project) if the project's consequent performance does not match expectations.[36]

While program design is ultimately an art, the earmarking of funds at the level of the kecamatan is not as allocatively efficient as earmarking funds across a number of kecamatans or even at the next highest jurisdictional level. Presumably, designers would need to (or did) weigh the marginal gains in allocative efficiency against the marginal transaction costs as either local governance wanes, social cooperation weakens, or computational complexity rises ("bounded rationality").

These design concerns suggest that villages might not have a particularly strong incentive to do a good job on implementation, other than the prospect of losing some of the expected benefits of the project. The project's institutional design tries to address some of the inherent principal-agent risks (moral hazard and adverse selection) of such an allocation mechanism. "The general formula is competition plus information leads to better decisionmaking."[37] For example, experts engage in extensive technical evaluation on all submitted proposals. The KDP implementation team actually looks at the occurrence of weak implementation

33. One could argue that this reputational effect is asymmetric: while achieving subproject goals may not increase a village's chances of repeat funding, failing to meet subproject goals may forfeit such chances.

34. This is in part a manifestation of the asymmetric information problem discussed in appendix D. The question is not just whether a project is financially viable or whether the variability of its returns is acceptable given *exogenous* risk factors, but also whether the project selectors are able to identify significant principal-agent threats beforehand.

35. Guggenheim, personal communication.

36. One can imagine that the village chief, to the extent that he heads the activity, might be seen to bear the responsibility for poor outcomes, and this may generate some additional governance if it motivates him to exert pressure for good results.

37. Guggenheim, personal communication.

incentives from the village's perspective. They ask, since it requires considerable effort to develop and promote a proposal all the way through the competition, why wouldn't a village implement it well?[38]

Their experience identifies the following reasons: ignorance or inadequate skills on how to implement the project, microincentives to steal, limited control over or access to all the variables that affect performance (for instance, small contractor oversight), and insufficient monitoring to detect when it goes off course.[39] The KDP believes, however, that compared with other donor and government projects, the difference in its approach is due to several factors.[40] First, there is a high but nonarbitrary level of effort required of the villages to get a proposal funded. Only after that does the village have access to project funds. With standard projects it is usually the other way around. Second, proposals are vetted by indicator and budgeting analysis, and the amount and types of inputs are determined with the help of KDP experts. Third, since the project offers funding only to poor villages for infrastructure that is greatly desired and with little chance of alternative funding, villages display strong ownership of each project they win. To this one might add that social capital and a village's desire to "save face" within the kecamatan may exert some pressure to refrain from opportunistic behavior during implementation.

The approach seems to be successful. For example, in 2004 when the government of Indonesia (GOI) was desperate to disburse funding for village projects, an unplanned (natural) experiment took place. The GOI argued that the reason projects were unfunded was because there were not enough donor funds to go around, not because of competition. It therefore offered to use its own funds to provide a second funding tranche to pick up the technically evaluated but rejected proposals. Apparently, these GOI-funded projects did not perform well at all.[41] World Bank staffers inferred from this experience that the KDP (input-based) competition did in fact exert positive selection pressures to identify good prospective projects.

On the other hand, villages do develop reputations, which are clearly valuable (see above), but these may only identify the top and bottom tier of quality, leaving much room for shirking within each winning team.[42] Nonetheless, funded tasks are demand driven, and the kecamatan level of fund allocation is likely to be rather efficient, relative to past alternatives.

38. I thank Scott Guggenheim of the World Bank for this suggestion.

39. The KDP technical team was almost always able to trace back the reasons why an implementation fails to one of these three causes. Guggenheim, personal communication.

40. Guggenheim, personal communication. Note that the source for this explanation is a World Bank field officer closely associated with the activity.

41. Ibid.

42. Ibid.

Still, from a PIJC perspective, the KDP project seems to have missed an interesting opportunity by not imposing any explicit conditional criteria on participation—neither at the kecamatan nor the village level—other than being able to produce a good project proposal. And there is no evidence provided to show that a winning proposal correlates with a serious effort at implementation. This suggests that the project may not have taken advantage of all the incentives a multiround competition might have generated. For example, the KDP could have demanded some sort of prior or concomitant governance improvement at the kecamatan or recipient village level as a quid pro quo for the right to KDP funds.[43] Of course, since the primary purpose of the project was to carry out village-level investment and not (necessarily) to improve governance, this may have been seen as potentially counterproductive, especially by the GOI. However, this is an empirical question. Given the large number of kecamatans, not to mention villages, some modest reform as a condition for participation might not have changed by much the number of proposal submissions, especially since jurisdictions with the enthusiasm to write good proposals might be correlated to jurisdictions willing to engage in some type of reform. A similar opportunity might have existed to regularize decision criteria for repeat funding of a village: a higher "bar" could have been set so as to equate the marginal distributional effect loss with the marginal gain in allocative efficiency.[44] These questions are considered again in chapter 6.

For the current purposes, then, one must ask, first, whether the ensuing costs of the KDP's institutional design are worth it, and, second, would an outcome-based tournament approach have been feasible and desirable? Put differently, was anything lost by not taking advantage of the theoretical benefits of the tournament approach? The first question is easy. The high internal rates of return make it unlikely that the institutional costs exceeded gross benefits. Likewise, to the extent that the alternative would have been to give the funds to the government ministries, as claimed by the KDP (2005), then the project was cost effective.

Turning to the second question, what if an outcome-oriented tournament approach had been used? On the one hand, this would have required that the KDP

—create a list of common activities from which villages could choose and compete,

—assign weights (shadow prices) to each allowable activity for use in aggregating performance,

---

43. An anonymous referee points out that one must be careful about theoretical design "improvements" that may not have been feasible in practice. This concern is addressed below.

44. Giving a village a second project presumably means it submitted one of the best proposals, hence strengthening allocative efficiency. This concentrates funding in fewer villages, however, and thereby narrows the distributional spread of benefits for the overall initiative.

—design and administer pre- and posttournament benchmarks pertinent for each approved activity, and

—calibrate a set of salient rewards to elicit tournament participation.

On the other hand, the KDP would *not* have had to

—assess the feasibility and business plan of each proposal across all the villages in all the kecamatans,

—create and implement forums in each kecamatan to prioritize and finally "pick winners" based on ex-ante expectations of success, or

—engage multilevel monitoring horizontally and vertically across jurisdictions.

To this cost-side calculus, one should add to the (theoretical) benefit side that many more times the number of projects might have been undertaken than actually were. This is because tournament incentives would have led not only funded villages to implement their ideas but also unfunded villages who thought they, too, had good proposals.[45]

But would an outcome-oriented tournament be feasible? First, the risks associated with the KDP grants were likely idiosyncratic, not systemic (common across all grants). As discussed in chapter 2, an idiosyncratic risk profile is more suited to a contract or certification approach rather than a tournament. Second, a tournament based on outputs (quality of performance) rather than inputs (proposal quality) would require an alternative way to fund the village projects. Presumably, any alternative would have placed project risk squarely on the villages, whose limited savings would have led to risk-averse investing and therefore fewer projects—at least for infrastructure (though not for governance or regulatory reform, to the degree such opportunities exist at the village level).

What if the funds were provided as loans that converted to grants for the winners? It is not clear that increasing the indebtedness of the poorest villages is in the long-term interest of a poverty alleviation activity, and the assumption of risk is still inefficient. What about providing partial cofinancing to villages (or requiring other costly inputs) that reverted to complete financing for the winners?[46] The share of initial cofinancing would have helped offset the capital constraints on villages but at the expense of increasing total project costs—exactly the opposite objective of the tournament approach! These dual objections might be mitigated if the indebtedness were at the kecamatan or even kabupatan level. In this way, middle-level government (or the forum organization set up by the initiative) would have a more internalized incentive to ensure that good projects were selected and, equally important, implemented to generate the performance

45. A fascinating question to investigate would be what share or number of village proposals not funded by the project were actually undertaken anyway.
46. This relates to whether the rewards included in the mechanism design were adequately calibrated for sufficient salience. Were they too high—could participation have been motivated with less than full outside funding? Were they too low—was there too little proposal writing because development costs were too high for some players?

expected. This consideration reveals a fundamental policy design challenge: at what point in the KDP design does the efficiency gain from reducing the moral hazard and adverse selection risks outweigh the losses caused by inefficient risk spreading?

To obviate mechanisms for reallocating project risk, an alternative project design would combine an input tournament with an output tournament. First, one would apply the current KDP design at the level of each kecamatan, as before. At the same time, players would know that the results at the kecamatan level would be embedded into an *inter*kecamatan competition in which winning kecamatans would be those with the highest average performance, according to a preestablished metric in the *intra*kecamatan (village) grant tournaments. A rigorous assessment of the feasibility and desirability of such a design, unfortunately, is outside the present scope of this book, which is to illustrate the power of analyzing government transfers and sponsor assistance from an institutional economics perspective and the opportunities that may exist once one is willing to go beyond the standard fiscal models.

As an aside, a less demanding alternative to the fully output-based tournament suggested above would be to add some conditionality, either on the kecamatan or the participating village, for qualifying to submit a proposal. Still, adding conditions for improvements in local governance, for example, would have further complicated the project and delayed disbursements, unless the tasks required were very simple and easy to verify. Whether this was bureaucratically feasible (acceptable), I do not know.

Whatever the answers might be to the aforementioned dilemmas, there are some additional PIJC components that could have been incorporated into the existing KDP design framework at little extra cost and, presumably, to great effect. First, it would seem to be a missed opportunity that uniform data or indicator collection was not required before the start of each funded project. This would have allowed policymakers to draw generalizable conclusions from the enormous number of activities funded by the KDP. Second, it would have been interesting to assess just how much was gained or lost by limiting the competitions to village-level proposals at the kecamatan level rather than pooling proposals across all villages across all participating kecamatans (or at least up to the kabupaten level). Third, the extended duration of the KDP initiative (eight years when this was originally written) makes it likely that villages could develop reputations for results-based performance (see above). In fact, extra projects apparently are discretionally granted to high-reputation villages. However, this externality could have been better used. For example, the KDP or the government could commit to promote high-reputation villages nationally (or even internationally). This would create an added incentive for the village to perform well—especially if the criteria for "high reputation" were set beforehand and without discretion, as done in the case of Galing Pook (see earlier in this chapter).

Finally, since decentralization, apparently "citizens spend far more time and effort on KDP processes than on local government participatory processes linked to formal accountability," though the latter have far more resources.[47] Moreover— and this would be the case for most interjurisdictional competition projects—the need to set up village facilitators and hold intervillage meetings would seem to be a direct admission of local government failure, since such organizational arrangements are substitutes for the normal, local, public sector investment allocation process. While upon reflection this is patently obvious, its implications are less so. First, how healthy is the implicit competition for effectiveness (or for political credit from the voter) between the KDP (funded directly through one central government ministry) and local government activities (predominantly funded by a different central government ministry but seen as local initiatives)?[48] Second, should donors be funding the creation of parallel local government institutions or using the funds to strengthen official agencies? Clearly, short-term poverty alleviation gravitates toward the former whereas long-term considerations may suggest the latter. Such considerations should probably be addressed on a case-by-case basis by donors during the formulation of such projects. Therefore, this important question is explored further in section 7.2.4.

IMPACT OF INITIAL CONDITIONS

The most obvious initial condition here is the existence of an appropriate hierarchical structure of local jurisdictions—from the kabupatan to the kecamatan to the village—and a sufficient governance arrangement at the kecamatan level to organize the selection meeting process. Moreover, the large number of villages permitted a wide array of proposals for a vibrant competition. The fact that within each kecamatan the villages had roughly the same level of competence in generating proposals means that there was likely to be a level playing field for each tournament

The dire state of the villages within the kecamatans participating in the KDP initiative suggests that initial conditions may not have been too important to the success of the project. On the other hand, some degree of literacy and local skills would be required if the same level of local participation were desired for the village facilitators and the local implementers. One obvious initial condition, however, that was used to advantage was the existence of women's groups. The KDP held special meetings with such groups (see figure 4-2) to encourage them to develop winning proposals for consideration. It is also the case that the World Bank's long-term perspective (eight years at the time of this writing) and the large allocation of funds have contributed to the project's success. Both of these factors

47. Written comments by an anonymous referee (January 2008) familiar with the application.
48. An anonymous referee (January 2008) has pointed out that when the GOI took over funding the KDP from the donors, a turf battle ensued within the government for control of the project, not a good sign for sustainability.

would have signaled to local stakeholders the value of investing in the KDP's "proposal game." Neither project length nor abundance of funding should be stressed as project preconditions, however, since the project could be (and was) tested first as a pilot with success.

SUSTAINABILITY AND SCALABILITY

The KDP initiative appears ideally designed for scalability. As additional kecamatans are added to the roster of participating jurisdictions, little additional bureaucratic burden is placed on local government, human, financial, or physical resources already involved in the exercise. (There would be some potential capacity constraint issues at the World Bank and at the level of the national government, for example, for evaluating the technical merits of proposal submissions.) Thus, to increase the number of village beneficiaries, the World Bank would simply increase the budget by the same percentage. Likewise, it is likely that the KDP's design would work well in most other countries with weak local government. This last condition is added because, as mentioned above, the organizations set up by the project to allocate the grants are in direct competition with (substitute for) the existing local governments. Where the latter are relatively strong or well organized, they might demand a "piece of the action." Perhaps having their representatives act as facilitators would be sufficiently co-opting, as was the case in the Middle East Partnership Initiative (MEPI) Morocco project (see discussion later in this chapter).

Any project concept that depends on outside funds for its operation is per se not sustainable *as a process*. The success of the KDP, however, seems to have led the government—both national and local—to agree to use their own funds to finance in part future phases of the project (KDP 2005). In principle, this would bode well for the sustainability of the *process*. Nonetheless, there is always a concern that a future government could view the KDP as purely a creation of the donor or a previous Indonesian government and would no longer be interested in continuing it; new governments like to clear the slate and have their own donor collaborations. Since this is understandable, it does point to the importance of ensuring sufficient involvement by senior management at the appropriate line ministries. Regardless, unless the project's specific goal was to institutionalize the project's process of grant giving, this theoretical future threat to process sustainability should not be seen as a serious flaw, especially if the project led to *product* sustainability.

The theory is (and often in practice) that projects with high levels of local buy-in and ownership are more likely to generate sustainable (*product*) outcomes than projects without these characteristics, regardless of whether one's own funds or grants are used.[49] In the case of infrastructure projects, there is always a hidden

---

49. No empirical information on this question was found in available sources.

future cost, namely, that of operations and maintenance (O&M). History suggests that poor communities with donated infrastructure often do not have the follow-up resources for O&M. Matters are made worse where there is no line ministry engagement, which seems to be partly the case here (as suggested in figure 4-1 and figure 4-2).[50] Although it is not known whether or not the KDP-funded activities provided for O&M, for example, by imposing user fees set at full-cost pricing, it seems rather unlikely—especially since the transaction cost of collection for many of its project grants (such as a short stretch of road) might be relatively high.[51] However, as a condition for grant funding, the donor could require, for example, long-term commitment by a higher level of government to annually fund O&M, payment of user fees, or some combination of the two. Such problems are not generally a major concern for PIJC projects that focus on "soft" reforms (see above).

4.2 Mixed Tournaments

In mixed tournaments a jurisdiction must both exceed a threshold performance requirement as well as attain a high rank in order to win or place. The three presented below are from Russia, the MCC, and Morocco.

4.2.1 Russia: Fiscal Reform Loan

STATEMENT OF THE PROBLEM

Since the breakup of the Soviet Union, a series of World Bank analytical reports have pointed to the need for extensive technical assistance in the area of fiscal federalism and regional fiscal reform within Russia to promote financial transparency, budgetary accountability, and strengthened fiscal management policies and practices at the regional level (World Bank 2001b). It was the crisis of 1997–98, however, that precipitated concrete World Bank action in the form of a loan to the Russian federal budget to support a broad range of reforms.

OBJECTIVE

The Fiscal Federalism and Regional Fiscal Reform Project had two objectives. The first was to strengthen the system of fiscal federalism in Russia. The second was to help the regions of the Russian Federation to develop and implement fiscal reform programs that promote financial transparency and budgetary accountability, and strengthen fiscal management policies and practices at the regional level. To address these objectives, the program was divided into two components:

---

50. I thank Johannes Linn of the Wolfensohn Center at Brookings for this point.
51. Note, however, that local infrastructure commons, such as waterworks, have survived and been maintained for centuries in developing country environments. See Ostrom (2000) for examples in the Philippines and Mexico.

the first "addressed the reform of the system of fiscal federalism and the second component supported the establishment of the incentive mechanism that rewarded successful regional reformers" (World Bank 2006a, p. 2). For present purposes, the focus will be on the second component, the regional fiscal reform project, since it contains a tournament mechanism.

SPONSOR AND IMPLEMENTERS

The donor was the World Bank, and the Ministry of Finance (Fiscal Monitoring Division) was the primary implementer of the project, through an interministerial working group.

PLAYERS

There were at least two major players in this tournament application. The first player was the Russian government, whose interests were represented by two organizations. The first was an interministerial working committee that comprised "representatives of key government agencies involved in the design and implementation of intergovernmental and regional reforms such as the Ministry of Finance, Ministry of Economy, and the Duma, and [had] decisionmaking powers commensurate with the task of carrying out intergovernmental and regional fiscal reform in the Russian Federation" (World Bank 2006a, p. 21).[52] The Fiscal Monitoring Division of the Ministry of Finance supervised the day-to-day tasks of the project. The second and most important set of players were the regional governments that were the target of the reforms and who participated in the project.

COST AND TIME FRAME

Regional governments were given one year to prepare their reform programs. Over the course of 2002–04, three tournaments were held. The amount of the World Bank loan for the component containing the tournament was $60 million, of which $40 million were earmarked for the rewards. While the technical assistance and rewards came through the loan to the Russian Federation, the costs of local government staff efforts to implement the institutional and legislative changes were borne by the regular operating budgets of the respective local governments.

RULES OF THE GAME

This project used a competitive grant mechanism to improve the fiscal performance of regional governments in Russia. Grant funding came from the Regional Fiscal Reform Fund (RFRF), which was established during the first component of the project (see above). The participating regions were divided

---

52. The Duma is the Russian parliament.

up into three cohorts comprising seven, ten, and ten regions, respectively. The regions within each cohort would compete in contests in which the "prize" was access to RFRF grants for regions that undertook significant fiscal reform.[53] Up to five regions from each cohort received awards from the RFRF "for budgetary support based on their fiscal performance and implementation of their fiscal reform programs" (World Bank 2006b, p. 12).

Applicants were "judged on the basis of how well they prepared and implemented regional fiscal reform programs" (World Bank 2006a, p. 3). Each region was allowed at least one year to prepare its reform programs, which were subject to minimal guidelines (thresholds) established by the World Bank and the implementing agencies. (It is the existence of these thresholds that makes this application a "mixed tournament.") The World Bank also provided each region participating in the competition with technical assistance on the design of its fiscal reform programs. When a participating region did not "implement its reform program or [was] disqualified, it [was] simply dropped from the competition, making the prospects of success for the other regions better" (World Bank 2006b, p. 12).

Using objective and clearly observable variables, the tournament selected winners according to weights: 15 percent for fiscal performance, 30 percent for quality of management, 45 percent for program implementation (the degree to which the reform program is implemented), and 10 percent for the planned use of funds.[54] The scoring system was "extensive and quantitative but allowed for variations in focus among regions and scored implementation on a relative basis to motivate regions with significantly different starting positions" (World Bank 2006a, p. 3).

REWARDS

First and foremost, "key benefits of the project include[d] improved fiscal management, greater budgetary transparency and accountability, more effective use of resources, and in the longer term, improved delivery of services at the regional level of government" (World Bank 2006b, p. iii). The contest also offered the winners a grant of $7 million to $9 million, an amount equal to 10 to 15 percent of the annual revenues of a participating region (World Bank 2006b, p. 12).[55] The large monetary prize provided powerful incentives for the regions to pursue fiscal reforms. The winners of the competition received the

53. These are essentially incentive-based transfers created from a line item in the Russian federal budget (World Bank 2001b, p. 71).

54. Program implementation was actually evaluated by two criteria: degree of phase-1 reform compliance (25 percent) and degree of phase-2 reform compliance (20 percent).

55. The grant was to be used as follows: 70 percent for reform implementation, 23 percent for debt servicing, 5 percent for "social infrastructure," and 2 percent for "socially important spending" (World Bank 2006a, p. 13).

grants in "two disbursements—initially, upon completion of the first phase of reforms, and subsequently, upon completion of the second phase of reforms" (World Bank 2006b, p. 12). Hence the program may be viewed as having had front-loaded conditionality on intergovernmental finance improvements. In addition to this reward and the benefits of having a well-designed and implemented fiscal reform, program participation was "expected to have reputational benefits for the regions" (World Bank 2006b, p. 12).

STATED OUTCOMES

Of the twenty-seven regions preselected and divided into the three cohorts, a total of twenty-four regions presented applications and reform programs, and nineteen regions took part in an actual competition for the RFRF grants (World Bank 2006a, p. 6). Of those regions that participated in the competition, five from each of the three cohorts, for a total of fifteen regions, were provided with grants. Thus, with respect to the second objective of the program, fifteen regions "improved their fiscal management practices through implementation of the two-stage programs of the budget reform" (World Bank 2006a, p. 4).[56] These included "gradual transition toward treasury principles of budget execution; adoption of more transparent regulations for both transfer equalization and tax sharing; new procedures to control budget commitments/liabilities; reducing the number of off-budget accounts; monitoring and capping tax exemptions; improved information and management of debt and monitoring of the consolidated public sector debt; improved asset management techniques; and strengthened internal audit of budgetary funds" (p. 4). Moreover, there appears to have been "clear spill-over effects," as many regions that did not receive grants still registered partial improvements and participated in the program's technical assistance workshops.

PIJC COMPONENTS

This World Bank initiative contained most of the necessary components of a full-fledged PIJC. First and foremost, it used a tournament mechanism—that is, winning depended on *relative* performance—to motivate regional efforts to engage in fiscal reform. Players (regions) were divided into groups to ensure a level playing field. The tournament mechanism was also subject to minimum performance thresholds that any winner had to exceed. The competition was prospective, with each region knowing that it was participating as well as the exact nature of the rules and rewards. As proposed in chapter 2, not only was participation voluntary but the particulars of reform implementation were left to each participant, though technical assistance workshops were offered by the World Bank. The required reforms themselves, however, were dictated by the World Bank, so in a strict sense, the reforms were not demand driven or self-selected. The fiscal tournament used

56. These were the conclusions of an independent assessment carried out for the World Bank.

a scoring system to objectively assess performance to help to create a bright set of incentives. Among the "targets for outcomes were . . . performance of the treasuries, debt management, public procurement, financial planning systems, [and] settlement of arrears."[57] These are described in appendix B1.

The project design also included a statistical evaluation of the intervention that compared player performance along many dimensions to that of regions that did not participate. For almost all the indicators, participating regions performed better.

ASSESSMENT

Of the projects presented in this book, the Russian fiscal project is among the closest to being what chapter 2 calls "a full-fledged PIJC." As such, this application is examined in somewhat greater detail, first by summarizing the independent assessment done for the World Bank, and then by considering whether missing PIJC components, design differences from a full PIJC, or other conditions led to the shortcomings identified or benefits generated.[58]

The World Bank evaluators deemed the regional fiscal reform component of the Fiscal Federalism and Regional Fiscal Reform Project "successful" (World Bank 2006a, p. 31).[59] In addition to the successful implementation of the five winning regions' fiscal reform plans, there were also "clear spill-over effects, as many improvements were made by regions, which did not receive grants (they may have implemented only parts of their budget reform programs or have simply participated in workshops under the project)" (World Bank 2006a, p. 4). Furthermore, comparative analysis of regional performance conducted by the World Bank in 2003 suggested that the "regions participating in the . . . Project out-performed their peers in a number of important areas, especially with respect to the speed of their fiscal adjustment and expenditure restructuring" (World Bank 2006a, p. 5).

The World Bank attributed the success of this program to two factors. First, the size of the loan ($120 million) allowed the grants to be large enough ($7 million to 9 million) to provide powerful incentives for the regions to participate in the competitions. The second factor was the "exemplary commitment from the counterparts in the Russian Government, who have been active in developing and

---

57. World Bank (2006a, p. 10).

58. The independent assessment was carried out by the Independent Evaluation Group at the World Bank. Still, one referee of this chapter who indicated a familiarity with the initiative advised skepticism regarding any organization's self-evaluation. While this may be true in general, it is not obvious why a large organization such as the World Bank would create an independent assessment group only to ask it to distort its opinions. Moreover, I personally know some of those who served as evaluators and can fully vouch for their professional integrity.

59. World Bank evaluators are a group of experts from within the bank who are assembled to assess the level of a project's success. Of course, they are not involved in the project being evaluated.

pursuing reform of fiscal federalism and improved regional financial management" (World Bank 2006b, p. 13).

The World Bank itself identified several lessons from (what it called) this "innovative model" of technical assistance delivery (World Bank 2006a, p. 9). First and foremost, it concluded that "the competitive model of promoting reform can be effective."[60] (Note that "competitive" meant that winning depended on *relative* performance.) Aside from the evident reforms implemented by the "winners," the World Bank was particularly surprised by the behavior of the "losers." These regions that did not perform well in past screenings still undertook serious efforts to prepare reform programs, often "redoubl[ing] their efforts" in subsequent competitions. In particular, the World Bank pointed to the fact that fifteen winners were rewarded out of a total of eighty-nine regions "without protest or complaint" from the "losers" as a sign of the success of the delivery model. This they attributed to the "critical role of transparency in the process." One could argue that another reason might be that since most "losers" still undertook benefit-producing reforms, they also gained from the exercise.

Second, the World Bank concluded that "technical assistance is more effective when it is reinforced by an incentive framework"—in this case, the lure of an award. Moreover, the World Bank specifically concluded that the technical assistance "would not have been anywhere as nearly effective had the incentives . . . not been present" (World Bank 2006a, p. 10).

Third, the World Bank concluded that "ownership matters." The Russian government (that is, the Ministry of Finance) maintained firm ownership of the activity as a quid pro quo for taking on more debt—the project was loan financed. In other words, the government's agreement to take the loan was contingent on retaining full control of the project and funds, contracting out only a very few technical tasks. Thus top officials were unlikely to "lose interest in the project" (World Bank 2006a, p. 10).

Finally, the World Bank believed that this project proved that "subnational fiscal reform can be a legitimate topic for policy lending," even for "implementing a wide range of common [fiscal] systems, policy changes, and even outcome targets" at the subnational level (World Bank 2006a, p. 10). In the present context, this lesson also may be viewed as an affirmation of local-level reform managed and overseen by the jurisdictions themselves.

The World Bank evaluators did have a number of concerns. They felt that the list of tournament tasks was too ambitious, did not permit variation in reform options across different regions, should not have dictated the sequence of task attainment, and was "not only extraordinarily difficult, if not impossible, to achieve in Russia, but risk[ed] holding the rest of the program hostage to meeting these conditions" (World Bank 2006a, p. 32). Moreover, the evaluators found

60. All the quotes in the rest of this paragraph are from World Bank (2006a, p. 10).

"that the selection criteria and formulation of the ranking are unnecessarily complex and not as transparent as desirable" and thought that their simplification would make it "easier for the regions to understand and comply" (World Bank 2006a, p. 4 and p. 35).[61] Related to these concerns, evaluators believed that there is a risk that the program of intergovernmental finance reforms proposed by the central government may take longer to implement than anticipated, thus hindering improved fiscal incentives in the relations between the center and the regions. Evaluators tied this into their earlier concerns by suggesting that the front-loaded conditionalities be geared toward the essential minimum requirements of intergovernmental fiscal reform to help to mitigate these risks.

Now is a good time to consider these concerns by determining which are not specific to PIJC and which are. While any ex-post evaluation of a reform program—and not the least under the difficult conditions of Russia—is going to identify problems, those found by the World Bank evaluators appear to be related to implementation idiosyncrasies and not to any conceptual weaknesses of the PIJC approach. For example, the problem of insufficient reform time is not a PIJC-specific issue since the tournament approach does not appear to require a significantly longer time frame per se than other delivery mechanisms that also aim at sustainability.[62] Likewise, if time had been limited, fewer rounds could have been implemented, or tasks could have been reduced; if time simply had been insufficient, then longer periods for competing could have been offered.

Regarding the ambitiousness of the reform list, this was not a PIJC-specific problem but rather a product of the program's owner, the Russian government, which simply overreached on the comprehensiveness of the reforms they wished to implement—especially given the allotted time frame. The government could have adjusted this in follow-up rounds. Finally, the complexity of the selection criteria for awards is not per se specific to PIJCs; any program using award criteria learns over time to calibrate their indicators to optimize the balance between maximizing participation and ensuring clear, ungameable measures of outcomes. In all these cases, it is likely that as a result of the experience, the Russian Ministry of Finance and the World Bank will adjust their ambitions in the future.

The design of a full-fledged PIJC anticipates the shortcomings identified by the evaluators and related to the tournament itself. The PIJC approach advises that the list of reform options be a superset of tasks acceptable to the sponsors and that participants be allowed to pick and chose what to implement according to local preferences and self-assessed capacities. This was not the case for the Russian

61. They also expressed concern that these complications could open the tournament to manipulation by both the government and "some of the more astute regions," but how and why this might be the case was not explained.

62. I add the sustainability qualification because it is possible to impose a top-down reform, with foreign implementation experts, but such an approach is very unlikely to lead to reform that is permanent and institutionalized.

project, which not only specified a one-size-fits-all set of reforms but also a single implementation sequence. Project documentation does explicitly state that the scoring system "allowed for variations in focus among regions and scored implementation on a relative basis to motivate regions with significantly different starting positions" (World Bank 2006a, p. 3). However, this probably refers to the three categories of performance criteria used, which would have allowed participants to gain points according to their varying strengths in each category. Nonetheless, the list of reforms was the same for all players.

The evaluators did not mention the potential for problems related to the formation of the cohorts used for each tournament round. First, there were very few players (between seven and ten per cohort). On the one hand, while this is fine for a pilot implementation, it could open up the possibility for collusion, a temptation often found in competitive environments with small numbers of agents. On the other hand, the fact that no collusion occurred and competition was vigorous suggests that a large number of players may not be necessary. Second, in the formation of each cohort, there did not seem to be any concern for creating a level playing field; instead, the project report appeared to indicate that the diversity of regions included in the cohorts was a good thing (World Bank 2001b, p. 74). This, as for many aspects of PIJC calibration, is an empirical question. However, experience suggests that in a tournament a given set of incentives provides greater motivation for reform action if players see themselves as competitive with each other.[63] (Note how this issue relates back to the evaluators' observation about the inflexibility of the task list.)

The evaluators did raise the concern about tournament manipulation, though without being specific. As mentioned above, there is the possibility of collusion due to the small number of players. In addition, the scoring of some of the inputs into the reward decision rule suggests that some discretion on the part of the government is possible.[64]

As noted in section 2.2, one of the features of a PIJC believed to be particularly powerful in motivating participants to play is social pressure; for example, "my region is/must be/should be better than your region." This effect requires that player scores be made available as well as easy to interpret by citizens. In the present case, it is not clear just what sort of baseline was taken or whether it was made public.[65] This may be symptomatic, given the penchant for government secrecy in Russia, or it may be a weakness in the project's design. To the extent that social

---

63. See the assessment of the Romanian project in chapter 3 for the perils in this regard.

64. So-called Group-3 indicators covering fiscal procedures, systems, and methodologies were scored using qualitative assessments by experts.

65. The World Bank (2001b, p. 72) indicates that the Ministry of Finance used a World Bank–approved methodology for "pre-qualification" of participants (regions) who apply to play. It is not clear whether this was the baseline measurement.

pressure was lacking, it may be viewed as one of the few PIJC components missing from this application.

There are several other incentive aspects of this implementation that provide lessons for future PIJC applications. First, the Russian project was approximately two orders of magnitude more expensive than other PIJC applications described in this book. In part this was due to the large size of the rewards budget ($40 million). This was, in turn, due to the high percent of participants preset to "win" (up to 50 percent of the participants!) and to the size of rewards (on average $8 million). Project documentation did not discuss whether these amounts were determined from pilot calibrations to generate the desired institutional behavioral responses, given the political constraints. If such calibration did not occur, then doing so might have resulted in *lower* project costs (if local decisionmakers had revealed that lower reward amounts would have had a sufficient incentive effect) and yet *higher*-powered participation incentives (if pretests had identified additional or alternative ways to motivate participation). Moreover, by addressing some of the missed incentive opportunities mentioned above, the application might have been able to reduce the need for such large rewards.

Another lesson about incentives comes from the fact that the RFRF project design gave full control to the Russian government (Ministry of Finance), which encouraged its full participation and ownership, in keeping with the PIJC approach developed in chapter 2.

Finally, the World Bank evaluators made two additional points worth noting. First, they pointed out how the design of the RFRF mitigates the risks to the government (and donor) often encountered in the implementation of (other) programs at the regional level. Such risks include changes in regional governments that may lead regions to alter their support for the reform programs, and the possibility that regions may be unable to fulfill their programs. These risks are mitigated by the design of the RFRF, which focuses on a competitive allocation of funds to those regions that successfully fulfill their programs. Those regions that do not fulfill their programs simply do not receive resources. Second, the World Bank evaluators noted that "one of the principal outcomes of this project is to improve data available on [in this case] regional finances" (World Bank 2006a, p. 33). While this would be true of any project that generates quantitative indicators, a PIJC is likely to produce higher quality data since the values of the indicators are highly salient, transparently collected, and subject to close scrutiny by many opposing interested parties.

IMPACT OF INITIAL CONDITIONS

First of all, the time was right. With the country coming out of a chaotic decade, "there was a positive attitude toward budget reform."[66] The economy had started

---

66. The quotes and factual information in this section come from World Bank (2006a).

growing and, therefore, so too did public coffers, especially as oil prices had taken off. Top government officials sent a strong signal of their support for the project's budget reform goals. However, the transparency and credibility of the rules of the game for the participating regions is what cinched their enthusiastic participation. The Ministry of Finance had a very competent team and the interministerial working group performed well, which minimized delays. In addition, the reforms were of a technical, not political, nature.

Finally, though "at the time, no Bank loan had ever supported such an approach," it was felicitous that a group of donor staff members had "the willingness to craft a project supporting this innovative model competition reform," a fact that evaluators called "the major Bank contribution." Nonetheless, outside of Russia, the written statements by World Bank and Russian implementers suggest that because of the incentive-compatible mechanism design, the initial conditions were not too critical, except that it helped to have a technically strong and committed team in the Ministry of Finance.

SUSTAINABILITY AND SCALABILITY

While time will tell, there is evidence that the reforms (the "product") engendered by the project will be sustainable. For example, the fiscal reforms seemed well enough established to make the Ministry of Finance feel confident about applying the program to other SNGs. More impressive has been the sustainability of the project mechanism (the "process"), which became a part of the regular operations of the Russian federal government and of many subnational governments. Moreover, the Ministry of Finance has continued to use the RFRF for competitions in 2006 and, as of this writing, has budget plans to do so without continued World Bank funding up through 2008. I would argue that the eagerness with which SNGs chose to participate is due to the long list of incentive design features described in the assessment above and inherent in the PIJC concept.

With twenty-seven regions of the country involved, it is fair to say that this initiative has already proved it can be effective on a rather large scale. Perhaps for that reason, it has already begun to be replicated elsewhere in Russia. As final evidence of the potential for replicability and scalability, so powerful has been the effect of this project that the Russian government has begun to apply the tournament methodology "between Russian ministries, agencies and services in the context of gradual transformation towards performance based budgeting principles" (World Bank 2006a, p. 7).

4.2.2 Millennium Challenge Corporation

Given its conservative reputation, it was a surprise to some that the Bush administration, while dismantling the Iraqi state, was simultaneously launching the Millennium Challenge Corporation, a highly innovative initiative in the field of economic development assistance.[67] Equally surprising is that the mechanism employed is a mixed tournament. As will be seen, however, the tournament mechanism only applied to the eligibility process and not to implementation.

STATEMENT OF THE PROBLEM

In 2002 the Bush administration called for a "new compact for global development," which would link greater contributions from developed nations to greater responsibility from developing nations.[68] It came to this conclusion by noting that

—aid is not very effective when applied in an environment without sound political, economic, and social policies;

—development plans unsupported by a broad range of stakeholders and where the recipient country does not have primary responsibility and "ownership" are much less likely to succeed; and

—most aid projects lack serious monitoring and evaluation (M&E) and so lack effectiveness, accountability, and the transparency with regard to how taxpayer resources are used.

OBJECTIVE

The Bush administration proposed a concrete mechanism to implement this compact: the Millennium Challenge Account (MCA), which would fund development assistance for those countries that rule justly, invest in their people, and encourage economic freedom. The Millennium Challenge Corporation (MCC) was established in 2004 to administer the MCA. The corporation has been designed, in principle, to support innovative strategies, ensure accountability for measurable results, and make maximum use of flexible authorities. By 2008 over $5 billion had been requested for the program, and the Bush administration had pledged to increase annual funding for the MCA by $5 billion in the future. There are two main objectives of this initiative. The first is to "reduce poverty through economic growth—the MCC will focus specifically on promoting sustainable economic growth that reduces poverty through investments in areas such as agriculture, education, private sector development, and capacity building." The second is to "reward good policy—using objective indicators, countries will be selected to receive assistance based on their performance in governing justly, investing in their citizens, and encouraging economic freedom" (MCC 2006).

Two other key MCA principles are closely related. The first requires demand-driven project selection. "Operating as partners . . . with the MCC, countries that

---

67. The following discussion draws heavily from and often paraphrases material from the Millennium Challenge Corporation website (www.mcc.gov).

68. Monterrey Declaration, March 2002, Monterrey, Mexico.

receive MCA assistance will be responsible for identifying the greatest barriers to their own development, ensuring civil society participation, and developing an MCA program—MCA participation will require a high-level commitment from the host government" (MCC 2006). The second requires "focusing on results, [dictating that] MCA assistance will go to those countries that have developed well-designed programs with clear objectives, benchmarks to measure progress, procedures to ensure fiscal accountability for the use of MCA assistance, and a plan for effective monitoring and objective evaluation of results. Programs will be designed to enable sustainable progress even after the funding under the MCA Compact has ended" (MCC 2006).

SPONSOR AND IMPLEMENTERS

The MCC is an executive branch agency, so there is a chief executive officer appointed by the president and confirmed by the Senate. The agency is then overseen by a board of directors, mostly comprising directors of other executive agencies. This setup provides the organization some protection from politically motivated congressional interference and short-termism. Within the MCC are departments with different sectoral responsibilities and specializations, a point examined in greater detail below.[69]

Funding comes from the MCA, which is administered by the MCC. Project proposals come from the recipient government, which, in turn, typically uses a series of public participation mechanisms to develop a draft "compact" between all stakeholders. The compact is then approved by the MCC. Implementers can be U.S. citizens or recipient country nationals. The implementation is monitored by a special unit called a Millennium Challenge Authority (confusingly also called an MCA, and it is this meaning that is used for the rest of this section), which is set up by the host government, generally headed by an international expert hired by the MCC, and staffed by host country nationals. The role of the MCC (that is, those in Washington) is limited to technical assistance with compact formulation and oversight related to disbursement and M&E.

In theory, the MCC has a very limited role in the selection and monitoring of the projects constituting the compact. The idea is that the recipient government must take "ownership" of the activities and that anything imposed by the MCC would weaken the ownership incentives. For any given compact, there is a set of activities, each with its own set of local beneficiaries, national and foreign consultant implementers, and host government monitors. In practice, the MCC provides rather substantial support for the M&E component of the compact's projects, since this component must be designed into the front end of each activity in order to provide prospective assessment.

---

69. There are departments on agriculture and other key economic sectors, on economic analysis, and on monitoring and evaluation, among others.

The MCC gaming concept operates at two explicit levels. The first is among countries vying for MCC eligibility within income groups (similar to those of the World Bank). The second level is entered once a country is awarded a compact. At this level the players include a potentially large number of special political, business, and civil society interest groups, which compete to get their pet project included as part of the compact—that is, they take an active role in project identification. This compact formulation process is managed by a number of compact committees, including those that focus on project identification, M&E plan, rate-of-return analysis, and general coordination. To these players must be added the host government, with its participating agencies, and the MCA, an MCC-funded agency of local staff selected by the recipient government to manage the compact implementation process, including putting the M&E plan into practice.

COST AND TIME FRAME

As of this writing, eleven countries have received compacts. These include (with the compact's total value in millions in parentheses) Armenia ($236), Benin ($307), Cape Verde ($110), El Salvador ($461), Georgia ($295), Ghana ($547), Honduras ($215), Madagascar ($110), Mali ($461), Nicaragua ($175), and Vanuatu ($66). It is apparent that the funding for these compacts varies widely. Unlike World Bank projects (IDA excepted), these compacts are funded by grants, not loans. The value of the compact is roughly determined by the type and size of the projects proposed by the country, though there must be some indicative limits imposed by the MCC. Simple regression suggests that, with the exception of island economies (which receive amounts out of proportion to their size), per capita compact sizes are well explained by population, starting with a fixed value of $67 million and decreasing by about $2.60 per additional inhabitant.[70]

With most of the administrative support provided by the MCA, the in-country management team of local project staff selected by the recipient government, the implementation compliance burden on the recipient government is, in theory, light. In the case of Vanuatu, administrative and M&E costs are budgeted at $3.63 million and $1.37 million, respectively (about 5 percent and 2 percent of compact value, respectively). For El Salvador, administration and M&E together come to $44.9 million (or about 10 percent of compact value). To support these efforts (and an expansion to twenty country compacts by the end of 2007), the MCC in Washington planned to increase staffing from 175 to 300 in 2007 (45 percent of the MCC administrative budget). For a total level of committed funds of $1.7 billion, the annual administrative budget in 2006 was estimated at $75 million (MCC 2006), or about 4.5 percent.

---

70. Compact value per capita (in millions) = 67.5 + (222.9 * island dummy) – (2.59 * population), where $N = 11$ and adjusted $R^2 = 0.958$.

Compacts must be completed within a five-year period and, if successful, are open to renewal.

RULES OF THE GAME

The methodology for allocating the substantial funds managed by the MCC is based on an explicit tournament (game) and (at least) two subsidiary games (which, of course, comprise a series of subgames). The tournament relates to the process for qualifying as an MCC candidate, while the two other games relate to the compact creation and implementation processes.

No doubt the most innovative part of the MCC process is that it explicitly uses a tournament mechanism to identify candidate countries. A country must score above the median performer of its group to be eligible for funding.[71] The median performer is quantitatively determined by the aggregation of sixteen independently measured, objective indicators related to governance and economic and social performance.[72] In addition, the successful candidate country must exceed a preset threshold on a corruption indicator. The country must remain above the median in order to continue to receive MCC assistance.

Once a country has become a candidate for MCC funding, it enters into a public compact with the MCC that includes a multiyear plan for achieving development objectives and that identifies the responsibilities of each partner in achieving those objectives. In practice this requires the candidate to go through an elaborate process of consultation with stakeholder groups across the country in order to develop its own set of projects. This may be seen as a subsidiary game to the main intercountry tournament since these groups engage in an intense political struggle for a piece of the action. The only selection restrictions the MCC places on project choice are that it must directly address at least one of the MCC's objectives (see above), be assessed as feasible, and be within MCC funding limits for the country.

A second requirement relates to monitoring and evaluation. The project design and implementation plan for each component within the compact must be amenable (and subjected) to rigorous outside monitoring and evaluation.[73] The M&E plan essentially has two parts. One part consists of a set of extremely clear and transparent statutory indicator milestones and final targets related to compact performance that must be attained or else the host country is in international legal violation of the bilateral agreement. The other part consists of an impact evaluation plan, in which the default methodology is randomized treatment assignment. This plan is developed (in theory) in conjunction with the detailed

71. Countries are divided into income categories, so, to use a sports analogy, countries compete within their "leagues" or tiers.

72. At the time of this writing, an environmental indicator had just been added.

73. The expectation is that, where feasible, randomized evaluation methods would be used (MCC 2005).

implementation plan of the compact's activities so that the evaluation is properly prospective (as recommended in section 2.4). For these reasons the impact evaluation plan is primarily the work of international experts, though significant attention is given to the formation of a local M&E team.

Once the compact has been approved and implementation is under way, a second subsidiary game begins. This relates to the quality of implementation and the degree to which the recipient country feels motivated to ensure that the M&E plans are executed and the targets are met. If there is genuine ownership of the compact, then there is reason to believe that sincere efforts will be made. The MCC endeavors to make ownership incentive compatible by explicitly making future MCC funding contingent on the application of "best efforts" as assessed by the MCC, presumably with major input from M&E occurring throughout the compact's implementation.

REWARDS

MCC funds are provided to qualifying countries as grants, so there is no interest and monies are not repaid. This makes the already rather large amount of funds offered to a country all the more attractive. On top of this, the funds are not earmarked but (with a few weak restrictions) are used for purposes democratically determined by the qualifying countries themselves. Examples of what the funds have been used for include large-scale irrigation, airport expansion, and bridge and road network upgrading.

STATED OUTCOMES

It is now well known that the MCC has had a series of teething pains, not unusual for a new organization with such ambitious goals.[74] Now, however, the flow of signed compacts is growing—there are 11 as of this writing—and at least 10 of them have been tendered for independent, international M&E. Until these assessments are made publicly available in about five years, it will not be fully possible to know how this very innovative approach will fare.

PIJC COMPONENTS

The MCC system incorporates most of the PIJC incentive mechanisms. It uses indicators for performance baselines for candidate eligibility and benchmarking as part of M&E. It contains a tournament in that eligibility depends on both the candidate's performance and others' performance. Moreover, a threshold score is

---

74. One such glitch was the slow pace of disbursement, which some say was the reason the first head of the organization was eventually replaced. I believe some of the problem partly was caused by a near obsession with doing everything in a state-of-the-art way, the institutional imperative not to push money at the recipients, and a desire not to repeat any of the perceived "errors" of USAID. Likewise, there seems to have been a fear that a fraud or governance scandal might compromise the future of the organization as a result of congressional meddling or presidential backpedaling.

required on the corruption indicator, making this application a mixed tournament design. The projects that constitute the compact are selected by the recipient country, so project selection is clearly demand driven. Monitoring and evaluation are a critical component of the MCC process. Finally, the MCC dispenses output-based technical assistance (more or less) to the recipient country in that the technical assistance comes once the country qualifies as an MCC candidate; similarly, additional technical assistance comes as the projects in the compact evolve and meet performance-monitored targets. However, while these components are all found in the MCC aid configuration, they do not all operate in each of the three games identified above, a situation that, according to the assessment below, affects their ultimate effectiveness.

ASSESSMENT

Perhaps the biggest doubt surrounding the MCC enterprise is that it is not clear that the availability of relatively untied MCC funding acts as a lure for pre-candidate reform.[75] Rather, it seems to be a windfall to those countries that, for other reasons, intentionally or unintentionally raise their MCC indicator scores above the telltale median required for funding consideration. This peculiarity may also be a sign of the times: the tide has definitely turned toward the view that donors must only supply funding to cost-effective projects and that this priority takes precedence over project opportunities from less capable countries, which unfortunately tend to be the more needy ones.[76] On the other hand, this tournament approach does achieve the goal of identifying more capable target countries.

The tournament for MCC eligibility also suffers from the standard effects of using country classifications. The MCC uses these to create a level playing field so that countries compete to exceed the median score of countries at a similar level of development. Unfortunately, this means that a country near the upper limit of its group (for example, Cape Verde) has an incentive to moderate its growth performance so as not to loose its favored MCC status. To wit, by being the highest above the median score for one group, a country may then "graduate" to become a below-median performer in the next higher group.

One of the most interesting surprises from the assessment of the MCC program is that while the MCC process explicitly includes a tournament where countries compete on the basis of their precandidacy policy performance, the actual allocation of MCC funds is *not* competitive. Once a country qualifies for MCC funding, the quality of its proposed projects is not directly pitted against that of

75. This point was also voiced by Stuti Khemani of the World Bank, personal communication, 2007.

76. It may have been the Bush administration's unwritten policy to separate countries into those capable of meeting MCC qualifications and the rest, to be served by a reoriented USAID, which is already shifting its focus toward "MCC threshold" countries, in addition to "fragile states" and disaster relief (USAID 2005).

project proposals from other eligible countries.[77] On the other hand, the MCC does use benefit-cost analysis to help in the selection of approved projects that have been identified by the qualifying country. Thus one might view the within-country allocation of funds as a tournament among proposed projects, with the ranking based on the economic rate of return. But there is no competitive pressure to exert effort once the compact has been signed.

While the efficacy of incentives to stimulate precandidacy policy reforms remains an open question, the incentives for performing well on a compact also appear rather weak, since they basically only depend on the success of the compact process to generate a feeling of ownership for the recipients. In particular, the incentives on the project implementation side of the MCC process are not much different from any other standard aid delivery vehicles—even though the compacts include milestone monitoring of output-oriented targets.

First, a project's impact will be necessarily limited over the somewhat short time horizons of a compact, so pinning down its efficacy will be somewhat speculative.[78] Second, note that the enforcement mechanism is time inconsistent.[79] For example, how does the MCC know that maximum efforts have been expended in the case of mediocre performance? In this case, funding tranches are likely to continue anyway unless there is outright failure or fraud midproject. This especially became the case given the increased pressure to place the MCC funds following the replacement of Paul Applegarth, who had been the MCC's chief executive officer. The pressure to continue funding the activity is likely to be strong, both for the overseeing staff as well as organizationally. What about the case of outright failure? If the recipient continues to exceed median country scores for its category, then once a new political administration takes over—whether through revolution or democratic due process—it is likely that the compact will be renegotiated rather than terminated. One need only look at the muddied signal created from several countries that have not satisfied all the MCC conditions (for instance, Georgia with regard to corruption) but have nonetheless been awarded MCC funding.[80]

77. This point has also been made to me by Lael Brainard; see Zinnes (2006).

78. Since compacts have a five-year duration and time is required to launch implementation as well as administer M&E, when all is said and done, the effective impact period available for the various project components probably averages between one and three years. Still, this is generally a much longer period than that used by other donors.

79. Time inconsistency refers to the property of a decision rule regarding how to act in the future, which while reasonable to make ex ante, is not rational to carry out once the future has arrived. For example, a threat that is not credible is time inconsistent. In the present case, while it is rational for the MCC to threaten to cut off a country for poor compact performance, it is not rational (nor politically expedient) to do so ex post once a country has exhibited poor compact performance.

80. A possible explanation for Georgia's luck is ironically recognition of one "limitation" of the performance-based approach: it is based on performance! A new regime requires time to develop a reputation—or, in this case, higher scores on the MCC indicators.

Another novel MCC requirement is that compact design use benefit-cost analysis to remove some subjectivity from selecting projects for inclusion in a compact. While this is surely a good thing, it carries several risks. First, benefit-cost analysis tends to focus on technical coefficients and is necessarily ex ante. Hence it is no substitute for rigorous impact evaluation, which is both prospective *and* assesses outcomes. Moreover, technical coefficients invariably miss the idiosyncratic shocks that plague project implementation. The MCC tries to compensate by performing "sensitivity analysis." While this is commendable, the resulting analysis is neither quantitatively risk based nor is it typically able to foresee where to allow for *implementation* glitches. This has a bearing on project incentives since the reliance on benefit-cost analysis may be interpreted as a compensation device for the time-inconsistency problem described above, and may actually act to *reduce* the government's sense of accountability in project selection since projects must pass the benefit-cost "test" to be approved by the MCC.

One consequence of the incentive structure of compacts is that the MCC still needs to play a prominent role in M&E—even where there is an ex-ante contractual agreement to use a statistically verifiable evaluation methodology (such as randomized trials). This is because compacts are not de facto performance based. Incorporating heavy public participation in the design and monitoring of compact projects does not eliminate this consequence of the incentive structure.

Within the MCC are departments with different sectoral interests and specializations. Interestingly, there appears to be some competition among them to influence which sectors a compacts addresses.[81] This can play out in spite of the use of benefit-cost analysis to evaluate (ex-ante) project proposals since the MCC frequently provides countries technical assistance for project identification if requested. So, for example, if the MCC sends out its agricultural staff, these experts are unlikely to identify industrial projects. Hence the use of "objective" indicators does not completely eliminate discretion from project selection. This is a consequence of basing funding decisions on ex-ante proposals instead of on ex-post performance.

In conclusion, while much has been done to design a system to select recipient countries, in reality, the system to align recipient and MCC objectives by placing ownership squarely on the former is not as incentive compatible as it first seems. Significant monitoring and intervention by the MCC still remain necessary during project execution, as is true for a standard donor program.

IMPACT OF INITIAL CONDITIONS

Perhaps the best way to assess the role of initial conditions is to consider the donor and the recipient separately. In the case of the donor, several characteristics seem important. One is the ability to have a flexible yet accountable organizational

81. Observations based on personal experience with the MCC.

structure that can tailor the compact incentives to the conditions prevalent in a particular country. Another is the ability to pay salaries in excess of those of the GS system, which constrains USAID. These salaries—together with a reputation for trying to do things rigorously and right—have allowed the organization to attract a high-quality, young, and hard-working staff. This youthfulness may contribute an open-mindedness to new ways of implementing aid. Still, given the MCC's short track record—and in spite of its hands-off rhetoric—eligible countries have had a tough time inferring what type of projects will pass muster. A successful project, therefore, requires that MCC staff be able to nudge the recipient government in as neutral a way as possible to find "good" project proposals that also meet MCC acceptance criteria. Given the rivalry among MCC departments, this can be a challenge. Finally, one should add that having a huge budget to give away is probably necessary to get the recipient to go through the extremely protracted—often requiring several years—and often methodologically arcane compact process.

On the recipient side, the most obvious initial condition (to receive MCC funding) is the ability to exceed (and continue to exceed) the median score on the MCC good governance indicators. Regarding the initial conditions required for a successful implementation of projects within the compact, this obviously depends on the nature of each project and the extent to which the projects selected have truly come from and not simply been accepted by the government.

Finally, another important determinant of compact success will likely be the quality of the impact evaluation plan, which ideally should be prospectively integrated into project design and carefully developed ex ante by outside, independent experts. This relates to relevant initial conditions because most countries give short shrift to the M&E plan, considering it a waste of otherwise productive funds, and do not have local skilled experts for the MCA to hire to implement the plan. The less these factors are the case, the more likely is project success. Moreover, these factors reinforce the MCC's own institutional ambivalence to M&E, with its M&E department carrying little weight in project design and implementation. In particular, the MCC sector staff does not treat M&E as an integral part of project design but as an add-on, which means that evaluations—and therefore performance incentives—are not as powerful as they could be.

SUSTAINABILITY AND SCALABILITY

There are several aspects of the MCC concept that affect sustainability and scalability. Consider first the sustainability of the reforms a country implements to attain MCC candidacy status. This raises the empirical question of whether the lure of MCC eligibility motivates reforms at the national level. Be that as it may, excepting the unexpected occurrence of a coup or natural disaster, the highly aggregated nature of the indicators the MCC uses to assess country eligibility suggests that rescission of those reforms is unlikely.

Next consider the sustainability of the outcome of a compact's projects. Surely the MCC's demand for a high degree of participatory development in the compact's projects across the segments of the candidate's society augers well for sustainability. So does the use of compact milestones, M&E, and the MCC's radically hands-off approach for selecting and approving projects to include in a compact (an approach intended to stimulate local ownership). Finally, conducting interventions only in well-governed countries should prima facie improve a donor's track record. However, while the MCC uses a tournament incentive structure to select recipient countries, once a country is selected and its compact is approved, the incentives for compact performance are much less powerful. As pointed out above, it would be time inconsistent for the MCC to threaten to disqualify a country because a previous government administration did not make good on a negotiated compact. Admittedly, this discussion is all theoretical and speculative. I am simply not aware of any systematic, rigorous comparative study of the sustainability of activities funded within an MCC compact versus those resulting from a more standard approach.[82]

Similar arguments apply regarding scalability. The MCC selection process is eminently scalable, both in the number of competing countries as well as in the number of indicators upon which countries must compete. The only real obstacle is the MCC's internal capacity to negotiate and monitor compacts. Whether the individual projects included in compacts to date are themselves more scalable on average than projects developed under other donor mechanisms is an open question.[83] The orientation toward randomized impact evaluation means that compact project designs explicitly include multiple treatment and control groups, which should make it easier to scale up. On the other hand, the large budgets involved in MCC projects and the high degree of public debate a compact entails (an MCC requirement) may, if anything, make the MCC approach *less* scalable than other projects.

4.2.3 Morocco: MEPI Pillars

While this case illustrates a stillborn application of a full-fledged PIJC, it nonetheless provides several lessons regarding donor interest and project selection modalities. For this reason it is included as an example here, and additional details of its application are provided in appendix C.[84]

82. It is not even clear whether such a comparison should be done against other sponsors' grant programs, projects (regardless of the financing method), or projects of the same type and size (for example, drip irrigation).

83. To the best of my knowledge, this issue has not been researched. From personal experience with the agricultural component of the Cape Verde compact, I have reason to believe that the project ideas being tested out would be both scalable and replicable, especially if monitoring and evaluation were carried out in a rigorous way that allows for learning, as is officially claimed.

84. This section draws heavily from Meagher and Zinnes (2004) and the Center for Institutional Reform and the Informal Sector (IRIS 2005).

STATEMENT OF THE PROBLEM

There were several motivations for the eventual formulation of a PIJC for Morocco. First, the initial conceptual development of a Moroccan application was requested by the UN Industrial Development Organization (UNIDO) as a result of frustration at the inability of its own Investment Promotion Office to generate bankable SME projects outside the major cities of the country. UNIDO attributed this failure to the lamentable level of local governance and its negative impact on the business and investment environment. Second, the IRIS Center of the University of Maryland recognized the value of the PIJC methodology as an effective means to address the thorny issues (four "pillars") facing the U.S. Department of State's Middle East Partnership Initiative (MEPI), a group giving grants for collaborative proposals from U.S.–Middle Eastern nonprofit organizations. The four pillars were

—the problematic position of women in Morocco, particularly as an underutilized economic resource and source of entrepreneurship;

—the simmering crisis of youth unemployment in the countryside;

—the need for greater "region-wide economic and employment growth driven by private sector expansion and entrepreneurship"; and

—the lack of "an expanded public space where democratic voices can be heard in the political process . . . and [where] there is respect for the rule of law".[85]

OBJECTIVE

The goal was to organize a competition among municipalities (communes) in two regions of Morocco. The purpose of the competition was to improve local governance and the business environment through the mechanism of a tournament that encouraged the communes to carry out the necessary reforms. The program would strengthen newly enfranchised local governments and accelerate women's integration in the economic sphere in their own jurisdictions.

SPONSOR AND IMPLEMENTERS

The donors would be the U.S. State Department (through MEPI) for project design and implementation coordination and analysis, and the UNIDO Investment Promotion Office (UNIDO-IPO) in Rome for technical assistance. The IRIS Center was the main implementer. IRIS's main Moroccan partner was the Moroccan government's Center for Regional Investment (CRI) for Doukkala-Abda, which would host the project team. Moroccan project partners included Development Associations of Safi and of El Jadida, the National Association of SMEs, the Moroccan Association of Women Entrepreneurs, and the Union of Moroccan Women.

85. U.S. Department of State, "MEPI Standing Program Announcement (May 2004)" (http://mepi.state.gov/27603.htm).

PLAYERS

The project would implement two tournaments in the Doukkala-Abda region of Morocco, home to two provinces comprising eighty-nine communes. At the lower level, communes in each province would compete. At the higher level, the two provinces would compete for the best average performance of their communes.

COST AND TIME FRAME

While funds were never actually disbursed, the projected budget was to be provided from the following sources: MEPI, $900,000; UNIDO, $250,000 (for cofinancing of the tournament's rewards and in-tournament technical assistance); University of Maryland, $150,000 (cost sharing); CRI for Doukkala-Abda, $50,000; and participating Moroccan NGOs, $50,000 (cost sharing). In addition, the competition built on about $250,000 of IRIS's prior work, funded by UNIDO, to meet with Moroccan officials, conduct some twenty focus group meetings in communes across Morocco, and design the tournament program described here.

The project was planned for seventeen months, starting in late 2006. More time (an extra seven months) and more resources (about 15 percent more) would have permitted a wider competition (and therefore greater impact) and the addition of more complex tasks.

RULES OF THE GAME

The tournament among communes focused on policies, services, and governance practices that relate to the climate for entrepreneurship and investment. The project made explicit what is implicit: firms have choices about where to locate and localities make choices that affect the willingness of their own citizens or outsiders to engage in entrepreneurship.[86] For example, local councils "decide" on the ease of business licensing, degree of public participation in communal decision-making, quality of public spaces, and investment in certain infrastructure. By introducing structure and measures of outcomes to such competition, the project harnesses the power of this competition toward the MEPI pillars, trains local officials and enterprises, and rewards localities that were more proactive. By establishing quantitative measures of accomplishment for each task a commune implemented, the program also would have permitted targeting of donor assistance and rigorous evaluation of outcomes.

At the level of the region, there was a de facto supertournament: at the end of the tournaments within each province, the province with the highest average score also would become a winner, with its local government receiving rewards analogous to those given to the winning communal governments. The purpose of this innovation was to stimulate the proactive cooperation of higher-level government,

---

86. This insight is really just a variation of Tiebout (1956) applied to firms.

which could contribute to better outcomes by helping to coordinate intercommunal tasks dictated by the competition and by addressing province-level obstacles in the business environment.

The focus of the tournament was a menu of concrete tasks associated with each MEPI pillar, from which communes could choose to achieve on-the-ground outcomes. Tasks on the menu derived from economic theory, policy research in Morocco and other countries, and previous focus group interviews with over a dozen communal councils and with Moroccan entrepreneurs. At the start of the project, IRIS would have used additional local focus groups and stakeholder surveys organized by the project's team of Moroccan partner associations to further tailor and fine-tune the task menu, calibrate the reward schedule, and orient the pre- and posttournament public relations campaigns. The project team then would have organized an interjurisdictional competition that would

—stimulate communes in each province of Doukkala-Abda to voluntarily compete against other communes within that province to implement tasks to make themselves more attractive to domestic and foreign investors, as well as to facilitate the economic integration of women and youth;

—use advances in survey techniques and second- and third-generation indicators to establish outcome measures for each reform task;

—collect baseline and endline (pre- and posttournament) data for each commune;

—make technical assistance available to communes (that exceed a threshold of initial reform) during the tournament to enable communes to implement reform;

—offer additional rewards to the private sector in communes that are most successful in the tournament; and

—develop and run pre- and posttournament public relations campaigns, the former for encouraging tournament participation and the latter for dissemination of results and as part of a "blame or brag" signal, alerting investors to laggard communes and promoting investment in laudable ones.

The project's implementation strategy specifically proposed the use of communication and bright incentives to encourage local parties to overcome differences, and used public hearings, council votes, and public letters to government officials to ensure stakeholder buy-in and reduce the risk to local decisionmakers of getting too far out in front of their constituencies. This had the extra benefit of increasing the legitimacy—and thus, presumably, the sustainability—of the reforms undertaken more than might otherwise be the case through direct donor negotiation.

In sum, the project would have encouraged a greater exercise of and adherence to new democratic practices for participation in local decisionmaking, which should have led to more effective—and therefore sustainable—changes in the business and investment environment, increasing opportunities for all citizens—including women and youth. The project design also leveraged donor funds since a fixed amount of funding would stimulate many more municipalities to improve than would the standard "contractual" approach.[87]

REWARDS

While some rewards that flow from the steps aimed at improving governance and the business climate would have been immediate, many would have occurred after the period of the project. Recognizing this, the project design offered rewards during the tournament. First, communes that were able to realize governance improvements exceeding a modest threshold (often "stroke-of-the-pen" reforms) would receive technical assistance during the tournament period. This would be in the form of a two-day workshop for each task category, held in each province, in which representatives from all communes exceeding the threshold would be invited to participate. Second, top-scoring communes (the number of which depended on the rewards budget) would receive a variety of modest in-kind rewards, such as technical assistance (for commune administration as well as for SMEs in a priority sector for the commune), investment promotion, access to international trade shows, and technology tours abroad for local firms. Though these rewards were necessarily modest, they would help motivate the private sector to encourage (pressure) the commune's council to be diligent and progress in the tasks of the tournament.

Third, a Michelin-type star classification would award placers with an explicit program of national and international publicity to attract investors. This reward would provide the placing communes with more visible, immediate recognition of accomplishments that would have paid off over a longer time period. This visibility would have accelerated communication to both local and other entrepreneurs about the localities that were distinguishing themselves by their concrete improvements.

STATED OUTCOMES

Given that the rewards and tasks were suggested by the potential players, that the representative of King Mohammed VI and the governor in the participating region were strongly supportive, and that the rewards were to be calibrated using economic gaming experiments, the expectation was that a substantial number— perhaps one third—of communes would engage in some level of reform. Of course, since the U.S. State Department turned down the funding of this application, all these purported "outcomes" are pure speculation.

PIJC COMPONENTS

For obvious reasons, this project contained all the components described in chapter 2 for a full-fledged PIJC.

87. See appendix D for a theoretical treatment of the leverage property of tournaments.

ASSESSMENT

Since it is perhaps of limited use to evaluate an activity that did not take place, this assessment instead addresses the following question: if the Moroccan project design was so clever, so good a fit, had such great cofinancing, brought to bear so much local knowledge, and had so much Moroccan support, *why* was it ultimately rejected by the donors (MEPI, the World Bank, and USAID)?[88]

Though addressing this question is one of the reasons for presenting this case, I do not pretend to have the definitive answer, only some intuitions based on past personal experience. First, the donors operate in a world of "stovepipes," that is, their institutional and intramural departmental substantive mandates are very specific. For example, if a donor environmental department's project to reduce scrap tire waste begins to create a recycling industry, that project may run afoul of the same donor's industrial development department. Thus UNIDO's mandate to promote SMEs by improving the governance side of the business and investment environment ran afoul of those at UNIDO who felt that governance was the World Bank's purview, not UNIDO's.

Second, some donors, in spite of their lip service to the contrary, are reluctant to innovate beyond the margin. A donor will quite sensibly ask, "Where has this million-dollar approach been tried before?" If the answer is "nowhere," then even though its individual components have a well-known track record, the donor remains skeptical. This is the case even when the donor has routinely spent hundreds of millions of dollars on activities that have a track record, albeit a reliably checkered one. Such a response is not always due to individuals within the organization but rather is part of the institutionalized culture of big bureaucracies. MEPI, for example, is run by a very staid agency, the U.S. Department of State. It is used to funding grants for U.S. NGOs to train Middle Eastern academics or SME entrepreneurs. A project that instead trains these actors through empowerment by addressing regulatory obstacles impeding the exercise of entrepreneurship may have been simply too radical or perhaps too complicated for their project reviewers to contemplate.[89]

Third, donors often lose interest or fail to follow through in activities that take time to bring up to speed or require several phases; they tend to like quick results, such as those a business development services training session provides. This loss of interest is sometimes the result of an unstable management environment, which causes departmental objectives and strategies to shift over the project cycle or senior staff to periodically transfer elsewhere in the organization during the project. Such was the case with the Moroccan project: changes in political leadership in Italy affected UNIDO-IPO, leading to the replacement of those who had been

88. Several unsuccessful attempts over the period 2006–08 were made to obtain World Bank funding, including through its internal discretionary trust funds.

89. The author has actually been on project proposal evaluation panels for MEPI. The quality and degree of innovation embodied in these proposals was rather unexceptional, to be kind.

supporting a PIJC intervention to empower local government in Morocco with others who had little interest in the subject.

Finally—and there are many other reasons the reader no doubt could add to this litany— projects often need support from certain quarters to be accepted. For example, when MEPI failed to fund its Moroccan proposal, IRIS approached several different departments and groups within the World Bank, both substantive and geographic. Many offered to sponsor ("permit") seminars on the idea, but none was ever organized.

Likewise, getting an initiative implemented by a big donor requires being in the right place at the right time and knowing the right people. A senior manager of a large donor doing governance work in North Africa told IRIS that while he thought the proposal was impressive, he would not do it because his group was already overextended and in any event would only do it if the donor's mission in Rabat required it. The donor's mission, it turns out, was tied to the agenda of the Ministry of Finance, which had no interest in SME governance in rural areas. The Moroccan project's supporters would need to lobby the Ministry of Finance to request that the donor consider the project. This may all be as it should, but that is the point: getting a donor to adopt an activity requires a strong "project champion" from certain quarters of the organization. It would be fascinating to compare, for example, the experiences of those at the World Bank who successfully elicited support for the Nigerian scorecard project, the Russian grant tournament, or the Kecamatan Development Program in Indonesia.

IMPACT OF INITIAL CONDITIONS

Morocco proved to be an exceptionally propitious location to implement a PIJC. First and foremost, interviews throughout the two provinces showed that there was strong motivation within the communal councils to take up the challenge of reform. This is partly attributable to the recent passage of devolution legislation to increase the statutory and fiscal powers of local government, as part of the new king's effort to create a democracy in Morocco, and the inexperience of these newly elected councilmen (some of whom were illiterate), which meant they were hungry for ideas and support to distinguish themselves to their constituencies and to the king's representative in the province (the *wali*). Second, due to the long-standing familiarity and relationships the IRIS team had with experts in Morocco, a tremendous amount of local knowledge was available for the project's implementation. This is reflected in the quality and quantity of Moroccan NGOs who lined up as cost-sharing collaborators with IRIS for the initiative. Third and partly due to the preceding factor, the governor of the region was a strong proponent of the intervention, offering his own concrete suggestions for tasks to include in the menu of options. Finally, the king had recently developed a chain of "one-stop" investment promotion shops—one for each region—that were anxious to (individually) distinguish themselves to the king as well as for their region.

Of course, I can only speculate about sustainability and scalability since the project was never completed. First, the strong communal, provincial, and regional government demand to participate in this voluntary effort speaks volumes for the likelihood that their ownership of the reforms would make them successful and sustainable. Second, the likely reform tasks were suggested from the bottom up and would have required no further higher-level support to be sustained. Finally, the close (coincidental) similarities between this initiative and the World Bank's Russian project (described above), which appears to have been both successful and sustainable, suggests similar outcomes for this project in Morocco.

During the early stages of project design, many provinces showed an interest in participating. Moreover, UNIDO-IPO debated whether to pilot the project on the national level or on the provincial level. It was clear to them that the fixed costs of project development would be the same. In the end, the constant returns-to-scale nature of the reward and indicator measurement requirements dictated that, given the previously established budget available, the provincial pilot go first. UNIDO-IPO's ultimate goal was to use the approach for municipalities across whole countries within the Middle East. I mention these comments to suggest that at the time UNIDO viewed the approach as being highly scalable. Again, evidence from the World Bank's Russian project appears to substantiate this claim.

Of course, these points attempt to address *product* sustainability. *Process* sustainability—that is, the likelihood that future tournament rounds would have occurred—is even more speculative. Still, it is my experience that while donors are timid about initiating innovation, they love to jump on the bandwagon once an approach has shown success—witness, for example, the enthusiasm demonstrated for funding red-tape analysis and microfinance applications.

5

Review of Other Relevant Experience

I n the PIJC cases presented in chapters 3 and 4, the operative competitive mechanisms were either a certification or a tournament. Those applications exhibited many of the desirable PIJC design characteristics shown in table 2-2. The goal in examining those cases was to assess the efficacy and feasibility of the PIJC approach with actual real-world applications. For each case, I sought to infer whether any observed weaknesses were due to an inherent problem with the approach, the absence of certain PIJC design characteristics, or other causes associated with particular initial conditions or poor implementation.[1]

As outlined in section 2.5, a second tier of the strategy for assessing the PIJC approach is to examine the success of projects containing only one or a few PIJC components. Such an analysis can increase confidence in the feasibility of a full PIJC application by confirming whether its individual components already have a reputable track record.[2] Therefore, this chapter provides a nonexhaustive compendium of past and current applications across diverse substantive fields, as summarized in table 5-1. The table entries are organized alphabetically by field of implementation and are described in more detail in appendix A. Items were selected for inclusion based only on whether they contained a PIJC component

---

1. "Poor" in the sense that the PIJC could have been feasibly implemented under the conditions present but was not due to idiosyncratic but remediable errors.
2. It would also permit one to ask how the outcomes of those applications might have improved with additional PIJC components—and whether such additions would have been feasible.

Table 5-1. Summary of Initiatives with PIJC Components, by Substantive Category

Sector	Substantive project activity	PIJC component(s)	Assessment
Agriculture	Improving irrigation	Performance-based incentives, internalizes asymmetric information	Output-based aid to increase coverage of Paraguay's *aguateros*[a]; deemed "successful" by the World Bank
	Animal beauty pageants	Information revelation, tournament	Successful way for breeders to pick their inseminators or stock
Aid effectiveness	Donor (such as IDA, ILO, MCC) aid allocations	Competitions and tournaments, often with indicators	Sixteen public expenditure management indicators are used to evaluate progress in heavily indebted poor countries, and grants by IDA depend on such progress[a]; reduces arbitrariness of aid allocation.
	Linking donor budget support to fiscal performance (EC)	Indicators, incentive aligned	See box 1-1 for details. Requires high-quality (reliable) official data
	Millennium Development Goals; 1995 Copenhagen Declaration	Benchmark targets	Focal points of concrete and broad social and economic targets for donors to aspire to for increasing the quality of life in developing countries; so far, these have been mostly just inspirational.
	Policy reform aid conditionality	Certification with reward	Very mixed history (Svensson 2003); little local ownership in reforms, which are often not sustainable
	GlobalGiving Foundation[a]	Pecuniary certification	Certified development microprojects compete for web donations
	Commitment to Development Index (Center for Global Development)	Benchmark rating	Three-year-old grading system of rich countries' multisectoral policy friendliness toward poor countries

Business	Conglomerates investment allocation from retained earnings	Tournament	Ayala Corporation, one of the most successful in the Philippines, extracts funds from own firms for use with its firms with the best profit opportunities.
	Consumer Reports, Michelin guides	Information revelation, "voting with feet"	Very effective, as evidenced by long number of years these have been profitably operating
	Corporate Governance Scores—(Standard and Poor's)[a]	Voluntary, uses benchmark indicators, competition	Triggers strategic behavior by companies who want high ratings to attract investors; investors compare firm scores.
	UK supermarket sector Race to the Top project	Accountability benchmarking, participatory development, tournament	Tournament among supermarkets, in collaboration with NGOs, to improve firms' social consciousness standards
	Inward investment promotion at the country level	Tournament	Poland and Czech Republic compete for Toyota plant, using incentive packages and country characteristics.[a]
Education	Michigan Universal Tuition Tax Credit program[a] plus Michigan School-of-Choice program (charter schools)[a]	Benchmark indicators, tournament among districts	Tax credit issued if parent uses private school; School-of-Choice program allows parents to select school type.
	Canadian Education Freedom Index	Benchmark	Measures by province the freedom parents have to educate their children if the public system is unsatisfactory to them.
	Montgomery County, Md. Choice process[a]	Government-managed (limited) competition	After exam, students choose (public) high school based on school-specific academic specialization; program has been in service many years.
	"Cash on Delivery"[a] concept of Center for Global Development	Pecuniary certification	Donor gives $100 per child certified as attaining standard education; versions of this concept have been fielded in other sectors and several countries (for example, Progresa in Mexico).
	Public-private partnerships	Participatory development	See discussion of charter schools in chapter 1.

(continued)

Table 5-1. *Summary of Initiatives with PIJC Components, by Substantive Category (Continued)*

Sector	Substantive project activity	PIJC component(s)	Assessment
Environment	Green labeling (such as Rainforest Alliance standard for export agriculture[a] and Forest Stewardship Council seal[a])	Benchmarking, certification, voluntary disclosure	Sustainability of timber sources or agricultural practices; several competing certification programs, which can blunt signal to consumer. Rainforest Alliance has 10 million acres certified and worldwide certification network.
	Green Globe Project[a]	Benchmarking and certification services on four alternative standards	Focus on travel and tourism companies and communities to maintain good environmental and social practices
	Blue Flag Project[a]	Certification reward for local action, public awareness campaign	Awarded to beaches and marinas; builds on competition to attract tourists
	Cleanest and Greenest Town Award (Philippines)[a]	Tournament, cash prize plus citation	Run since 1999 by the local government of Samar Province and is open to all municipalities there
	Clean Development–Joint Implementation mechanisms in Kyoto Protocol	Public-private partnerships stimulated by cap-and-trade emissions system	Requires country buy-in to Kyoto process; some carbon sequestration projects are controversial due to questionable long-term effectiveness or difficulty in monitoring.
Finance and banking	Microfinance	Peer selection-monitoring, benchmarking, reputation creation, dynamic rewards, voluntary participation	Banco Sol, Bolivia; Grameen Bank, Bangladesh. Transaction costs can be high, leading some programs to require subsidies. Recently, lack of regulatory supervision has led to some interest rate gouging and unethical repayment pressures.
	Venture capitalism	Participatory development, risk sharing, peer monitoring, competition, baseline and benchmark indicators	Shown to be preferred financing method for high-risk start-ups; like pharmaceutical research, it works best for firms with many such projects so that the successful ones "pay" for failures.
	Moody's and Morningstar investment rating service	Benchmark indicators	Successful; taken very seriously by investors

Health	Changemakers Innovation Award (Center for Global Development)[a]	Tournament; also has NGO-business partnership award	Actual solutions for low-income or marginalized populations, ranging from health education and prevention to health financing, health care delivery, or pharmaceutical development
	Mosquito netting programs	Information provision, voluntary	Poor track record when free, since "free" has bad connotation for users; when sold, acceptance high
	Research and development contests	Tournament with rewards	Gates Foundation race for malaria and HIV vaccines
Infrastructure and service delivery	Buenos Aires water and sewage infrastructure concession;[a] road maintenance	Bid competition	Two-envelope method works well if pricing or demand forecasts are accurate. Yet there is a danger of renegotiation and bilateral hold-up problems. Least-revenue, present discounted value approach is better.
	Municipal bus service provision, Indianapolis[a]	Tournament	Public and private agencies bid or compete to win government service contracts; also seen in Latin American and Asian countries through the licensing of minibuses
	Enhancing Municipal Service Delivery Capability (Asian Development Bank)[a]	Benchmarking, information sharing, public participation	Networking and continuous improvement program; scalability evidenced by extension from three to nine municipalities
	National Solidarity Program[a] community grants	Public participation	Community-developed proposals receive grants for building projects in Afghanistan; community provides free labor.
	Public service demand surveys; citizen report cards	Preference solicitation	Either commissioned by local government or civil society (see Jharkhand case in chapter 3). Efficacy depends on agency incentives for follow-up or public reaction, respectively.

(continued)

Table 5-1. *Summary of Initiatives with PIJC Components, by Substantive Category (Continued)*

Sector	Substantive project activity	PIJC component(s)	Assessment
	French river basin management; also used for rail in some countries	Yardstick competition used to award concessions based on firm's prior performance in other basins	Has created some world-class water management companies, as well as state-of-the-art water management. Requires multiple concessions with similar conditions to serve, good concession law, and some regulatory sophistication.
Labor	Employee promotions	Competition, voluntary	May not engender teamwork
	Human capital investment (such as university degrees)	Signaling	In some fields this is very successful as means to stand out in job market, but it can also create a barrier to entry.
	Fair-trade labeling	Information revelation with shaming	Often used to publicize child labor, "slave wage," or prison labor practices. Effective when backed up by civil society boycott campaign.
	Teams	Tournament for bonuses	Toyota assembly plants have used this very successfully.
	Employment incentive programs	Voluntary task implementation with rewards	Not generally sustainable employment-wise but does yield some training
Public administration	Decentralization	Participatory development, policy ownership	Can lead to better matching of preferences and public expenditure, tax collection, local innovation
	Red tape analysis	Information revelation	*Doing Business* series (World Bank, various years)
	Community Development and Livelihood Improvement "Gemi Diriya" Project for Sri Lanka[a]	Scorecards, devolution, competitive grants, coordination mechanisms, voluntary tasks	Deemed "successful" by independent evaluation group at the World Bank

EU accession	Certification with reward and mammoth injections of cash and training	Program has led to huge impetus in eastern European countries to reform; still, height of and occasional movement of "bar" has created recipient backlash; program cost-effectiveness and net benefits hard to assess
Public Service Accountability Monitor (South Africa)[a]	Government department-level scorecard, wide dissemination	Administered by Rhodes University; government departments compete for most favorable scores
Government Performance Project (Pew Charitable Trusts)[a]	Scorecard on government management effectiveness	Implemented by Maxwell School, Syracuse University; active since 1996
Anticorruption programs (for example, officials' asset declarations)	Information revelation	Transparency International Corruption Perception Index, World Bank Worldwide Governance Indicators, Global Competitiveness Report, Heritage Foundation–*Wall Street Journal* Index of Economic Freedom, Fraser indicators
Provincial Competitiveness Index[a]	Pure tournament	Nine business friendliness characteristics aggregated for forty-two provinces in Vietnam; since 2005
The Clean City Program (ADIPURA) in Indonesia[a]	Certification, public disclosure	Long-running; seven governance and equity indicators for local government
Blue-ribbon city and country competitiveness competitions	Certification or tournament, voluntary task implementation	These are quite popular: Innovations in American Government Program[a]; Most Business-Friendly City in the Philippines (since 2001)[a]
Public finance — Federalism–revenue-sharing mechanisms; intragovernmental grants and transfers	Tournament, indicator targets	Sometimes revenue grants are allocated based on past performance (see section 1.3 for examples).

(continued)

Table 5-1. *Summary of Initiatives with PIJC Components, by Substantive Category (Continued)*

Sector	Substantive project activity	PIJC component(s)	Assessment
	Social service grants in Bosnia and Herzegovina[a]	Competition, participatory development, collective action, output based	Community Development Project helps citizens gain a voice in shaping municipal financing priorities.
	Tax competition	Tournament with indicators	While efficient fiscal system is important, it sometimes degenerates to low taxes *and* poor public services, leading to a "race to the bottom."
	Procurement	Tournament, information revelation	If there is no corruption or fraud, and government side is properly trained, this means of acquiring outside goods and services is very powerful.
	Performance-based budgeting	Competition between budget lines	Generally successful since the technique is widely used
Public participation	Civic action initiative grants, training, and capacity building	Some competition, participatory development, informational transparency	World Bank operational policies include public participation–social accountability directives for its lending; Freedom House and Transparency International indicators are focal points for international and domestic action.
	Grants	Tournament	Gates Foundation, Rockefeller Foundation, U.S. State Department, USAID, and many others use this mechanism.
	Radio (for example, shaming poor performance, information dissemination, facilitating community initiatives)	Coordination device, information revelation	Sometimes highly effective, where repercussions from consumer or civic action are feasible; can reduce tax evasion and can increase trust in a community and lead to cooperative projects
Regulation, other	Radio spectrum auctions	Tournament	In Europe a failure (led to massive overvaluation and subsequent bankruptcy) due to no-resale clause, but very successful in United States

	Corporate Average Fuel Economy (CAFE) standard (National Highway Traffic Safety Administration)	Baseline and benchmark indicators	In use for many years, but they do not stimulate much innovation to surpass the standard, and firms have discovered how to game the system.
Research and development	Research and development and patent races (such as Human Genome Project)	Tournament	All-or-nothing format sometimes leads to slow implementation and disputes on what should be patented.
	Firm incentive programs, including university royalty sharing	Rewards for employee initiatives	Depends on outside option for researcher and whether program is a retroactive taking in disguise
SME development	USAID-IRIS Philippines Business Development Services trainer incentives	Tournament with clear measurement and reward	Results sensitive to proper calibration of incentives and output metric
	Business in Development[a] business plan competition	Tournament, networking	Entrepreneurs compete by proposing business plans for particular countries and situations; process also generates mentor-investors and international SME network
	Dominican youth entrepreneurship program (Inter-American Development Bank)[a]	Tournament	Entrepreneurship training and business plan competition to form business partnerships among youth for start-up funding
Sports	City competitions (such as hosting the Olympics, World Cup)	Tournament, creates cooperation among sectors of each city or country	This is a winner-take-all contest; can be discretionary
	Draft picks	Tournament	System for allocating best college players into the major leagues
	Walkathons, bikeathons	Tournament, voluntary task implementation	A veritable explosion of these games underscores their success in raising money for worthy causes.

a. See appendix A for details.

and had available documentation, not on whether they were successful.[3] Still, the possibility of selection bias limits the rigor of inferences derived from this table.[4]

While table 5-1 covers much ground, it is still the tip of the iceberg in terms of donor, government, and business use of incentive mechanisms to deal with the contractual challenges of principal-agency risk, asymmetric information, incentive alignment, project ownership, and efficient risk spreading. Nonetheless, this bird's-eye view of the field allows one to draw several tentative conclusions regarding the effectiveness of the PIJC components.

First, column 3 in table 5-1 shows that the use of quantitative, measurable indicators is pervasive. This reflects the importance placed on objectivity, transparency, and accountability in most of the projects listed. Together such indicators also encourage participation since they promote fairness and minimize discretion. Success, though, depends on how the indicators are incorporated into an incentive scheme. For example, the indicators and their methodology must be known to the beneficiaries or implementers in advance to properly align incentives. Box 1-1 provides a perfect example, describing how the European Commission links member state budgetary support to performance. Of course, the effectiveness of indicators depends on the availability and quality of the data they require, which in turn depends on the skills of the implementers. Rewards or penalties for performance based on the indicator results must also be clear and "bright." Some of the schemes in the table score by mixing indicator results with discretionary judgments based on "other considerations" (for example, World Bank loan conditionality); this can either weaken or strengthen performance-based incentive schemes depending on the degree to which it is common knowledge that the considerations are truly exogenous. This suggests that the prospective nature of a PIJC is critical to its success, as is keeping discretionary elements to a minimum.

Second, column 4 in table 5-1 reveals that incentive mechanism rewards need not be purely pecuniary. Many incentive schemes in the table (for instance, the Green Globe and Blue Flag projects) use intangible rewards, such as free positive (and negative!) public relations. The degree to which this produces salient rewards depends on cultural, social, and technical factors. Organizers of these types of awards must be careful to manage the award's reputation carefully by selecting consistently high-quality winners and by reinforcing public perception that the award is not subjective but well earned. Organizers must also be able to engage professionally in effective information dissemination, using the appropriate media targeted at the relevant (for the winners) populations. These considerations can have bearing on whether, for example, scorecards should be sponsored by the government or by an independent NGO. They also clarify the extent to which a

---

3. In short, this is a purposeful, not a random, sample.
4. I thank an anonymous referee for drawing this to my attention.

PIJC can operate with an intangible award or will require additional, concrete rewards.

Third, table 5-1 confirms that there is a variety of incentive mechanisms in use—certification, competitions, and tournaments. Recall that the degree to which certification succeeds in motivating change depends on how high or low the bar is relative to the median performer and on the relative size of the costs and benefits of achieving change. Where achievement is not easy, then certification can be seen as a competitive game in which the benefits accrue to having it when others do not (for example with the PROPER program in Indonesia) or as a prerequisite for entry (as in the case of the Forest Stewardship Council seal). As the preceding chapters have made clear, certification-based competition is quite different from a tournament since only in the latter is the bar for attaining the reward set endogenously by the performance of one's competitors. Nonetheless, the impression one gets from the variety of applications listed in table 5-1 is how often competition is used to stimulate players to draw upon their idiosyncratic information to achieve high performance, innovation, and implementer creativity.

What is particularly interesting is the endlessly varied use of competitive mechanisms, regardless of whether the players are individuals or legal persons (organizations with a legal standing before the law) or jurisdictions. Depending on the application, donors, companies, individuals, developing countries, and even projects can be players, sometimes acting as a bidder or a seller. In the former they are one of many competing to acquire the same item; in the latter they are the one offering the item. Countries are bidders when they compete for foreign direct investment (as well as donor attention) and sellers when they run procurements for infrastructure concessions. Donors are bidders when they seek funds from their benefactors (for example, Congress or whatever entity allocates national budgets) and from providers of cofinancing (for instance, the World Bank solicits "trust" funds). Donors, of course, also act as sellers when they offer to provide technical assistance to a country.[5] Companies can be bidders, of course, seeking contracts to provide consulting services or infrastructure construction, but, as the web-based Business in Development Network illustrates, companies can also offer investment, business plans, and even experts to less developed countries on a pro bono basis.[6] The web-based GlobalGiving Foundation even exemplifies an application in which projects compete against each other for funding from nontraditional donors.[7]

---

5. However, if the country faces multiple competing offers to fund a project that, for some reason, several donors desire to acquire, then those donors become bidders.

6. More information on the Business in Development Network is available at www.bidnetwork.org.

7. More information on the GlobalGiving Foundation can be found at www.globalgiving.com. Note that before being put up for bid, the projects are themselves subjected to certification by GlobalGiving.

A fourth conclusion one can draw from table 5-1 is that the effectiveness of projects that use indicators appears to depend upon the scope for public action. This is also a central limitation of freedom-of-information projects. Knowing that a public utility is a poor performer or that a politician is corrupt does not bring change if there is no channel for action that involves relatively low transaction costs. The presence of such channels generally relates to existing laws as well as to the capacity and incentives for coordinated public action. Moreover, the power of incentive mechanisms based on shaming (negative rewards) to deter poor performance (such as Transparency International's various corruption indicators) also depends on the existence of such channels for citizen (and even foreign) action. These points are important for two reasons: first, a PIJC usually endeavors to stimulate collective action in the player-teams who compete; second, the more effective the dissemination of information is in mobilizing collective action, particularly with regard to poor performance, the more cost-effective a sponsor's initiative becomes.[8]

Since PIJC components are so tied to public participation, it is worth taking a detour to note the World Bank's assessment of its experience with public participation in those of its projects listed in table 5-1.[9] First the bank stresses that public participation has been the key to the success of social accountability–based conditionality attached to their development policy loans (DPLs).[10] It finds that such success was achievable in many sectors, including public finance, forestry, infrastructure, public expenditure management, procurement, social programs, and decentralization. While the bank acknowledges the key role of access to information and of the enabling environment's legal and policy frameworks for civil society organizations—especially to ensure sustainability of impact—it concludes that there are other conditions required for success (Word Bank 2005a, p. 19).

Foremost among these other conditions, according to the World Bank, is that public participation must be "accompanied by measures to simultaneously ensure citizen voice in . . . formulation, planning and monitoring."[11] Second, "if participatory implementation mechanisms do not also include internal [to the government administration] and external [to the public] accountability mechanisms,

---

8. Cost-effective here refers to a kind of "leverage" in that a given amount of funding leads a greater number of jurisdictions to undertake the reforms pursued by the sponsor. See appendix D for a technical treatment of leverage.

9. To be clear, the World Bank experience described here goes beyond the projects listed in the table to cover all DPLs.

10. Note that as budget support loans, DPLs have shortcomings: they cannot provide direct support to civil society nor can they provide financial resources to promote capacity-building in public agencies or civil society groups, which should accompany public participation lending conditionality. The bank addresses this by drawing on complementary sources of support, such as bilateral donor trust funds (World Bank 2005a, p. 27).

11. More explicitly, citizen voice requires providing a legal basis for establishing client power mechanisms.

[projects with public participation] can become as faltering as more traditional public sector mechanisms with weak accountability systems." Finally, the bank's evaluation of in-house experience cautions that "if the mechanisms only provide a space for civil society to execute programs or services planned by the state without having a voice in their design, planning and management, they will also lack accountability" (World Bank 2005a, p. 20).

Regarding the use of incentive mechanisms with trigger and benchmark conditions, in addition to urging that these be "measurable, clear and not subject to ambiguity," the World Bank analysis recognizes the importance of "[focusing] on actions that are within the realm of control of the government and can be met within the timeframe of the operation" (World Bank 2005a, p. 37). More generally, when dealing with mechanisms that impose some sort of de facto conditionality, the bank recommends "actions that can be implemented relatively quickly, but that are capable of having medium and long-term impacts" (World Bank 2005a, p. 20).

A fifth conclusion one can draw is that in contrast to the historical use of conditionality (which is essentially a form of certification), voluntary self-selection by player-beneficiaries seems to lead to more sustainable results. One need only compare the effectiveness of recent "cash on delivery" programs (very successful) to past donor efforts (usually unsuccessful) to push poverty alleviation conditions (or program designs) on recipient countries.[12] The incorporation of voluntary self-selection also keeps the donor "honest" since projects that do not generate sufficient player participation provide a clear signal that the beneficiaries are not on board with project goals. Of course, this possibility can be reduced through participatory development practices, not only by consulting with the beneficiary community but giving it a primary role in defining the project, objectives, and mode of implementation (as in the Community Development Project providing social service grants in Bosnia). These observations appear to substantiate earlier assertions that part of a PIJC's power resides in its ability to generate cooperation among hitherto untrusting parties in a collective and that a PIJC with goals that are not aligned with those of the beneficiaries is not likely to generate sustainable outcomes.

As stressed in chapter 2, a central challenge to increasing development effectiveness is overcoming principal-agent problems, whether between voters and their officials, ministers and their line bureaucracies, or donors and the chain of intermediary implementers. Where the alignment of principal and agent incentives is poor, monitoring by the former of the latter can become costly. In general, the greater a project's incentive design internalizes ownership among the beneficiaries (and thus aligns their objectives with the sponsor's), the less the sponsor

12. For a summary of cash-on-delivery schemes, see Barder and Birdsall (2006).

will have to monitor—assuming that the beneficiaries possess both the background knowledge and access to channels through which to act in their own interest. The community development initiatives shown in table 5-1 all implicitly capitalize on this insight.

It is no surprise, therefore, that many of the projects in the table implicitly provide solutions, of varying effectiveness, to the principal-agent problems that could arise from the services or products they endeavor to deliver. Some of the best projects create incentives either for the players themselves to monitor other players or for members within each team to monitor other members of the team.

In the former instance, consider irrigation projects in which water users monitor each other so that no one exceeds his or her quota or shirks his or her obligations to maintain the common waterworks. Another example would be revenue-sharing from the central government down to SNGs, where competing SNGs keep watch on each other for cheating on targets in the competition for budgetary transfers.

In the latter instance, where team members monitor each other, consider these examples from table 5-1:

—charter schools, where teachers and management have to cooperate to win more students and charter renewal;

—EU accession, where interest groups within a country have to moderate their opportunism and cooperate with other groups to enhance their country's chance for entry; and

—investment promotion agencies across the world, which have to address administrative weaknesses so that their region (their team) might win the tournament.

This property of incentive alignment is often observed in those projects that generate a feeling of ownership among the participants and, as such, suggests that the critical team-generating nature of PIJCs is one of their powerful characteristics—and one that is often feasible to employ.

This encouragement of teamwork points to a broader inference one can make from table 5-1, that is, many of the applications focus on increasing cooperation and coordination, and on signaling. PIJCs that harness cooperation can reduce existing "prisoners' dilemma" situations where useful action would otherwise not be taken (for instance, cooperation among competing interest groups in Poland at the start of its EU accession process). Rather than pitting players against each other to compete for a larger piece of a limited pie, recognition programs (either using a certification or tournament mechanism) stimulate local special interests to cooperate toward enlarging the pie so that there's more to share.

Coordination is a big issue for overcoming principal-agent issues, as the many examples of certification illustrate. For example, coordination among citizens' groups can generate a better response to scorecard initiatives. Coordination can also mitigate race-to-the-bottom tax competition when tax authorities in competing (and often adjacent) jurisdictions agree on a common set of rules for attracting investors. Without donor coordination, recipients can play donors off against each other (former president Moi's specialty in Kenya). The Global-Giving Foundation coordinates individual donations by certifying small project plans. Comparative country indicators on local business conditions can be seen to help investors and serious hosts coordinate their actions. Finally, note that both cooperation and coordination generally require some signaling device as a focal point. Thus many of the initiatives listed in table 5-1 involve the dissemination of some indicator or award of a certification.

While it is impossible to generalize with regard to scalability, table 5-1 does list several applications at different levels of scale. Certifications, such as scorecards, are a good example. Infrastructure benchmark competition for management contracts is another. However, community-based development initiatives (for example, the National Solidarity Program in Afghanistan) seem less amenable to scaling up in terms of the size of the jurisdictional unit able to cooperate, although they are more amenable to scaling up in terms of the number of communities competing, as the KDP case in section 4.1.3 illustrates. This could be due to the more idiosyncratic conditions training must confront. On the other hand, higher-education programs often have excellent signaling properties that scale up nicely. Finally, information dissemination appears to scale up easily if the content to be disseminated and the media are appropriate to the scale. For example, investment opportunities (such as those Business in Development promotes) are ideal for broader dissemination whereas something like the Race to the Top program, which promotes supermarket social consciousness, is not.[13]

The question of sustainability is examined in the next chapter, so the only point to make at this juncture is that a majority of the applications listed in table 5-1 have been in existence for many years. That these are the very programs one is likely to find documented misses the point. Rather, their persistence illustrates that many of the components of a full-blown PIJC have a track record for sustainability—and in varied sectors.

---

13. See appendix A for details on these programs.

6

Synthesis and Analysis

Chapters 3 through 5 provide a rich foundation for assessing the experience to date with prospective interjurisdictional competition as well as with applications utilizing some of its various components. The present chapter provides a synthesis of this substantial experience to identify lessons learned concerning the effectiveness and relevance of the PIJC approach. This is viewed from several angles. First, section 6.1 examines the importance of the PIJC characteristics for project effectiveness, as listed in table 2-2. What do the case studies reveal about whether missing desirable design characteristics were necessary or superfluous—especially regarding the choice of incentive design mechanism (certification, competition, auction, bidding, and tournament)? With this analysis as a basis, the next two sections examine the effectiveness of the case study projects in terms of other performance criteria such as allocative efficiency and cost effectiveness (section 6.2), and sustainability and scalability (section 6.3). Section 6.4 considers the influence of initial conditions on the choice of incentive design. The final section of this chapter (6.5) applies the preceding analyses to the process of selecting the appropriate incentive design in different situations. Table 6-1, which reflects actual project implementation, summarizes the degree to which the case studies presented in chapters 3 and 4 mirror the characteristics of a full-fledged PIJC as well as succeed in meeting various criteria for project effectiveness.[1]

---

1. While these measures of success provide some indication of the extent to which the projects worked as intended, a fuller discussion is found in the respective project's case study section.

6.1 Influence of PIJC Design Characteristics on Project Outcomes

As argued in chapter 2, to effect change or reform successfully, a sponsor's intervention must explicitly or implicitly resolve several informational and incentive issues. For this reason, table 2-2 offered a list of "desirable" characteristics that one could incorporate into a PIJC design to address as many of these issues as necessary and feasible. With the design steps introduced in section 2.1 as a guide, one can examine the case studies to determine whether their degree of project success or failure was due to the inclusion or exclusion of these characteristics—or whether they were superfluous. Each step begins with a brief summary of its applicability.

6.1.1 Assessment of Problem

The successful intervention will need to begin with a correct assessment of what is "broken." Such an assessment may be done by the sponsor or by the recipients or their representatives—for example, government. (Recall from table 2-2 that all incentive designs are amenable to being driven by beneficiary demand and by collective action, in particular.) This assessment has two parts: identifying the symptoms and identifying the causes.

Recipients may not be aware of causal symptoms since they have lived under them for so long. Thus symptom identification can benefit from the observations of an outside authority. However, a recipient may not agree that the symptoms are a problem so that any further intervention by a sponsor may encounter resistance. In the case studies, assessments are carried out by the recipient (Galing Pook, Senegal literacy initiative, and KDP), the donor (Russian fiscal reform, Nigerian LEEMP scorecard, Honduran *mancomunidades* project), both (MCC), or neither (in the Indonesian PROPER, it is done by the regulatory authority).

It is even less likely that recipients will be aware of the true causes of the symptoms under which they suffer. It is not surprising, therefore, that identification of causes is typically the purview of the sponsor or initiating NGO, which also draws up the final list of goals to certify or reward. In PIJCs with a small number of participants, these can be based on stakeholder input, as was the case in the Jharkhand report card and the KDP. In PIJCs with a large number of participants, such input is harder to solicit (Galing Pook) but not impossible (the Romanian "Simple and Fast" deregulation reform). When the sponsor has its own view of what constitutes merit, then no stakeholder input may be solicited. This is the case for MCC candidacy and for the Russian fiscal reform project.

There can be a role for sponsor facilitation here. Sponsors can educate stakeholders about the existence of symptoms and their causes, as in the case of the Russian fiscal reform, mancomunidades project, and Jharkhand report card. They can create the organizational structure for problem identification, as with KDP. And they can encourage collective action for identification, as with the Moroccan

Table 6-1. *Comparison of Characteristics and Impacts of Case Studies Assessed*

	Donor intervention					
Item	Romania "Simple and Fast"	Galing Pook	MCC	Nigerian scorecard	Russian fiscal reform	MEPI Morocco
PIJC component						
Ex-post output-based reward	√	√	√[a]		√	√
Leveraging of technical assistance	√	...			√	√
Game participation voluntary	√	√	√[b]		√	√
Actionable indicators and use of benchmarking	√[c]		√[a],√[b]	√	√	√
Recipient selects tasks to implement (participatory development)		√	√[a], √[b]	√		√
Tournament (T), pecuniary certification (P), certification (C), minimum score(M)[d]	C	T	C[a], T-M[b, e]	P	T, M	T, M
Leveraging of sponsor project funds		√	√[a]		√	√
Tangible reward (beyond reputation and reform)			√[a], √[b]	√	√	√
Social capital (power of peer pressure)						√
Collective action	√		√[b]			√
Strategic communication	√	√	√[a]	√		√
Demand-driven targeting of technical assistance	√	...	√[b]		√	√
Use of local know-how to overcome asymmetric information	√	√	√[a], √[b]		√	√
Use of outside coordinators-referees	√	√	√[a], √[b]		√	√
Minimal need for sponsor on-site monitoring	√	√	√[a]		√	√

	Donor intervention				
Senegal PAPF	Mancomunidades, Honduras	KDP, Indonesia	PROPER, Indonesia	Jharkhand report card	USAID R4
			√		√
√				...	√
√		√			
	√		√	√	√
		√		...	√
P	T (muni.)[j] P (manc.)[j]	T	C	C	C
	√ (muni.)[j]		√	...	
√	√	√	√[k]		
		√	√	√	
√		√			
			√	√	
√		√	√	√	
√		√	√	√	√
√	√	√	√		
√			√	...	

(continued)

Table 6-1. *Comparison of Characteristics and Impacts of Case Studies Assessed (Continued)*

Item	Romania "Simple and Fast"	Galing Pook	MCC	Nigerian scorecard	Russian fiscal reform	MEPI Morocco
			Donor intervention			
Impact of intervention[f]						
Subjective success rating	Medium	High[g]	Uncertain[h]	Low	High	[i]
Cost-effectiveness	High	High	Low	Low	High	[i]
Allocative efficiency	High	High	Low[b]	Unknown	Medium	[i]
Sustainability	High	High	Uncertain	Low	High	[i]
Scalability	High	High	...	Medium	Medium	[i]
Relevance	High	High	Medium	High	High	[i]
Donor(s)						
Sponsors-organizers	USAID	Ford Foundation	MCC	World Bank	World Bank	UNIDO

Note: ... = not applicable

a. The precompact game in which countries in the same income group compete to exceed the median MCC indicator score for their group and thereby become eligible to negotiate an MCC compact.

b. The postcompact negotiation game between the country and the MCC in which the country's MCA executes the compact.

c. Uses dichotomous stars and no baseline.

d. Indicates whether winner must also exceed threshold score.

e. One of sixteen indicators (corruption) has a minimum score requirement.

f. *Allocative efficiency:* degree donor resources are distributed among opportunities to maximize donor goals; *cost-effectiveness:* degree a given intervention has been done at the least cost; *sustainability:* degree inter-

project where IRIS organized focus groups of stakeholders and communal councils to examine areas of reform as specified by UNIDO, MEPI, the World Bank's International Finance Corporation (Private Enterprise Partnerships, Foreign Investment Advisory Service), and others.

Despite the risk of pushing the "data" too far, one might consider whether table 6-1 contains any evidence to tentatively test some of the arguments put forth in chapter 2.[2] In this regard, I begin by examining whether the table suggests a potential correlation between greater recipient engagement and agreement on the nature of the problem, on the one hand, and more successful project outcomes, on the other. The former are proxied by the rows in table 6-1 indicating whether

2. As discussed at length in section 2.6, the case studies included in this book, while not chosen with any known bias, are not the result of rigorous random selection procedures. Thus, to the extent that any of the hypotheses analyzed statistically in the rest of this chapter involve variables that are in some way also correlated to the hidden selection variable, were it to exist, the statistical results stated may be spurious. Whether the consequence strengthens or weakens the inferences made here cannot, by definition, be known.

	Donor intervention				
Senegal PAPF	*Mancomunidades, Honduras*	*KDP, Indonesia*	*PROPER, Indonesia*	*Jharkhand report card*	*USAID R4*
Medium	Low	High	High	High	Low
Medium	Uncertain	High	High	High	Low
Medium	Uncertain	High	...	...	Low
High	Uncertain	High	Medium	...	Low
High	High	High	High	High	High
	Uncertain	High	High	High	High
World Bank	USAID	IDA	Government of Indonesia	PAF, World Bank	USAID

vention successes will remain after donor disengagement; *scalability:* degree project model can be replicated successfully; *relevance:* degree the reforms selected were appropriate and a priority for the country; *subjective success rating:* author's assessment, based on available literature, of the degree to which sponsor goals were met at project completion.

g. Insufficient information on impact of dissemination.

h. "Uncertain" means that an evaluation of performance is in progress.

i. It is too early to assess this intervention.

j. The project had two games, one for municipalities (muni.), and one for mancomunidades (manc.).

k. Reward is avoidance of a regulatory fine.

or not the project is based on "participation," that is, voluntary reform, recipient selection of tasks, collective action, demand-driven technical assistance, and use of local know-how. The latter is proxied by the row headed "Subjective success rating."[3] While panel A in table 6-2 would suggest a correlation—witness the diagonal cells are the largest—the relevant statistics shown in panel B are just a little too weak to allow an unambiguous rejection of the hypothesis of *no* correlation.

6.1.2 Identification of Solution and Tasks

There can be several ways of addressing problems that are identified. Here, again, the solution may be developed by the donor, the recipients, or both together. Even more than with the problem identification step, this process requires that the sponsor tread a fine line since it has more knowledge of past applications and technical expertise, but the recipient better understands the local conditions and the likely behavioral responses of stakeholders.

3. See table 6-2, note c, in for further details.

Table 6-2. *Case Study Correlations of Task Participation and Resulting Project Success*[a]

Panel A[b]					Panel B
	Subjective Success Rating[c]				Pearson chi-square (2) = 2.8929,
Participation	Low	Unclear	High	Total	Pr = 0.235
No	2	1	1	4	Likelihood ratio chi-square (2) = 2.9430, Pr = 0.230
Yes	1	1	6	8	Cramér's V = 0.4910
Total	3	2	7	12	Gamma = 0.7391, ASE = 0.261
					Kendall's tau-b = 0.4693, ASE = 0.246
					Fisher's exact = 0.265
					Number of observations = 12

a. MEPI Morocco is not included; the competition for MCC eligibility and the MCC bilateral compact execution game are treated as two separate observations. See footnote 2 for possible biases in this table.

b. In spite of these large values for the diagonals, the correlation of the table's two ordinal variables is *not* significant at the 10 percent level.

c. The subjective success rating is a Likkert variable based on the author's inferences from published assessments of the projects and running from 1 to 5, with 5 being excellent and 1 being poor. See note "f" in table 6-1 for additional details.

Table 2-2 suggests that the choice of specific tasks to achieve the reforms need not be dictated by the incentive mechanism selected. For example, in the case of the Romanian certification, while the implementer (IRIS) suggested how to implement the reform, the recipient had an equal if not greater say on how to accomplish the change. In the Nigerian scorecard project, however, the World Bank placed specific implementation demands on local governments, too. Likewise, tournament format does not dictate the choice of tasks. For instance, in the Russian fiscal project, which dealt with a highly technical kind of reform, the donor's input appears to have been more hands-on, but it was the Russian Ministry of Finance and the local jurisdictions that were firmly in the driver's seat. The KDP, however, allows the villages to choose an activity on their own (constrained only by a short negative list) as did the MEPI Morocco project, though both offer optional suggestions and technical assistance. Still, PIJC designs generally place the onus on the recipients to initiate the reform and to decide what approach to take (with the offer of technical assistance coming *once* a recipient has undertaken a threshold of efforts on its own). In fact, this is the main virtue of the approach: full ownership based on the premise that the beneficiaries know their work environment best.

This discussion suggests that the findings from the case studies are somewhat nuanced. For Romania and the Honduran mancomunidades, the insistence on implementing five specific reforms may have contributed to the relatively low number of winners. The Galing Pook, Senegal literacy, and Indonesian PROPER projects fall at the opposite extreme, with no donor guidance on what tasks to undertake and a large number of recipient contributions (and awards). Unfortunately, an analysis similar to that found in table 6-2 is insufficient to resolve empirically whether project performance is superior when the sponsor or the recipient determines the solution tasks to implement.

6.1.3 Technical Assistance Requirements

There are three aspects to this component. First, the setup of a PIJC may be new to the players and therefore require sponsor input to help players initiate the steps in the process. While all the PIJC incentive mechanisms would benefit from start-up technical assistance provision, a tournament does require more up-front training of players than would a certification program or standard aid contract. (Acceptance of the technical assistance is at the discretion of the local recipient.) In the cases of Russia, Romania, the KDP, and Senegal, technical assistance was provided in advance, and it is likely that such assistance was critical for outcomes. The more complicated a project is, the more help is needed and the greater its likelihood of failure, ceteris paribus, without it. This is borne out in the case studies. The simple certifications (Galing Pook, PROPER) rarely use technical assistance at setup while the more complicated tournaments (Russian fiscal reform) do.

The second aspect to this component relates to technical assistance offered for the specific purpose of identifying the problem and alternative solutions. In this case the donor has greater knowledge of past applications and technical expertise, which could be invaluable to the project stakeholders.

The third aspect is the issue of who receives the technical assistance. Its provision to those who do not take advantage of it is wasteful. In general, the best PIJC designs require that players display a threshold of effort before they are eligible to receive any technical assistance related to the reforms. This is one way a sponsor can improve the cost-effectiveness of its resources. In the MEPI Morocco project, initial technical assistance was conditional on the recipient completing a precommitment process, including a letter of commitment sent to the king's representative (see appendix C); other midproject technical assistance was conditional on promulgation of threshold (usually stroke-of-pen) reforms. A sponsor also can take advantage of economies of scale by using regionally based workshops (and even interactive web teaching applications) for technical assistance delivery to the large number of jurisdictions (or players) associated with PIJCs. In Romania, for example, IRIS provided technical assistance in the form of group seminars to representatives of all participating municipalities.

While withholding technical assistance from those unprepared to use it may seem obvious, what if the reason a jurisdiction is in need of reform is its inability to engage in collective action—the very thing precommitment requires! For example, the Senegal literacy project required the local community to organize itself together with an NGO provider in order to receive services. Those too disorganized to do so received no literacy training under this program. This sponsor dilemma may be addressed with a call for clarity. The sponsor needs to decide as a matter of policy whether and to what degree a particular program is to be disbursed with horizontal equity and with horizontal efficiency. As long as this is clearly set by the sponsor, then a program's effectiveness can be judged appropriately and fairly. Again, this sounds obvious, but many (most?) sponsors apply performance measures to programs that include implicit horizontal equity disbursement requirements. The result is that neither equity nor efficiency is well served. A possible example of this phenomenon is the Nigerian report card (LEEMP) project, where several of the states most in need received the least assistance.

Contrary to the case above where technical assistance can be superfluous, in the case of USAID's R4, some experts (Clapp-Wincek and Blue 2001) speculate that the program's poor performance was due to too little technical assistance (training). In the Honduran mancomunidades project, no technical assistance was provided—though here I believe the project might have been more successful with more up-front assistance. For MCC candidacy there is no technical assistance since supramedian scores along the sixteen indicators must be attained (often with other donor assistance) before engagement with the MCC is allowed.[4] In the case of Galing Pook, there is no technical assistance offered, though after a tournament round the winners are paid to promote their innovation as a form of ex-post technical assistance to other jurisdictions who are interested.

6.1.4 Type of Incentive Mechanism

The influence on outcomes of the type of competition mechanism employed by a project is one of the central concerns of this book. While many more alternative incentive mechanisms exist—as evidenced in table 5-1—the selected case studies utilize just certification (simple and pecuniary) and tournament (pure and mixed). These are indicated in the top part of table 6-1 (the sixth row under "PIJC component"). The case studies illustrate how each of the associated incentive mechanisms creates some sort of competitive interaction among players. The sponsor-designer can focus the object of player action (that is, the manifestation of a player's strategy) on several levels: inputs such as project proposals (KDP), outputs such as project results (Galing Pook, Russian fiscal reform, MEPI Morocco), or even as preproject participation requirements (MCC). The concern here is the influence of the incentive mechanism design on project impact along diverse dimensions.

Among the implications of the theoretical arguments presented in section 2.3 was one suggesting that the more desirable characteristics a design had, the more

---

4. However, this is not always true since the MCC, through its Threshold Program with USAID, does have relations with countries on the cusp of exceeding the median scores for their income category.

likely it would have a good impact. Likewise, it was argued that the success of a project intervention would depend on how all of its components worked together, not just on the effectiveness of one component or the other. While these are difficult propositions to test empirically—a point revisited below—the case studies provide some suggestive evidence, both qualitative and empirical.

While the reader will surely note several such sets of mutually reinforcing PIJC characteristics, the power of actionable indicators provides a good qualitative example of the role of synergies among PIJC characteristics. Although the use of actionable indicators is prevalent, the success of projects that use them appears much enhanced if they are accompanied by a strategic communications plan. Such a plan, for example, could be used to spread the message of jurisdictional performance and thereby up the incentive stakes for the player's decisionmakers. The Nigerian scorecard, MCC compacts, and the mancomunidades projects all lack a focused strategic communications plan and also do not score highly on a subjective measure of success. On the other hand, the most successful projects that employ benchmarking also include a strategic communications plan.

From a more empirical perspective, it is possible to "test" whether PIJC designs that incorporate more of the "desirable" characteristics (described in table 2-2 and graded in table 6-1) also have better subjective success ratings.[5] First, the correlation of a project's number of desirable PIJC characteristics and its subjective success rating is 0.76 (with a level of statistical significance greater than 1 percent). To investigate this further, the former is regressed on the latter while accounting for the potentially different needs of certification and tournament projects. The results, shown in table 6-3, suggest that a greater number of desirable PIJC characteristics is associated with better overall project performance (statistically significant at the 1 percent level), and the effect may be even more important for tournaments, though the evidence is not statistically significant.

It would be nice to test the effectiveness of one mechanism over another for a given situation. For example, a recurring theme in this book is whether one can determine the conditions, situations, and necessity under which a tournament design is preferable or, alternatively, even feasible compared to the other types of designs. There are two empirical difficulties with such a test. First, the designers proactively chose one mechanism over the others. While it is possible that the designers were ignorant of the other options, simply made a mistake, or were too timid, there may have been unobserved situational characteristics (hidden variables) that led them not to choose the others. The cause for this could be that the other mechanisms were either infeasible or inferior for some other reason. Hence, a priori, one would have a difficult time hypothesizing the nature of the underlying relationship to test.

---

5. See table 6-2, note c, for a description of the subjective success rating variable.

Table 6-3. *Effect of Desirable Characteristics on PIJC Project Success*[a]

	Dependent variable: subjective success rating[b]					
					95 percent confidence interval	
Independent variables	Coefficient	Robust SE	z	P > t	Lower limit	Upper limit
Number of characteristics[c]	0.535	0.135	3.96	0.000	0.271	0.800
Tournament * number of characteristics	0.123	0.116	1.06	0.289	−0.105	0.352
Summary statistics						
Wald chi-square (2)	15.79					
Pr >chi-square	0.0004					
Pseudo-R^2	0.3237					
Log pseudo likelihood	−12.312					
N	12					

a. Results are for an ordered probit multivariate linear regression with robust standard errors. MEPI Morocco is not included; the competition for MCC eligibility and the MCC bilateral compact execution game are treated as two separate observations. See footnote 2 for possible biases in this table.

b. See note "c" in table 6-2 for the definition of this variable.

c. "Number of characteristics" is the sum of desirable characteristics on which a project is graded, as listed in the "PIJC component" rows of table 6-1.

Given this caveat, there are a number of preliminary analyses that would enable one to grapple with the issue. One set relates to the mechanism of choice under particular policy objectives. Such objectives include generating maximum effort, avoiding substandard effort, and maximizing participation. Another set relates to the power of ex-post output incentives. Each is considered in turn.

Chapter 2 notes that one benefit of a certification design over a pure tournament is that it ensures that a minimum standard is achieved in order for performance to be acknowledged, whereas a player could, in principle, win a tournament either without exerting maximal effort or—and this is a different concern—without exceeding a threshold of performance acceptable to the sponsor. (One of the jurisdictions in the Romanian project exhibited the former problem whereas one of the jurisdictions in the Nigerian project demonstrated the latter.) In fact, the mixed tournament was devised precisely to address this design weakness of a pure tournament. Table 6-4 tests whether this intrinsic design issue was taken into account by the project designers. To do this, a dichotomous variable was created that codes each project as to whether or not its documents indicate a concern for achieving a minimum level of performance. The relatively larger diagonal elements in the frequency table (panel A) would suggest that designers implicitly took into account this minimum performance concern in their choice of mechanism. This conclusion is confirmed by the summary statistics in panel B,

Table 6-4. *Case Study Correlations of Substandard Effort Concern and Mechanism Design*[a]

Panel A[b]				Panel B
	Mechanism design			Pearson chi-square (2) = 4.286,
Substandard performance concern?	Certification or mixed tournament	Pure tournament	Total	Pr = 0.038 Cramér's V = −0.5976 Gamma = −1.0, ASE = 0.0 Kendall's tau-b = −0.5976, ASE = 0.161
Yes	5	0	5	Fisher's exact = 0.081
No	3	4	7	One-sided Fisher's exact = 0.071
Total	8	4	12	Number of observations = 12

a. See note to table 6-2.
b. Variables are significantly correlated at the 5 percent level.

which shows the correlation between these two variables to be −0.598 (statistically significant at the 5 percent level).

A similar exercise can be carried out for the policy objective of maximizing participation (getting the most possible attempts at reform). Here again chapter 2 argued that certification or a mixed tournament would attract more participation than a pure tournament. Turning to the case studies, evidence provided by the relatively larger diagonal cells in panel A of table 6-5 seems to support this view. Likewise, panel B shows a correlation of −0.507 (statistically significant at the 10 percent level), suggesting that projects with an explicit participation objective are less likely to use a pure tournament design.

It also has been argued here that projects based on an ex-post output incentive would be, ceteris paribus, more motivating and therefore lead to a greater impact than other types of performance incentives.[6] Testing this revealed a positive relationship, as required to support the hypothesis, but unfortunately, the correlation was statistically insignificant.[7] This may be because there are simply too few observations or the signal is too weak. More likely, the relationship is more complicated or nuanced than a simple bivariate correlation could reveal. For example, we limited our coding to projects having output-based ex-post incentives whereas some projects that had ex-post incentives measured inputs (for example, KDP). When we include both types of ex-post incentives, we get a correlation of 0.69 (statistically significant at the 1 percent level) between performance and use of ex-post incentives. Likewise, the diagonal cells in panel A of

6. Recall that an ex-post output incentive refers to a game in which the player's performance—whether for the preparation of reform inputs or reform outputs—is assessed *after* a period of play, that is, after players have had a chance to react to the incentives created by the project.
7. The bivariate correlation was 0.33 with a *p* value of 0.29.

Table 6-5. *Case Study Correlation of Participation Objective*
           and Choice of Pure Tournament[a]

Panel A[b]				Panel B
	Mechanism design			Pearson chi-square (2) = 3.086,
Maximum participation concern?	Certification or mixed tournament	Pure tournament	Total	Pr = 0.079
				Likelihood ratio chi-square (2) = 3.256,
				Pr = 0.071
				Cramér's V = −0.5071
Yes	5	1	6	Gamma = −0.818, ASE = 0.231
No	2	4	6	Kendall's tau-b = −0.5071,
Total	7	5	12	ASE = 0.245
				Fisher's exact = 0.242
				One-sided Fisher's exact = 0.121
				Number of observations = 12

a. See notes to table 6-2.
b. Variables are significantly correlated at the 10 percent level.

table 6-6 are supportive of this more inclusive supposition, also with statistical significance as shown in panel B.

6.1.5 Motivating Local Ownership of the Reform Process

Since, by assumption, reform is not occurring on its own, it is likely that the sponsor needs to play some role in facilitating, stimulating, or organizing local cooperation, interest, and self-motivation to champion the reforms under consideration. This could be as simple as providing education, for instance, about the impact of current pollution levels. The PIJC approach employs several incentives to create local ownership. These include having a well-advertised game serve as a focal point for preexisting preferences for reform, using rewards (both for the jurisdiction's citizens as "principals" as well as for the SNG as their "agent"), self-

Table 6-6. *Case Study Correlations of Ex-Post (Input or Output) Incentives*
           and Project Success[a]

Panel A[b]					Panel B
Ex-post–based input or output incentive	Subjective success rating				Pearson chi-square (2) = 5.78,
	Poor	Unclear	High	Total	Pr = 0.056
					Cramér's V = 0.694
No	2	1	0	5	Gamma = 0.917, ASE = 0.109
Yes	1	1	7	7	Kendall's tau-b = 0.661, ASE = 0.175
Total	3	2	7	12	Fisher's exact = 0.045
					Number of observations = 12

a. See notes to table 6-2.
b. Variables are significantly correlated at the 1 percent level.

Table 6-7. *Case Study Correlations of Project Sustainability
and Voluntary Participation*[a]

Panel A[b]				Panel B
Game participation voluntary	Likely sustainability			Pearson chi-square (2) = 3.438, Pr = 0.064
	Low	High	Total	Cramér's V = −0.5590
No	3	3	6	Gamma = 1.0, ASE = 0.0
Yes	0	5	5	Kendall's tau-b = −0.5590, ASE = 0.169
Total	3	8	11	Fisher's exact = 0.182
				One-sided Fisher's exact = 0.121
				Number of observations = 11

a. See notes to table 6-2.

b. Variables are significantly correlated at the 10 percent level.

selecting reforms and their solutions by players, and providing a framework for enhancing or diminishing reputations.

Recall from chapter 2 that creating ownership is important for several reasons. Recipients are much more cooperative when they feel in charge of their future environment. When the recipients feel they own an activity, the activity suddenly becomes legitimate. As such, stakeholders are more inclined to share and apply their own idiosyncratic local knowledge in the interest of the project. These factors also bode well for a project's sustainability. And there is some empirical support for these arguments from the case studies. The correlation of project sustainability and whether participation in the project's game was voluntary is 0.56 (statistically significant at the 10 percent level). Table 6-7 provides additional details of this relationship.[8]

Beyond empirics, a review of the case studies also reveals a wide range of options for creating ownership of the process of change. In Romania the main purpose of the game was to act as a focal point for local action.[9] In the cases of the KDP, Senegal literacy project, and, perhaps, Russian fiscal reform, the possibility of a reward led potential players to overcome their prior reservations about the transaction costs of cooperation with other potential "teammates." For USAID's R4, the mancomunidades, the Nigerian scorecard, and Galing Pook, the reward

8. Recall that there are two types of sustainability: process and product. The variable in this analysis and in table 6-7 refers to product sustainability unless the project's output was a process, in which case the variable refers to process sustainability.

9. Surely a fundamental question is why didn't, say, Giurgiu, one of the winning jurisdictions in Romania, carry out the reforms without the project, since the project offered no pecuniary rewards? The project's designers might claim that the promise of investment promotion for winners was enough to overcome the principal-agent transaction costs embedded in the jurisdiction's initial conditions. Another possibility is that the project offered costless access to technical assistance, both to help identify as well as address local government administrative weaknesses.

does not seem to have generated an ownership effect. In the case of Nigeria and R4, however, the exact nature of the reward was vague or simply the absence of a penalty.

Nonetheless, as confirmed by the number of desirable characteristics found in table 2-2 related to it, no particular incentive mechanism is per se better at generating legitimacy.[10] In the case of simple certification, the degree of ownership depends on the value that the participating party places on the certification. In Romania's "Simple and Fast," the allure of publicity to attract investors appears to have galvanized municipalities into taking ownership of the reform opportunities, something they had not chosen to do before certification was offered.

Note that certification can be a voluntary act, as in the Romanian project, or an involuntary act, as in PROPER. Somewhat counterintuitively, this distinction did not always line up with motivating ownership through project legitimacy. Rather, legitimacy resided in the public's perceptions of the objectivity and pertinence of the certification, not in the certified party's perceptions.

Also, simple certification can induce competitive behavior, especially in competitive markets when being certified is deemed salient. For example, while "Simple and Fast" offered five stars, in principle, to any jurisdiction that chose to participate, it was understood that only a few *could* achieve the performance required for certification. Hence, in the competitions for entrepreneurial talent, donor attention, and investment, jurisdictions saw attainment of certification as a competitive advantage.

Finally, note that while the other incentive mechanisms described below are more sophisticated than simple certification, they can also include a certification element. For example, the winners of the Galing Pook prize or the high scorers in the mancomunidades tournament were also able to advertise the certification that the prize implicitly conferred.

There are many reasons, however, why a reputational award, such as that conferred with simple certification, may be insufficient to generate a meaningful sense of ownership and, therefore, player response. This is especially true when the decisionmaker and the beneficiaries are not one and the same, and when costs and risks associated with an "output" (for example, a reform, improvement of a service, or regulatory performance) to be certified are not distributed efficiently. Then the decisionmaker may choose a course of action—or inaction—that is not in the interest of the beneficiary; in other words, there may be severe principal-agent problems. Other related situations where nonpecuniary certification may fail to motivate production of an output are

—where the expected transaction costs of collective action make cooperation unlikely,

—where success is generally perceived as unduly difficult,

10. At a minimum, these would include items 3, 5, 8, and 9.

—where exogenous shocks are likely to have an impact on performance, or

—where accountability (or the length of the hierarchical chain of responsibility) is spread among so many actors that any reputational effect of certification is blunted.

In these cases the addition of a tangible reward that is strategically targeted may help to create a stronger feeling of ownership by offering something that is privately capturable and can be shared by the reformers, thereby encouraging them to internalize the project's objectives. For example, making the outcome of the R4 process ratings salient by, say, providing a bonus to the project backstopper at USAID (the Contracting Officer's Technical Representative or COTR in USAID-speak) would surely have had a major impact on R4 performance.[11]

When certification is for an input, for example, for a business plan worth funding, then there is no reputational effect, even in principle, and an alternative concrete reward must be provided. This is because the project requires implementing an investment for a cause external to the prospective provider of the inputs. The Senegal literacy project is an example here, where certification meant approval of funding for an applicant's literacy training proposal. Likewise, removing the infrastructure grants from the KDP project would have indubitably killed the activity.

As with the other incentive mechanisms, the achievement of local ownership under a tournament design is the result of a combination of factors, including the use of clear benchmarking, salient reforms, reputational benefits, and participatory development practices. Of course, the main difference is that participants cannot know ex ante whether they will win—that is, the tangible portion of the reward is probabilistic, a point returned to below. This, however, means that those players who engage in reform do so with the expectation that the benefits of reform itself must be the main motivating factor in tournament participation. Galing Pook is no doubt the shining example of this since the reforms are literally finished before play starts. In the case of the KDP, a village has no guarantee that its proposal will be accepted by the kecamatan selection forum.

The MEPI Morocco project is quite instructive here on how to motivate local ownership.[12] Participation was conditional on holding stakeholder meetings in each area where the communal council wished to compete, and a letter of commitment was sent to the king's representative. These tasks were important since the goal was to harness civic pride and social capital. Participating and nonparticipating communes alike were told that they would be benchmarked and that (simplified) indicators of municipal quality in the areas under the competition would be disseminated for all to view. They were told that a star system would be

11. Whether the impact would have been positive or negative would have depended on the details of the institutional design.

12. Although the project was not completely implemented, the dozen communal councils that met with IRIS were anxious to carry out the precommitment activities described in this paragraph. In fact, they suggested them.

promoted internationally on the Internet. Finally, they were told that intermediate and final rewards would be given to winning and placing communes and their communal councils, as well as consolation prizes to communes achieving threshold improvements.

In discussing the issue of motivation, it is worth responding to a common concern raised about the use of tournaments as a development delivery mechanism. There is a fear—or philosophical aversion—that tournaments operate by instilling competition among players and thus either erode cooperation or create a "race to the bottom" in terms of some quality dimension of the development enterprise. This concern is addressed once one determines the exact nature of the competitive component in the Russian fiscal reform, the KDP, and the MEPI Morocco projects, as well as in the MCC candidacy program. In each case the players are not individuals but teams—large municipalities, villages, and countries, respectively. In order to win, members within each of these jurisdictions must work together and exert effort to achieve (relatively) high performance. Thus winning entails teamwork—that is, cooperation. In short, *inter*jurisdictional competition stimulates *intra*jurisdictional cooperation. Hence, in a PIJC there is really no trade-off between competition and cooperation; they are mutually reinforcing!

6.1.6 Evaluation and Monitoring (M&E)

As explained in section 2.4, M&E can serve several important purposes in the context of PIJC. First, since it benchmarks where recipients stand, both absolutely and relative to their respective peers, it may play a role in motivating players. Second, M&E can be considered part of education or transparency, leading to accountability through follow-up action, whether through civic pressure, mitigation, or avoidance. Third, during projects—and especially the more involved ones—monitoring intermediate outcomes is often critical for keeping players on track so that long-term objectives are met. Only through monitoring can midcourse corrections be made. Fourth, if an award or certification is to be provided, then objective evaluation may be critical to ensuring recipient faith in the fairness of the sponsor's conditions. If sponsor contributions or rewards are to be contingent on improvements being made (as opposed to simply having the highest score), then evaluation must occur on a pre- as well as postproject basis. Finally, rigorous M&E is the most powerful way for a sponsor to derive lessons learned from project experience, both for the specific case at hand as well as for general scalability.

All the incentive design mechanisms discussed are in principle amenable to rigorous M&E. Data for M&E can be qualitative (for example, from subjective interviews) or quantitative. Likewise, there can be greater or lesser emphasis on project inputs or outcomes. While the latter is preferred from an incentive compatibility perspective, historically the former has been evaluated, perhaps because inputs are easier to monitor and less subject to exogenous impacts, issues revisited in chapter 7. Of course, when evaluating types of projects across several implementations, statistical inferences are only possible about the average performance of a method, not about a specific case.[13]

The PIJC approach is particularly amenable to the use of randomized impact evaluation (trials), which must be prospectively built into the project's design. This means that the target population would be randomly divided into control and treatment groups suitable for randomized trials.[14] Care must be taken to include in the sampling frame those who want to participate and do, those who want to participate but are prevented by the experimental design from participating, those who do not want to participate but are persuaded to, and those who do not want to participate and do not.[15] Due to contamination concerns, some nontarget population units are included in the benchmarks to complete the control group. In principle, a partial benchmarking could be run on a subset of indicators midway through the PIJC to monitor progress by task.

So, was rigorous evaluation used where feasible in the case studies? With regard to certifications, they can be a one-time or ongoing affair. For instance, the Senegal and Romania projects fit the former category whereas the Jharkhand report card and PROPER projects fit the latter. More important, the sponsor can certify inputs or outputs. So while a sponsor can monitor aspirants in either type of application, it happened more intensively in projects where inputs were certified.

More specifically, those applications that measure future performance subsequent to the start of the game reduce the costs of monitoring during the project. This is borne out by the pairwise correlation of −0.598 (significant at the 5 percent level) between the use of ex-post output incentives in projects and their intensity of monitoring, and shown in table 6-8, where the off-diagonal cells contain the larger values. Thus the MCC paid close attention to the execution of its compacts (a certification of ex-ante inputs), but IRIS did not have to closely monitor reform activities during the Romanian project (a certification based on ex-post performance).

The Senegal literacy project was clearly hampered by weak M&E. Had the sponsors required it—say, by having implementers compare test results across service providers—they would have discovered earlier that many of their service

---

13. For example, one can unambiguously compare the performance of centralized and decentralized fiscal system reforms, but from such an analysis, it would be hard to infer that a specific country would have done better (or worse) with the other system.

14. Briefly, to avoid political backlash, an alternative would be either to run a second tournament for those jurisdictions in the first tournament's control group after the first tournament has been evaluated, or to offer jurisdictions in the control group the statistical expected value of the benefits of being a jurisdiction in the treatment (tournament) group.

15. When a protocol includes steps to persuade this third group (those who do not want to participate) to participate, this constitutes what is called "encouragement design" in the statistical evaluation literature.

Table 6-8. *Case Study Correlations of Ex-Post Output Incentives and the Need for Greater Monitoring*[a]

Panel A[b]				Panel B
Heavy use of monitoring	Ex-post output incentive		Total	Pearson chi-square (2) = 4.286, Pr = 0.038
	No	Yes		Cramér's V = −0.598
No	0	4	4	Gamma = −1.0, ASE = 0.0
Yes	5	3	8	Kendall's tau-b = −0.598, ASE = 0.161
Total	5	7	12	Fisher's exact = 0.081
				One-sided Fisher's exact = 0.071
				Number of observations = 12

a. See notes to table 6-2.
b. Variables are significantly correlated at the 5 percent level.

providers were doing substandard work. Such an outcome could have been remediable through a multipart reward incentive. For example, a part of the service provider's payment could be withheld subject to follow-up trainee testing.[16] The sponsor could randomly assign a remuneration package comprising a fixed fee at the outset, an up-front per student fee that would randomly run from some percent below cost to 100 percent of cost and disbursed at a point during the training, and pay the remainder, up to 100 percent (or higher) of cost, depending on the performance of the course participants.[17] (I return to the question of why sponsors did not take greater advantage of the lower monitoring intensity for ex-post and output-based projects, a strong attraction of PIJC incentive mechanisms and a source of their simplicity.)

When certification is used to stimulate change, then the implementer must first evaluate the potential players to confirm that none of the reforms has already occurred. Then a reevaluation generally takes place at a preannounced interval to determine which players met the certification criteria (the baseline). Needless to say, the incentive effects of certification depend on whether it is done before or after the target population has been given warning of the exercise and time to modify behavior if it so chooses. The Jharkhand report card project did not do so in its first implementation, so had service providers not expected future enumerations, there would have been no way to quantitatively confirm that change had occurred. (Note that this is different from having an incentive effect, since there could still have been public pressure from a comparison of the quality of service provision across providers due to the single survey cross-section.)

16. Alternatively, a base fee could have been offered followed by a bonus subject to satisfactory trainee test results.
17. Options for the performance standard could be an absolute level of proficiency or the median performance of all training course participants, as used by the MCC.

It is possible to construct a simple certification program based on randomized trials (see Duflo 2005), though none of the case studies in chapter 3 did this. The inclusion of randomized trials would allow one to assess the certification's incremental impact on performance. For projects within a country's compact (a bilateral certification), the MCC generally requires the randomized trials approach as its preferred M&E method. On the other hand, it is clear why randomized trials were not used in the case of PROPER since it would have been politically difficult to color code some firms (the treatment group) but not others (the control group). Instead, the environmental regulator already had time series discharge and emissions data across several sectors for large firms on Java and was easily able to evaluate the PROPER implementation to show the impact of certification on large firms. Moreover, in theory one could carry out a national certification program in which different dissemination methods are used regionally to evaluate the importance of dissemination mode to certification effectiveness.

So far it has not been necessary to make a distinction between simple and pecuniary certification. Therefore it is worth noting that the use of pecuniary rewards makes one more element available for testing via randomized trials. Here the size of the reward attached to certification may be varied randomly by class of player (for instance, the sector or jurisdiction).[18] This can be important since the salience of the reward strongly affects the performance outcome as well as the donor's budget. Lower but sufficiently salient rewards would allow a given budget to offer a tiered reward structure for different levels of certification. For example, a World Bank debriefing of Nigerian officials related to the LEEMP project found that the size of the pecuniary reward was too low to attract the sort of reform efforts considered necessary to effect change. Such a design feature could have been calibrated (pretested). For example, the sponsor could have offered different size rewards to randomly selected jurisdictions.[19]

In the case of pure tournaments, since the level of performance required for winning is unknowable in advance, evaluation is critical to the operation of this incentive mechanism. First, a clear metric with which to objectively compare performance across players (jurisdictions) is necessary for legitimacy and in order to motivate sufficient player participation. Second, a sponsor will want to know that its resources have actually led to the highest level(s) of performance (that is, that the observed results can be attributed to its funding).

As in the case of certification, ex-ante and ex-post tournament designs require different levels of M&E. In the case of ex-ante input tournaments such as the

---

18. Such a test could also be done during the project pilot as part of calibration, an important aspect of any PIJC design.

19. An alternative is to offer a schedule of rewards, each associated with a particular reform. The reward here would act as the price the sponsor would be willing to pay for the reform, and jurisdictional responses would be an indication of demand.

KDP, extra monitoring is incorporated as proposals are evaluated by technical experts before the kecamatan selection forum judges them. Moreover, the KDP's project design had to compensate for using ex-ante input competition by incorporating community peer monitoring to reduce the World Bank's workload for overseeing the thousands of proposals that were implemented under the KDP. While this appears to have worked effectively, without rigorous evaluation such a claim cannot be corroborated. Moreover, opportunities to learn from the process were likely missed, especially concerning project selection and peer monitoring.

At a minimum, three mechanism design issues could have been tested. First, does the project's incentive design lead to the best proposals being selected? Here one could randomly select villages with standing proposal committees and, before implementing the actual proposal selected by the committee, compute ex-ante economic rates of return (ERR) for those proposals not selected. The null hypothesis to test would be that the selected proposals do not have the highest ERR. Second, do proposals fulfill their promise? Here one could compare the ex-ante values of the quantitative indicators used to select the proposal from other contenders facing the committee to the ex-post values of the same indicators. The null hypothesis to test would be that the implemented proposals do not on average achieve their ex-ante performance predictions. Third, one could randomly implement the nonselected project with the highest ex-ante ERR among nonselected projects and compare it ex post to the average performance of each committee's selected projects.

In the case of the Honduran mancomunidades (and the Nigerian scorecard), though output performance (curiously, self-reported in the former) was used, benchmarking measurement was done ex ante, so there was no incentive for jurisdictions to exert serious effort. Hence follow-up implementation of reform funding needed to be monitored just as with any standard bilateral donor application. The project's documentation makes no mention of an attempt to do rigorous evaluation, however. In this case—as in the case of the Nigerian scorecard—randomized trials could have been used to assess the impact of the follow-up pecuniary reward, as with the MCC compacts. In the case of the Russian fiscal reform project, ex-post output performance was used (though it was self-reported). Still, no randomized impact evaluation was considered.

To emphasize the role of evaluation, consider again the structure of uncompleted MEPI Morocco activity. It begins with a baseline using household or firm surveys and local government data, which should be collected *before* the competition is announced to minimize gaming by respondents. The benchmarks then provide input to participants as to where they stand relative to others, which helps them to select the tasks on which to compete.[20] An identical follow-up under-

20. Recall that the tournament is formulated so that not all tasks need be accomplished but rather that the player allocates its efforts across that subset of eligible tournament tasks to achieve the highest number of total points.

taking occurs at the end of the tournament. Of particular note is that benchmarks are taken of both participating and nonparticipating jurisdictions so that a jurisdiction's fear of embarrassment by being benchmarked cannot influence its decision to compete or not.

Since randomized impact evaluation is the preferred and state-of-the-art method for M&E, one must ask why its use has been so limited in the case study projects. As the theoretical discussion in section 2.3 explains, randomized trials take time, add to project expense, require greater implementation skills, and are applicable only where an intervention can be targeted and performed on many similar decision units (hence preventing the Jharkhand initiative from statistical evaluation), and where a control group can be created without contamination or political liability. These are eminently practical considerations. So, what can one learn about this from the case studies, and, in particular, why wasn't rigorous evaluation used where feasible?

A careful reading of the case study reports suggests several tentative answers to these questions. In particular, the following factors may have had a bearing on apparent the lack of rigorous evaluation:

—Lack of familiarity with how to structure the experimental design.[21] This possibly applies to the Romanian "Simple and Fast" project, though an important factor to consider is that it was done on a "shoestring" and with inadequate staffing.

—Particular legal, administrative, or institutional project constraints, making the additional effort required for M&E impractical. When the sponsor is a governmental or multilateral entity, some types of random assignment of treatments (that is, the tasks and benefits associated with a project) can run afoul of uniform horizontal and vertical equity statutes, a problem potentially faced by the regulators who designed PROPER in Indonesia.

—Lack of desirability (for example, for political reasons or avoidance of accountability). The politics of education policy in Senegal—and the World Bank's involvement—were extremely delicate during the execution of this literacy project, which may have made the sponsor reluctant to impose the kind of strict accountability on players that evaluation would have entailed.

—No *effective* institutional demand or incentive within the sponsor for staff performance (or, more generally, for accountable results) or interproject learning. At the risk of being accused of cynicism, I believe that this is the case for most institutional donors. Statutory rigidities and constraints on the nature of civil service remuneration are part of the reason; other reasons include complex and countervailing objectives, a highly indirect chain of accountability between the recipient and taxpayer, and "stovepiping" (which especially limits cross-project

---

21. While not the case for the Romanian project, an additional related explanation is ignorance of the opportunities and benefits afforded by M&E.

learning).[22] These explanations are particularly germane to understanding why the USAID R4 initiative did not apparently do any formal analysis with its R4 database, though individual projects were monitored closely with repeated benchmarking. An interesting contrast is the aggressive use of M&E at the MCC, a new organization and one with much more flexible staff compensation.

—Measurement challenges. Some projects have objectives with outputs that are difficult to measure or, equally challenging, to attribute to project outcomes. Good examples of the latter are macrolevel reforms and project sustainability. For example, the R4 system had a notoriously hard time attributing increased economic growth to USAID projects.

6.1.7 Rewards for Success

While the motivating benefits to engaging in reform should be the direct changes engendered by the reform or the new infrastructure or services, most of the case study PIJCs offered a panoply of additional benefits to proactive efforts associated with the project. Political benefits included increased power for incumbent officials who helped to achieve the reforms. Economic benefits came in the form of increased output and attraction of investment. Social and health benefits accrued if reforms focused on improving health outcomes, gender or minority equality, or the strengthening of human rights. A combination of the previous two also increased civic pride or other utility communities get by knowing that their jurisdiction was somehow superior to neighboring jurisdictions. This list could be easily extended. Some of these benefits were costly for the sponsors; others were free.

A sponsor's project designers must be clear as to the nature and cost of these additional rewards to reformers and associated local project champions when setting the size of the funded reward portion. On the one hand, rewards should be salient enough (together with the indirect benefits) to overcome principal-agent or transaction cost problems and thereby encourage the collective action necessary for a jurisdiction to compete in the PIJC. If this is not the case, then the sponsor risks either "bribing" jurisdictions to do what they do not want to do—which runs diametrically against the PICJ approach—or, at the very least, distracting the jurisdictions from other tasks they would otherwise prefer.

On the other hand, the total ex-ante perceived benefits should not be so large as to attract jurisdictions only interested in the sponsor's funds and not in implementing serious reform.[23] The PROPER and Honduran projects tested the rewards through pilots.[24] The MEPI Morocco project planned to use laboratory

---

22. There is a huge literature on this, some of which is referenced in chapter 1.
23. As indicated in chapter 2, economists call this adverse selection.
24. In fact, the Honduran project *was* the pilot.

experiments with decisionmakers to calibrate salient expected rewards.[25] More-over, what ultimately matters is the expected value of the benefits and not just their nominal value. Hence the designer should estimate the probabilities of winning and the number of winners (and placers) when establishing the size of the reward budget.[26] Where these are not clear to the jurisdictions, the incentive design risks lower participation rates than otherwise.

So what were the case studies' experiences with certification and tournament rewards?

As defined, a simple certification's only reward is the outside, reputational ben-efits conferred by being so marked. Hence the four certified municipalities in Romania could advertise their distinction. The mechanism's incentive properties were strengthened by promising visits by the U.S. ambassador and other VIPs. These modest rewards may explain the small number of jurisdictions that com-pleted the reform program. Still, the Romanian activity was based on ex-post outcomes. The Galing Pook initiative, though it has garnered much praise—and imitation in other countries—offered its awards for *prior* reform and with no pecuniary component. Since it has not been subjected to rigorous evaluation, one must therefore remain skeptical of Galing Pook's reform-stimulating impact. Still, the initiative probably has been effective in terms of its ability to identify success-ful and *feasible* reforms in a local context (though, again, without rigorous evalu-ation, this observation is circumstantial).

So when is pecuniary certification used—and when should it be? It has been argued that its use can stimulate team members to overcome the transaction costs associated with an activity desired by the sponsor.[27] Some empirical evidence from the case studies seems to support this view. First, the correlation between the need to generate collective action for project success and the offer of a large pecuniary reward was 0.85 (significant at the 1 percent level; table 6-9, panel B). Second, as the frequency chart in table 6-9 clearly illustrates, sponsors feel compelled to offer a large reward when they recognize that collective action is required for project success.

Large rewards might also be necessary—especially ex ante—when the spon-sor's objectives require that the jurisdiction make a physical investment, and the jurisdiction either does not have access to sufficient capital or is reluctant to

25. This would have entailed having the decisionmakers anonymously interact (in a classroom or office setting—"the lab") with others through computer games specially designed to infer willingness to pay (or accept) particular benefits or costs related to their potential roles in the project. Such a lab setting offers a degree of control over exogenous factors that is not generally feasible in a survey-based (field) pilot.

26. See appendix D for a technical treatment of this issue.

27. Again, examples of transaction costs could include acquiring information and organizing col-lective action.

Table 6-9. *Is the Need for Collective Action Associated with Larger PIJC Rewards?*[a]

Panel A[b]				Panel B
Large reward used[d]	Collective action required[c]			Pearson chi-square (2) = 8.571, Pr = 0.003
	No	Yes	Total	Cramér's V = 0.845
No	6	0	6	Gamma = 1.0, ASE = 0.0
Yes	1	5	6	Kendall's tau-b = −0.845, ASE = 0.137
Total	7	5	12	Fisher's exact = 0.015
				One-sided Fisher's exact = 0.008
				Number of observations = 12

a. See notes to table 6-2.

b. Variables are significantly correlated at the 1 percent level.

c. A subjective dichotomous variable based on table 6-1 and reflecting whether the PIJC tasks required collective action in order to succeed.

d. A subjective dichotomous variable based on the author's assessments of the reward size given the number of players and degree of task difficulty.

assume the inevitable risk. Some empirical evidence from the case studies seems to support this view. First, the correlation is 0.68 (statistically significant at the 1 percent level) between the dichotomous variable on whether the sponsor's funds are given before a player makes an expenditure required to compete in the PIJC and the dichotomous variable on whether a large investment is required. Second, this result remains even after controlling for whether the PIJC is a certification or tournament, since, as shown in table 6-10, the coefficient of the large-investment-required variable is both positive and statistically significantly at the 10 percent level.

When certification is for an input or when certification is for an output of low value to the recipient but requires some investment to attain (such as training), then reputational benefits are generally insufficient to generate change. One option is to offer tangible rewards to certified parties. Examples would be guaranteed access to funding, as in the Senegal literacy or Nigerian scorecard projects. The case of R4 is more subtle. Here one might argue that the tangible prize was the avoidance of a penalty, which was theoretically threatened for projects not meeting their threshold certification values (intermediate indicator targets). Seen in this way, most state regulation may be seen as a form of pecuniary certification. Noncompliance—loss of certification—leads to penalties, that is, negative pecuniary rewards.

While Jharkhand and PROPER were both scorecard-type projects, they had different reward profiles. The Jharkhand report card, categorized as a simple certification, was "marketed" as including follow-up donor technical assistance to facilitate the needed reforms. Here, however, sponsor funding carried an unknown probability for the service providers, so its salience was likely muted.

Table 6-10. *Do Sponsors Give Funds Up Front to Winners of PIJCs Requiring Large Investments?*[a]

| Independent variables | Dependent variable: funds given ex ante[b] | | | | | |
| | Coefficient | SE | z | P > t | 95 percent confidence interval | |
					Lower limit	Upper limit
Large investment required[c]	1.510	0.844	1.79	0.074	−0.145	3.165
Tournament	0.432	0.821	0.53	0.599	−1.177	2.041
Constant	−1.291	0.759	−1.70	0.089	−2.779	0.198
Summary statistics						
Wald chi-square (2)	3.28					
Pr >chi-square	0.194					
Pseudo R^2	0.215					
Log pseudo likelihood	−6.395					
N	12					

a. Results are for a probit linear regression. MEPI Morocco not included; the competition for MCC eligibility and the MCC bilateral compact execution game are treated as two separate observations. See footnote 2 for possible biases in this table.

b. A dichotomous variable equal to 1 if the sponsor gave the winner the funds before carrying out a substantive investment.

c. A subjective dichotomous variable based on the author's assessments of whether a project required a substantial investment to be successful.

For PROPER the pecuniary benefits took the form of avoiding environmental fines and closures. Firms probably had clear prior beliefs ("priors") on the probability of such regulatory compliance action, allowing them to estimate the expected value of participating in the PIJC.

In the design of the rewards, the case studies suggest that special attention must be given to who captures them. They may be fully publicly captured if the reward is the computerization of the local public administration. The Nigerian project fell into this category. They may be fully privately captured if the reward is a series of trade and investment missions for local SMEs, as in Romania or Morocco. Or they may be a bit of both, as in the case of Senegal, where both the public as well as the private training companies benefited from the reward.

While the introduction of pecuniary rewards may greatly increase the salience of the incentives, it is also likely to increase the incentive for opportunism, cheating, and even corruption. These can lead to reduced objectivity in the certification process, and that, in turn, can lead to a downward spiral: loss of certification credibility reduces the value of certification, which requires increasing the pecuniary prize to maintain the salience of the mechanism, which increases the incentive for cheating, and so on. Perhaps due to the way the case studies were selected, there are no examples of a project that deteriorated due to corruption.

In the case of tournaments, the most obvious rewards are those offered to winners (see table 6-11). These could be a fixed amount for the top-ranked performers, as in the cases of the Russian fiscal reform project and the Nigerian scorecard, where a municipality could receive up to $9 million and $7 million, respectively. In the case of R4 and the mancomunidades (and, according to post-project debriefings, the Nigerian project as well), the size of the expected rewards does not appear to have been big enough to generate the results desired. Alternatively, the rewards could be for a declining scheduled amount, as in the case of the MEPI Morocco project. In the Moroccan project, rewards could also entail earmarking, such as offering winners cofinancing or access to special investment funds. Finally, the pecuniary reward could be for almost nothing at all: in the long-lived Galing Pook program, it was just $250, illustrating the high nonpecuniary value the player community placed on the certification.[28]

Just like for certification, rewards for tournament winners could also be nonpecuniary. Some sponsors used the tournament to reveal which jurisdictions (or their firms) could take greatest advantage of technical assistance (MCC, MEPI Morocco, mancomunidades). In the Moroccan project, winning jurisdictions were set to receive free participation in international trade shows for local firms as well as international promotion of the jurisdiction to foreign investors. This illustrates the potential for the strategic use of rewards. Here, by giving some of the reward to the private sector in municipalities that organize themselves to successfully implement reforms, the project created a link of private rewards for public action and established a pressurefeedback mechanism between the private sector and local government institutions. It also encouraged public-private partnerships to achieve winning performance.

Depending on their complexity, duration, and distribution of risks, tournaments often offer a mix of strategic secondary rewards. For example, some case study tournaments included "consolation" prizes that went to those players that exceeded a preset threshold for a task (for example, certain municipalities in the Russian fiscal reform). This threshold is set so that it corresponds to some necessary and concrete improvement but not so high as to be unattainable by conscientious players. A third level of reward is found in many competitions (for instance, the Romanian, Nigerian, and MCC projects) where technical assistance and sometimes information technology equipment are provided to participants who meet the precommitment requirements during the early stages of the tournament. In the Moroccan tournament, public officials involved in maintaining a jurisdiction's momentum were set to receive perks during the tournament, such as trips to workshops, a computer, and Internet access.

---

28. This sort of leveraging of sponsor funds by investing in reputation is explored further in appendix D. The high participation rate despite the lack of salient pecuniary rewards may also be due to the low entry costs of competing.

Table 6-11. *Summary of Case Study Game Objectives, Costs, Duration, and Number of Players*[a]
Units as indicated

Project (sponsor)	Objective	Project size[b]	Number of players	Duration of activity	Number of winners	Unit reward[b]
Russian fiscal reform (World Bank)	LG fiscal reform (budget, tax, expenditure, debt, audit, SNG transfers)	$120 million for rewards	7+10+10 regions eligible; 24 played; 19 finished	3 rounds, 3 years	3 × 5 =15 regions	Average of $8 million
Romania "Simple and Fast" (USAID)	Red-tape reduction	$150,000 plus cost of post-game TA	80 cities eligible; 29 played	1 round, 1 year	4 cities	Press coverage; U.S. ambassador visit; TA
Galing Pook, Philippines (Ford Foundation)	Encourage LG innovation	$1 million endowment	10,000 LGs eligible; 2,440 competed	11 rounds, 11 years	175 municipalities (2 tiers)	$250, publicity, national demo tour
Mancomunidades, Honduras (USAID)	Improve LG quality	?	298 eligible municipalities	1 round, 6 months	35 municipalities	TA
Jharkhand, India, report card (PAF)	Report card on rural credit, education, health, water	?	4 public service sectors	12–18 months	...	Good or bad publicity; possible assistance
Nigerian scorecard (World Bank)	LG fiscal, community responsiveness, administration, and budget quality	+$70 million	~190 LGs in 9 states	~5 years	~12 LGs (2 each in 6 states)	~$7 million per LG; $15 million per state
Senegal PAPF (World Bank)	Outsourcing literacy, BDS training	~$20 million	~300 proposals a year; 100 chosen	6 years?	200,000 trained women	$51 per trainee[c]

(continued)

Table 6-11. *Summary of Case Study Game Objectives, Costs, Duration, and Number of Players*[a] *(Continued)* Units as indicated

Project (sponsor)	Objective	Project size[b]	Number of players	Duration of activity	Number of winners	Unit reward[b]
MCC (U.S. government)	Incentive to improve governance; infrastructure and large project funding	$10 billion?	Over 100 countries	MCC 4 years old; Compact approval 2–3 years	11 countries	$100–500million
KDP, Indonesia (World Bank)	Village infrastructure grants	$1.3 billion	69,956 eligible villages	+7 years; 5 rounds	34,233 villages (40–60 percent ERR)	<$35,000 per village; $50–150,000 per kecamatan per round
PROPER (Indonesian government)	Reduce large industry pollution	$100,000 annual budget	43 large industries	12 years	…	Fines avoided; good or bad publicity
R4 (USAID)	Improve aid effectiveness	$270 million[d]	70 bureaus, thousands of projects, staff, and contractors	5 years	…	…

Note: … = not applicable; ? = data could not be obtained.

Source: Various primary and secondary documents (see text).

a. MEPI Morocco project concept not included in this table since implementation was aborted by donor for political reasons (see section 4.2.3). BDS, business development services; LG, local government; TA, technical assistance.

b. Costs are nominal as of the year of the project (unless otherwise noted) and hence may not be directly comparable.

c. This is the official 2003 dollar average over the project period. Comparable "corrected enrollment" according to Nordtveit (2005) is $78. See section 3.2.2 for further details.

d. Author's unofficial estimate.

Beyond positive ("carrot") rewards for doing well, some tournaments, like the Russian fiscal reform, MEPI Morocco, and (in theory) the mancomunidades include negative ("stick") rewards for those who do poorly or, worse, choose not to participate at all. The stick is administered by broadly disseminating participant scores so that people on the street (as well as investors, higher levels of government, and other donors) are able to objectively assess the level of performance of their municipality and, equally, their elected officials.

The introduction of rewards means that the tournament designer needs to address calibration challenges related to their size and the probability of winning them. While the same consideration exists in the case of pecuniary certification, calibration is more difficult in the tournament approach. This is because the "cost" to the player of receiving a reward—that is, the needed level of effort for a winning performance—is not known ex ante.

It is ironic that the existence of competitions at the local jurisdictional level is, in some sense, an admission of government failure. For example, in the case of the KDP, allocation of grant funds as a reward would normally be part of the local pubic finance responsibilities of the government at the kabupatan or kecamatan levels. That the donor had to set up a separate organization to perform this function (the forum, in the present example) is a case in point. This concern is covered in more detail in chapter 7.

6.1.8 Dissemination of Results

The case studies show that dissemination of results plays a central role in mechanism design effectiveness and, therefore, should not be seen as simply part of a sponsor's efforts at self-promotion. First, the ex-ante knowledge that objective postproject results would be disseminated often provided an additional motivation for player decisionmakers to distinguish their jurisdictions—and themselves—as seen in the Romanian and Galing Pook projects. Likewise, a jurisdiction may have had greater difficulty in attracting sponsor assistance for reform if previous project failures generated "bad press," as was the case for some communities in the KDP project.

This encouragement effect had two impacts, one on the decision to participate in the PIJC and one on how much effort to apply once participating. The case studies reveal that, depending on local culture, peer social pressure and community pride can reinforce these two effects or be used by decisionmakers to motivate collective action. With Galing Pook the only reason to participate was the opportunity for positive exposure from dissemination of results. Note, however, that neither of these dissemination effects need be present in a PIJC, as can be seen, for example, with the KDP project, where such dissemination was not part of the reward structure. This also illustrates the tendency for the motivating effect of dissemination to be more powerful for output-based rather than input-based PIJCs. (Of course, as mentioned below, where certification is for an input, then dissemination may still be important for knowledge generation, as in the Nigerian scorecard.)

The introduction of the World Wide Web has given new motivating power to the offer (or threat) of results dissemination. For example, in the Romanian and Moroccan competitions, players were told that their score (the number of "stars" their jurisdiction rated) would be publicized internationally on the Internet.

The effectiveness of dissemination should come as no surprise: a secret certification has little motivating value. Projects that included funding for dissemination seemed to encourage greater participation in the PIJC because players feared that public benchmarks would potentially reveal how poorly they were doing relative to their peers. This is what IRIS found in setting up the Moroccan PIJC. The power of PROPER in the beginning lay with the concern firms had about the negative impacts that could arise from dissemination of poor scores (though firms later realized that good scores had a positive value in advertising).

Still, some sponsors could have made more and better use of dissemination. In the Romanian project, for example, while some newspaper coverage was given to the awards ceremony, and while USAID, the funder, was extremely satisfied with the results, little formal dissemination occurred. For instance, to my knowledge, there is still no published working paper on the activity. This may explain both why so few municipalities were motivated to achieve full marks (five stars) and why USAID did not replicate the initiative elsewhere in the world.

A second use of dissemination is to demonstrate the applicability of interventions in order to encourage replication in other jurisdictions. Thus, for example, the Galing Pook project publicizes the local government innovations of its awardees to demonstrate feasible options to other jurisdictions. This is also one of the intents of the Nigerian and Jharkhand activities, and may also apply to PROPER. However, the Senegal literacy project and the KDP did not appear to take advantage of this possibility, though in the latter case, the kecamatan review committees clearly used the level of a village's success in project implementation to assess its later proposals. In the Moroccan project, workshops were to be held for sharing both experience and lessons learned with other participants as well as to facilitate network formation among participants during the tournament and at the closing ceremonies.

A third use of dissemination is as a substitute for or complement to project rewards. It may be cheaper for the sponsor to invest in certification reputation (for example, by improving its objectivity and value, and by promoting it through public relations) than to incur the direct out-of-pocket cost of paying for tangible rewards. The case studies show the inclusion of dissemination in project design to be very cost effective in leveraging sponsor funds in a PIJC with many players. Moreover, given the requisite expense of advertising the initiative, the additional cost of disseminating the results is often minimal. In some of the case studies, dissemination of results was the sole reward (Galing Pook and Romania's "Simple and

Fast") for good performance or the sole penalty for poor performance (Jharkhand report card and PROPER).

Some tentative empirical evidence for this third effect can be found by calculating the statistical significance of the correlation between the size of the pecuniary reward and the effectiveness of a project's public dissemination of jurisdictional performance.[29] The correlation is −0.71, statistically significant at the 1 percent level. This correlation is consistent with several possible considerations that PIJC designers may have taken advantage of, by explicitly reducing the cost of pecuniary rewards through cost-effective publicity or compensating for a small reward budget by using cost-effective publicity, or by implicitly acknowledging the incentive substitution potential between these two benefits.

Finally, notice that with the exception of simple certification, where there is no pecuniary reward offered, these three uses of results dissemination are not unique to certification or to tournaments.

6.2 Comparing the Effectiveness of Alternative Project Designs

So far, project effectiveness has been assessed in terms of the impact of adding or removing a PIJC characteristic or component. And this assessment reveals that the impact depends on the presence of other complementary characteristics, that is, characteristics work synergistically. In this section project efficiency and effectiveness are assessed by examining the degree to which the case study designs overcome the inherent obstacles from the strategic behavior caused by principal-agent problems and transaction costs. To clarify the sources of differences, several characteristics of a project's design are held constant. The reader may wish to refer to table 6-1, which describes the case study *incentive* characteristics, and to table 6-11, which summarizes each case study's *game* characteristics.

6.2.1 Informational Challenges

An intrinsic challenge to aid effectiveness is that the recipient knows much more about the implementation environment than the donor—and often has many reasons either not to reveal this information to the donor or to reveal it strategically or fallaciously. This "information asymmetry" generally combines with a donor's existing "imperfect information," meaning that the donor may not be able to know whether a poor project outcome was due to recipient opportunism (for example, shirking) or bad luck. Likewise, the effectiveness of an intervention depends on how recipients respond, often in a strategic game with the imple-

---

29. For each case study, these two variables were coded a 1 or 0 depending, for the former, on whether the pecuniary reward was considered salient or not and, for the latter, on whether the publicity campaign disseminating a jurisdiction's PIJC performance was effective enough to be deemed salient by evaluators. See section 2.6 on the possibility of sample selection bias.

menter or sponsor. Knowing what "type" of player the recipient is—honest or dishonest, patient or anxious, risk averse or risk tolerant—allows the donor to design more appropriate incentives into the project. Economists refer to the lack of such knowledge regarding a player's type as a problem of "incomplete information." As a result of all these information limitations, many projects are forced to include an expensive monitoring component. With this perspective in mind, I briefly consider some consequences of asymmetric and incomplete information for the various mechanism designs in the case studies. (Imperfect information is discussed in the next section.)

One of the most effective ways to deal with information asymmetries is to use an incentive that economizes on what the donor needs to know. As described earlier in this chapter, theory and practice have shown that the two most powerful ways to do this are to harness the power of incentives (Zinnes and Bolaky 2002), first, by giving the participants a central role in defining what is broken, what to fix, and how to fix it, and second, by making development assistance performance based. While this may sound obvious, it is rarely done. For example, historically, aid conditionality generally failed per se on the first count, and failed on the second count by rarely waiting for the conditions to be fulfilled before providing the assistance. The present case studies mostly avoided these mistakes, partly by using participatory development practices and partly through a mechanism design that offered rewards sufficiently small that only those who placed a high value on the intervention's goals were sufficiently motivated to play the game. However, only in some of the cases was full responsibility for performance placed squarely on the participants by making the reward *post* game and output based.

The certification approach relies on a preset hurdle to exceed. In the case of the Nigerian project, the hurdle was to exceed a particular governance score; for the Romanian project, it was to accomplish five tasks; and for the Senegal literacy project, it was to exceed a technical score on a training services proposal. Participants assessed their chances of exceeding the bar and then made their decision to exert effort (or initiate reform) accordingly. Hence a donor only needed to assess whether the hurdle was exceeded rather than to closely monitor recipient efforts to achieve a preset level of performance.

But in the presence of informational problems, what happens if the donor does not know where to place the hurdle? As has already been mentioned in other contexts, if the bar is set too high, then the certification approach will elicit few participants; if the bar is set to low, then too many win, and certification holds little meaning. Moreover, it is not always possible for even the participants to know in advance just how high a bar they could surpass, since the degree of difficulty may not always be apparent before trying. This is analogous to a golf tournament or horse race where no one really knows how contestants will perform in the heat of the contest. In fact, this problem arose in the Romanian "Simple and Fast" (certification) project where some municipalities were able to win with almost no effort, others won that no one suspected could win, while yet others did not even try to participate.

The tournament approach can resolve these informational obstacles. In addition to using the various incentive alignment features that have been discussed, tournament designers try to include enough players so that the best players themselves define the limits to what performance is achievable—that is, where to set the bar. Hence, with the tournament approach, it is *not* necessary for the donor, let alone the participant player, to know for certain what degree of success is required to win. This dose of competition has the added benefit that tournaments can bring out unexpectedly high levels of performance from participants. Of course, such a mechanism design is more effective in tournaments with *post*game rewards and even more effective for *output*-based postgame rewards.

This self-setting performance bar feature of tournaments, however, leads to the concern that some players may be discouraged from participating ex ante by realizing that there are other players that are much better than they are. The case studies show that this problem can be overcome in several ways during the design of the project. First, the donor can make certain that the jurisdictions eligible for participation are of similar levels of ability (which often translates into having the same initial conditions). For example, in the MEPI Morocco project, only rural municipalities were eligible to participate, not the big cities such as Casablanca or Rabat. In the KDP project, only kabupatans with poor villages were included. Second, donors can offer a "consolation" prize or participation award, as in the case of the Moroccan project's reward for threshold performance (which is the certification component of the mixed mechanism design). A similar feature was included in the Russian fiscal reform project.

6.2.2 Exogenous Performance Factors

The discussion of uncertainty back in section 2.1 pointed out that there is systemic and idiosyncratic risk for the principal when it comes to evaluating agent performance. When there is much systemic risk, tournaments are theoretically preferable since all competitors are affected in the same way by exogenous factors. Rather than a reward being conditional on achieving a *specific* score, as in a contract, the tournament rewards the *best* scores, regardless of the impact of intervening exogenous shocks. Another way to say this is that since task completion depends on both the player's efforts as well as exogenous factors, under certification some or all participants could miss the bar through no fault of their own if the exogenous factors dominate. Knowing this could diminish the ex-ante power of the incentives. Consider an analogy with golf. In a contractual scheme with a required score to reach to win, few might participate on a day with high winds since there is a low likelihood of achieving the needed scores. Rather than developing a set of contingent contracts based on wind speed (or direction or variability), the tournament incentives encourage players to exert high efforts regardless of the conditions since all players face the *same* wind conditions.

For example, in the USAID R4 initiative, contractors could miss their intermediate targets due to an unexpected devaluation of the national currency, national work stoppages, or for less obvious causes uncorrelated to their efforts or scope for action. In the Jharkhand report card project, if the local government officials were convinced that exogenous though unknown political events at the state level would affect their municipality's performance—for example, vagaries in budget allocations—the report card might not motivate them to engage in reform. In short, it is possible that participants will recognize the likelihood that uncontrollable factors could hinder their performance, thus blunting the effectiveness of a given set of incentives, or worse, causing some participants to opt out of the initiative altogether.

Statistical analysis does not find any correlation between the substantial likelihood of exogenous risk and the choice of a tournament. While this is surprising, two factors make it more understandable. First, several of the case study PIJCs were based on pregame performance, so game risk was likely irrelevant. Second, none of the case studies selected were subject to a substantial likelihood of exogenous risk in practice, with the exception of the USAID R4 project. Interestingly, in the USAID R4 project, the indicator system was ignored over time and eventually was dropped. This may in part be due to the failure of the designers to choose a PIJC mechanism whose incentives were relatively independent of the degree of systematic exogenous risk (common shocks).[30]

6.2.3 Reward Effectiveness

From a theoretical view, the greater the degree of difficulty of a reform or the greater the perceived political risk to the decisionmakers who ultimately spearhead such efforts, the more important are donor-provided—and privately capturable—rewards for creating sufficient incentives to pursue such reform. While only suggestive, evidence from the case studies indicates that the bivariate correlation between the size of the reward and the perceived political risk or degree of difficulty is 0.63, statistically significant at the 5 percent level.

Though both the certification and tournament approaches may be enhanced by offering concrete rewards beyond recognition of performance, the pecuniary certification approach is theoretically less able to make use of rewards as effectively. The reason for this is twofold. First, as discussed in section 6.5, under the pecu-

---

30. One has to be careful here since USAID would not want its staff undertaking excessively risky projects or ignoring risk altogether. However, USAID is forced to implement projects in an inherently risky environment while at the same time being held accountable for the results, which presumably requires a way to attribute outcomes to staff action. The discussion in the text refers to the identification of an incentive mechanism for balancing the latter tradeoff (that is, attributable staff action in the face of systematic exogenous risk).

niary certification approach, the sponsor cannot predict the number of winners ex ante. Thus while a tournament budget can be set in advance, the budget for a pecuniary certification cannot. Under certification any number of players may achieve a particular performance, either costing the organizer more (or less) money or, if a sharing rule is used, reducing the promised payments and therefore incentives. Second, it is often possible under a tournament to leverage the reward funds so that a given rewards budget can serve to attract a greater number of players (reformers) than under certification. Of course, the tournament approach has a flip side in that it risks expending reward funds for little improvement since there is no fixed bar for contestants to surpass. Recall, however, that this concern is easily remedied by requiring thresholds to be met in order to win.[31]

The role of rewards and, consequently, the choice of incentive mechanism depend on the nature of the project, which, as the case studies listed in table 2-1 show, can fall into several types. Among these there are three situations of particular interest. In the first situation, the reward is given for a finished output that would *not* have been achieved without the prize, as in the Russian fiscal reform and MEPI Morocco projects. There are two reasons for this situation: the reforms are themselves highly valuable, so the reward only needs to compensate for the transaction costs of overcoming distrust (or act as a focal point) within the team; and the reforms would otherwise only be considered a priority by the donor and not by the recipient.

In the second situation, the reward is given for a finished output which *would* have been done without the prize; this occurs in the eligibility phase for MCC compacts and in the Galing Pook and R4 projects. Here the reward acts to attract *outsider* attention to the quality of work, essentially signaling a demonstration project.[32]

In the third situation, the reward is for an input, such as the proposals in the Senegal literacy and KDP projects, that would not otherwise be provided without the lure of the reward. Here, the reward stimulates the search for value-added opportunities for sponsors to fund. There are two likely scenarios: first, the sponsor wants many applications (as in the Senegal case), and second, the sponsor has a limited budget relative to the likely opportunities available and wants to pick the best proposals, say, for demonstration purposes (as in the KDP, mancomunidades, and Morocco cases). In the first scenario, a pecuniary certification would be the best option, and the donor would only need to establish that the input met a minimum quality level to make success sufficiently likely. In the second scenario, a tournament approach would lead to a more efficient outcome. Note that in the

31. The threshold would be set at that level below which the sponsor would deem its initiative no longer cost effective.

32. Demonstration projects are used by donors to introduce a new method or approach to a common problem faced by many similar actors. The latter are able to evaluate the suitability of the method to their situation before deciding whether to adopt it.

second instance, the donor could also provide some seed financing for implementation with the promise that the best results would receive an additional prize.

Again, while only suggestive, evidence from the case studies indicates that the bivariate correlation between the size of the reward and the designers' assessment that the sponsor's objectives would not be achieved without the offer of a substantive reward is 0.50, statistically significant at the 10 percent level.

As discussed in section 6.1.7 in relation to rewards for success (with a detailed example for MEPI Morocco in appendix C), the PIJC approach allows rewards to be used much more strategically than simply providing the winner qua jurisdiction a reward, which has often been the practice under certification or tournaments. The PIJC approach suggests that the project designer should first comprehensively assess who the decisionmakers are whose buy-in is critical for project success and who the parties are, whether private or public, that will bear the risk. Based on this assessment, rewards would then be targeted at the motivational weak points of implementation, subject to the caveats described in the aforementioned subsection. This design consideration is as equally applicable to pecuniary certification as it is to tournaments.

In practice, these insights have been applied to some of the case study projects. For example, the Nigerian, Romanian, Russian, MCC, and KDP projects all involved providing valuable technical assistance—a type of reward—to players during the competition process. The Moroccan project proposal offered a computer workstation to jurisdictions whose initial efforts during the tournament met a threshold and more specialized technical assistance at the midpoint of the competition for those meeting a second threshold. Such strategies may also be targeted to particular groups within a player's team. For example, the Moroccan project advocated offering cofinancing and trade missions to businesses within winning jurisdictions. This reward design both directly contributes to SME assistance and uses the lure of privately capturable project rewards to create reform pressure on local government by key constituents. Finally, the creative use of rewards may also offer a way to address the concern that an incentive mechanism could lead to cumulative disappointment or boredom.[33] However, to the extent that such concerns are relevant—and the dozen case studies provided no evidence of this—there is no reason to expect them to apply to just the tournament approach.

6.2.4 Partial Credit

Given its design, certification is typically seen as an all-or-nothing approach. For example, the Senegal literacy project only funded proposals exceeding a quality score threshold. In Romania a task was either completed and received a star or not. Without partial credit, however, it is more likely that if a player

---

33. I thank Johannes Linn of the Wolfensohn Center for raising this concern in a January 2006 seminar on the tournament approach.

doubts its chances to fully succeed, it may not try at all; partial attempts or efforts are thus implicitly discouraged. Pure tournaments, on the other hand, do not suffer from this problem (though at the cost of risking that a substandard performance can win). The case studies illustrate how designers have addressed this problem. On the certification side, steps can often be built into the certification program. For example, the PROPER project provides several increasingly strict levels of environmental compliance (certification). On the tournament side, designers can introduce a minimum performance threshold (certification) into the tournament to create a mixed tournament (as introduced in section 2.3). Under these circumstances, if a jurisdiction believes it can exceed the task threshold, then it will exert additional effort even if it does not believe that it can win the tournament.

6.2.5 Project Efficiencies

As national governments have become increasingly interested in what their aid budgets are achieving, the issue of efficiency has come to the fore. While economists employ many types of efficiency concepts (allocational, distributional, informational), just two are used here. *Allocative efficiency* describes the degree to which resources are distributed among assistance opportunities to maximize sponsor goals. This concept is associated with the idea that funding is scarce and that funds have opportunity costs due to other possible projects foregone by a funding decision. This concept should be applied to the two sides of the aid game. On the demand side, is the sponsor choosing to fund the "right" type and quantity mix of projects?[34] On the supply side (and often overlooked), does the project's selected design encourage the targeted potential recipients to allocate their time and effort across project tasks efficiently?[35]

Cost-effectiveness describes the degree to which a given intervention has been done at the least cost, that is, there was no other way to achieve the same end at a lower cost (or, alternatively, there was no way to achieve greater ends for the same cost), given that the benefits exceeded these (least) costs. As is the case with allocative efficiency, the project should be designed to provide the recipients the necessary incentives to want to pursue least-cost options. Since a player can be given incentives to allocate its time across almost any distribution of reform activities, the risk here is that the design might create incentives that would lead the recipients to engage in tasks to the point where the marginal costs of provision are far from the marginal benefits of the reform (or investment)—or worse, to produce off the "supply" curve.

---

34. I ignore here the issue of whether the sponsor has enough information to be able to select the highest priority projects for the recipient and whether the recipients have the necessary understanding to see these as the highest priority and thereby consider the activities as fully legitimate.

35. Recall that several PIJCs, for example, those in Romania and Russia, allowed players to select which activities to engage in—and to what extent.

Underlying both these concepts is the issue of asymmetric information, that is, the dilemma that the sponsor must set project objectives—and incentives—while the recipient possesses much of the requisite information about implementation costs and local factors relevant for project success. Note that the other type of information asymmetry typically confronting local public service provision relates to the government's limited knowledge of recipient preferences for such services. In the present context, however, this may be less of an issue since, typically, the sponsor wishes to impose "merit" goods or services on the beneficiaries (though a high degree of sponsor-recipient divergence on preferences can degrade project legitimacy).

The issue of a project design's efficiency can be clarified further by revisiting the typology shown in table 2-1, which points out the distinction between input-versus output-based performance measures (for winning). Only the cases where performance is measured ex post are considered, since this is the only arrangement in which the sponsor can influence efficiency or costs. A certification-based approach requires the sponsor to set the level of inputs or outputs desired. When the sponsor sets the required threshold for inputs, there is no guarantee that the ensuing output produced from them will be efficient.[36] Worse, the sponsor has no guarantee that players will maximize its objectives, since these are generally based on outputs. This is true regardless of whether the sponsor or player-producer is paying for production. When the sponsor's design sets (certifies) the required levels of inputs and *is* paying for production, it also has no control over whether the output, which is what will ultimately satisfy the sponsor's objectives, will be provided cost-effectively. A tournament, on the other hand, allows the player to choose from a continuum of inputs associated with the range of alternative tasks. Unfortunately, this still does not resolve any of the aforementioned concerns (though it does encourage efficient production of inputs) since there may still be no perceivable benefit to the player for generating the highest level of outputs.

In the case of ex-post output-based performance PIJCs, there is still no guarantee that certification will lead to an efficient output mix since the sponsor may not know the provider's (player's) cost function. If the player is paying for production, it *is* likely that production is cost-effective, however, since the player is the residual claimant.[37] If the sponsor is paying, then this favorable property will disappear unless addressed separately. A tournament design under ex-post output-based performance measurement, however, is inherently better than a certification approach at encouraging efficient allocation of reform efforts. A properly

36. Here efficiency refers to the marginal costs of provision being equal to the marginal benefits (as perceived by the sponsor) of provision.

37. "Residual claimant" is a term from principal-agent theory. It refers to the party that receives the leftover revenues (or unused output) once the costs of production or provision have been covered. Usually, the residual claimant is the party incurring the risks associated with the production or provision.

designed tournament scheme elicits the socially optimal amount of effort across multiple reform tasks by encouraging the players to minimize input costs and face the shadow prices (marginal rates of substitution of benefits across tasks) of the sponsor. Consider another athletic analogy, that of the Olympic decathlon. Here a group of athletes competes across ten events with points accumulated according to quality of performance in each event. Athletes must pace themselves (allocate effort) across the events so as to maximize the number of points.

Moreover, as shown by the case studies, the points awarded for each task in a tournament can be adjusted to reflect the sponsor's relative value placed on the various tasks. This can cause the players to provide an efficient level of output (since they will set their marginal costs equal to the ratio of award points for each pair of tasks). Returning to the decathlon example, one could set up an award point system to give a long-distance runner an advantage over a shot-putter. The setting of a point system is thus critical in determining who chooses to participate in a multitasking tournament and also how, given participation, each will choose to train or compete. A question for the tournament designer in this example is whether the shot-putter should be encouraged to run in the 1,500-meter event or perhaps just jog, watch from the sidelines, or train for the shot-put.

When a donor foots the bill for a reform, then the recipient has a lower incentive to minimize costs than when the recipient is the residual claimant to cost savings. This issue is especially problematic when project aid is input based since the sponsor has limited knowledge on how the inputs are then used. To address this, sponsors usually take an active role in the appraisal of project proposals and put elaborate (and costly) monitoring systems into place when they expect to foot the bill for the consequent reform (or investment). The problem normally does not exist for output-based aid if the player pays for production. When the donor is not sure where to set the bar ex ante for encouraging output, a tournament approach will encourage more cost-effective output. Exemplification of these points can be found in the MCC program. First, MCC eligibility is a tournament, so no monitoring needs to be done by the MCC regarding country performance. Once an MCC compact is signed, however, a certification game begins, and at that point the MCC monitors the country *very* carefully.

The project design, therefore, is like the proverbial Walrasian auctioneer.[38] Its creates an institutional framework within which the demand side reflects sponsor objectives and recipient benefits, and the supply side reflects the sponsor's financial costs and the recipient's implementation, reorganization, and redistributive costs. The "ideal" project design, therefore, would provide the incentives so as to lead stakeholders to expand the project up to the point where

---

38. Economists, following the lead of nineteenth-century Swiss economist Leon Walras, use the concept of an imaginary auction of buyers and sellers to illustrate the way the price mechanism in a "perfect market" would equate supply and demand.

the additional benefits would just equal the additional costs entailed in generating them.

In light of these theoretical insights, it seems that the designers of the case study mechanisms either selected and calibrated an appropriate incentive mechanism or took ad hoc measures to address the inefficiencies a "wrong" choice created. Consider the certification case studies. The "Simple and Fast" Romanian certification, which was ex-post output based, required a municipality to complete five tasks (reforms) in order to be certified. The sponsor partially addressed the threats to allocational efficiency caused by information asymmetries by conducting many meetings in an attempt to identify *which* five tasks needed to be done across all eighty eligible municipalities. Still, the project design was not amenable to inferring whether the project outcomes were sensitive to the five tasks chosen. Might there have been some municipalities that would have been better off with a different set of five tasks? And why not reward those who achieved just four of the five tasks—and, if so, would all tasks be equally important? What about the other certification case studies? Since the Jharkhand and Nigerian projects were ex-ante games, the PIJC mechanism had no influence on efficiency or cost-effectiveness. The PROPER initiative addressed the problem of cost-effectiveness for certifications by offering a multitiered certification program, which allowed players some flexibility in matching their marginal costs to the regulator's signal of social marginal benefits.

Finally, the USAID R4 (certification) system was not designed to address inter-task (or project) allocative efficiency. The internal indicators also were not used as an incentive for the countries receiving services. Rather, USAID staff worked out the indicators either internally or in collaboration with contracted implementers. Hence their impact in the first instance was on cost-effectiveness and, to a lesser degree, on motivating USAID staff monitoring of the efforts of its contractors. I am unaware of the extent to which—if at all—the R4 indicators made their way into private implementer contracts. To the extent they did, when implementers were paid a lump sum for their output, this encouraged cost-effective provision but required close monitoring of quality (unless the contract stipulated how it would be quantitatively measured ex post). When an implementer had a "cost-plus" contract (typically for more risky production requiring uncertain levels of effort), all its costs were covered by the sponsor, so even more monitoring would have been required to overcome additional reduction in the incentive for cost-effectiveness.

How did the tournament case studies s fare in terms of allocative efficiency and cost-effectiveness? The Honduran mancomunidades project was a one-shot ex-ante tournament, so there was no opportunity for the sponsor to influence efficiency or cost-effectiveness. In the MCC PIJCs, the eligibility game is an example of a donor mechanism that endeavors to allocate monies efficiently, if one accepts the hypothesis that a better policy environment leads to better project outcomes. Once a recipient country enters a compact, the MCC allows the country to select the projects to propose, which further contributes to allocative efficiency. The MCC then pays the bill, whose price tag is set in the compact ex ante. The MCC has endeavored to address the inherent weakening of incentives for cost-effectiveness that this arrangement creates through extensive ex-ante use of international experts for the implementation plan. Nonetheless, ex post several of its compacts have come to resemble USAID cost-plus contracts.

In the KDP tournament, the World Bank placed few restrictions on use of funds, so objectives were set by each kecamatan's project committee. Since those proposing the projects were in some sense also represented in the kecamatan's project committee, one may conclude that this arrangement internalized the demand-supply decision process and encouraged expected marginal costs and benefits to be equalized. Still, this PIJC was based on input performance, so in principle the game could have lacked cost-effectiveness ex post. According to project reports, the mechanism design dealt with this in three ways. First, the PIJC was created as a repeated game. Project reports indicated that players believed that the potential to win in future rounds meant that reputations for cost-effectiveness were worth developing. Second, since the PIJC award was strictly intended to overcome a financing constraint and not to galvanize collective action or overcome related transaction costs, there was a strong alignment of village and sponsor objectives, again encouraging cost-effectiveness. Third, the strong intervillage social peer pressure tended to mitigate postaward opportunistic behavior in winning villages.

Finally, the Russian fiscal reform and Moroccan MEPI projects, as mixed tournaments, had the most intrinsic support for allocative efficiency and cost-effectiveness. Here the point systems transmitted to the players the shadow prices (that is, marginal benefits) of the sponsor while allowing the players to implement the reforms they selected with maximal flexibility (that is, allowed them to adjust their marginal costs). This improved allocative efficiency. And having the player as the residual claimant in reform implementation efforts encouraged cost-effectiveness.

6.2.6 Use of Benchmarks

One of the main attractions of certification is its simplicity—a yes or no decision is involved—and this strengthens the mechanism's legitimacy and hence motivational power. Benchmarks can contribute to the power of the incentive by increasing player perceptions of objectivity and hence fairness of scoring. Interestingly, all the case study certifications employed benchmarks, even those that judged ex-ante performance.

While both the certification and tournament approaches in the case studies used quantitative benchmarking methods, the tournaments required benchmarks with greater graduation. This is because a tournament requires greater dispersion in scores in order to be able to rank players once the benchmarks of the many tasks have been aggregated into one indicator. For example, the MCC's eligibility game aggregated sixteen indicators, which created good score dispersion. Similarly complex scoring was observed for the Russian fiscal reform and Nigerian LEEMP initiatives. In fact, with the latter two, independent evaluators raised the concern that the scoring was needlessly complex. The Galing Pook project, on the other hand, depended on the subjective evaluation of independent experts rather than benchmarks. However, since in this case the reforms had been previously completed, this otherwise weaker motivational method of scoring did not lead to any negative strategic behavioral consequences for the incentive mechanism.

6.2.7 Time Dimension

There are two main comparisons to make when considering time requirements among alternative incentive mechanisms. The first is between a certification PIJC and a standard bilateral contract (where each recipient to be targeted receives a contract).[39] Toward this end, it is useful to examine the time requirements of each step in a canonical certification application, as described in section 2.1. Regarding problem identification, objectives setting, and establishment of task, a fair comparison requires that one first hold constant

—the number, type, and priority of tasks to accomplish;

—the efforts of local participants in identifying problems and establishing the task menu; and

—the type and complexity of the commitment mechanism.

In addition, this comparison assumes no impact evaluation step. Finally, since the main sponsor contributions to recipients in bilateral contract situations are technical assistance, investment funding, and other services (such as training and trips abroad), one must compare the standard bilateral contract with pecuniary rather than simple certification.

Under these qualifying conditions, a little thought reveals that the only likely source of difference between these two approaches would come from how the recipients are selected. Normally, under the standard approach, the sponsor proactively identifies eligible candidates to receive assistance and thereby incurs search costs and expends time. Under a PIJC certification, the sponsor does not generally search for eligible candidates. Rather, it sets the conditions (certification criteria) for benefits eligibility and waits for candidates to apply. While the certification criteria should be the same as those used for candidate selection under the standard aid case, the sponsor must now also incur costs and expend time to develop and implement a strategic communications plan for informing the target jurisdictions of its offer. As for the calendar time required under each approach, in the case where the sponsor knows the recipients it wants to target, then clearly

39. With only one recipient, the standard bilateral aid contract *is* identical to a certification, so there would be no differences between the two!

the standard approach is quicker. In the case where the sponsor has little idea of which jurisdictions are best to target (that is, ones that are both able *and* willing), then it is likely that the certification approach would be quicker.

The second comparison to make is whether a certification takes less time than a tournament. At first blush, the obvious answer would seem to be yes. Yet one should not confuse observations from typical applications with a mechanism's inherent characteristics. To address this question, the steps in a canonical application are used again, and the same features are held constant as above. And again the comparison must be with pecuniary rather than simple certification, this time because of the risk of confounding the time intensiveness of establishing reward structures (which are not a component unique to tournaments) with that of the incentive mechanisms being compared.

This may still leave additional time-consuming tasks under a tournament. First, even once the specific tasks have been identified, the choice of benchmarks for a tournament can still entail greater complexity than for a certification since a tournament may necessitate greater dispersion in scoring in order to generate a clear ranking. Second, if the sponsor is concerned about a jurisdiction winning with a performance that in hindsight the sponsor would not have considered worth the cost, then additional energies and time would be required to establish performance thresholds. On the other hand, if the establishment of such (minimum) thresholds would take significant time, the setting of stimulative certification requirements takes even longer. Third, while certification approaches also have rules of the game, the underlying concept of certification is generally much less foreign and easier to grasp. This may mean that game manuals, public relations to encourage participation, and player training may be quicker to implement in a certification than in a tournament.

Some case studies from chapters 3 and 4 are useful for putting this discussion in a real-world context. Consider the Romanian "Simple and Fast" program. From a time perspective, it is very likely that a sponsor of a standard bilateral approach would have required more time to work with each of the eighty municipalities to find out which were suitable and interested in undertaking specific reforms and then to write contracts and collaborate with each of them to do so. Here we see that the certification approach was certainly a better choice for USAID than its standard bilateral approach. Would a tournament have taken more time than the certification, ceteris paribus? I believe so, because the concept would have been foreign to the prospective players and thereby have required more training and public relations. On the other hand, what if the MCC used a certification rather than a tournament to determine eligibility? If fewer simpler indicators were used, then the process would be quicker. With the actual set of indicators, it is likely that the two methods would be equally time consuming. (Moreover, it is hard to believe that the MCC would be able to pick the optimal certification levels.) In the case of the KDP project, a similar story obtains. If the same economic rate of return indicator were used to set the level of acceptance for a certification or as the basis for ranking in a tournament, it is likely that both approaches would have been equally time consuming. In the case of a certification, if a simpler indicator had been used to check business plan suitability, then it would have been quicker to implement.

So why does it seen obvious that standard aid contracts are much quicker and easier than certifications and that certification is quicker and easier than tournaments? I believe the answer is that the greater sophistication of the latter in each comparison allows them to be used in more complex and time-consuming applications. To give but one example, it is clearly more time consuming to run a certification of a country's or region's SNGs than it is to conduct a technical assistance project with one SNG. Likewise, it is clearly more time consuming to conduct a tournament to determine which jurisdiction has the most reliable municipal water service than it is to run a certification of whether a jurisdiction's piped water system delivers at least five hours of daily service. But phrased in this way, it becomes obvious that these are not appropriate comparisons: the former compares assistance to one versus many jurisdictions; the latter compares a complete service ranking system to a measure of minimum service. Moreover, in the latter instance, how would one know that five hours is a satisfactory or achievable target as opposed to four hours or six? The absurdity of comparisons becomes even starker when certification without pecuniary rewards is compared to tournaments with such rewards. Note, however, that I am not arguing that the time it takes to provide assistance is independent of choice of incentive mechanism. Rather, it is likely to be other factors aside from time that will dictate which mechanism is best suited to a *particular* application.

Finally—and conversely—note that for a given set of tasks, it is likely that the tournament approach will yield outcomes *sooner* since certification programs are generally open ended while tournaments impose a time limit as part of the "finish line."

Absent from this discussion and perhaps of greater import for timing is whether the selected PIJC mechanism incorporates prospective, randomized impact evaluation. This entails extra steps in the design of a project as well as in its implementation since a control group must be identified and benchmarked. This might add three months to a project, two during the design stage and one for post-PIJC assessment. Of course, randomization also provides potentially large benefits, including the ability to assess and attribute impacts, extract lessons for improving outcomes, and evaluate project scalability and replication.

6.2.8 Complexity

By now it should be apparent that the issue of PIJC complexity is closely entwined with that of timing, and thus much of what was discussed above applies here as well. What I do argue here, however, is that a hands-off incentive mechanism is *more complicated* to design than a standard bilateral aid agreement: under the latter, "mistakes" can be easily corrected during the implementation period, so less foresight is demanded; under the former, once the rules are set, the sponsor needs to let the game play out until the next round. Likewise, a tournament can accommodate more subtlety and fine-tuning in outcomes and targeting, so it permits greater complexity *if desired* (since the preceding discussion made clear that much of this kind of difference disappears when an "apples-to-apples" comparison is made).

Complexity can come from several sources, such as the number of tasks to accomplish to meet a sponsor's objectives, the sophistication of the benchmarking technology, the structure of rewards (and their calibration), and the inclusion of randomized trials. Some of these considerations increase the player training component of a project, which generates its own additional complexity. Likewise, more complex tasks probably require more sponsor technical assistance, which itself increases implementation complexity for the sponsor. Since such sources of complexity can be found in either mechanism, there is no intrinsic reason for a tournament to be more complex to implement than a pecuniary certification *with similar ambitions.* For example, it is unlikely that the Galing Pook program was more complex than the PROPER program. Both required an assessment, the former of an SNG initiative and the latter of a firm's environmental profile. In practice, however, certification programs tend to be dichotomous in their attributions and much more modest in their scope, and for this reason, the commonly held view is that a tournament is more complicated than a certification. Compare, for example, the Moroccan tournament to the Romanian certification. Both targeted SNGs, but the Romanian initiative only addressed five discrete items and produced five certified jurisdictions whereas the Moroccan activity was aimed at a much more complex set of reforms, anticipated dozens of reforming jurisdictions, and was set to distribute large rewards in a manner that aligned public and private interests.[40]

6.3 Sustainability and Scalability of PIJC Applications

An important issue for the sponsor is the influence that mechanism design has on project sustainability and scalability. Recall that the former refers to the degree to which the benefits of a project endure in the long term after the sponsor has withdrawn its support and that the latter refers to the degree to which the project may be geographically extended within a country or the project model may be replicated in other countries or in other sectors.

40. Additional examples from the case studies that would illustrate some of these arguments can be inferred from the preceding discussion on the time dimension.

6.3.1 Sustainability and Incentive Design

First, it is necessary to distinguish between the degree to which an *organization* established under a project is sustainable versus the degree to which the *results* of the organization's *outputs* are sustainable. One might refer to this as process-versus-product sustainability. In addition, a *project* will be considered sustainable if it achieves product sustainability and, where it aimed to create an ongoing organization, if it achieves process sustainability.

Consider process sustainability first. Galing Pook, the KDP, the MCC qua organization, and (possibly) the Jharkhand report card are examples of projects with purpose-built delivery processes or organizations created to encourage process sustainability (but not generally its products).[41] In these examples process sustainability also has an institutional side (Did the project create an organization to provide the desired outputs, or was it simply done through a temporary office with international experts?), a supply side (Does the location have the skills and other inputs to provide the expected outputs in the long term?), and a demand side (Do the recipients value the outputs, and is there political or governmental support for the activity?). These factors generally combine to determine process financing. Organizations require a continued source of funding to be sustainable. This can come from a government budget, a user fee, an NGO budget, or from the private sector. The latter two sources are not generally sustainable. These sources, of course, can be mixed. The Senegal literacy project, for example, charged a user fee, which was set below the amount participants were willing to pay. This reduced the portion of additional funds required for sustainable financing.[42] The rest was paid by the World Bank with the expectation that the central government would expand or replicate the activity.

Hence process sustainability, where full-cost pricing is infeasible, requires political support more than program success or popularity—though the latter clearly facilitates the former. Since politics is by nature fickle, such sustainability is difficult to guarantee. PROPER has lasted for many years, through changes in government and even a "revolution," perhaps because it was a regulatory initiative and had a firm seat inside the executive branch of government. At the other extreme, Romania's "Simple and Fast" had no bureaucratic home and ended after the first application, even though it led to sustainable outputs, was on budget, and was highly regarded by USAID and even the U.S. ambassador. Between these extremes lies the equally successful KDP project which, after the substantial donor funding had ended and central government budget support began, had its institutional basis threatened as two opposing ministries fought over its functional

---

41. Inclusion of the Jharkhand project depends on the extent to which the Public Affairs Foundation was set up by the project as a long-term provider of scorecards or as a product of the activity.

42. Because of the positive externality from education, economics indicates that the efficient level of the fee would be below the cost of service provision, with the government paying the difference.

terrain. Similar vagaries can occur in the nonprofit sector. The Ford Foundation, for example, ended its support of the Galing Pook initiative after a dozen successful years of operation and much imitation in other countries. (The program did find outside financing and has continued.)

A related way to establish funding is feasible where there is a strong public demand for the organization. For example, a trade organization may be sustainable if there is a critical mass of its members who find its services worth funding. One such service could be the assessment of red tape or of product characteristics (to prevent forgery, for example). Thus, for example, Galing Pook has continued because there was considerable public support for its certification services. The sustainability of the MCC as a corporation has depended on vague promises from the Bush administration for continued funding, and future sustainability will depend on whether the MCC continues to maintain public support for long-term funding, at least for the duration of the Obama administration.

Generally speaking, product sustainability, like process sustainability, requires institutional or organizational assistance for the continuation of a product resulting from a sponsor's initiative.[43] For example, the sustainability of a sponsor-financed fleet of vehicles depends on the quality of the recipient's maintenance organization.

There are several commonalities in the characteristics of projects that led them to become sustainable.[44] First and foremost, project sustainability depended on the degree of legitimacy attached to the project's goals and process of implementation. Thus, for example, projects that included the recipient in goal setting and in establishing the key variables for performance metrics to be used in certification or tournaments tended to lead to sustainable outcomes. The KDP, Senegal literacy, Romanian "Simple and Fast," USAID R4, and Russian fiscal reform all took pains to include participants in such details. Furthermore, in each of these, the players participated in project implementation. Second, projects where participation was voluntary tended to lead to more sustainable outcomes. The Romanian, KDP, and Russian projects were voluntary, but the USAID R4 and Nigerian projects were not. The former projects led to sustainable outcomes while the latter did not.

Third, projects where a successful outcome was demanded by a strong group of local stakeholders tended to lead to more sustainable outcomes. The KDP, Russian, and Senegal projects are good examples of this tendency.

43. Since a sustainable project first has to be successfully completed, the focus is on those case studies with completed projects. However, since concrete data on output sustainability were scanty, the observations here are rather speculative.

44. The present paragraph, which discusses characteristics common to sustainable projects, *necessarily* refers to either process, product, or both since both are required for project sustainability. Moreover, ascribing a characteristic to either process or product sustainability can often be like splitting hairs. Hence, in the following discussion, particular commonalities are not ascribed to process or product sustainability specifically but to project sustainability in general.

Finally, players (for example, jurisdictions) with a more homogeneous population generally engaged in more collective action than those with a heterogeneous one and, therefore, tended to do better. For example, KDP villages appear to have done better in creating outputs than did Nigerian regions.[45] And Moroccan communal councils showed more interest in success than did the provincial governments of the province they were in.[46]

The World Bank seems to concur with these observations. It concludes that "to facilitate [project sustainability], we find that it is important to identify and build on existing practices and capacities, promote local ownership of the reforms, and focus on building the capacities in government and civil society, as well as help put in place systems and mechanisms to ensure their institutionalization. Support to ad hoc practices . . . can be effective as a first step to help institutionalize processes and practices in later phases" (World Bank 2005a, p. 44).

The case studies point out that sponsors often run PIJCs where winning is based on pregame performance. With such a design, they are forced to base their assistance decision on *pre*project indicators as a proxy for *post*project sustainability. This makes perfect sense when the goal is to "advertise" and disseminate a best practice; it makes less sense when the goal is, say, to fund SNG capacity building. Sponsors have chosen to deal with this limitation in several ways.

Some interventions have begun to use indicators of the general policy environment as proxies for the likely future performance of a specific sector or situation being considered for assistance. MCC compacts, for example, are awarded based on a country's prior, general, policy environment (input) and not on the performance of previous interventions similar to the proposed project (output). Thus the potential sustainability of the Cape Verde compact for drip irrigation was not proxied by the sustainability of past drip irrigation in the country but on a set of national-level economic and governance indicators.[47] Where a compact is for something previously not available in the country such an approach seems appropriate. Still, the case studies seem to suggest that it is less effective to use input-based evidence of sustainability than output-based evidence of sustainability where the latter is available, and that it is even better to use ex-post performance-based evidence. For example, the Nigerian project evaluated SNG suitability for funding based on indicators of past local government performance whereas the Russian project evaluated such suitability based on performance improvements during the project period in the areas to receive funding; the fund allocations in Russia appear to be generating longer-lasting results.

---

45. Granted, this is not a perfect comparison since the countries were different as were the activities the players were engaged in.

46. Recall that provinces in the Moroccan MEPI project would be competing against other provinces based on the average score of their communes.

47. See section 4.2.2 for details.

Other interventions have chosen to provide assistance based only on project-specific measures of performance, and these have also encouraged sustainable outcomes. For example, although sponsor assistance had been available both to enterprises in Indonesia and to service providers in India, it was not until color codes and scorecards, respectively, were introduced that sustainable change occurred. Some sponsors, on the other hand, have chosen to provide assistance to recipients where no project-specific measures of performance are taken, with the apparent result of less sustainable projects (just as the absence of performance measures tends also to lead to less effective outcomes). Again, in the Nigeria scorecard project, the local government grants that the World Bank provided to municipalities were based neither on project performance nor on the scores of the recipient municipalities but rather on ex-ante performance scores of other municipalities in the same state. Based on the limited evidence, this did not result in sustainable outcomes. Finally, the Honduran mancomunidades project could be interpreted as using either environmental or project-specific indicators. While it computed ex-ante sustainability scores to identify municipalities with policy environments deemed more likely to encourage sustainable projects, project rewards were for just such policy capacity-building support. It is still too early to tell whether the ensuing outcomes actually will be sustainable.

So what is the answer to the sponsor's key policy question? Are environmental or project-specific precompetition indicators better at guiding sustainable project outcomes? First, as the preceding discussion makes clear, there is no substitute for salient, incentive-compatible indicators for project implementers. Second, as long as the sponsor's initiative is micro in scale and below the political radar of the central government but supported by the local SNG, then project-specific rather than country-level policy environment indicators are probably a better choice for sustainability. Third, where the indicator measured inputs to the long-term success of the product, then the less gameable and the more central to performance the input, the better it was for sustainability.[48] Where the indicator measured previous output performance, the sponsor risked subjection to recipient opportunism unless the institutional nature of the product ensured that pre- and postgame performance would be highly correlated.

The case studies also highlight another interesting challenge in incentive design. How or when are process and product sustainability linked, and can the incentive design influence the link? As pointed out earlier, it is generally possible to offer a large enough incentive payment so that a recipient does whatever a sponsor wants, just as long as the incentive signal is clear and sufficiently well aligned to the sponsor's objective. The problem is that while brighter, larger incentives may produce a more "successful" immediate outcome, they

---

48. "Gameable" refers to the property of being open to manipulation by a player's strategic behavior in ways unrelated to the designer's original intent.

Figure 6-1. *Potential Linkages between Process-Product Sustainability and Incentive Design*

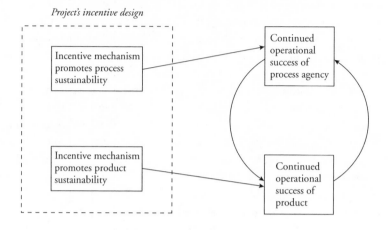

may not lead to a more sustainable project (product) outcome. There are two reasons for this. First, the local factors responsible for short-term project performance are different from those required for long-term project effectiveness. Second, securing an organization's (process) sustainability requires different types of support than that required for the sustainability of its outputs (product). One need only think of what is required for Galing Pook's organizational sustainability versus the sustainability of the innovations its awards promote. These challenges can occur while the donor is still funding the process or while those trained or employed by the donor are still involved with the activity. A sustainable project, however, requires that the institutional environment supporting the project in the long term have an interest in continued project output—think of the Ministry of the Environment's continued enthusiasm for PROPER. This usually requires some type of accountability feedback linking the preferences of the project's ultimate beneficiaries back to the product providers. Conversely, a good institutional environment does not necessarily guarantee that the project generates sustainable product outcomes. The latter depends on the incentive compatibility of the project design and on implementation considerations that are often very different from the initial institutional environment. These relationships are summarized in figure 6-1. As shown below, there is also a potential for sustainability-reinforcing links between process and product.

To extract further inferences from the case studies on these linkages, table 6-12 identifies the key process and product sustainability links as well as the characteristic of the incentive mechanism that supports it. In general, two of the main links between product and process sustainability are that a delivery process that fails to

Table 6-12. *Incentive Design Influence on Link between Process and Product Sustainability*[a]

	Type of sustainability		*Incentive design impact on sustainability or linkage*	
Case study	*Process*	*Product*	*Process→product*	*Product→process*
Romania "Simple and Fast"	Temporary IRIS project office	Administrative reforms	Temporary nature of initiative may have reduced number of counties participating	None
Jharkhand, India, report card	Public Affairs Foundation (PAF), apparently meant to be long term	Local public service provision quality/ quantity improvement	Newness of PAF and of process may have dampened player responses	Success of product reinforced PAF to solidify its LT existence
PROPER, Indonesia	Ministry of the Environment	Enterprise compliance	Lead role of state institution encouraged firms' LT efforts	Success of compliance enhanced ministry's stature
USAID R4	USAID missions, D.C. bureaus	Full range of development assistance	Large institutional commitment encouraged adoption of products	Weak impact on product sustainability led to loss of support for process
Nigerian scorecard	Purpose-built (presumably temporary) state and federal project support units	Administrative capacity building and TA	Project units certainly improved outcomes, but other design weaknesses mitigated LT impacts of process	Product may have had process impact in states that responded to process incentives
Senegal literacy	Financial management and oversight by ministries and a QUANGO; provision by existing and new-for-opportunity NGOs	Women with basic literacy skill and some miscellaneous business or artisanal skills	Process led to formation of strengthened village associations, supporting LT product success	LT success of product led to replication of process
Galing Pook, Philippines	Special local office created	Certified SNG initiatives	Professionalism of administration enhanced award reputation	LT record of selections before award reflected well on Galing Pook organization

(continued)

Table 6-12. *Incentive Design Influence on Link between Process and Product Sustainability*[a] *(Continued)*

	Type of sustainability		*Incentive design impact on sustainability or linkage*	
Case study	*Process*	*Product*	*Process→product*	*Product→process*
Mancomunidades, Honduras	ARD (U.S. consulting firm)	Administrative capacity building and TA	(More elapsed time needed to evaluate)	(More elapsed time needed to evaluate)
KDP, Indonesia	Kecamatan Project Committee, with oversight by various ministries	Village-level infrastructure projects	Repeated game feature led committees to help monitor each award	Success of village projects strengthened LT political support from national government
Russian fiscal reform	Specialized office within Ministry of Finance	Local public finance administrative reform and budgetary support	Ministry of Finance presence provided LT regulatory and TA support	Success of reforms reinforced ministry's LT commitment
MCC eligibility	MCC staff collect indicators from outside agencies	Countries certified as MCC eligible	Perception of LT existence of MCC encourages country efforts to make LT improvements	Extent to which countries make LT improvements increases political support for process
MCC compact execution	MCA, a local office created to oversee compact design and implementation	Mostly infrastructure outputs	LT nature of compact ensures LT support to product	Product durability increases chance of postcompact funding for product and thus for MCA
MEPI Morocco[b]	Temporary office within the regional investment promotion agency	For SNG: administrative capacity building, TA; for private sector: cofinancing, trade, and investment promotion	...	...

Note: ... = not applicable

a. LT, long-term; QUANGO, quasi-autonomous NGO; TA, technical assistance.

b. PIJC implementation not completed.

generate sustainable products is unlikely to survive due to a lack of beneficiary demand and political support, and where beneficiaries may receive repeated assistance (as in the KDP), successful products may generate the political support needed to maintain the delivery process.

Table 6-12 also illustrates the possible links between process and product sustainability in terms of the various categories of a sponsor's products:

—*Infrastructure financing* may result in, say, a road successfully built (product), but the sustainability of the road depends on future operations and maintenance financing, which in turn depends on institutional (process) sustainability. USAID infrastructure projects have had a spotty record of sustainability: USAID generally tried to ensure such follow-up commitments of support from governments whose infrastructure was being funded, but the R4 system did not (and could not) apply to governments. The KDP project did not establish any process support that I could identify with its various village rewards, though presumably the winning business plans required the application to explain how operations and maintenance would be handled (and financed).

—*Policy reform* comprises the de jure change, its implementation, and eventual compliance. Here the first two may be considered the product, with the last being the establishment of the institutional support (process). Compliance is a measure of process sustainability. MCC eligibility required success in all three areas and was (in theory) forfeited if the third process was not sustained. Eligibility was handled through a pure tournament and then was recertified annually.

—*Administrative reform* is like policy reform in its product and process characteristics. Here, however, de jure change and implementation were probably the hardest to achieve, since it entailed fighting entrenched interests. Sponsors typically had to use a significant pecuniary incentive to ensure this product's sustainability (for instance, in the Russian and Nigerian projects). USAID did not use such an approach and often had poor results in this regard. Once implementation was achieved, however, compliance (process) sustainability could be achieved through a long-term source of domestic financing and political support. PROPER and perhaps the Senegal literary project are case study examples here.

—Achieving the sustainability of *local public service delivery* projects has focused on creating capacity and instilling a commitment to service quality and quantity.[49] These kinds of projects tend to be a mix of administrative reform, training, and securing an institutional home and financing for the provider. Project incentive designs often contribute to sustainability by creating salient feedback from the beneficiary to the provider. In the case studies, incentive mechanisms for creating sustainable capacity took many forms. The Jharkhand project's demand-driven approach used customer satisfaction surveys that encouraged service providers to

---

49. While service delivery is a service, it is still the "product" of the project according to the framework here.

accept and even seek outside assistance in capacity building. USAID's supply-driven approach endeavored to use the R4 incentives to improve the quality of its contractors' efforts to strengthen public services. The former appears to have worked well; the latter, less so. For service quality and quantity, sponsors have had the most success with certification (Jharkhand, Romanian, and PROPER projects, and the World Bank's *Doing Business* rankings), though the results from tournaments seem very promising (Transparency International's Corruption Perceptions Index and the World Economic Forum's *Global Competitiveness Report*).[50] Even PROPER, in certifying an enterprise's level of compliance, may be thought of as giving the provider (of pollution control services) feedback from the beneficiary (the citizen through its regulatory representatives) services.

—The provision of *training* may be seen as product, with its sustainability dependent on adequate opportunities for trainees to apply their new skills. In the Senegal literacy project, for example, the World Bank established a rather successful process to deliver the training. The project created many new "education" NGOs that sought to apply for training funds. As these organizations multiplied, it likely gave a boost to continuing the project. The sustainability of the product—literate women—depended on the latter's need to read. This was cleverly built into the project by having participation in the training be voluntary. Moreover, the project spontaneously morphed into also offering artisanal and business skills development and women's associations. These, in turn, strengthened the returns to literacy and thereby supported the sustainability of the underlying institutions (process). Many of the other case study PIJCs included training of some sort. Often it was supplied through the process organization (as in the Romanian, Russian, and Moroccan projects). Here, the incentives were reinforcing since better product sustainability in turn strengthened political support for continuing the process, aiding the sustainability of the latter.

—*Regulatory compliance* is a reform that especially calls for political support since often the requisite private sector actions are financially costly. No sector is a better example of this than environmental compliance. Often these were the least successful of USAID projects under R4. In contrast, the design of the PROPER incentive mechanism addressed both process and product sustainability. First, the initiative jurisdictionally located the process in an intrinsically sustainable institution, the Ministry of the Environment. Second, its use of culturally based public certification indicators was clever since the targeted enterprises' color ratings were constantly visible to the public, creating a long-term incentive to maintain compliance. Third, PROPER's product incentive mechanism led enterprises both to install new capacity as well as to acquire greater environmen-

50. See World Bank (various years); World Economic Forum (various years); Transparency International, "Corruption Perceptions Index" (www.transparency.org/policy_research/surveys_indices/cpi).

tal expertise. Once enterprises made these kinds of investments, they then had a long-term stake in the continuance of the process providers, which reduced the ministry's future costs of enforcement for existing firms as well as for new entrants. The Jharkhand process, which was more independent of political support, still had the full cooperation of the service providers (who were government entities). The process implementer (PAF) endeavored to increase product effectiveness and hence its own raison d'être (that is, sustainability) by providing technical assistance to the providers. Financing, always a weak link for sustainability, could be addressed through some increase in user fees: the modest improvements in service quality—in response to pressure from the survey results—could provide political cover and legitimize the increase in the eyes of the beneficiaries. These fees could contribute to the capital improvements that regulatory compliance might require (for example, equipment for laboratories and mobile monitoring facilities), which, in turn, would further improve service quality, creating a virtuous cycle for sustainability.[51]

As donors come to grips with the long germination periods needed for true development, it will become more difficult to base rewards solely on final results. Some other type of incentive mechanism is needed to ensure local dedication over the long term. Some projects have used what one might call the threat of future penalties if project results are not maintained or do not materialize according to a work plan. In essence the MCC does this by threatening the country with the risk of having current assistance curtailed or follow-up compacts eliminated. Unfortunately, this incentive mechanism is what economists call "time inconsistent," because if the country falls out of compliance with the MCC compact at a later date, it is not likely to be in the MCC's interest to cut off future funding. While the success of a compact's implementation is the primary responsibility of the government, national governments come and go. It does not make sense to penalize a country when it throws out a "bad" government for a new one. In a way, the MCC implicitly admits as much in another context regarding its treatment of Georgia. At the time Georgia was announced eligible to enter negotiations for an MCC compact, it did not meet the MCC criteria for candidacy, particularly due to its low scores on corruption. Regardless, Georgia does have a compact. The MCC argued that the corruption score was due to previous governments and that the then-new government was serious about eradicating corruption.

An alternative and probably more successful approach to sustainability is seen in the Russian fiscal reform, Galing Pook, and KDP projects. In each of these cases—though they use different mechanisms—continued good results are

---

51. Though perhaps it would be economically efficient, one should not expect to be able to set a user fee sufficiently high enough to fund the capital budget for a regulatory agency. Such levels would likely be politically unacceptable as well as potentially regressive if the distributional impact falls on the poor (which is not the case for PROPER).

ensured by the existence of strong indigenous demand from the beneficiaries and stakeholders of the specific project.

The issue of player disillusionment, touched upon elsewhere in this study, also has implications for sustainability, especially *process* sustainability. Casual experience suggests that people—be they children or staff offered recognition incentives—eventually lose interest in "games," and the same players can become habitual winners or losers.[52] Does experience with jurisdictional competition bear this out? There is some evidence for this outcome—donor fatigue—in the case of projects that require more time to set up. The R4 and Moroccan case studies under USAID and UNIDO, respectively, might exemplify this phenomenon. In the USAID case, donor fatigue was due to a faulty incentive design, so there was never any interest in the game in the first place, and the only solution would have been a redesign of the incentive mechanism. In the UNIDO case, donor fatigue is probably a misnomer: higher-level political changes led to a change of director at the UNIDO Investment Promotion Office, and the new director did not have sufficient interest in the activity to fund it to fruition. Neither of these cases, however, provides evidence of stakeholders losing interest in an ongoing game.

In point of fact, there is no evidence from the case histories of fatigue among beneficiaries in well-run and well-designed contests. Such projects create their own legitimacy and reputational momentum. For example, at the time of this writing, the Galing Pook competition had been running for twelve years, and it does not even involve a pecuniary prize. The Indonesian government's PROPER initiative has run for over a decade and has been copied domestically and internationally. The World Bank's KDP project ran for five years and still continues as of this writing, even though there has been a regime change. Aside from its track record of successes on the ground, which garnered strong support at the local level, this project may persist because it was established and implemented with broad and active involvement at several levels of government, up to the highest political level.

Another possible reason for the absence of player fatigue is that, unlike the challenge of motivating a *specific* person on one's staff, a fixed incentive in a repeated game with jurisdictions or teams as players confronts *different* individuals over time. Local government officials change over time, and the stakeholders and beneficiaries of project activities change with each tournament—consider, for example, those who would benefit from a red-tape reduction activity versus a literacy campaign activity.

It is true that in the case of the KDP, some villages were awarded grants in several tournament cycles, and in the mancomunidades project, some jurisdictions never won anything. Nonetheless, were a project designer to observe the same jurisdiction always winning (or losing), there would be ample scope to adjust the parameters of the tournament to ensure a better distribution, if that were deemed

52. I thank Johannes Linn for pointing this out.

important.[53] For example, in the Galing Pook initiative, the designers created a special category of distinction for jurisdictions that won repeatedly, and this actually served to *increase* overall participation in the tournament over time! In fact, from a developmental point of view, such information would be very useful. The donor should be able to learn from such outcomes—especially if they occur within the context of a randomized evaluation—the underlying factors that contribute to winning and losing and, thereby, adjust the upfront technical assistance or training built into the PIJC rounds. However, even in the worst case where a tournament is "only" repeated five times and then discontinued—hence curtailing *process* sustainability—there is no reason to think of the original project as unsuccessful or unsustainable since the tasks completed during the five tournaments probably would have led to long-term benefits streams—that is, *product* sustainability.

6.3.2 Scalability and Incentive Design

With regard to scalability, the case studies also provide some potential lessons for three kinds of follow-up applications: those in which the scope is the same but larger populations are targeted in the same or a different country; those in which the size and scope are the same but the application is to occur in other locations within the same country (replicability); and those with a different scope (for example, treating a different sector or a different set of problems within the same sector). In fact, a number of the case studies (the Jharkhand, Romanian, and Moroccan projects) appear to have been pilots for just such scaling.

More generally, a careful reading of the case studies reveals that another nice feature of PIJC projects is that their horizontal and vertical hierarchical design naturally lends itself to easy scalability. Horizontally scalable opportunities exist by increasing the number of jurisdictions that are permitted to participate. In the case of a tournament PIJC, however, as the number of jurisdictions increases, two effects need to be considered. One is that each jurisdiction becomes less familiar with its competitors, entailing the risk that the motivation to compete may wane. The other effect is that it becomes harder to maintain a level playing field. Hence at some point it may be wise to establish a number of parallel interventions, for example, multiple simultaneous tournaments that take place in different regions of the country.

Vertical scalability is possible in two ways. First, one can simply carry out a successful PIJC at a higher level of jurisdiction. The Jharkhand report card (or the Nigerian scorecard, for that matter) could have been run at the level of each Indian

---

53. There is no reason to assume that good opportunities or "low-hanging fruit" are uniformly distributed in the PIJC target region. Hence it may well be the case that some jurisdictions simply face better opportunities for major improvements (or the converse). If this is so, then the PIJC's distributional objectives would have to be weighed against its economic efficiency objectives, taking into account the incentive effects on other players of having perennial winners and losers.

(Nigerian) state, rather than within just one. The KDP grants could have been awarded across kecamatans rather than within them. In a sense, the *Global Competitiveness Report* and the World Bank's *Doing Business,* with individual countries as the units of observation, were versions of the Moroccan application scaled up to the international level.[54]

Second, one can embed a PIJC at one jurisdictional level into another at the next jurisdictional level (or the reverse). For example, in principle, one could have allocated future rounds of KDP funding to those kecamatans with the "best results" (however measured) at the village level. The Moroccan project design envisioned a provincial tournament among those provinces that each had their own commune-level tournament. The province with the highest average commune score would win. This had the added virtue of stimulating provincial governments to pursue province-level reforms that would help boost the scores of all their competing communes. Likewise, to the extent a sponsor established a separate PIJC in several countries, there then could be a final international tournament based on some aggregation of each country's PIJC score at the national level (perhaps accompanied by an international conference to discuss the results and how to improve the overall structure of the intervention). Alternatively, a sector-level PIJC could be organized across sectors (say, related to corruption or to the number new workers trained), to be followed by some aggregation of each sector's PIJC score for a PIJC at the national level.

Still, there are some generic factors that might inhibit the extent to which both forms of certification and tournaments can be scaled up. First, the players in the case studies are not individuals but groups or teams. The cohesion of a team and its ability to engage in collective action becomes more difficult to maintain as its size increases (Olson 1965), though cultural idiosyncrasies influence at just what size this effect sets in.[55] For example, the "Simple and Fast" competition, which had no pecuniary prize, appears to have worked across counties in Romania, but to achieve the same actions across countries, the MCC had to provide substantial pecuniary rewards (the compacts) to overcome the transaction costs of collective action at a larger scale. Likewise, the Senegal literacy activities may have worked well at the village level but probably would not have been feasible at the municipality or regional level. Certainly, at the country level, the national government must have a leader to focus team efforts. Prime Minister Blair, for example, took on this role in London's bid to get the 2012 Olympics.

Second, not all PIJC mechanisms are likely to be equally easy to scale up in a given situation. For example, since the tournament form is a less well known game, training costs per additional (marginal) player may be higher than for certification as the scale increases.

Third, aside from the benefits of the reform itself, the rewards offered in several of the case studies were reputational in nature. Depending on a host of complex factors, however, as the size of each team increases, the importance of the team's reputation to the individual team members may decrease. For example, social capital, peer pressure, and the value of signaling may depend on the size of the jurisdiction. On the other hand, the reputational value to winning generally increases with the number of contestants and with the size of the population from which the contestants are drawn. For example, the incentives of PROPER would not likely have been so powerful had only a few firms been subject to certification or if the scheme had operated in only one kabupatan. Finally, there may be economies of scale in public relations, which is the key input in generating participatory interest in and promoting winners of certification or tournaments. Such economies would facilitate scale. On the other hand, these mechanisms depend on the public's belief in the objectivity of the referee. As the project's scope or target population size changes, the ability of the referee to maintain objectivity may be affected. This seems to have occurred in the Senegal literacy project: as the number of providers increased, the quality of oversight decreased.

Analysis of the case studies also suggests that the fixed and variable costs of a project's design, the initial conditions in the operating environment, and other factors can influence a project's scalability. Each of these is considered in turn.

Projects entail fixed (that is, not dependent on scale) and variable (dependent on scale) costs. The establishment and operation of the implementing organization and the design of the incentive mechanism are examples of fixed costs. Proposal evaluation (as in the case of the KDP and Senegal literacy projects) and indicator and target preparation and measurement (as in the case of USAID R4) are examples of variable costs. Likewise, in the tournament for country eligibility, the MCC could probably increase the number of countries competing for eligibility without any problem: the indicator values of the new country, already available from indicator providers, are simply entered into the database (the additional albeit minimal variable costs), and the same computer program along with the existing staff (the much larger fixed costs, which were already amortized into pre-existing MCC activities) calculates the rankings. On the other hand, the MCC's ability to oversee the design as well as monitor country compacts eventually *would* run into capacity constraints due to limitations in the size of its headquarters and its technical staff (again, fixed costs). Galing Pook uses pro bono experts to evaluate projects, but it too would eventually run into capacity constraints if it were expanded without addressing its fixed costs. The Russian fiscal reform, USAID R4, Romania's "Simple and Fast," the mancomunidades project, and the Nigerian scorecard all could be expanded without hitting organizational capacity constraints.

These case study examples reveal an important aspect of fixed costs in the context of scaling up. While for modest increases in participation rates fixed costs are, by definition, fixed, it is the fixed costs that ultimately pose a bottleneck to scaling up as one approaches capacity constraints.[56] Thus, for example, if the MCC adds one agricultural project to a compact, it simply hires a few more agricultural experts to augment its existing agricultural department. At some point, however, the number of agricultural projects to design and monitor would grow to such size that the MCC would need to put an additional management structure in place—an increase in fixed costs due to scaling up. Likewise, a compact project to build an airport could be handled with a few additional outside consultants; if all compacts had airport construction, the MCC would need to expand its in-house capacity and set up a whole new technical department (for infrastructure). Box 6-1 presents a revealing example, in a completely different context (EU accession), of the effect of scale on the incentives created by a tournament approach.

The examples in the last paragraph, of course, are not specific to PIJCs. Examples that are specific to PIJCs would occur when scale is increased through simultaneous, horizontal replication or through vertical PIJC embedding. Consider "horizontal" examples. Each new country Transparency International adds to its rankings requires the establishment of a completely new office and local monitoring infrastructure. A similar set of new fixed costs would confront the World Bank if it were to set up a Senegal-style literacy program in an additional country. Similarly, in the context of vertical scaling, if the KDP competition were to be embedded in a national-level tournament, a new (fixed-cost) committee structure would be required at the kabupatan level.

Since the role of initial conditions and other factors on project success is examined in section 6.4, it is enough here to note that with the exception of the inherent obstacles laid out above, many of those key conditions that make for project effectiveness also contribute to project scalability (for example, strength of social capital, existence of sufficient legislative framework, propensity to cooperate, homogeneity of population, and availability of local organizations in the sector of interest). For example, just as one would want a level playing field for jurisdictional players in the Russian, Nigerian, or Romanian reform-oriented projects to ensure participation and motivation, so too would one want a level playing field among the superjurisdictions for the simultaneous tournament at the higher level within which the first one was embedded.[57]

56. Economic theory states that for a given scale of operations, there is an optimal size for an organization that minimizes its fixed costs.

57. Note that not all PIJCs have as a complementary objective the fairness implied by a level playing field. For example, the Galing Pook project wanted to identify the *best* SNG innovations and not just the best innovations among SNGs of a given local capacity level. The same can be said for the PROPER program.

Box 6-1. *The EU Accession Game*

The EU accession process provides some interesting insights on scalability and the tournament approach. There is general agreement that the lure of playing the "EU accession game" has been very successful in encouraging central and eastern European states to radically reform their economies and even their societies. It is likely that in the 1990s there was a sense of competition among candidate states in the belief that the door might close to later entrants as the EU encountered the social and economic costs of assimilation. A similar contest may have operated to a lesser degree between Romania and Bulgaria, since the government of either would have been vociferously blamed for failing to get in while the other country did. Ten years on, however, with Turkey, the Ukraine, and even Georgia knocking at the door, the accession process is clearly showing severe signs of political strain and is at risk of grinding to a halt.

First, what kind of game is EU accession? Is it a certification or a tournament? To the extent that all newly current member states *believed* they would achieve entry if they accomplished the tasks in the *Acquis Communautaire,* it is fair to see the game as one of certification. To the extent that some of these new entrants believed that only the first few would succeed, then the game was a tournament. This view may be strengthened by recognizing that the game had the characteristics of a mixed tournament, as described in section 2.3, where tournament milestones in the form of task thresholds had to be achieved in order to stay in the accession game (and reaching those thresholds ensured competitors some preliminary benefits to playing—access to PHARE or TACIS funds.[1]

The current growing pains of the EU offer some qualitative lessons for PIJCs. First, while a PIJC may flourish at an intermediate scale of operation, that does not imply that further successful expansion is guaranteed. Clearly scalability is nonlinear. Second, variation in player characteristics should be kept within limits, as was done with the target population for the PIJC in Morocco where urban areas were excluded from play. In the case of EU accession, Turkey clearly pushes these limits. Third, the success of staging a PIJC depends on its legitimacy and the backing of all participants. The political nervousness the currently queuing members are exhibiting

1. Both PHARE and TACIS (Technical Assistance for the Commonwealth of Independent States) were funding programs of the European Union to assist former communist countries with their transition to market economies. The acronym of the PHARE program originally referred to *Pologne, Hongrie Assistance à la Reconstruction Economique.* The program subsequently expanded to include all the countries of central and eastern Europe.

(continued)

Box 6-1. *The EU Accession Game (Continued)*

suggests that the process may have lost these preconditions. Fourth, the explicit rules of the game—the EU constitution—may be in need of revision. This corresponds to the fine-tuning that inevitably occurs in repeated PIJCs. In fact, the recent rejection of a new constitution for Europe is probably itself symptomatic of the current limits to scalability facing the association. According to Johannes Linn, a former vice president of the World Bank, it may also reflect, as scale issues often do, the increasing misalignment of incentives between members of the EU government in Brussels and Strasbourg as "agents" and their constituencies in their home countries as "principals."[2]

2. Johannes Linn of the Wolfensohn Center made this observation at a January 2006 seminar on the tournament approach.

Finally, the case studies shed some light on the World Bank's observation, related to its considerations for scaling up one type of incentive mechanism, that "in some cases, it can imply starting with more actions of a more temporary character to pilot and test new social accountability mechanisms, gradually scaling them up until they become institutionalized. In other cases, it can start with putting in place the legal framework, while then moving on to operationalizing systems and processes to ensure their implementation."[58] The Romanian and Jharkhand projects started with temporary local offices (IRIS and PAF, respectively) for the running of the PIJC. Each was viewed as a pilot initiative, and neither required an additional legal basis. The Romanian program never scaled up, and the office ultimately closed.[59] The Jharkhand program expanded, and its office is still operating many years later. Though there were many additional factors involved, the Romanian office was mostly populated with foreign experts while the PAF was a strictly local organization. Over time, the success of the scorecard initiative gave the PAF credibility that no doubt contributed to it sustainability and scalability. In contrast to these two projects, the very successful PROPER program started out as a pilot administered by a permanent organization—the Ministry of the Environment. From the start the program was given a legal basis in regulatory statutes. The ministry scaled up the program by expanding the sectors and reducing the minimum enterprise size required for inclusion.

58. World Bank (2005a, p. 40).
59. The office closure had nothing to do with Romania's "Simple and Fast." Recall from section 3.1.1 that this innovative activity was an afterthought for this USAID project, developed quickly during the course of other previously contracted tasks. The contractor's (IRIS) office in Romania closed on schedule once its original tasks were accomplished.

6.4 Role of Initial Conditions and Other Requirements for Successful PIJC Applications

One of the main lessons for development effectiveness from the policy reform literature is that a project must be tailored to the idiosyncrasies of the local environment. Moreover, the "enabling" environment, which goes beyond the immediate project operational environment, is also likely to have a major impact on outcomes. The enabling environment refers, inter alia, to the quality of the country's macroeconomic and fiscal environment, the predictability and security of property rights (including the court system), and the regulatory environment.[60] The literature on sectoral reform (and policy reform in general) already discusses the importance of initial conditions, including the local environment and the enabling environment, so that discussion need not be repeated here.[61] Rather, the focus here will be on the initial conditions required for the incentive mechanisms used in the case studies. First, the initial conditions common to all of the incentive mechanisms are identified, followed by an examination of the specific conditions required for mechanisms that provide tangible rewards. This section then ends by considering an important, if unexpected, kind of initial condition—the nature of the aid sponsor itself.

6.4.1 Common Conditions

Each of the incentive mechanisms requires the preexistence of the necessary legislation—in particular, concerning public finance and administration—to empower the jurisdictions to carry out the actions required to play in the PIJC game. For example, in both Nigeria and Morocco, previous legislative reforms had created a rich, new, decentralized, de jure set of powers for municipalities, though in the latter country, there was no experience in exercising them. Moreover, as these two examples illustrate, a prior history of strong unitary government made the recently elected local officials nervous about using these powers.

To repeat an important point, successful projects strategically use community and participant input in the formulation and development process. To do this, the incentives must be such that the sponsor can elicit the participation of an existing organizational structure, such as preexisting NGOs or community-based organizations (as was the case in the Senegal literacy project). Tapping into existing organizations tends to increase project legitimacy better than setting up new ones, thus improving the chances of sustainability. Likewise, since incentive mechanisms that require benchmarking require some sort of local data collection, the

---

60. While it is semantics whether to include social and cultural norms and conventions into the definition of the enabling environment, these can be equally important. For example, one would want to make certain that a PIJC were not introduced into a Muslim country as a form of gambling.

61. See, for example, Zinnes, Eilat, and Sachs (2001).

availability of local firms with survey experience in the sector of study is usually important. The Jharkhand and Nigerian case studies demonstrate this. Some countries have public or semipublic agencies with experience in contract management and monitoring. If these are of sufficient quality or can be trained, then using them increases the likelihood of project sustainability. This was of critical benefit in the Senegal project since without the AGETIP to execute the financial side of the activity, the project would have had to set up a whole new department or agency, or risk potential loss of (process) sustainability. Even then the staff of the new office would not have had the field experience that AGETIP staff had.

Finally, with the exception of the KDP, all the case study projects depend on having an impact on the player's (team's) reputation or on causing the constituency of the team's decisionmakers to react in a way that affects the decisionmakers personally.[62] This means that the project's dissemination component is critical to the salience of the reward. The value of the reward, the rules of the game, and the results of the project all require effective public relations and dissemination. Hence an important initial condition for the success of the incentive mechanisms is that there exist local media channels and, ideally, local expertise on how to effectively advertise and disseminate project materials.

For projects such as the Jharkhand report card, the Nigerian scorecard, and Romania's "Simple and Fast," success required a target audience for dissemination of project results. This audience was expected to react to the new information and then put pressure on their representatives for change. For this to work, several conditions need to be in place. First, the public must be sufficiently educated to be able to interpret what the information is saying. Some projects made this condition less stringent; for example, PROPER disseminated technical noncompliance data to the innumerate public by translating it into simple color codes. Second, there must be legal channels through which the newly informed public can act without incurring prohibitively high transaction costs. The size of such costs is influenced by the degree to which the local culture is comfortable with inter- and intragroup cooperation and collective action. More homogeneous populations tend to experience lower transaction costs. For example, villages in Nigeria were able to act jointly on publicly provided information about the local education budget to redress local corruption, but such a response did not occur in reaction to equally egregious state-level corruption. A variant of this factor is whether the initial conditions allow for the necessary communication between different levels or branches of government. The Nigerian LEEMP project was less effective, for example, because of poor communication between municipal and provincial officials. Likewise, several of the vertical scale-up examples in section 6.3.2 might not

---

62. Even in the KDP project, a village that failed to properly implement a funded proposal would risk creating a poor reputation, which would jeopardize its chances of consideration in the next round of funding in the kecamatan.

work properly without the existence of adequate cooperation between the requisite levels of government and their agencies.

Reexamination of table 2-2 reveals that there are several design characteristics available to a PIJC—items 5, 8, 9, 10, 11, and 13, in particular—that can increase the adaptability of any given design choice. These characteristics are the design features that encourage players to voluntarily participate and excel, and in so doing apply their own superior, asymmetric knowledge so as to adjust their own game behavior to the idiosyncrasies of initial conditions. Similar flexibility is often gained by using an output-based instead of an input-based design since the former offers further flexibility to the players to adapt the rules of play to local initial conditions. While a sponsor must still do its homework in order to match its incentive design process and products to local initial conditions, the more a PIJC design incorporates the aforementioned six characteristics, the less onus there is on the designer to create a perfect fit from the start.

6.4.2 Simple Certification

With this mechanism the only reward contributing to the incentive is the positive or negative effect certification has on player reputation or constituent backlash. The requisite initial conditions, as discussed above, for informing a target population and having that population able to interpret and respond to the certification score are particularly important.

6.4.3 Pecuniary Certification

The offering of pecuniary rewards requires that certain provisions in local public finance legislation allow jurisdictions to receive the funding (for instance, central government revenue transfers or grants, as in the Russian project) or goods promised by the incentive mechanism.[63] (This condition applies to tournaments as well.) To this one may add other initial conditions required to make operative the areas that Brook and Petrie (2001) say make an output-based application successful:

—Is there local capacity to participate in or implement an assessment of what quality and scope of service would be required?

—Would the behavioral responses on how to set the incentive structure from prior applications be relevant or would new studies be required?

—For project sustainability, how would the rewards of games be paid for, and do local conditions allow for the sources proposed from prior applications?

—How would the bidding process (and the variable it would be based on) be structured to be most consistent with social and cultural conditions?

—Does the reward compensate for player disutility from implementation and from the transaction costs of team organization?

---

63. See Steffensen (2007) for a detailed discussion of the funding aspect of this issue.

—Where a PIJC application involves user fees, is the instrument used to determine the willingness to pay (contingent valuation) applicable to the particular application's conditions?

6.4.4 Tournaments

Aside from the conditions specific to pecuniary rewards, as described above, there are cultural and even religious characteristics that should be taken into account in the design of a tournament application. While these would be impossible to list exhaustively, suffice it here to provide a few examples. In the Moroccan project, designers had to exercise care not to portray the tournament as a "betting" game, since Islam prohibits gambling. Likewise, cultural conditions can affect the incentive power of a tournament when it comes to maintaining competitive interest within the players' teams and with regard to attitudes about being a winner or loser. Some analysts have expressed concern that boredom during the tournament or disillusionment at not receiving a reward could hamper the effectiveness of the tournament approach.[64] Each of these concerns is considered in turn.

Clearly, a project's success depends on how well it is presented to the targeted players, and this depends on taking into account their cultural and social beliefs and conditions. Similarly, each country and even different parts of a country (for example, rural versus urban) have their own tolerance for the length of a game. (Americans have no interest in cricket, which can take days to play, while many outside of the United States find baseball too slow to maintain their interest.) It is prudent, therefore, for project designers to assess what the appropriate length of a tournament should be for it to remain motivating. While this concern is sensible in the context of tournaments, it is equally applicable to certification mechanisms. In fact, since parties often delay certification for years, it is likely that, far from being inhibiting, the tournament approach, with its intrinsic imposed deadline, may stimulate participant action.

The issue of player disillusionment in a tournament was covered earlier in the discussion on reward effectiveness (see sections 6.2 and 6.3). The arguments and ways to minimize this concern presented there will be more or less relevant depending upon the initial conditions. While none of the case studies, under their respective sets of initial conditions, report such an issue arising, in the Nigerian LEEMP project, the players indicated that the rewards were not motivating enough. Since the rewards were for several million dollars, this underscores the point that Brook and Petrie (2001) make on importance of calibrating incentives to local conditions.

---

64. See footnote 33 in this chapter.

6.4.5 Sponsor Environment

Initial conditions within recipient countries are not the only important issue. As stressed in the literature (Zinnes and Bolaky 2002; Espina and Zinnes 2003), the incentive conditions *within the donor* can be equally critical to project effectiveness. These include the donor agency culture and the donor's relationship with its funders (in many cases, the executive and legislative branches of government).

The culture within a donor agency can have a big impact on the effectiveness of the incentive mechanisms. This is because historically most donors have not placed much emphasis on project effectiveness, in spite of lip service to the contrary. There are several reasons for this. First, donor agencies are not generally *development* agencies but rather *aid* agencies that have (at least some) nondevelopment motives in their mandates.[65] Thus the agency is often the subject of political interference from the executive or legislative branch of the funding government. Second, donors usually have a large number of simultaneous objectives (for example, "fly American," use only EU experts, alleviate poverty), with project effectiveness being just one. Third, parts of a donor's budget are often earmarked by the funding source, constraining or even dictating project formulation or implementation. Such limitations can interfere with incentives for effectiveness all along the project chain and, in the extreme case, make a mockery of any incentive mechanism (such as threats) that might risk project or program cancelation. Finally, the bureaucracy within a government or donor is usually ideologically opposed to decentralized solutions—a characteristic of PIJCs—preferring to exercise its own discretion instead. (A similar change in mind-set was necessary in the last quarter century regarding acceptance of the market price mechanism over government price controls.)

The impact of sponsor environment can be seen, for example, in the many restrictions World Bank member countries place on the use of trust funds they contribute. USAID provides another example, for it is likely that its internal environment was responsible for the difficulties in implementing the R4 system. In this case congressional earmarks meant that USAID had little discretion over most of its budget. Other examples from USAID include the lack of salient (that is, career impinging) feedback to staff about project successes or failures, and the bureaucratic use of "stovepipes" to organize projects by reform, thereby being unable to take advantage of the multidisciplinary nature of change. One can argue that the MCC's organizational design was intended to create initial conditions that would redress such problems. The MCC is a much more flexible organization, with project effectiveness and monitoring and evaluation, in particular, a central theme in its project designs. Its indicator approach to the country candidacy tournament not only ensures that projects take place in good enabling

---

65. See footnote 19 (and associated text) in chapter 3.

environments but also helps protect the MCC as an institution from political interference regarding which countries to assist. (Still, Georgia became eligible for MCC funding despite its failing score on corruption.)

6.5 Selecting the Appropriate Incentive Design

In this book I have identified several classes of PIJC incentive mechanisms and have endeavored to evaluate them and their applicability in a dozen real-world situations. Some PIJC applications were more complicated to develop, pilot, or implement than others. In general and ceteris paribus, tournaments seem to pose more implementation challenges than certifications, and the addition of pecuniary rewards further complicates any application. Likewise, some PIJC mechanisms placed different informational demands on the designer or monitoring demands on the sponsor. One question not yet directly tackled, however, is whether the greater sophistication of a given design is worth the benefits; if not, then common sense would dictate that the simpler mechanism be selected. This question will be considered from two perspectives: by PIJC mechanism and by project type.

6.5.1 When Is Greater Sophistication Necessary?

To address this question, the various PIJC mechanisms will be compared in order of their apparent sophistication.

PECUNIARY VERSUS SIMPLE CERTIFICATION

Here designers must ask themselves whether pure reputational effects are sufficient for the application at hand or whether the extra level of complexity generated by the provision of tangible prizes is necessary. In the two pecuniary certification case studies, it appears that the designers made the right choice. In the Senegal literacy project, simple certification—approval of a business plan— would clearly have been inadequate since the only motivation for the players was to have the project pay for service provision. With the Nigerian scorecard, the nature of the steps for certification and the low value placed on reputational effects meant that greater sophistication was necessary: the certification had to have a pecuniary component. Given the initial conditions in Nigeria, it is simply unlikely that a PIJC could have been conceived based on reputational rewards alone (simple certification). The one exception to this scenario would have been if legal means were used as an incentive. For example, the government could have passed a law or issued a statute that SNGs below a certain performance threshold would be subject to administrative sanctions.

Could the case studies utilizing simple certification have attained better results with a pecuniary certification? In the case of R4, I argued in section 3.1.4 that its failure to motivate the desired changes partially was due to its fuzzy reward structure; therefore one may suppose that not only were additional rewards (or penalties) necessary, but they should have been applied more rigorously. From my own experience in Romania, I would say that the "Simple and Fast" project would have had greater participation had there been pecuniary rewards. Unfortunately, the budget available for this pilot exercise did not permit such an option.

In the case of the Jharkhand report card, the rating was a retrospective "one-shot" game (that is, not repeated) among government agencies. Thus reward salience was immaterial. If it were announced that the rating exercise would be repeated, say in one year, the salience of rewards, were they reputational or pecuniary, would likely depend on the political pressure the public could bring to bear on the leadership of the respective ministries and on the latter's degree of accountability to the public. To the extent that there were substantial managerial and administrative inefficiencies to address, pecuniary rewards would probably not have been necessary per se; to the extent that poor service was due to inadequate or run-down infrastructure, the offer of pecuniary award assistance—say, allocation of a capital budget—would have been appropriate. From a separate perspective, in the Jharkhand report card, project performance had a strong regional influence, so comparisons across jurisdictions would be tricky; moreover, many of the indicators were subjective. Given this situation, the report card was, to some extent, more focused on tracking change over time *within* a jurisdiction and pointing out for which public agencies relative dissatisfaction was higher so that it could be corrected. Since all agencies needed to improve their performance, there was little sense in trying to make this happen by dichotomizing the agencies into winners and losers.

TOURNAMENT VERSUS CERTIFICATION (NONPECUNIARY)

Recall that in section 6.2 a careful decomposition revealed that there is often no major intrinsic difference in implementation difficulty between a certification and a tournament, but rather it is the nature of the specific application that makes a tournament typically seem more challenging. Moreover, since pecuniary rewards can be added to tournaments and certification alike, such rewards do not necessarily distinguish one as being more sophisticated than the other. Hence the question of tournament versus certification needs to be addressed in two steps: first, the choice of mechanism where the reward for the certification or tournament is not pecuniary, and second, the choice where it is.

As argued earlier in this chapter, aside from the initial conditions, the choice of incentive design must be based on

—the number of jurisdictions the sponsor's objectives desire to acknowledge;

—whether there exist substantive systematic or exogenous risks that might influence player motivation;

—the extent to which the application needs to identify "the best" performance under particular initial conditions (for example, best practice);

—whether the sponsor's objectives would be better served by a mechanism that encourages universal participation;

—whether there is a need for a minimum level of performance (either for the application to make sense or for the sponsor to feel that the activity was worth its attention and funding); and,

—in the case of ex-post competitions (see table 2-1), whether the donor has a clear idea of what performance is either possible or required.[66]

Tournaments generally lead actors to exert more effort than a certification for two reasons. First, if the certification bar is too high, then potentially low scoring aspirants will not try too hard, believing their situation to be hopeless, or they may even decide not to participate. Second, if the certification bar is too low, then potentially high scoring aspirants will also not try too hard since they know they are already close to satisfying the necessary criteria. This latter phenomenon occurred in the Romanian certification project, where one of the few jurisdictions to receive certification exerted little effort to meet certification criteria but certainly would have engaged in further reform had it been competing in a tournament. By the same argument, it is likely that the Moroccan project would have been less effective had it used a certification approach.

The change in the effectiveness of the Galing Pook initiative, were it to be a certification program instead of a tournament, would depend on how stringently it set the threshold for innovation. If it were set too low, too many municipalities would "win," thus devaluing the certification. If it were set too high, then too few municipalities would submit innovations to be judged.[67] By choosing a tournament design over certification, the Galing Pook organizers implicitly acknowledged the difficulties they would have in setting a threshold that would best reflect what could be achieved in the environment facing local government in the Philippines.

As discussed in chapter 2, the risk of systemic or exogenous shocks can affect motivation. Had the Russian fiscal reform project been a certification rather than a tournament, it is possible that the risk of exogenous shocks—great, given the volatility in Russia—may have dulled the other incentives and reduced participation or level of effort.

---

66. Of course, one option sometimes used is to set a series of certification levels, as is done in most hierarchical organizations such as academia and government bureaucracies.

67. If the Galing Pook rules could have specified objectively the characteristics for a minimum acceptable innovation they would want to promote (disseminate), then a certification incentive might have been appropriate. This would be similar to dynamically setting (that is, ex post) a cut-off for the number of players who may place (that is, receive a reward for coming in second, third, and so on, but not first) in a tournament. Since ex-post cut-offs are open to discretion and corruption, they have a dulling effect on incentives. In such a situation, the certification would constitute a superior incentive design.

In the case of PROPER, a tournament approach would not have been appropriate. The fact that the program was codeveloped with the Ministry of the Environment means that there was precise information about the technical capabilities of the regulated community and a multilevel color code could be created to cover the range of likely performance. Moreover, for environmental health the level of pollution matters, not simply whether one firm does better at controlling it than another. On the other hand, the Honduran mancomunidades project would have fared better as a tournament since the actual certification process implemented did not stimulate any efforts to improve local governance or administration. It simply assessed the status quo.

The USAID R4 project is an interesting situation in that its indicators could have been used for a certification or a tournament. The certification would have satisfied the organization's need for accountability and a tracking system while the same indicators could have formed the basis of a tournament (of, say, average project performance within a department or office at a mission) to motivate staff managerial efforts. In reality, the USAID R4 system suffered from lack of salient penalties, which weakened its effectiveness.

TOURNAMENT VERSUS CERTIFICATION (PECUNIARY)

There is an extra level of complexity entailed by a pecuniary reward, regardless of whether it is part of a certification or tournament mechanism. Aside from the reasons listed above for selecting one mechanism over the other, the inclusion of a pecuniary component generates some additional implementation issues to consider: budgetary control and leveraging of reward funds.

The first type of implementation issue that distinguishes certifications and tournaments with regard to pecuniary rewards is that pecuniary certification does not allocate funds according to budget constraints, nor does it allocate funds efficiently. Consider, for example, the Senegal literacy project, a case of input competition. Without knowing in advance how many proposals would technically qualify for funding, the donor would not know the cost of its program when it set a quality threshold (certification) for proposal funding. At the same time, no one would prepare a proposal without knowing its prospects for funding. Had the World Bank project "run out" of funds, the initiative would have had to stop early with, presumably, some embarrassment to all concerned. Since no donor has an unlimited budget for such funding, and donor credibility is an important ingredient for future PIJCs, the donor simply could have stated that the project would end after the first z satisfactory proposals were funded. This would have placed a burden on those NGO providers who had made the effort to collaborate with a village only to find out when they submitted their proposal that the project had ended. The tournament approach offers an alternative where the sponsor instead prospectively provides the criteria for proposal quality and announces up to V dollars for the x best proposals meeting the criteria, where $x = \text{int}\{B/V\}$ and B is the total budget the donor has available.[68]

This is exemplified by the KDP project, which would not have worked without a tournament approach *at the level of the proposal* (an input to the final desired outcome). The KDP gave each participating kecamatan an amount B and a limit of V ($\leq\$35,000$) to fund x proposals. Curiously, the MCC tournament for candidacy does not ensure budgets are respected, since the allocation of compact funding is disconnected from a country's eligibility scores. Here the standing MCC offer of candidacy for countries with supramedian scores uses the tournament format to stimulate countries to do their best even though just how to do so and what can be achieved is uncertain to all—including the MCC. The onus is thus squarely placed on the prospective candidate, not the donor.[69] Nonetheless, some in Congress and in policy circles expressed concern recently about the appropriateness and impact on incentives of the MCC's need to promise future funds that have yet to appear in a federal budget approved by Congress.

In the Senegal literacy project, the budget issue is more complicated. Here it is likely that a tournament approach would have led to a much more cost-effective program.[70] This would have mattered to the extent that training proposals were being turned down for lack of project funds, that is, a more cost-effective project would have left funds for more literacy training. On the other hand, if the project sought to generate the maximum number of training courses irrespective of their effectiveness in alleviating illiteracy, then the limitation of access implicit in a tournament would have been welfare reducing. This is of particular relevance for poorly performing training firms that sought repeat funding.

A second type of implementation consideration when choosing between a pecuniary certification and a pecuniary tournament is the latter's potential for leveraging sponsor funds in any ex-post–based PIJC.[71] This operates in two ways.

First, a donor's challenge is typically how to stimulate the most reform possible given its budget constraints. The answer, as any compliance program illustrates, is to offer an attractive prize (or costly penalty) but with a less-than-certain probability of winning, that is, to organize a tournament. This means a fixed budget can motivate a large number of active participants. Second, from the sponsor's operational perspective, a tournament format does not require writing a contract

68. The need to preestablish V is itself a source of potential economic inefficiency, since some proposals may prove to merit greater levels of funding.

69. Just how salient the MCC incentive is remains open to question. However, it does ensure that only countries with relatively better policy environments receive MCC assistance. This leads to an important policy question: should donor budgets be used primarily to stimulate change or as an investment in only the best environments?

70. An example of such a tournament would be one where the winning NGOs would be those that provide the service at the lowest cost per trainee receiving a passing grade on a standardized literacy test.

71. This is demonstrated mathematically in appendix D.

for each potential recipient but only, at most, for the winner(s). The main limit on the number of players then becomes the cost of pre- and posttournament benchmarking and the impact on player incentives as the probability of winning falls, issues that calibration can address (see below).

Finally, two comments are in order with regard to the mechanism design choice between pecuniary certification and tournaments. First, most incentive mechanisms can be designed to generate "ownership" among recipients. Conditions that are typically important in order for players to feel ownership are that their participation is voluntary and that they have the opportunity to feel in control, say, by having an active role in various aspects of PIJC design, such as selection of tasks, the nature and structure of rewards, and design of benchmarking. Thus, for example, the R4 mandatory initiative did not generate much ownership while the Senegal literacy initiative did. Second, prospective evaluation (for example, randomized trials) can be incorporated into each of the mechanism designs, especially during pilot stages, to help determine which incentive scheme would be most effective and to assess the need for pecuniary rewards (whose size would then have to be calibrated for salience).

6.5.2 Is There a Preferred Incentive Design for Each Type of Intervention?

In the comparisons above, there is a risk of concluding that one PIJC incentive design might dominate all other designs independently of the nature of the application. But does it really make sense that the preferred incentive design for infrastructure investment would be the same as that required to stimulate literacy? To address this question, the issue of incentive design will now be considered from the perspective of the type of objective a project might have. For each type of objective, I suggest what the preferred incentive design would be; then, where a different design was actually used in a case study, I speculate why the preferred approach was not used. For each type of objective, table 6-13 summarizes the major characteristics of the preferred design versus those of the design actually used in the relevant case studies.

PHYSICAL INVESTMENT

Here what matters is whether implementation is to be provided mainly by outside (probably foreign) experts or by those associated with the local beneficiaries. In the former instance, proposals generally would be judged on either least-cost provision of a given economic rate of return (ERR) or the highest ERR for a given budget, in each case with some governance mechanism to adjudicate penalties for failure to meet ex-ante performance criteria. The MCC, for example, used the threat of compact abrogation. The choice of investment, however, often has an equity and distributional element, leading to political considerations that may not be reflected in the ERR. If competing proposals were for complex projects, then they would likely be expensive to prepare since accurate ERRs would be necessary.

Table 6-13. *Choice of PIJC Incentive Design by Project Type*

| | Preferred approach[a] | | | | | | Case study approach[b] | | | | |
| | Mechanism | | | | | | Mechanism | | | | |
Objective (situation)	Type[c]	A/P	I/O	P/NP	Why preferred	Name	Type[c]	A/P	I/O	P/NP	Why preferred approach not used
Physical investment (limited local implementation)	T, M	P	O	P	Sets minimum ERR standard and encourages project proposals to compete for best use of funds	MCC compact	C*	P	I*	P	Choice of funded activities probably too political for purely quantitative criteria. Proposal prep probably too expensive. Who bears risk of under-performance?
Physical investment (mainly local implementation)	T, M	P	I &O	P	Sets minimum ERR standard and encourages project proposals to compete for best use of funds (I); additional funds require success of prior fund use (O)	Indonesia, KDP	T, M	P	I &O	P	…

Training (women's literacy)	C	P	O	P	Some part of compensation should be based on pupil postcourse test scores	Senegal, PAPF	C	P	I*	P	No good reason not to track provider performance to receive additional contracts; use of pupil test scores may have been logistically difficult or open to corruption.
Administrative and regulatory reform (SNG level)	T, M	P	O	P	Ensures that all jurisdictions participate and exert significant efforts to place or receive consolation award	Romania, "Simple and Fast"	C*	P	O	NP*	Donor too bureaucratic or timid to fully commit to the new approach.
						Philippines, Galing Pook	T, M	*d	O	NP*	Here the goal was strictly to identify and disseminate successes, not to stimulate them; so pecuniary reward was unnecessary.

(continued)

Table 6-13. *Choice of PIJC Incentive Design by Project Type (Continued)*

Objective (situation)	Preferred approach[a]						Case study approach[b]					
	Name	Mechanism				Why preferred	Name	Mechanism				Why preferred approach not used
		Type[c]	A/P	I/O	P/NP			Type[c]	A/P	I/O	P/NP	
							Honduras, mancomunidades	T	A*	I*	P	Technical assistance offered only to those municipalities that met preconditions related to their administrative environment; ex-ante performance was sufficient, but opportunity was missed to reveal who was motivated to reform.
							Morocco, MEPI	T, M	P	O	P	…
							Nigeria, scorecard	C*	A*	O	P	Sponsor may not have wanted to wait for performance and may have worried that corruption would invalidate official data used to judge contest.

Policy and regulatory reform (central government)	T	P	O	P	Results-based and reduces informational demands and performance monitoring required for donor	MCC eligibility	T	P	O	P	...
Budget funding (grants to SNG)	T, M	P	O	P	Overcomes central government needing to know degree of performance possible	Russia, fiscal reform	T, M	P	O	P	...
Improve accountability of donor aid delivery process	C	P	O	P	Each project is different so no use in finding best, only that each achieves a modicum of success; yet, accountability requires signaling "praise," not blame	USAID R4	C	P	O	NP*	Civil service regulations do not permit bonuses; high turnover of USAID staff on project; targets not independently set; much of outcome was outside of staff's control.

(continued)

Table 6-13. *Choice of PIJC Incentive Design by Project Type (Continued)*

Objective (situation)	Preferred approach[a]						Case study approach[b]				
	Type[c]	Mechanism			Name	Why preferred	Type[c]	Mechanism			Why preferred approach not used
		A/P	I/O	P/NP				A/P	I/O	P/NP	
Regulatory compliance (firm improvements)	C	P	O	NP	Indonesia, PROPER	Dissemination of firm's anti-social behavior in Indonesian context is sufficient punishment	C	P	O	P*	The prize (exemption of regulatory fine) was perhaps a political quid pro quo for having the large firms accept the initiative when it began.
Service delivery (local)	T	P	O	P	Jharkhand, scorecard	Ideally, agencies for a given service to compete across jurisdictions; benefits for improvements could be staff bonuses; if service is privately provided then engage in yardstick competition and award concessions accordingly	C*	A*	O	NP*	Within a single jurisdiction, agencies from different service sectors competed for beneficiary rating of service performance.

Note: ... = not applicable

a. All projects are preferable with ex-post, output-based performance.

b. * indicates where case study design characteristics differ from our "preferred" design.

c. "Type" refers to incentive design (see table 6-1, row 6 of PIJC component section for codes). A/P, ex ante or ex post, referring to whether players act before or after game begins; I/O, input- or output-based performance competition; P/NP, pecuniary or nonpecuniary (usually reputational) awards.

d. It is not always clear whether players viewed this PIJC as a stimulus to engage in reform or just as an opportunity for free publicity for reforms undertaken for independent reasons.

The sponsor may not want to bear such costs. If a penalty were placed on the recipient ex-post for underperformance on the ERR, then the agreement on risk sharing might be problematic.

If the beneficiaries are the main implementers, then they will internalize the cost of both a poor proposal choice as well as sloppy implementation. Therefore, allowing the beneficiaries more flexibility on proposal choice makes sense. This was the case for the KDP.

TRAINING

This activity could be implemented using either certification or a mixed tournament, depending on whether or not the playing field is level. If it is not, then a certification based on ex-post performance (generally test-score based) is indicated. The challenge is how to construct the pecuniary or in-kind reward for the service provider. If such providers are already certified, then the threat of losing certification due to underperformance may be enough to maintain effort. Of course, this requires tracking of actual individuals within the provider organization, since they may otherwise simply request certification under a different NGO name. (Such shenanigans were actually observed over the course of the Senegal literacy project.)

SNG ADMINISTRATIVE AND REGULATORY REFORM

In a multijurisdictional reform effort with a level playing field, the mixed tournament is really the way to go. This incentive design generates the most player effort in the case where the sponsor has imperfect knowledge about what is achievable. Where this approach was not taken in the case studies, it was due to bureaucratic obstacles not directly related to tournaments, a schedule that had insufficient time for assessing player performance using a game format, or a framework in which prior performance was considered a proxy for future (*post*game) performance, therefore making a game unnecessary.

The recommendation for an ex-post design (see the note to table 6-13) is predicated on the application in question having the goal of *encouraging* administrative reform in addition to disseminating best practice in this field. One case study (Galing Pook) had only the explicit goal of disseminating best practices. In this more modest context its ex-ante tournament design should be considered appropriate.

POLICY REFORM

Donors have come to realize that sustainable policy reform without an indigenous demand for it is an oxymoron. As such, conditionality should be replaced by tournaments that allow countries to signal their suitability for further reform through their actual reform efforts. This is especially the case when one considers how hard it is for a donor to estimate what level of improvement is feasible for a given level of development. This is what the MCC eligibility indicators achieve by identifying those countries at a given stage of development whose policy performance is above the median for their group.

BUDGET FUNDING

If the amount of budgetary support is limited, and one wishes to encourage local public finance reform, then running a tournament is a clear solution to identifying both which jurisdictions are trying hardest to improve and what level of improvement is feasible. The Russian fiscal reform projects may be considered an example of this best practice.

DONOR ACCOUNTABILITY

The success of many of a donor's more ambitious projects is held hostage to beneficiary government action (and sometimes acts of God). This makes it difficult to assign blame for their failure to donor staff (or even their contractors). To make matters worse, donor staff move from project to project, and their civil service regulations strictly limit rewards that staff may receive. How does one impose accountability on such projects in such an environment? While the answer to this question again depends on the exact nature of the intervention, having those being held accountable set their own targets, confirm whether they have been met, and be immune from the ensuing praise or blame does not seem to be the best solution. Instead MCC compacts offer another kind of approach. Here the beneficiary is asked to bear the opportunity cost of a poor project choice (or its execution) by forfeiting the additional benefits that an alternative project would have generated. (The MCC avoids principal-agent problems related to project choice by requiring selection via multi-interest committees and by imposing a minimum ERR.)

An additional—and not mutually exclusive—option that is feasible only in cases where quantitative outcome indicators are possible is to allow the donor staff to state the criteria under which a project is selected and then to contract the project's statistical assessment to an independent evaluation firm. (The MCC does something like this.) Such a practice would allow an assessment of whether the outcome could be attributed to the donor's actions and, in the case of failure (which, by the way, is actually a relative concept and not usually dichotomous), test the extent to which the donor's (or its consultants') efforts were at "fault."

REGULATORY COMPLIANCE

In theory regulatory compliance is a simple cost-benefit calculation for the firm, just like tax compliance. In each instance there is a probability of being found out of compliance, an ensuing probability of being convicted, and then a probability of the conviction being enforced. On the cost side are also the transaction costs that both the regulator and the regulated must incur. Under a weak regulatory and legal system, it may be worth it for the regulator to publicly shame the noncomplying party rather than incur the transaction costs of conviction with uncertain outcomes. The question is then how to implement such a system and to avoid any potential political interference. Ideally, the noncomplying firm should pay the fine associated with being out of compliance as well as incur the social stigma. In some cases the "price" of initiating such a system is to agree not to impose any fines, with the understanding that the social stigma will cause the noncompliant firm to mend its ways. Later, once the stigmatizing system is in place and working well, the savvy regulator can reintroduce the pecuniary or operating-restriction sanctions. The PROPER project is a good example of a successful application of this approach (see section 3.1.3).

SERVICE DELIVERY

If one is interested in assessing the performance of a local-level public service provider, as was the case in the Jharkhand report card, comparing (certifying) beneficiary satisfaction may be a good place to start. Will such an undertaking motivate improvements? If politicians put pressure on their agencies or if they themselves feel embarrassed enough to allocate the agencies additional resources, then the answer may be yes. Otherwise, without the "threat" of repeated future surveys, these service providers may not undertake reform. This is especially true if the comparisons of the single cross-section survey are between agencies from different sectors (for example, forestry versus health services). The way to proceed, then, is to ensure that the surveys generate salient consequences for the service providers. One way to achieve this is to make comparisons *across* jurisdictions but *within* the same service category (an analogous approach was used in the MEPI Morocco project). Such comparisons, triggering civic pride, may generate public pressure for change. Using pre- and postcompetition surveys (or repeated surveys of a preannounced frequency in the case of long-term reforms) stimulates even more concerted action. Once several jurisdictions are part of a comparison, the competition becomes an implicit tournament.

6.5.3 Sachs-Easterly Debate

Coincidentally, a healthy debate has been taking place between two thoughtful development economists, Jeffrey Sachs and William Easterly (Easterly 2006a, 2006b; Sachs 2005) that is quite pertinent to the PIJC enterprise.[72] While the

72. See also William Easterly, "Dismal Science," *Wall Street Journal,* November 15, 2006, p. A18; Easterly, "The U.N. Millennium Project for Ending World Poverty," *Wall Street Journal,* December 5, 2006, p. A19; Nicholas Kristof, "Aid: Can It Work?" *New York Review of Books,* October 5, 2006, pp.41–44; Jeffrey Sachs, "Vibrant Economies, High Taxes, and High Social Welfare Spending," *Wall Street Journal,* November 27, 2006, p. A13; Sachs, "How Aid Can Work," letter, *New York Review of Books,* December 21, 2006, p. 97. I thank Navtej Dhillon of the Wolfensohn Center for pointing out the connection to me.

debate has a fine intellectual pedigree, especially in the twentieth century, and its current rendition encompasses many nuances, at heart it is about the speed and manner in which outsiders can facilitate the development process.[73] For the current purposes, this debate can highlight several development effectiveness issues that the PIJC approach has sought to address.

First, the debate asks whether there is a role for planning as a tool for directed development. Sachs believes that the rich nations have a moral obligation to offer to act as outside coordinators for consenting developing countries and to assist them in developing and executing a series of sectoral development plans.[74] Toward this end the rich countries would contribute an order of magnitude increase in their current levels of financial assistance so that a "big push" may occur to overcome the "poverty trap" in which these countries find themselves.[75] Easterly (2006a), seeing this orientation as a return to central planning and as the creation of a welfare state, believes that both historical and recent development experience on the ground discredits these "utopian" notions.

Second, Sachs believes there is an important role for large dollops of public sector investment, both national and international. Easterly believes that such investment would be poorly utilized. Rather, he urges support for microlevel activities initiated by the recipients themselves. Sachs sees his approach as leading to quicker development; Easterly sees his approach as leading to gradual development, which, he believes, is the only speed at which true socioeconomic development can occur.

Both these issues underscore radically different views of the role of government. Underlying Sachs's view is the belief that the existing weak governments in developing countries are a consequence of poverty and morbidity whereas Easterly's view is based on the diametrically opposite arrow of causality.

Third, with regard to project feasibility, Sachs appears to place more emphasis on the technical (agronomical, environmental, medical, technological) aspects while Easterly places more emphasis on the behavioral (incentives, transaction costs, principal-agent) aspects. Sachs observes that technical and cost-effective solutions are readily available to drastically reduce morbidity and mortality so that citizens would be able to get on with the business of economic development. Easterly agrees these technical solutions are available, but their adoption—especially where infrastructure and government policy are required—

73. These nuances include the relationship between creating a welfare state and freedom (as posited in Friedrich Hayek's *Road to Serfdom*), the role of macro versus micro donor initiatives, whether the effect of large aid inflows is immiserizing, whether donors should help all governments or only democratic ones, and whether the OECD countries have lessons for less developed countries.

74. Sachs, "How Aid Can Work."

75. See Easterly (2006a) for a discussion as to whether there is any empirical evidence for the poverty trap.

depends on social norms, culture, and political institutions whose behaviors may be based on information and incentives not aligned with those of the wishful project proponent.

While this is not the place to resolve this debate, and while it is easy to be sympathetic to Sachs's plea for an order of magnitude increase in international assistance for poverty alleviation, the PIJC approach conforms to the Easterly orientation. This can be demonstrated by drawing on the insights of the previous chapters to show what the PIJC approach implies for a radical increase in sponsor financial assistance, the role of government in citizen welfare, central planning, externally imposed solutions, and technical versus behavioral feasibility.

The PIJC approach is a mechanism for delivering development assistance and not a call for an increase thereof. In fact, since tournaments focus this assistance and leverage the funds that are available—recall that it encourages many more players to exert efforts than the number who will actually receive financial assistance—one could argue that its application would *reduce* donor expenditures. Of course, the consequent increase in development effectiveness might stimulate additional commitments in development assistance and thereby reduce or reverse this economizing effect.

PIJC operates on bottom-up incentives and encourages—in fact, demands—grassroots participation to solve one's own problems, all as suggested by Easterly. The approach firmly acknowledges the information asymmetries between the donor (or initiating government) and the recipients. Since the approach endeavors to reward only performance, it helps only those who take the initiative to help themselves. Players exert effort only on those tasks they are motivated to address. All this is in the spirit of Easterly's philosophy; PIJC is an incentive-compatible approach.

At the same time, since the design and initiation of a PIJC application often—though not by necessity—comes from an outside body, the approach also operates from the top down, as suggested by Sachs. This is because an outsider usually needs to kick-start an activity among parties suffering from coordination failure.[76] Nonetheless, the decisions regarding PIJC participation, the tasks subject to competition, and the solutions to apply generally originate voluntarily from the beneficiaries themselves, not from an outside entity. In this sense, Easterly's asymmetric information, principal-agent, and transaction cost concerns are directly addressed. Moreover, the intention of the PIJC is to strengthen through use the existing political, legal, and legislative institutions, not to circumvent or replace them, even though they are inevitably weak.

---

76. The reader is urged not to confuse coordination failure with a poverty trap or other threshold nonlinearity motivations, which have been the basis for the "big push" arguments of Paul Rosenstein-Rodan and Paul Romer (see Murphy, Shleifer, and Vishny 1989).

In short, the PIJC approach, while initiated by outsiders, is a local empowerment enterprise similar in spirit to devolution and decentralization. By overcoming coordination problems, jurisdictions find locally invented solutions to local problems. These solutions also generate demonstration effects that compete in the marketplace of ideas to be freely taken up by other jurisdictions. This cost-effective approach, therefore, is far removed from a central planning or welfare-state orientation.

7

Conclusions and Scope for Future Applications

In chapter 6, I endeavored to identify as many lessons as possible from the case studies of chapters 3 through 5. The numerous results were purposely case specific. The present chapter restates the nature of the mechanism choices in the starkest terms and then, in light of the findings of chapter 6, considers the pros and cons of the prospective interjurisdictional competition approach—and of tournaments in particular. The ultimate goal, however, is not instrumental but project oriented, namely, how to apply the incentive mechanisms to improve sponsor effectiveness in tackling the substantive areas of their interest, such as poverty alleviation, local public services and red tape, corruption, youth unemployment, tropical disease control and eradication, and even global governance. These clarifications allow one to identify potential opportunities to simplify the approach. The chapter ends by pinpointing some remaining sources of uncertainty, areas requiring further research, and application opportunities for the future.

7.1 Clarifying the Fundamental Issues

7.1.1 Statement of the Problem

The sponsor wishes to influence entities in a target population either to produce a good or service or to modify a law or procedure. This requires some motivational device or "incentive mechanism." Historically, the mechanism sponsors have employed has been a bilateral contract with the recipient (or its legal representative). Some of these contracts carried (generally policy) conditions or a quid pro quo.

Such contracts were laboriously negotiated, were intensely monitored by the sponsor over the contract period, and offered no assurance that the recipient's compliance with the conditions would continue once the sponsor's obligations were fulfilled. Under such circumstances, scaling up an intervention to multiple jurisdictions was impractical.

An alternative class of mechanism—the PIJC—has the potential to overcome some of the incentive-compatibility weaknesses and the limited jurisdictional coverage of the bilateral contract approach, and the principal goal of the research in this book has been to evaluate its suitability from both a theoretical and experiential perspective. In so doing, the research also underscores the importance of other components of the project within which the mechanism operates. These include the components that establish how and who identifies the "problem" and how to address it, how to assess participant performance, and what the rewards are and what the technology is for implementing them. Thus, while incentive mechanisms are the focus, this story must also touch on the presence and use of these other components, which, fortunately, are not generally mechanism specific. The participating "entities" or "players" in all but one of the dozen case studies are political "jurisdictions," so these three appellations are used interchangeably in the ensuing discussion.

In reading the case studies presented in chapters 3 through 5, one cannot help but be impressed with the diversity of applications for which PIJC incentive mechanisms have been applied; however, in the majority of cases, PIJCs have been used to increase citizen empowerment, government accountability, and transparency, and to stimulate local governments to improve their output quantity, quality, and efficiency by unleashing the forces of competition (and its effect on innovation) in the government sphere. Incentive mechanisms (such as auctions and competitive procurement) have also been used to allocate investment (primarily in infrastructure) and to generate employment in small business. However, PIJC techniques can be applied to such diverse tasks as location choice (such as for the Olympics), adoption of disease avoidance and mitigation methods (mosquito netting), and cost-effective road maintenance.

7.1.2 What Is Being Evaluated Here?

At first glance, each of the dozen case studies appears to have a unique incentive mechanism to motivate effort in the target population. As the analysis here revealed, however, PIJCs essentially entail just three types of core incentive mechanisms, as well as combinations thereof:

   —simple certification, in which a project-sponsored body grades some aspect(s) of player performance against an absolute preset "bar(s)," and where the grade itself is the only reward each certified party receives;

   —pecuniary certification, which is the same as simple certification except that certified parties also receive a tangible reward; and

—tournaments, in which a preset number of parties (less than the total number competing) who achieve the best grades for their performance over a preset time interval—with no absolute threshold to surpass—are declared "winners" and receive a grade and possibly a reward.

One particular combination of these, referred to here as a mixed tournament, appeared in two case studies. Like a tournament, it prospectively offers awards and prizes to a limited number of jurisdictional contestants for achieving the best performance on a set of tasks beyond a preset threshold; like a pecuniary certification, it offers consolation prizes to jurisdictional contestants who exceed the preset threshold.

Sponsors utilize these core mechanisms in projects to stimulate the production of either inputs to a process (such as investment proposals or improvements to the policy environment preconditions) necessary to achieve their objectives, or outputs of the process that achieve the objectives themselves (for example, the satisfactory functioning of the investment or meeting of the reform target). The inputs and outputs can be "produced" before, during, or after the project's incentives are in place. The incentives may target a participant's *level* of performance or the *change* of level. Beyond the inherent benefits of achieving the specific project goals, winning can confer to the successful participant either direct benefits from the project—for instance, a reward such as a grant—or indirect benefits that arise from recipient performance on the project—for example, a project award that signals investors to do business (or not) in the jurisdiction. When one considers the possible combinations of all these key incentive attributes, the rich array of incentive designs observed in the case studies is no longer surprising.

A particular benefit of developing a comprehensive model of the variations in PIJC incentive mechanisms is that it provides a perfect opportunity to investigate how various PIJC components contribute to project success or failure. This then enables one to examine what the benefits would have been of a less (or more) complicated incentive design, whether such a modification would have been feasible, and, if so, why it was not implemented.

7.1.3 Disentangling the Mechanism Differences

When analyzing the effectiveness of alternative PIJC mechanisms, it is important to compare "apples to apples" and not "to oranges." Thus I first tried to be clear about what are *not* intrinsic differences between various approaches.

Both standard bilateral contracts and PIJC approaches are amenable to a participatory orientation in the conception and implementation of a project. Also, both standard bilateral contracts and PIJC approaches may use quantitative benchmarks as well as focus on producing "inputs" or "outputs." Regarding intrinsic similarities between the certification and tournament approaches, a sponsor can have a participatory focus regardless of whether it designs a tournament- or certification-based project. Likewise, regardless of which incentive mechanism is used, the project design can include a metric for winning or certifying that depends on the value(s) of graduated or dichotomous benchmarks. Both certifications and tournaments may be designed with a baseline measurement followed by a "finish line" benchmark or may only use the latter.[1] In both cases, the project may deliver technical assistance before, during, or after the benchmarking period. Both mechanisms can have a retrospective design (mechanism judges past performance) or a design based on prospective incentives (mechanism stimulates performance); independent of this distinction, the design can score either inputs or outputs.

Once these commonalities are understood, a number of insights become clear. First, standard donor contracts (with or without conditionality) are really just special cases of certification in which there is but one player. On the other hand, unlike certification, standard donor bilateral contracts must have pecuniary or in-kind rewards since the reputational awards from winning are generally of limited value if there are no other players. Second, neither certifications nor tournaments are inherently more time consuming to run ceteris paribus; it is only the inclusion of additional design elements—which could be integrated into either mechanism—that leads to greater complexity. Third, neither mechanism works properly unless several components are present and well implemented, that is, success requires that project components work synergistically; so having the "right" incentive mechanism alone is not enough. For example, having a reward with no benchmarking or benchmarking without a reward makes a huge difference in project effectiveness.

In theory, certification and tournament design differences boil down to whether the performance bar is absolute or relative, whether or not a reward is directly provided, and the number of contesting jurisdictions that can win or place. In short, the three core mechanisms essentially form a continuum of incentive design options. *In practice,* the main differences among the types of PIJCs are in the incentives for generating group action; the size, control, and structure of costs; sponsor informational requirements; and the creation of positive externalities.

7.1.4 The Effects of Missing and Unnecessary PIJC Components

While both the similarities and differences among the core incentive mechanisms are subtler than first thought, success depends on adapting the incentive design to the idiosyncrasies of the initial conditions. An examination of the case studies suggests that several of them might have achieved more had they adopted one or more of the PIJC components they were missing. For example, the Romanian

---

1. In fact, in a retrospective or ex-ante PIJC, if one measurement is taken, it is semantic whether it is called a baseline or finish line.

"Simple and Fast" project would have had greater success if its rewards had been more salient. An evaluation component would have increased the cost-effectiveness of the Senegal literacy project. It is also likely that the Honduran *mancomunidades* project would have had a greater effect had it followed an ex-post rather than ex-ante performance design; that is, the design was weakened because rewards were given on the basis of performance that had taken place *before* the project's incentives could have an impact.

Of course, the relevant question is not where in theory one could improve an incentive design but whether such an improvement would have been feasible in practice. While answers to this question must remain speculative, a careful reading of each of the projects just mentioned suggests that the adoption of the missing PIJC components would have been feasible had the designers wanted to do so. On the other hand, while table 6-13 proposes concrete design improvements for many of the case studies, it also indicates that in most cases there appear to be good reasons for their omission from the design. These reasons, however, did not call into question the infeasibility of the proposals per se. Again, in the Romanian "Simple and Fast" project, the lack of pecuniary rewards was due to the USAID project officer's decision to try out the project concept with funds already available within an existing project rather than take the time to acquire the additional funds such rewards would have required (not to mention the possible need to run a new consultancy procurement).

In addition, weaknesses in projects adopting the PIJC approach did not seem to be intrinsic to the mechanism but rather were the result of short-comings in a specific application's design or implementation. For example, the potential achievements of the USAID R4 system and the World Bank's Nigerian scorecard project were *not* limited because the PIJC approach but rather because the rewards were not sufficiently salient. Thus one should not confuse weaknesses in project design with intrinsic limitations in its incentive mechanism.

Finally, no case study presented a situation where there were redundant (unnecessary) PIJC components.

7.2 Pros and Cons of the PIJC Approach

There is a clear trend for projects to include some sort of certification mechanism in their design. The appearance of indicators and interest in evaluation are notable manifestations of this development. The examples in section 1.3 and in chapter 4 suggest that in some situations tournament approaches can offer even more powerful ways to incorporate incentive compatibility into project design. At the same time, an exhaustive search through the literature of sponsor experience does not turn up many examples of tournament applications. Why the apparent contradiction?

Many observers have pointed to a gamut of concerns and even explanations for this observation.[2] I have tried to address many of these in this book, including

—PIJC approaches are too sponsor driven for outcomes to be sustainable;

—sponsors end up working with *receptive* local counterparts who are fundamentally at odds with other key organizational actors;

—players are only interested in the financial rewards, so reforms are reversible;

—tournament approaches only target ad hoc unimportant reforms;

—tournament approaches require other reforms be to effective or only address a first step in a long reform process;

—it is difficult to build a neutral system (institution), and implementer objectivity will be elusive;

—the desired outputs of PIJCs take too long to obtain; and

—there are many countries or regions where competitive approaches would be considered too confrontational to be accepted and, in the case of tournaments, where cultural norms of a subgroup would not be amenable to an approach based on rankings.

This section revisits these issues by summarizing the pros and cons discovered in the preceding chapters' analyses of past experience with PIJC components. In doing this, one needs to decide whether to compare the properties of a PIJC against either the theoretically possible properties or the de facto properties (that is, those typically implemented) of alternative mechanisms. Likewise, while section 7.1 identified many *theoretical* commonalities between certification and tournament approaches, some theoretically favorable properties of certification are not often observed in practice. The following assessment addresses the pros and cons of features that are typical of practice while pointing out the theoretical exceptions.

The discussion begins by summarizing the potential benefits of PIJCs over conventional approaches. It then considers the circumstances in which certification, tournaments, and even conventional approaches can have special advantages over one another. For the reader's convenience, table 7-1 summarizes these comparisons.

7.2.1 Benefits of Incentive-Compatible Approaches

The idea of an incentive-compatible approach is that if the recipient of assistance shares the same objectives as the sponsor, then the former will be more collaborative and exert more effort than otherwise. In addition to making the attainment

---

2. This paragraph draws on one Brookings referee's concise enumeration of these concerns, which I have heard frequently when presenting the PIJC concept. On the other hand and as explicitly stated in section 2.6, the case studies selected for this book were not drawn randomly from the population of possible sponsor projects; rather, they reflect the author's perception of what a representative sample of *completed* PIJCs would look like. As such, the notion of there being "too few" tournament applications is somewhat speculative.

Table 7-1. Comparison of Complexity and Cost of Alternative Project Designs[a]

Step	Characteristic	Incentive mechanism		
		Conventional	Certification	Tournament
Design of indicators and weighting	Complexity	Generally qualitative and based on presumption of "best efforts"	Depends on number of reform tasks; can be qualitative	Depends on number of reform tasks if based on surveys
	Cost	Part of initial negotiations for assistance	Borne by sponsors; more modest than in tournaments	Sponsors bear pecuniary costs; stakeholders contribute feedback via meetings
Reward structure	Complexity	Aid must be given to each jurisdiction, which requires idiosyncratic rewards for each one; so, singly simple but jointly complicated	Provided only to certified parties; probably simplest of all mechanisms	Provided only to winners, placers, and those meeting threshold; relatively complex
	Cost	Borne by sponsors; each jurisdiction must receive aid, so mechanism is very expensive	Borne by sponsors; only certified parties receive rewards, so less costly than conventional approach	Borne by sponsors; less expensive than conventional approach
Treatment design	Complexity	None ex ante; retrospective methods feasible, cheaper, but less reliable	Simple (complexity depends on evaluation method)	Most complex (depends on evaluation method); if randomized trials, requires government acceptance
	Cost	Least expensive; minimal country burden	Not expensive but more than conventional method	Most expensive and information intensive

(continued)

Table 7-1. *Comparison of Complexity and Cost of Alternative Project Designs*[a] *(Continued)*

		Incentive mechanism		
Step	Characteristic	Conventional	Certification	Tournament
Preimplementation public relations	Complexity	Not often used; otherwise basic	Moderate	Moderate (complex for mixed tournament)
	Cost	Minimal	Sponsors (government) cover privately (publicly) owned media costs	Sponsors (government) cover privately (publicly) owned media costs
Player training	Complexity	…	Simple	Moderate (complex for mixed tournament)
	Cost	…	Low; borne by sponsors	Moderate; borne by sponsors
Contracting	Complexity	Complex, since provided to all jurisdictions	Minimal; a pamphlet explains rules to prospective participants	Modest; a pamphlet explains rules to prospective participants
	Cost	Expensive	Minimal, excluding assessment	Modest, excluding assessment
TA (needs, conditions, schedule)[b]	Complexity	Simple (only 1 package required) in-project delivery	Moderate; needs are same as conventional case; more likely provided to all who request it via workshops.	Moderate; provided to groups of players via workshops (mixed version: provided in stages as thresholds are met)
	Cost	Very expensive since it is generally provided to all jurisdictions separately	Potentially expensive if there is high demand; cost unknown up front	Least expensive; mounts with number of workshops if players geographically spread out
In-project monitoring	Complexity	Complex	…	…
	Cost	Most expensive since there is little player ownership or incentive to excel	In theory none, but depends on degree sponsors pretested mechanism	Limited but more than under certification; depends on degree sponsors pretested mechanism

Benchmarking	Complexity	... [c]	Limited to checking certification requirements	Complex because all jurisdictions, whether they play or not, are measured
	Cost	...	Modest	High, perhaps $100,000 for sponsors; none for government
Evaluation protocols	Complexity	Moderate, if done rigorously	Moderate, if done rigorously	Complex, if randomized trials used
	Cost	Less expensive than for tournaments; borne by sponsors	Less expensive than for tournaments; borne by sponsors	Prospective methods more expensive than retrospective but more believable; borne by sponsors
Postimplementation dissemination	Complexity	Not required for mechanism	Simple but can be costly; critical for sustainability of mechanism	Less simple than certification; can be costly; critical for sustainability of mechanism
	Cost	...	Sponsors (government) cover privately (publicly) owned media costs	Sponsors (government) cover privately (publicly) owned media costs

Note: ... = not applicable

a. Comparison assumes the same size target population and reform objectives.

b. This technical assistance is separate from any provided in the package of rewards.

c. If sponsor applies conditionality, then project is classified as one-player certification.

of objectives more likely, this also reduces the costs to the sponsor of monitoring and sophisticated governance mechanisms. Sponsors have long realized this and therefore have tried to adopt more participatory approaches.

The challenge for the sponsor is to design an institution—a set of rules, payoffs, and beliefs—that triggers players to adopt those best-response strategies that would be most consistent with attaining the sponsor's objectives. As I have argued, limited information about initial conditions makes it hard for sponsors to infer what is possible to achieve, resulting in time-consuming and costly negotiations. A principal insight of the PIJC approach is that competition, by providing the player maximum latitude and flexibility to draw on its own creativity and skills, offers a way to redress these information asymmetries.

The bilateral nature of standard sponsor assistance contracts, however, limits the sponsor's ability to reduce principal-agent problems by harnessing the power of institutional and competitive incentives as part of project design.[3] On the one hand, this is because much of the required design comes from the competitive effects of multiple possible recipients for assistance. Moreover, in bilateral assistance, the sponsor's historical mindset of focusing its efforts on a single jurisdiction accustomed the sponsor to engaging in substantive monitoring and governance without the need to develop the incentive-compatibility side of the contract. On the other hand, assistance has historically been a rather micromanaged activity.

The closest bilateral assistance has come to creating incentive compatibility has been through conditionality, where the recipient agrees to do X as a condition for receiving Y from the sponsor, where X and Y are unrelated. Experts have argued (see section 1.1) that conditionality does not work well, especially where sustainable change is sought. However, in a PIJC design, X and Y are not just related but integral to success. For example, the technical assistance offered in the Moroccan and Honduran PIJCs would not have been useful without the concomitant administrative environment required to receive it. The extra budgetary funding in the Russian fiscal reform project would have been hard to receive and manage without first having implemented the fiscal reforms required. Similarly, PIJCs often act as coordination devices to overcome the transaction costs of the collective action necessary to achieve ends most parties within a jurisdiction already desire.

PIJC approaches offer a direct way to create competitive, institutionally based incentive compatibility. In comparison to conventional approaches, a "race-to-the-top" competitive approach generates the following particularly attractive benefits.

---

3. Recall that according to new institutional economics, "institution" covers a lot of ground, including such things as culture, written constitutions, government, firms, NGOs, language, and black markets.

COST-EFFECTIVENESS

A competitive approach leverages a sponsor's funds in a significant way so that each dollar spent generates more output or reform than a conventional approach would.[4] The latter requires preassessment, negotiation of a one-on-one aid agreement, and allocation of funds for each jurisdiction of interest whereas a competitive approach enables the donor to use a smaller amount of funding since those who can best use the resources "self-select"—via their performance—to receive project benefits, be they from certification or a tournament. Self-selection is a bottom-up approach in which players within the target population select what *they* believe is important to address, so change is driven by local interest, not government (or sponsor) pressure.[5]

Moreover, less funding is needed to motivate a larger number of jurisdictions to compete. For example, if a government considered providing jurisdictions with $50,000 of assistance, then a region of, say, fifty jurisdictions would require an aid budget of $2.5 million under conventional methods. Experience shows that many—perhaps a third to two-thirds, depending on the activity— would not make good use of such donor assistance. But which ones would? Under a certification or tournament approach (which awards and publicizes each player's "grade" and takes advantage of social capital and peer pressure), the government might offer either to award the $50,000 of assistance only to those who become certified—that is, those who signal through their grade that they are serious about using it—or to award $250,000 to $500,000 to the top three scorers in a tournament. In the first scenario, the certification would require a budget of $1.25 million if half the jurisdictions were certifiable.[6] In the second instance, the tournament would require a budget of $750,000 to $1.5 million. Not only is the budget smaller under certification and tournaments than under the conventional approach, but the effects may be bigger: many more of the fifty jurisdictions would have tried their best to do well—and have taken positive steps, regardless of whether or not they had won. Even better, in this example the additional costs of negotiating a conventional aid agreement with each jurisdiction are now unnecessary. Furthermore, as the Russian fiscal reform project nicely illustrates, spillover effects seem to be more pronounced in underperforming jurisdictions in certification or a tournament projects than they would be in a standard "demonstration" project. In short, the only losers are those who take no steps at all!

4. See appendix D for a more precise statement of many of the suppositions in this subsection.
5. Self-selection and "participatory development" are the properties that make community-driven development so effective.
6. Here one needs to assume that high scores on the certification criteria are highly correlated to performance in a conventional contract as well as in a tournament.

ENCOURAGEMENT OF COLLECTIVE ACTION

When a project uses competition incentives that require *team* action, then, paradoxically, *inter*jurisdictional competition also stimulates *intra*jurisdictional cooperation and collective action. Since winning (or becoming certified) requires that many segments of local society *cooperate* toward the common goal, interjurisdictional competition applications, whether via a certification program or a tournament, can forge an alignment of incentives among private sector, civil society, and government actors, encouraging collaboration in order to win, place, or become certified. This generates a consensus among diverse groups to rise above petty interests and engage in real reform, to the benefit of all members (interest groups) of the team (jurisdiction). The Russian fiscal reform and the Indonesian KDP projects are good examples of this for the cases of output and input competition, respectively. The SNG reforms in the Romanian "Simple and Fast" project were desired by most interest groups within each *judeti* (county), but it took a competition to galvanize them into action to work together politically. The Senegal literacy initiative created incentives for providers and consumers of literacy services to work together to develop business plans for sponsor funding. In a conventional project design, conversely, the selected jurisdiction gets the rewards regardless of how much effort it exerts. Likewise, the incentives for interests to draw upon inherent social capital to excel as a team are at best muted since there are no strict performance criteria to meet in order to receive the aid. "Us-versus-them" (in- versus out-group) forces of competition do not exist.

CREATION OF POSITIVE EXTERNALITIES

This encouragement of collective action means that there are benefits beyond the direct economic ones—that is, positive externalities—from the project. By allowing players to experience firsthand the benefits of cooperation *during* the project—that is, players learn that cooperation is not a zero-sum game—the project leads to greater future trust among members of teams *after* the project is over. In short, both competitive certifications as well as tournament designs based on competitive teamwork create indirect benefits through stimulating local democratic processes, civil society, and even public-private partnerships (which are created to address some of the tournament tasks). Such designs also often lead local civil society groups to play a role in monitoring government commitment (as MCC compacts demonstrate).

A related positive externality arising from the competitive team approach is that demonstration projects take on a new meaning. Under a conventional approach, the donor may support an intervention in order to show its feasibility to other potential reform units. However, the transaction costs associated with cooperation and latent in-group cohesion forces may mean that the demonstration effect falls on deaf ears. In a competition-oriented project intervention, the process of creating and training teams reinforces teamwork and stimulates group identity so that the resulting more internally cooperative jurisdiction is more receptive to demonstration effects from other jurisdictions.

SELF-SELECTION FOR BETTER AID TARGETING

Analysis of the challenges regarding aid effectiveness identified two classes of problems donors face: incomplete information and asymmetric information. The incomplete information problem relates to the fact that the sponsor (or an investor) cannot generally distinguish serious from nonserious reformers. In conventional projects the sponsor decides where to allocate aid based on political motives or fact-finding assessments. However, neither of these allocation methods takes into account a recipient's actual reform behavior on the project's tasks. This problem is sometimes exacerbated by the fact that even the jurisdictions themselves do not always know whether or not they are really serious about reform. With incentive-compatible projects, participation requires that before the (potential) recipient receives sponsor assistance, it must engage in some project tasks or signal its competence on tasks deemed to be correlated to success. Either way, the onus is on the recipient, who must demonstrate through its efforts its worthiness for consideration. The potential disutility of this effort acts to prevent "adverse selection," that is, nonserious "reformers" will find the requisite efforts not worth the expected benefits of the sponsor's help, thus eliminating themselves from the sponsor's consideration.

The asymmetric information problem relates to the fact that sponsors do not generally have enough local knowledge to establish how much reform—either in quantity or quality terms—is achievable by a given player (jurisdiction). In either case, strategic considerations would limit the amount of truthful information a recipient would care to provide to a sponsor. Each incentive-compatible approach addresses this problem in its own way. In a project based on certification, differential rewards, either pecuniary or reputational, encourage player-recipients to draw on their own knowledge to perform to the point where the (perceived) marginal costs of further effort would exceed the (perceived) marginal benefits. In a tournament-based project, not only is the informational disadvantage avoided, but the sponsor does not even have to worry about getting the certification gradations right! By simply agreeing ex ante to give the rewards to the best performers, the jurisdictions themselves establish the limits of what is attainable. The tournament thereby causes the players to draw upon their informational advantage *as if* they had accurately passed it on to the donors.

At the risk of redundancy, one can contrast the significant differences in the source of design difficulty between a PIJC approach and the standard "contract" approach historically used by sponsors. In the standard approach, the onus is squarely on the sponsor to identify the tasks, decide how and when to implement them, and closely monitor their execution. As a result of the enormous information asymmetries between the sponsor and the local beneficiaries, these activities introduce many avenues for opportunistic behavior that may compromise success. On the other hand, the type and amount of the reward or sponsor assistance is rather "easy" to set since they are not crucial to the intervention outcome. With the tournament approach, it is exactly the reverse. Identification, implementation, and monitoring are relatively straightforward. Here, since interests are aligned, the beneficiary-implementer wants to do a good job. On the other hand, one of the most difficult aspects of PIJC design is calibrating the appropriate type, number, sizes, and amount (value) of rewards for the midproject, winners', placers', and consolation rewards—both for the jurisdiction as a whole as well as for key individual team members. This calibration usually requires that preferences be elicited through an initial survey, focus group assessments, "lab" experiments, or even a pretest to establish the appropriate incentive structure and who needs it.

GREATER LEGITIMACY

In a conventional project, sponsors relentlessly monitor to impel the recipient to exert maximum effort. The result is often that the recipient feels no ownership in the reform. In the case of reform carried out within the framework of an incentive-compatible project, reform and effort are essentially voluntary and, as explained above, collective action is stimulated and ownership of the reform is internalized, thereby enhancing its legitimacy.

Nevertheless, there is considerable evidence (Cowen 2007) that people do not like to be played with, manipulated, or told what to do, even when compensated. Might such psychological factors limit PIJC effectiveness, too? The answer depends on whether the beneficiaries want the reform being encouraged and on how the problem is framed. Bribing your children to take out the garbage is a different dynamic than bribing them to play harder to win their soccer game. If the PIJC is used to pursue ends whose benefits are desired by the players, then the sponsor's rewards act as a coordination device to encourage collective action—hence the importance of player collaboration in task identification.[7] This issue also points to the importance of education. If the target population does not realize that a particular reform is in their interest, then it will be indifferent to the PIJC's objectives.

EVALUATION AND LEARNING

There are three separate motivations for a donor to include evaluation (and announce ex ante how it is to be carried out). First, evaluation permits the use of performance-motivating incentives since the outcomes of a recipient's use of aid can be objectively measured. Second, if evaluation is carried out during as well as after the recipient's project activities, then the sponsor is able to

---

7. It is basically a question of framing: if the players believe that a PIJC task should not be their responsibility, even if the benefits are manifest, then player cooperation will also be reduced.

adjust project parameters in response to unexpected exogenous shocks or even design flaws. Third, evaluation allows the donor to learn lessons, regardless of whether the recipients succeed in implementing the project activities. (Perhaps one should add a fourth motivation—but for the donor's overseers: rigorous evaluations provide those who allocate the funds a transparent and objective means of assessing the *donor's* performance, thereby strengthening the aid system's overall accountability.)

Under conventional project approaches, evaluation is typically cosmetic and retrospective (Clapp-Wincek and Blue 2001). Little if any serious thought is given to evaluation during project design; it is simply tacked on as a final task for the consultant. This is not surprising since evaluation requires performance indicators, and there is little need for indicators when incentives are not a consideration in project design. The result is that the incentives that influence recipient behavior are usually unintentional, implicit, and often perverse (that is, counter to the sponsor's actual objectives). While a conventional project can generate substantial learning from retrospective analysis (using the so-called modeling approach to evaluation), it is often harder to generate the kind of strong and indisputable results possible from a prospective design approach, such as from randomized trials. The prospective approach is *generally* not possible under conventional projects since it imposes specific constraints on overall project design that can be inimical to the requirements of a conventional project.[8]

I said "generally" since, as alluded to at the start of this chapter, one can design both standard bilateral contracts as well as PIJC projects to include randomized impact evaluation. The difference is that the evaluation of a PIJC takes place *across* (that is, at the level of) the players, which is obviously not possible in standard bilateral donor contracts where there is only one player. On the other hand, the standard bilateral donor contract *does* provide the opportunity to design statistical evaluations at the level of the intervention, something that might be difficult to achieve in a multiplayer setting. For example, in its Mali compact, the MCC was able to design implementation around random assignment of resettlement and irrigation options within the *Office du Niger* lands. Such a complex intervention design would probably have been infeasible to implement across a significant number of jurisdictions at the same time.

PIJC applications *in principle* are particularly appealing because the large number of players leads to application designs with monitoring and evaluation (M&E) integrated into them in a natural way. PIJC brings together several emerging methodologies in the field of governance and experimental economics. These include second-generation governance indicator design (Knack, Kugler, and Manning 2001), strategic communication, participatory development, and

8. For example, conventional approaches like to "pick winners" (assign treatments to particular beneficiaries), a no-no under prospective evaluation.

behavioral assessment of stakeholders through lab (gaming) experiments with salient rewards.[9]

I emphasize "in principle" because very few projects base their design around randomized trials. For example, with the exception of the Morocco project, which has been fully designed but not yet implemented, not one of the tournaments described in chapter 4 included randomized trials.[10] One is forced to ask why randomized evaluation is so rare if it is so powerful. The matter is all the more intriguing because economists and social scientists have been applying these methods to public policy questions (Greenberg and Shroder 2004; Duflo and Kremer 2005). Cook and Payne (2001), for example, asserts that one should not need to look for reasons to use randomization but rather require a sound rationale *not* to use randomization! They suggest that "randomization should only be forfeited where (a) it may simply not be feasible or may not work, despite repeated attempts; (b) crossovers from control groups may dilute the results; and/or (c) there are solid, in-depth studies on the interrelations between, and effects of, specific interventions on targeted outcomes" (p. 2).

One possible explanation for the dearth of randomized evaluation in foreign aid projects in general, despite its ubiquitous use in health and education sectors, is concern about the political acceptability of the exclusion requirement. While this matter is discussed in detail elsewhere (Duflo 2005; Azfar and Zinnes 2003), some of the ways to address this concern include randomizing over time rather than space, judiciously choosing regions from which to select treatment and control groups, and using techniques to compensate for imperfect random selection or assignment.[11] While referring to a slightly different context, the Russian fiscal project reports explicitly state that there was no political backlash or formal regrets registered by the tournament's "losers."

Regardless of how one comes down on randomization, one can design and implement a PIJC without doing randomized impact evaluation just as one can conduct randomized trials to evaluate the development effectiveness of an intervention not based on a competitive incentive mechanism.

EQUITY AND DISTRIBUTIONAL CONSIDERATIONS
Since PIJC offers allocational improvements over standard bilateral approaches, it is natural to dwell on economic efficiency when selecting the appropriate incen-

9. The last technique may be used to assess the likely success of a hypothetical policy change without the need for expensive field pilots. This is done by running lab or survey experiments to evaluate the responses of key stakeholders whose behavior determines the outcome of the policy change. See Azfar and Zinnes (2005) for details.

10. On the other hand, a number of sponsors have begun to embrace randomized impact evaluation, including the MCC and the Gates Foundation.

11. For example, selection could be based on a natural break separating the treatment and control groups that is uncorrelated with the probability of treatment outcomes and then use regression discontinuity analysis.

tive design. Of course, policy and project instrument decisions must also take equity and distributional concerns into account, particularly because the sustainability of an intervention depends on its perceived legitimacy, which may be at risk if such concerns are not addressed.

While an approach is only as good as its implementers, the steps in the design of a PIJC include many elements that encourage taking distributional considerations into account. First, a sponsor can use measures of distributional outcomes as performance measures (or apply weights to subindicators contributing to an overall score). Second, a sponsor can ensure a level playing field (see below). Third, performance may be based on the degree of improvement rather than the absolute level of performance, further leveling the playing field. Fourth, the success of a team is improved when all parties within the team are cooperating, even the poorest, and a sponsor can encourage this participation. For example, the MCC required MCAs within a country developing its compact to organize public hearings to select the activities to be included. In the Jharkhand initiative, distributional equity was ensured by the proper design of a representative sample for report card surveys.

Still, intervention designers are faced with the following dilemma. If the inability of a jurisdiction's interest groups to engage in collective action contributes to its low level of economic development, then an approach that only provides assistance to those displaying serious effort—which requires collective action—fails to address the root of that jurisdiction's problems. However, if an approach provides scarce resources to those who are not serious about using them, then the resources are being wasted. What did the case studies have to say on these issues?

First and foremost, while economic development and collective action are linked, a sponsor should not confuse poverty with ability to work hard or work together. In particular, the case studies showed that it is generally incorrect to infer that groups within a jurisdiction with weak rule of law or unaccountable government institutions are unable to engage in collective action. True, such groups may lack experience and models of successful nonmarket institutions, follow norms discouraging trust of outsiders, and believe all action to be a zero-sum undertaking.[12] Some of the case studies (for example, Senegal, Romania, the KDP, Morocco, and Russia) illustrate that even in such cases, a PIJC, in reducing the transaction costs of collective action, encourages it and generates results that ultimately also demonstrate its power. In short, a sponsor should not automatically rule out collective action approaches without first doing its field-based homework. Nonetheless, it is worth briefly considering what a sponsor's options are both when collective action appears feasible for an underprivileged target population and when it does not.

In case studies, when an underprivileged target population appeared capable of engaging in collective action, the project design paid particular attention to

12. That is, if one group gains, the others must lose.

creating a level playing field. This was seen to encourage higher levels of participation. For example, only the poorest *kecamatans* were eligible to participate in
the KDP initiative; the Nigerian LEEMP included only less developed states; and
the Moroccan MEPI project's targeted municipalities excluded any of the country's
bigger cities. Likewise, because the PIJC approach offered great flexibility and
adaptability under diverse initial conditions, case study projects displayed a high
level of ingenuity in motivating "humble" target populations to implement substantial interventions. For example, even for an issue as complex as environmental
compliance, a PIJC was designed in Indonesia to generate civic action among an
illiterate population to address pollutant emissions.

When an underprivileged target population does appear *incapable* of engaging
in collective action, a sponsor still has several options. First, a jurisdiction's capacity
for collective action is not an all or nothing proposition. Hence a sponsor has the
option of scaling back its objectives to allow the use of a PIJC with a less demanding level of collective action. A second strategy would be to treat basket cases directly
using a standard bilateral approach and then implement a PIJC for the other
jurisdictions. In this way, one or a few jurisdictions do not weaken the effectiveness of remaining funds for everyone else. Finally, even when a standard bilateral
approach is selected for a jurisdiction with an insufficient capacity for collective
action, the sponsor should still determine whether the given initiative is worth the
effort under such conditions or whether more a modest intervention is in order.

COMPLEXITY AND COST CONSIDERATIONS

The power and effectiveness of an incentive-compatible project design does
not come without additional complexity. It requires that the project have more
components than a conventional approach. However, this does not always translate into additional costs. This can be understood by examining complexity and
cost considerations according to the phases of a project, as described in section 2.1.
A comparison between conventional and PIJC approaches is summarized in
table 7-1.

In the first phase, the sponsor identifies the problem, objectives, and target
population using focus groups, interviews, and surveys. In conventional approaches
the sponsor needs to assess each jurisdiction in the target population so as to
negotiate and contract a bilateral agreement later. This is time consuming and
expensive; as such, conventional approaches generally restrict themselves to more
limited target populations. Under certification and tournaments, the sponsor
typically assesses a sample of jurisdictions in order to determine the distribution
of problems and the capacities of the jurisdictions, a less expensive process.

In the second phase, the sponsor establishes the reform tasks; indicators;
relative value of each task (that is, how to aggregate the indicators); project design
(incentive mechanism, treatment protocols, and controls); rewards; technical
assistance requirements, conditions, and delivery schedule; in-project monitoring;

evaluation protocols; preimplementation public relations and player training; and postimplementation dissemination. Ideally, the more sophisticated an incentive mechanism is, the more upfront calibration is required.

One of the lessons learned from the case studies is that the motivational effect of the overall incentive environment depends on how the various project components work together. Thus, while one can design any of the approaches listed in table 7-1 without including any testing, this may vitiate the potential benefits of the more sophisticated mechanisms. Hence the levels of rewards should be calibrated using some combination of surveys and lab experiments, and pregame public relations and dissemination strategies must be tested for motivational effectiveness.[13] With conventional approaches these steps are usually skipped, and instead sponsors pay for extensive monitoring of the recipient's use of the technical assistance and aid. Training of jurisdictions on how to compete (play the "game"), while unnecessary in conventional approaches, goes from straightforward technical assistance for certification mechanisms to more complex and involved training for a mixed tournament, especially where there are opportunities to compete along multiple tasks.

With the first two phases completed, a project design may optionally include an evaluation protocol. While any method may be subject to retrospective evaluation using a model approach, prospective methods (such as randomized trials) are the gold standard of evaluation. As discussed earlier this chapter, conventional approaches and certification and tournament approaches are suitable for different levels of impact assessment. If evaluation is included, the amount of project development time is increased—substantially so during the design period since a treatment plan must be created. The treatment plan generally requires nontrivial modifications to most aspects of the project since the sponsor's interactions with each treatment and control unit must be strictly limited (that is, discretionary action and modifications during project implementation must be very limited), and the design must address and prevent contamination of control groups.

In the third phase, the sponsor implements the project. Whereas the first two phases present the more difficult challenges for certification and tournaments, it is the third phase that is most difficult for conventional approaches since it entails extensive contracting, tailoring of reform requirements to the specifics of each jurisdiction, and, of course, continuous monitoring—and all of this must be done for every jurisdiction in the target population. With certification and tournaments, the cost of implementation depends on the nature and number of indicators and, most critically, on whether a pregame baseline is taken or only an endgame benchmark.[14]

13. When the rewards are nonpecuniary (for example, funding a trade mission or provision of technical assistance), a sponsor would be wise to use valuation methods to determine whether the reward would be sufficiently salient to stimulate the actions desired of winners.

14. If the sponsor is interested in the degree of improvement a jurisdiction achieves, then both baseline and endgame benchmarks are required.

In the fourth phase, the sponsor conducts postproject dissemination and completes the evaluation as necessary. This phase is typically not a part of conventional projects. For certification and tournaments that include reputational rewards, the dissemination strategies developed during project design are implemented. If evaluation includes assessment of project sustainability, then it must wait until dissemination has been in progress for a predefined period. Otherwise, sponsor consultants, often in collaboration with local experts, process the data collected at the end of project play.

It is interesting at this point to juxtapose the assessments of the Russian government and the World Bank with regard to the Russian fiscal reform project. The former hailed the project and its tournament incentive mechanism, and began using its own funds to finance both additional rounds with other jurisdictions as well as new applications of the approach in other sectors. The World Bank, while rating the project as "successful," raised several cautionary notes regarding the project's complexity, which it felt emanated from the inclusion of too many tasks in the tournament. Given the broad experience of the World Bank, it is safe to say that while the new generation of incentive mechanisms offers donors the hope of much more effective outcomes, a sponsor would be well advised to match its ambitions to the environment and capacity of the target country's local jurisdictions.

SUSTAINABILITY

The case studies revealed two types of sustainability: process and product. The former refers to the long-term capability of the institutions created by the project to provide the products the project aims to generate whereas the latter refers to the durability of the products themselves. Process sustainability, where full-cost pricing is infeasible, generally requires political support more than it does program success or popularity (though the latter clearly facilitates the former). Since politics is by nature fickle, such sustainability is difficult to guarantee, though it is helpful if the process has a "home" in a government agency or has strong public support.

With regard to product sustainability, the case studies underscored the importance of the perceived legitimacy of the project's goals and process of implementation. They also confirmed that products tended to lead to more sustainable outcomes where project participation was voluntary. Furthermore, this book recommends using ex-post, output-based performance incentives. Those PIJCs where awards were based on ex-ante (pregame) performance (for example, in Honduras and Nigeria) were forced by definition to use preproject indicators as predictors of project sustainability. For obvious reasons these had mixed success. However, the case studies identify a neat way, where applicable, of dealing with this conundrum: use of a repeated game. Under this design, while the first reward is based on performance that occurred before the incentive offer, future rounds depend on prior round performance.

Where such a solution is not possible, however, this poses a key policy question, namely, whether environmental or project-specific pregame indicators are better at selecting (forecasting) sustainable product outcomes.[15] The case studies did not find that one orientation dominated. Generally speaking, where the indicator measured inputs to the long-term success of the product, then the less gameable and more central to production the input was, the better it was.[16] Where the indicator measured previous output performance, the sponsor was more vulnerable to recipient opportunism unless the institutional nature of the product ensured that pre- and postgame performance would be highly correlated.

Another consideration is whether the case studies reveal linkages between process and product sustainability. In general, there are two main links between product and process sustainability. First, a delivery process that fails to provide sustainable products is unlikely to survive, due to the resulting lack of beneficiary demand and political support. Second, where beneficiaries are able to receive repeated assistance (as in the KDP), successful products may generate political support to maintain the delivery process. A related question is whether these linkages depend on the category of product (six were identified) and the role of the incentive.[17] Where the process organization was able to withdraw certification (for example, in regulatory compliance) or the reward (as the MCC can do with both eligibility and compacts), the PIJC design process stimulated product sustainability. Where the PIJC design was based on reputational considerations (as with Galing Pook) or on providing a valuable service (the Senegal literacy initiative), then the sustainability of the winning product (be it a reform, good, or service) enhanced the respect for the PIJC process organization (respectively, the Galing Pook selection organization and the NGOs providing training), thereby contributing to the sustainability of the latter.

In sum, this presents a challenge. On the one hand, the case studies suggest that from a pure design perspective, it is best to base a PIJC on ex-post, output-based performance incentives. On the other hand, as donors come to grips with the long germination periods for true development, it would be disingenuous to believe that one could withhold the rewards of a PIJC until the long-term viability of final results is proven. The allure of the PIJC approach is that by design it offers players a much higher level of flexibility, independence, and participation in project conception and implementation. This strengthens player feelings toward project ownership and legitimacy, which in turn support project sustainability. Likewise, since the PIJC approach stimulates many jurisdictions to generate outcomes,

15. The quality of underlying policies is an example of the former, and the quality of a project proposal is an example of the latter.

16. See chapter 6, footnote 48.

17. The six product categories are infrastructure financing, policy reform, administrative reform, local public service delivery, training, and regulatory compliance.

it increases the likelihood that *some* will prove sustainable. Standard bilateral contracts, on the other hand, place all the sponsor's hopes on just one jurisdiction, thereby increasing the probability and risk of failure.

SCALABILITY

The case study examples make clear that certification and tournament mechanisms have the potential for wide applicability. What these incentive mechanisms do require, though, is a latent demand in the beneficiary community for the reforms desired by the sponsor and a sufficient level of jurisdictional identity or social capital upon which to build team competitive spirit (as with international soccer, where the country's population unites regardless of existing hostilities among its groups). With the presence of these "initial conditions," the sponsor can act as a facilitating outside coordinator or referee by offering incentives to encourage team members to overcome the transaction costs of collective action and compete in the (voluntary) game, whether it is a certification or tournament. While these two conditions act as a constraint on scalability, the sponsor is able to harness local incentives rather than fight them, and the intervention acquires a legitimacy it would otherwise not have. Within these limits the incentive-compatible approach may be applied at several levels of sophistication and, therefore, can be scaled up to fit the local context.

At the simplest level, a certification can be dichotomous or multitiered. The "Simple and Fast" project in Romania and the PROPER project in Indonesia illustrate how a multitiered certification program can operate—in the latter case, even within a poor and illiterate population if the dissemination strategy is appropriately thought out. Pecuniary certification adds the challenge of dealing with corruption and fraud, since the stakes to winning are more immediate and tangible. The implementation weakness of the Senegal literacy project illustrates that ensuring the conscientious application of in-project evaluation (measurement of candidate performance) is needed to limit this. Of course, standard bilateral contracts are no strangers to issues of corruption and fraud. The high level of monitoring—a task assigned to entire departments within a donor—exists specifically to control these problems. A PIJC with an ex-post, performance-based incentive design is much less susceptible to such opportunism. In fact, in many PIJCs the players themselves have the incentive to monitor and report on each other's cheating. Still, as scale increases, player monitoring becomes less feasible (competitors are further away and less familiar), and the expected return to monitoring decreases.

In the case of tournaments, there are several design parameters that can be adjusted to facilitate scalability. These include size and types of rewards, number of winners and placers stipulated, size of the jurisdiction, number of eligible players, amount and frequency of technical assistance provided during the tournament, the time frame, and strategic use of mass media.

As the size of the target population increases, however, so does heterogeneity. This means that in a contest with a given reward structure and number of winning positions, a jurisdiction's chances of winning diminish. This reduces the strength of the incentive in a pure tournament. Increasing the number of reward categories and placers can redress this. However, if jurisdictions are somewhat risk averse, then the sponsor may not be able to compensate sufficiently for the reduced expected reward by simply raising the stakes. Fortunately, the structure of PIJC provides solutions to this scalability dilemma.

For each of these incentive mechanisms, the sponsor can increase the scalability by varying the number of tasks and the sophistication of the indicators, and weakening the power of the evaluation (for example, reducing the number of treatment or control groups). Furthermore, the well-known lesson that projects succeed or fail to the extent that they are appropriate for local conditions is even truer for projects that endeavor to harness local incentives. Fortunately, a sponsor can reduce this danger, ceteris paribus, by investing in calibration, pilot testing, public demand surveys, and focus groups; paying attention to the existing legislative environment; and collaborating with local stakeholder groups. The sponsor then must use the behavioral and contextual information gained via these preproject methods to design an incentive mechanism appropriate to the interests, skills, and understanding of the target population.

MATCHING PROJECT OBJECTIVE TO MECHANISM SUITABILITY

Comparison of the case studies suggests that there is no preferred incentive mechanism. First, the mechanism chosen must suit the characteristics of the sponsor's objectives. In particular, the preferred incentive design will depend on the nature of the application: it does not make sense that the preferred incentive design for infrastructure investment would be the same as for literacy training. This issue is addressed here by considering what the ideal design might be for a sponsor's objective based on the six categories of intervention (see table 6-13). About one-third of the intervention types are best suited to certification designs, with the remainder better suited to tournaments. (The arguments for each category are discussed elsewhere in this chapter.) Still, where a case study application did not follow this ideal, the sponsor often had a justifiable, albeit idiosyncratic, reason not to do so (such as an exogenous budget constraint).

A sponsor's objectives will also have other characteristics pertinent for the choice of incentive design. For example, if the sponsor has a limited budget and wants to allocate it to generate the most effective outcomes, then, ceteris paribus, a tournament is the sponsor's best option. The KDP or Russian fiscal reform projects are good examples of this match. However, if the goal is to fund as many applications as possible as long as a predefined minimum outcome is likely, then a certification approach is indicated. A good example of this is the Senegal literacy project. If the sponsor places importance on a rigorous assessment of lessons learned across variations in initial conditions, then the certification and tournament approaches are the way to go; if the assessment is to determine what works best for a given set of initial conditions, then the standard bilateral contract approach is preferred.

Second, the relationship between the number of jurisdictions under consideration and the preferred incentive design is not always straightforward. True, if there are few or just one "player," then a standard bilateral contract approach is preferred over a PIJC. However, the choice between a certification and a tournament is not necessarily monotonic. Where there are few players, a certification approach is usually applied. For example, the MCC certifies the activities within a compact; it does not run a tournament on proposals submitted by the MCA. At the other extreme, when there are a hundred or more players (such as the Indonesian firms being assessed for environmental compliance), a winner-takes-all tournament can lose its motivating properties. It is between these two extremes that tournaments appear to have an important role.

Third, the choice of incentive mechanism design will also be influenced by initial conditions. The implications of this set of issues are addressed below.

7.2.2 Benefits of Standard Bilateral Contracts

Given the aforementioned virtues of an incentive-compatible design, one may wonder why a standard bilateral contract approach would ever be used. This would be going from one extreme position to the other. While this book argues that the default design for a sponsor's intervention should be based on incentive compatibility in general and a PIJC in particular, there are still some situations in which the standard bilateral contract approach is preferable to that of a PIJC, in particular where

—the intervention is to be in just one jurisdiction, so interjurisdictional competition is out of the question;

—the newness or complexity of the intervention for the player(s) requires one-on-one hand holding that would be impossible to provide well to a large number of jurisdictions simultaneously;[18]

—the size of the requisite investment by players during the game is so large that sponsor reward payment based on ex-post performance is either infeasible (for example, players would not have the funds) or perceived as too risky by the players;

—there is the potential for systematic exogenous events that might prevent all players from exceeding the certification bar or a tournament threshold; and

—the nature of the activity involves substantial risks of failure that a jurisdiction is unable to assume or spread, or that would be more efficient for the sponsor to bear due to the potential for positive externalities.

18. This case would also cover the situation where a subgroup of jurisdictions was too weak in some sense to compete in a PIJC. See the discussion of equity considerations in section 7.2.1.

A concrete example of a project fitting these characteristics would be a one-of-a-kind, large-scale infrastructure project.

Still, in almost every case, a sponsor can take steps to strengthen the incentive compatibility of the intervention. First, the sponsor should involve and empower the recipients in project identification and design. In particular, the project should be placed within an existing organization (that is, a temporary local institution should be created) with a stake in the outcome. Second, where there cannot be output competition, input competition (for example, based on proposals or on ex-ante performance) is often feasible.[19] Third, there may be time-consistent ways to create a repeated game in which future benefits depend on the success of the current intervention. Finally, where the service to perform, good to provide, or investment to make has been previously established, the sponsor should consider using competitive procurement.

PIJC, as a multiplayer incentive-compatible approach, requires clear (generally quantitative) measures of success. A standard bilateral contract may be preferred, therefore, if the development assistance situation does not warrant or permit the use of such data-based methods or if their use would not yield reliable results.[20] This is all the more the case since "several different impact measures [should] be used so that it is possible to run robustness checks on the results and increase confidence in them" (Azfar and Zinnes 2003). This generally means that at least two quantitative indicators must be developed for each task, which takes time and effort. This can create technical challenges, especially with the inclusion of randomized trials. First, each indicator must be constructed to correlate as closely as possible to a key characteristic of task outcome. Otherwise, as USAID's experience with the R4 system illustrates, players may find a way, intentionally or unintentionally, to maximize their score on an indicator without materially contributing to the reform. Second, for there to be a perception of fairness and hence legitimacy, the data used for the performance indicators must be objective. However, a common source of data is the players themselves, that is, official data from the jurisdictions. These are not always known to be of the highest quality, as illustrated by the Nigerian scorecard project. Third, indicator data may come from field surveys, say, of the jurisdiction's beneficiaries. On the one hand, the design of the instrument must suit the local context, the firm administering it must be sufficiently experienced, and the culture must be receptive to survey methods. On the other hand, regardless of the data collection methods used, project designers must be careful that the incentive to "game the responses" is minimized.

---

19. Also see the discussion of yardstick competition in section 1.3 as well as various entries in table 5.1.

20. Of course, even in standard bilateral aid contracts it is recommended that quantitative indicators be used as targets for focusing beneficiaries and implementing parties. MCC compacts provide excellent examples of this practice.

This last requirement is not always easy to meet, as some of the case studies demonstrate. For example, this was not well followed in the Honduran mancomunidades project since the direct beneficiaries of donor largesse were the ones who filled in the data forms upon which they would be ranked! In the Nigerian scorecard project, the protocol required that villages within jurisdictions providing the data would be excluded from receiving certification benefits. The result was that villages receiving a high rating for project suitability were banned from the project while villages receiving benefits were not judged at all and could have been much less suitable than average. In the Jharkhand report card project, beneficiaries could have biased their survey responses in an effort to influence which public service they wanted to look comparatively worst (best) in the hope that the service reform would be addressed sooner (later).

7.2.3 Benefits of Tournaments over Certification

I have argued above that the *theoretical* benefits of *some* certification-based project designs can rival the benefits of a tournament. One might be forgiven for asking what properties are left that favor a tournament. While I have whittled down many of the previous claims for tournament superiority over other project designs, there are still some powerful remaining benefits to a tournament approach that the present analysis has identified.

"BEST VERSUS THE REST"

The survey of incentive-compatible projects in chapters 3 through 5 revealed that some projects seek to allocate their funding to the best uses while other projects are not interested in achieving the highest performance by a few recipients but rather an acceptable level of performance (above a threshold level) by as many recipients as possible. These orientations call for different incentive mechanisms in order to align recipient incentives with those of the sponsor's. For example, for the KDP project in Indonesia, the government had a limited budget and wanted to identify a few of the best infrastructure or public service activities in each kecamatan. It chose a tournament mechanism to allocate funds. On the other hand, with the Senegal literacy project, the World Bank was not interested in funding the cheapest firms for conducting training everywhere but in funding the greatest number of literacy courses possible in the target region that would achieve acceptable outcomes. They chose a certification mechanism to allocate funds.[21]

---

21. As discussed in chapter 6, a sponsor would be wise to anticipate what to do with "losers" regardless of the delivery mechanism. The MCC excludes some projects proposed for a compact and includes others; when the World Bank provides technical assistance to one ministry, it excludes the others. Still, the evidence cited in this book does not support the contention that losers can feel excluded and become politically or otherwise restive. The likely reason for this is that most tournaments are explicitly designed so that the main reason for engaging in the requisite actions is to receive their direct benefits (for example, reforms), not a sponsor's reward. Hence a player recognizes that winning depends on its own efforts and that its efforts will bring benefits regardless of whether it wins or not. Of course, this requires that the game be perceived as transparent and fair.

INFORMATIONAL CONSIDERATIONS

These examples underscore the need for both absolute and relative approaches. In Senegal the donor knew a priori what an acceptable level of performance was when it chose the certification approach, but in Indonesia the donor did not know ex ante what level of performance was achievable or which villages would be able to provide it. Note that the KDP example also illustrates the power of a tournament under informational imperfections. Not only was the Indonesian government unaware of what performance was achievable or by which villages, the villages themselves did not know. Only through competition were parties able to determine this, and the tournament structure provided this framework.

Since the critical information required to make a project successful lies with the recipients, the sponsor needs to provide the recipients with incentives to apply their idiosyncratic knowledge to the project's objectives, which by assumption are consistent with those of the recipients. Interjurisdictional competition provides these incentives and thereby encourages the potential recipients (players) to strive to achieve the project's objectives. Furthermore, in doing so, interjurisdictional competition causes the players to reveal to the sponsor the benchmark or standard of what is feasible. At the same time, the process reveals which jurisdictions are the serious reformers and which are not. Note that these benefits cannot be achieved using certification—not even using a multitier certification design. This is because by assumption no one knows the range of possible collective action outcomes, so any preproject bars will be speculative and may lead to suboptimal exertion of effort by the players (as occurred in the Romanian "Simple and Fast" project).

EFFICIENCY CONSIDERATIONS

Where applicable a tournament approach will achieve a more efficient outcome than a certification. First, it creates *within-task* efficiency. This occurs as players endeavor to achieve the best performance they can on a task to the point where their marginal costs equal their marginal expected benefits. Hence, under a tournament, there is no alternative allocation of project funds that would achieve higher net benefits for a given task. Under certification, on the other hand, players perform up to the point that performance satisfies a preset certification bar, or if they believe the bar is set too high, then they exert no effort at all.

Second, a tournament approach leads to *across-task* efficiency by offering players a menu of reform tasks to choose from rather than the requirement to do all of them, as certification and conventional approaches demand. The sponsor begins by selecting the set of permissible reform tasks it deems important (hopefully in collaboration with potential recipients). In a tournament the sponsor may also assign weights or differential point values to each task to reflect its own valuation of the different activities. Players then allocate their efforts and resources to these tasks to maximize their point score. This requires that they equalize their own marginal costs per additional point across the tasks—which is also the condition

for efficiency! Since some tasks will appear to be inordinately difficult (for organizational, technical, or even political reasons), this means that for some players some tasks within the permissible set may not be addressed at all. Under
a conventional or certification approach, however, each recipient is forced
to allocate its efforts and resources to the same set of tasks (as in the Romanian
"Simple and Fast" project) to receive rewards, which is much less efficient. Thus,
if efficiency is a priority, a tournament is indicated.

COST CONSIDERATIONS

If a sponsor has a fixed budget, then a certification approach can lead either to
budget overruns or underprogrammed funds (which, ironically, a bureaucracy
finds worse than an overrun). This is because in a tournament the sponsor presets the
number of winners and placers whereas in a certification the number of qualifying participants cannot be known ex ante (though the sponsor can influence the
number by the placement *in advance* of the certification bar). A tournament may
also be less expensive than a certification under certain conditions, for example, if the objective is only to fund projects having the highest scores according to particular criteria.

IMPACT OF DEADLINE

As argued above, many of the benefits from tournament incentives can also be
achieved through a suitably designed pecuniary certification. In practice, however,
there is an important psychological distinction between these two classes of
approaches: a tournament has a beginning and an end whereas certification typically
creates an ongoing opportunity. This is a particularly important feature given the
teamwork required to achieve the performance needed to be certified or to place
in a tournament. Recall that many of the reforms that sponsors want jurisdictions
to implement require collective action or at least some level of cooperation between
interest groups. As has already been pointed out, the sponsor's project acts as a
coordinator for local action—and a "referee" in the case of certification and tournament incentive mechanisms. In many cases a time limit focuses the efforts of
teams. If given enough time, any team can pass the finish line, but the goal is to
get them to do it within the sponsor's time horizon. With an open time frame,
the transaction cost of coordination between players, who each have different
opportunity costs to their time, leads to serious problems. A tournament overcomes
these whereas placing a time limit on a certification program generally does not
make sense and so is time inconsistent.

GRADUATED TECHNICAL ASSISTANCE

The tournament's ability to better allocate project benefits does not just apply
to the allocation of rewards but also to the technical assistance provided before
and during the performance period. A tournament efficiently allocates technical

assistance in two ways. First, by incorporating the strengths of certification, a tournament establishes subtask completion thresholds for which players may receive graduated levels of technical assistance as tournament play evolves. Second, since a tournament efficiently allocates the primary reward, it also does so for the accompanying technical assistance component (hence USAID's choice of a tournament for the mancomunidades project). Thus the tournament design creates what is called a "separating equilibrium" since internal project incentives affect players differently. Payoffs and their prerequisites can be graduated so that the manifested demand for technical assistance corresponds to the degree of seriousness of the local reformers (who could use it to good effect). As such, the payoffs do not attract others—those who would squander the assistance (or simply want a donor's cash)—since they would not exert the requisite efforts to complete the associated subtask(s).

SUSTAINABILITY

With regard to product sustainability, tournaments are more likely to produce more sustainable winners, since by definition fewer and more motivated jurisdictions win a tournament than would receive certification. With regard to process sustainability, neither mechanism is inherently superior since this outcome depends on the specifics of the process and the place. On the one hand, because certification produces more winners, it creates a larger number of parties with a stake in the sustainability of the organization granting certification. On the other hand, tournaments generally offer much larger rewards, perhaps pushing tournament winners to be more vocal in their support of the process than certification winners would be.

SCALABILITY

Aside from the scalability options discussed for all incentive-compatible mechanisms, the PIJC mechanism as proposed in this book provides two additional solutions to the scalability dilemma that an increase in the number of players increases player heterogeneity, which has a negative impact on player incentives to perform. First, PIJC uses the concept of nested tournaments. For example, say a sponsor wants to scale up the PIJC in Morocco from the one province, Doukkala, to two provinces, Doukkala and Abda. One option is to simply run one tournament with both provinces' jurisdictions playing. The alternative proposed in section 4.2.3 was to run a PIJC with *three* tournaments, one among the municipalities in Doukkala, one among the municipalities in Abda, and one at the *province level* between Doukkala and Abda. In the last the average scores of the municipalities in each province's tournament are compared, and the province whose municipalities have the highest average score is declared the winner. This not only overcomes the heterogeneity issue but, during the municipal-level competition, encourages the provincial governments to identify provincewide reforms and actions that would increase all scores in their province. It is interesting to note that the KDP project in Indonesia implicitly recognized the first part of this option by limiting tournament play to village competition within each kecamatan rather than running one tournament in which all villages competed against each other.[22]

A second way that PIJC can address the scalability dilemma is through combining certification and tournament mechanisms to increase participation. To clarify how this may help, consider two situations, one where the sponsor only wants to identify the best performance and one where the sponsor *also* wants to motivate as many players as possible to fully engage. The KDP illustrates the former, since there would be no interest in motivating villages with mediocre ideas to develop proposals. The Russian fiscal reform project illustrates the latter case where the donor hoped all jurisdictions would do their best to undertake fiscal reform. In the KDP case, a tournament mechanism alone is sufficient to stimulate the generation of the best proposals, though a multitier certification mechanism to allocate technical assistance in proposal preparation is still indicated. In the Russian case, however, the multitier certification mechanism ("consolation prizes") could also augment the tournament performance incentives by rewarding lower-level reform achievers. This would encourage participation by those jurisdictions that otherwise might not have gotten involved if they viewed themselves as less capable reformers or felt they faced more intractable reform obstacles than other competing jurisdictions.

7.2.4 Limitations of Tournaments Compared to Certification

In spite of the theoretical and practical benefits of tournament designs, there are applications in which a tournament would *not* be the preferred incentive mechanism. Section 7.2.2, for example, discussed many situations in which a standard bilateral contract would be preferred. Even when a PIJC approach is applicable, a tournament mechanism still may not be preferable. For example, it would make no sense to use a tournament in microfinance and only to lend to the best women's group. In this section, therefore, I consider potential practical limitations to the tournament approach.

TECHNICAL CHALLENGES

A mixed tournament can be a powerful tool to elicit recipient efforts toward mutually held objectives facilitated by sponsor resources. This power comes at a cost. A project designed around PIJC is more complicated and sophisticated than the same project would be using conventional methods. While chapters 3 through 5 provide examples where the net result is positive, there are several technical challenges that must be assessed for feasibility in the context of the target site.

---

22. Note that while psychological considerations make the former preferable, neoclassical economics would "prove" that the latter would be more efficient.

A relatively obvious consideration is whether there are enough players to conduct a tournament. While there is no absolute number requirement, the number must be large enough to satisfy three concerns. First, given the number of winners the budget permits, the number of players must be sufficient to generate competitive pressures that create incentives to overcome the transaction cost impeding collective action, but that number cannot be so high as to cause the less secure teams to give up trying from the start. Second, with too few players, it may be possible to create perverse incentives that lead to collusion, that is, a situation in which some group of players strategically coordinates their efforts so as to control who wins and to minimize the effort needed to do so. However, practical likelihood of such collusion is small given that the project's target jurisdictions are selected precisely because they have been unable to cooperate *within* their jurisdiction to achieve the reforms most members wanted. As such, it is doubtful that such internally uncooperative players could nonetheless coordinate their behaviors *across* jurisdictions. Third, the number of players must be large enough for the sponsor to deem worthwhile the extra effort of running a tournament versus a series of aid contracts.[23]

In practice, the case studies demonstrate that the number of players does not necessarily need to be large for a tournament to overcome the aforementioned concerns. For example, the Russian fiscal reform project did not experience these problems despite having only seven jurisdictions participating per tournament. Of course, in the cases of Galing Pook and the KDP, the number of players was much larger.

Perhaps the trickiest technical issue for PIJC design in general and tournaments in particular is how to calibrate the parameters and values influencing the incentives themselves. Since by assumption the expected payoff of the tournament provides a salient incentive for player effort, factors affecting this calculation are critical for tournament success. Aside from issues common to reform in general (such as distributional impacts), box 7-1 lists many of these factors. Ideally, a project's designers need to calibrate and test the behavioral parameters underlying each of these factors. This takes time and expertise. Of course, such an incentive analysis would increase the probability of success in certification or even conventional projects, but it is rarely done. Finally, in addition to these calibrations, a project's designer should test the player's manual (containing the rules of the game) and the strategic communications procedures (used to generate public interest and later disseminate player performance scores) for ease of technical comprehension and cultural suitability.

23. An adequate number of players is also a factor if the tournament design includes randomized impact evaluation. A fairly large number of players is needed in order to achieve reasonable statistical power (usually of at least 80 percent) for an acceptable minimum detectable effect size (say, 30 percent). The exact number depends on many factors, including the degree of variability of the characteristics in the hypotheses to test as well as the proportion of variance captured by covariates.

Box 7-1. *Design Parameters to Calibrate or Set in a PIJC*

Design element
Number of players
Number of winners and placers
Type and salience of precommitment device (to qualify for participation)
Incentives (co-option) for risk-taking player-level decisionmakers
Threshold for consolation prizes
Value of the technical assistance (during tournament)
Value of the reform itself
Value of tournament rewards
Impact on reputation
Perceived difficulty of carrying out the competition tasks
Perceived political fallout from randomization (if using randomized
    impact evaluation)

The addition of randomized impact evaluation (which is not limited exclusively to PIJCs, though well suited to them) increases the complexity of project design and implementation in a number of ways.[24] First, the need to measure treatment impact increases the amount of measurement redundancy required to ensure robustness of statistical results, and this, in turn, increases the likelihood of encountering the data challenges described above. Second, the requirement that there be a control group (ideally, randomly selected from the same player population as those participating in the tournament, that is, the treatment group) poses challenges. This is because the widespread publicity recommended for generating interest in PIJC participation could "contaminate" the behavior of the control group, perhaps causing it to adopt reforms, either from demonstration effects or simply out of competitiveness with the treatment group.[25] Finally, harking back to scalability concerns, the larger the geographic area covered by the tournament, the harder it is to avoid contamination. There are, however, technical approaches to address or correct the contamination problem.[26]

---

24. Keep in mind that one can run a PIJC without evaluation or with evaluation not based on randomized trials. Likewise, one can incorporate randomized trials into conventional (non–incentive-based) and certification type projects.

25. In other words, what happens to or in the treatment group may influence the control group's behavior.

26. Alevy and Zinnes (2005) propose practical methods to overcome such concerns. The first uses statistical methods to compare the outcomes among players participating in the PIJC with those that choose not to participate. The second matches the tournament region with another region in the country that is outside of the range of the publicity campaign and then uses the same PIJC evaluation procedures to measure activity associated with the tournament tasks there.

EASE OF ADOPTION

Understandably, the greatest uncertainty in a PIJC relates to the susceptibility of the target population and its officials to the tournament approach and its rigors, such as they are. Design features such as the scope and number of tasks on the option menu and the point system for fulfillment of each task can become complicated if too ambitious, which can confuse players.[27] The motivational impact of an incentive diminishes the more confused about it the players are. However, descriptions of player reactions in the tournament case studies, as well as my own direct experiences in the field in Morocco and in the Philippines, suggest that players are quite attracted to the game approach. The trick is to program the tournament's level of ambition to be commensurate with the absorptive capacities of the players and their environment. It is particularly important that the actions and strategies required to play be legal and require no additional legislation to exercise. Laws take time to develop and pass; however, there is no need for the laws to have been previously implemented de facto since one of the purposes of the PIJC is to encourage players to put such de jure laws into practice.

Once the scale of the tournament has been properly dimensioned, success will depend on the quality of the tournament training materials, their use, and related publicity. Clearly, a tournament requires more training to explain the rules of the game to the players than a certification would. Hence close local participation is needed to ensure ease in explaining how to play the game to participants and their constituencies. Likewise, the quality of data collection will depend in part on the existence of experienced local survey firms.

GOVERNMENT AND DONOR RETICENCE

While evidence is scarce, in some situations governments and donors alike seem reluctant to use the tournament approach. With the former it is likely that politicians simply do not like having their performance measured—although this would also be an issue with certification. Undoubtedly the same applies to government offices and agencies. This reluctance is easy to understand given the historic lack accountability under which these officials have operated. Pritchett (2002) argues that program advocates generally make exaggerated claims about the success of their activities in order to mislead swing voters into providing their support. Transparent quantitative PIJC indicators (not to mention a rigorous program evaluation) would reveal their program's true performance.

Duflo and Kremer (2005, p. 225) offer a different twist on this matter, arguing that "policymakers are not systematically fooled, but rather have difficulty gauging the quality of evidence in part because advocates can suppress unfavorable evaluation results." They suggest that because standard retrospective regression analysis

---

27. The World Bank evaluators of the Russian project voiced this concern, for example.

tends to yield results with large error bars and specification biases, politicians rationally discount most evaluation estimates. In this environment Duflo and Kremer ask why anyone would conduct rigorous randomized trials, which are not subject to large confidence intervals, only to have their results discounted anyway in comparisons to competing project claims.

In my own work in Morocco, however, I found a counterbalancing propensity: a proclivity for measurement! In particular, in most communes where I conducted focus groups, communal council members expressed an urgent desire to prove that their locality was ripe for investment and other outside attention, but they did not know how to signal it. Participation in a PIJC offered them such an opportunity.

Regardless, the motivations behind government reticence do not appear to be good reasons for a donor to hesitate about encouraging the use of a tournament design if there is support within the electorate for greater accountability. However, this reluctance may explain why a certification (threshold) approach to motivate change is far more prevalent. Certification can be implemented by civil society organizations and without government support, whereas a tournament would be hard for civil society to organize without the active participation of the local governments.

Experience to date suggests that donors, too, are reluctant to sponsor a tournament. Private communications I have had with the developers of the KDP and Russian fiscal reform projects all indicate that they encountered stiff resistance to the concept in their respective organizations. (In the case of the Nigerian scorecard project, such resistance may have contributed to the project being designed as a certification.) My own interaction with the U.S. Department of State, the Soros Foundation, and USAID confirms their experiences. Why didn't USAID replicate "Simple and Fast," and why didn't the World Bank, MEPI, or UNIDO follow up on the Moroccan PIJC? I can only speculate as to the reasons.

One possibility is that donors are habitually conservative organizations, especially the multilateral ones. They are reluctant to try something new. Some may feel it is unethical to "experiment" on an unsuspecting population. On the other hand, donor reticence about tournaments, and their measurement component in particular, is probably more a concern at the level of their project staff since, from a bureaucratic point of view, the expected, private net benefits to innovation tend to be negative. First, the highly volatile environment in which projects take place not only makes it difficult to unambiguously attribute responsibility for performance but also limits the control donor staff have over outcomes. Second, donor institutions often subject their staff to a perverse asymmetry: they get little tangible benefit from managing well-performing projects but may be adversely affected if their projects perform poorly. Likewise, the sponsor employee's penalty for failure is much higher if the intervention had few precedents than if it was standard practice. Finally, the employee's reward for success via an innovative approach would be modest and probably not any different than if the individual had applied a standard approach. (Of course, the benefits to future applications from the innovation experiment could be large.)

A second possible cause for donor reticence could be the political concern that in a PIJC technical assistance is endogenously allocated according the tournament's (preset) rules of the game, and therefore players might claim differential provision of technical assistance as a cause for their failure to win, blame the process, and react belligerently. While this is a reasonable concern, experience to date provides no evidence that this has occurred. Perhaps this is because recipient communities have had long experience with workshop-style training—as well as with "train-the-trainer" programs. Alternatively, the type of technical assistance recommended for a PIJC may be provided to representatives of several player groups during the course of play. Hence no single jurisdiction or team could complain that it was somehow uniquely disadvantaged by unequal assistance. Moreover, the technical assistance training modules would be highly standardized (since, unlike individualized donor interventions, the task menu in a PIJC is also standardized). This would be especially true for a project design that includes randomized impact evaluation.

Third, a donor's reticence may come from its desire to implement other activities within the group of potential players. Such parallel activities, however, would likely compromise the effectiveness of a PIJC. For example, the PIJC in Morocco would have required that UNIDO not offer other technical assistance to the participating regions during the tournament period. Otherwise players might not have been willing to incur the tournament's reform "costs" when equally appealing UNIDO assistance would be forthcoming outside the tournament's reward framework.

Fourth, donors may be concerned about the political fallout of exclusion.[28] They may worry that losers can become angry or the control group may feel left out. Alternatively, "the random creation of treatment and control groups may also appear inconsistent to the donor and its goals, since randomization necessarily excludes jurisdictions that wish to participate in the tournament" (Azfar and Zinnes 2003). Section 6.1.6 presents a series of arguments showing how to handle these concerns and why they generally should not be an issue.

To conclude, while the potential for cumulative disappointment in and boredom from a tournament is theoretically possible, the only concrete evidence I have found comes from the Russian fiscal reform project. It is worth summarizing some of the lessons that the World Bank (the donor) identifies from (what it calls) this "innovative model" of technical assistance delivery (World Bank 2006a, p. 9).

---

28. In my monitoring and evaluation at the MCC, an organization well known for its interest in M&E, I still have found a rather strong reluctance, both by MCC staff as well as by local MCA field staff, to implement a treatment approach that requires withholding services from some (a requirement of randomization) for the benefit of learning related to later sustainability and replication.

First and foremost, it concludes that "the competitive model of promoting reform can be effective."[29] Aside from the evident reforms implemented by the "winners," the World Bank was particularly surprised by the behavior of the "losers." These regions, which did not perform well in past screenings, still undertook serious efforts to prepare reform programs, often "redoubl[ing] their efforts" in subsequent competitions. In particular, the fact that fifteen winners were rewarded out of a total of eighty-nine regions "without protest or complaint" is taken as a sign of the success of the delivery model. The report attributes this to the "critical role of transparency in the process."

CREATING A "CRUTCH"

A deeper but subtler issue concerns the institutional impact of the PIJC process itself. A PIJC mobilizes local cooperation to husband the jurisdiction's own public and private resources toward a good or service desired by most of its citizens. But this is the exact purpose of local government! Upon reflection, then, one might view the PIJC as a type of extrapolitical system operating parallel to the existing local government. Here the outside referee (donor and tournament rules) and rewards act as a system of accountability to compensate for accountability weaknesses in the functioning of the local government. At the risk of some exaggeration, should donors be funding the creation of parallel local government institutions?

In the short run, this is probably a good thing. Experience with PIJC should enhance trust within jurisdictions and demonstrate the power of collective action and due process. In fact, PIJC was designed with the explicit goal of encouraging the local government and its private sector partners to exercise statutory powers and legislated prerogatives. Moreover, as some of the case studies demonstrate, some PIJCs *are* designed and implemented by government (for example, the literacy initiative in Senegal and PROPER in Indonesia).

In the longer run, however, it is less clear whether the continued use of PIJCs across a group of jurisdictions would ultimately strengthen the functioning of local government, which is of more fundamental importance, or become a "crutch," retarding its development. The assessment here of the PIJC approach does offer some guidance on how to ensure that the latter does not occur.

First, sponsors must exercise due diligence when proposing a PIJC to substitute for services legislatively assigned to local public administration. Ideally such substitution would only occur when the services are sufficiently dysfunctional as to obstruct a critical path in local development.

Second, once higher-level government disbursement agencies become more accountable in the transfer of public funds, the sponsor's purpose for the PIJC in the locality can shift to encouraging other reforms. The KDP and Russian projects

---

29. This and the rest of the quotes in this paragraph are from World Bank (2006a, p. 10)

provide excellent examples of how long-term experience with PIJCs led the respective governments to adopt the approach officially once the donor's project finished, thereby ensuring its "process" sustainability (see section 6.3.1). Third, as jurisdictions develop, PIJC applications can concentrate on encouraging them to exercise their statutory authorities rather than substituting for them. Finally, the government itself can consider using PIJC as part of a fiscal decentralization system to distribute performance-based revenue grants or transfers (Steffensen 2007).[30]

7.3 Simplifying the PIJC Approach

In spite of the allure of the PIJC approach, it is not suitable for all applications or initial conditions. Fortunately, potential simplifications are possible at several levels of PIJC application, the most obvious ones relating to the embellishment of the certification approach. Lessons from the case studies can help identify the scope for feasible simplifications and their likely implications for project quality. While these simplifications can reduce the cost and complexity of a PIJC, in many cases the core benefits of the approach will still remain.

7.3.1 Motivations to Simplify

The most obvious constraint to an application is the *availability of funding*. There are several main decisions that influence the cost of a PIJC. The first and primary decision is whether the intervention should address one, a few, or many jurisdictions (or players, as the case may be). PIJCs entail two fixed costs—one for the type of intervention per se (such as hiring foreign experts to prepare a training or other service) and one for designing the tournament—and a variable cost (such as running a baseline survey for an additional jurisdiction). A virtue of the PIJC approach, of course, is that in providing assistance to many jurisdictions, a PIJC can spread the fixed costs across them, and the per jurisdiction cost falls accordingly. The variable cost tends to be modest since a PIJC uses local companies and applies the same methodology to each jurisdiction.

The second decision is whether there will be rigorous monitoring and evaluation. If the PIJC's design already requires quantitative performance indicators, then M&E may not entail much further pre- and postintervention data acquisition costs. (In fact, since standard bilateral contracts rarely have quantitative performance criteria, it is paradoxically likely to be cheaper to add M&E to a PIJC than to a standard bilateral contract, holding constant the number of jurisdictions targeted.) On the other hand, rigorous M&E usually requires the inclusion of additional jurisdictions (the controls), which would obviously raise costs.

30. Afonso and Guimarães (2008) make the excellent point that PIJC should not be used for the core funding of basic services since this would fly in the face of equity considerations and poverty alleviation policy objectives.

A third decision is whether to use pilot(s), which would likely be needed to calibrate reward and task response parameters as well as for pretesting written tournament materials for public dissemination. It is certainly the case that due to calibration requirements (see box 7-1), the role of a pilot is more critical for a PIJC application than for most other types of interventions. Of course, there are ways to reduce the scope of the pilot, such as involving local stakeholders in economic (gaming) experiments in the laboratory or relying on focus groups instead of surveys.

A second constraint that would motivate simplifying an application might be limited *local implementation skills*. Local skills may be required not just for tournament-specific implementation (such as baseline measurements) but also for reform implementation. This constraint is unlikely to be any different for a PIJC than for another delivery mechanism for the same technical assistance intervention. In both cases a more modest set of tasks would be indicated. If the required task is highly technical and must be implemented only by foreign experts, then a PIJC would *not* be an appropriate aid delivery mechanism.

Yet another type of constraint motivating the simplification of a PIJC application may be the *amount of time* for project implementation. A tournament approach certainly requires extra time to design and implement—especially if calibration or pilots are included. Depending on the complexity and scope of the intervention (see table 6-13), this could take up to an extra six months at each end of the intervention.[31] The costs of this must be weighed against the benefits of having a large number of jurisdictions trained and engaged in a set of reforms. Likewise, a PIJC is demand driven; therefore, stakeholders need to be consulted and opinions accorded before decisions are made, which also adds time to the process. Here, however, one must be careful. Any local-level, demand-driven reform process would (hopefully) draw on public participation, so this is unlikely to generate differential costs for a PIJC over that of a standard aid delivery project. Inclusion of rigorous evaluation also adds time to the process. Again, however, if the decision is to have the project monitored and evaluated, then the additional time required for the tournament over a standard intervention *for the same number* of monitored jurisdictions is narrowed considerably.

The *level of education, comprehension, social openness, and local pride* of the target population can also constrain the scope of a PIJC implementation. First, a PIJC is demand driven, and the ability to form a local consensus on reform will be limited if the stakeholders refuse to interact or find the appropriate, indigenous, institutional forums to do so. Second, the incentive effect of disseminating performance indicators may be weakened if the receiving population cannot decipher their meaning. Finally, the effect of peer pressure, social capital, and interjurisdictional

---

31. While calibration and pilots occur before the PIJC proper, ex-post output-based PIJCs require that endline data be collected in order to calculate player scores and identify the winners.

pride on the incentives to collaborate and reform will be more diffuse the weaker the level of these psychological attributes is in the target population. Of course, these limitations would also likely affect the standard aid delivery mechanism. The trick here—as any veteran of the aid business knows—is that the success or failure of an intervention depends on how well it is adapted to the local context. Being demand driven helps, but that alone is not sufficient.

In a similar vein, *political, cultural, and religious sensitivities* may also constrain a PIJC's degree of ambitiousness. A simple example is the view in Islamic countries that "gambling" is immoral. Thus attention is required to ensure that the tournament nature of the enterprise is not perceived as such.

The number of potential players available is also a limiting factor to running a tournament-type PIJC. In general, just as more competitors increase the efficiency of a market, so, too, do more players enhance the efficiency of a tournament. While in practice the number of jurisdictions required for a successful PIJC depends on those factors that elicit collusion versus those that generate constructive competition, on both theoretical and empirical grounds, the requisite minimum is generally quite low (see section 7.2.4).

7.3.2 Simplification Options

It goes without saying that the options for simplification depend on which type of intervention is planned (see table 6-13). Consider the case where the intervention is to stimulate policy, regulatory, or administrative reform. The first level of simplification would be to reduce the number and complexity of tasks on the menu of reforms subject to the game. This reduces the amount of technical assistance and benchmarking effort.

A second level of simplification would require an assessment of reform tasks, the local context, and, potentially, the sponsor's budget flexibility in order to determine whether a certification design can be used instead of a tournament. As explained in section 7.2.1, this has two aspects. First, does the sponsor know enough to set performance bars, or is the degree of information asymmetry between the donor and the potential recipients too large? Second, is there the potential for exogenous shocks across target jurisdictions to be correlated? If there is, then a certification approach may discourage participant effort. Note that in the case where the objective is to generate improvements in several jurisdictions, reversion to the standard bilateral contract approach may not be a simplification at all. Finally, a related factor to consider in incentive mechanism selection is implementation time. If the sponsor has a clear understanding of where to set the performance bar, then choosing certification in principle means quicker implementation.

The third level of potential simplification requires deciding whether evaluation is important and whether to use a randomized trials approach, and deciding on the nature, complexity, and diversity of tasks desired. These are interrelated since the nature of the tasks will determine whether it is possible to use simple benchmarks to assess initial and final participant performance. Moreover, complex tasks or tasks of uncertain (to the participant) difficulty may require rewards beyond the social benefits anticipated from a reform. (Keep in mind that a participant may consider the benefits stream from a reform to be uncertain.)

A fourth opportunity for simplification lies in reducing the "bells and whistles" of a PIJC implementation. This can include dropping the pilot tests to calibrate the requisite value of rewards, task points, and other related parameters, and removing player precommitment steps (which a jurisdiction must take to become eligible for participation and to receive the initial level of technical assistance). Likewise, in selecting tasks for the tournament, the sponsor can take into account whether they involve easy-to-document baselines (for example, no surveys required) rather than more sophisticated indicator metrics and surveys. Finally, the structure of rewards can be simplified to just broad dissemination of score publicity rather than any pecuniary compensation.

Finally, a more radical simplification would be to switch from an ex-post to an ex-ante performance design, which rewards past performance. Such a design works well for disseminating best practices, but it is unlikely to stimulate as much reform as an ex-post approach and can also dampen reform efforts because the time for a player's response is open ended. As discussed earlier, one way to address this is to engage in a repeated game in which the prior round's ex-post performance becomes the next round's ex-ante performance.

An analogous exercise can be done for each of the other categories of intervention shown in table 6-13. In each case simplifications will have their costs and benefits, though the former may be better viewed as risks to success. Incentive design, like intervention and project design, is ultimately an art, which means that practice makes perfect and that the designer must be ever attentive to adapting to the idiosyncrasies of initial conditions. While the accomplishments of the case study PIJC designs to date are surely impressive, this marathon through them has pointed to many unresolved questions, which are considered next.

7.4 Areas for Follow-Up Research and Testing

I hope that the reader will come away from this monograph with the impression that while major mistakes have been committed, development economists have a deeper understanding of the obstacles facing poor countries today and how to design incentive-compatible mechanisms to address them, given the right public participation. Moreover, examination of the case studies and other examples reveals that some sponsors have begun to incorporate these mechanisms and similarly motivated ideas of experts on the ground. These insights are based on recognizing that the source of development problems *and* their solutions is primarily institutional and informational.[32] Only institutional solutions have the chance of becoming sustainable since institutions, being "equilibriums" resulting from the interaction of participants (behaving under individually rational best responses, given their private information sets), stimulate and lock in the incentives faced by both decisionmakers and their agents on the ground.[33]

While there have been notable achievements, much still needs to be done, both in policy research and in more ambitious and innovative implementation. This section therefore focuses primarily on areas where further policy research is needed regarding the scope for greater use of tournaments, and only briefly touches on where changes on the donor side may affect them, thereby also requiring follow-up study.

Resolving Design Choice Mysteries

The descriptive analysis in chapter 6 and the current chapter points to a number of perplexing choices that sponsors have made in the selection of the incentive design for an intervention. One discovery to emerge from the comparisons shown in table 6-13 is that what first appeared to be a poor choice of incentive design often turned out to be appropriate once the sponsor's underlying constraints became known. Still, a number of "stylized facts" remain mysteries for future consideration:

—Why do sponsors favor ex-ante over ex-post incentive designs? Is it that the former are quicker or cheaper? Are sponsors able to deal with the former's weak performance incentives by engaging in repeated rounds?

—Why do sponsors favor input rather than output measures of performance? Are the latter harder to measure? Or is this design issue tied to a predilection for ex-ante incentive mechanisms?

—Why are there not more tournament applications? While a definitive confirmation of this observation must await the creation of a truly random sample, the intrinsic advantages of tournaments would in theory lead one to expect an abundance of tournament applications.

—Why was randomized impact evaluation not included in any of the PIJC applications? Is this simply because the methodological issues have yet to be resolved (see below)?

PIJC Implementation Issues

Aside from the actual substance of the reform, there are several other implementation challenges to overcome in order to have a successful PIJC. One concerns

---

32. The definition of "institution" here is broader than in the vernacular, as explained in the introduction to chapter 1.

33. There is an irony here. The very power of institutional equilibriums to lock in sustainable solutions is also the source of the original obstacle: institutional rigidities, formed by adaptation to past social, economic, and other realities, are now considered maladaptive and in need of change.

the calibration of optimal rewards and their structure. First, the project designer must decide whether to base the competition on achieving the highest *level* of performance or the largest *incremental improvement* in performance. Or should there be one set of rewards for best performers and one set for best improvers (Duflo 2005)? As discussed earlier, the latter is a more effective incentive when players are heterogeneous. Beyond this, however, is the question of how to determine the number of winning positions to offer and the size of each reward, given the number of players and their heterogeneity. A similar question concerns the need for adding certification thresholds in a tournament and the level at which to set them. Larger than necessary rewards can be distracting and encourage corruption while insufficiently sized rewards risk attracting too few players.

Closely related to the structure of rewards is how to set the number of players and their individual size so as to have the most effective tournament possible, that is, to stimulate the greatest number of reformers. The Russian fiscal reform had seven jurisdictional players, the Moroccan project anticipated eighty, and Galing Pook potentially had hundreds. There are many factors to consider, and some research-based guidance on this matter would be helpful.

The standard way to resolve these questions has been with focus groups, rules of thumb, and inferences from experience elsewhere. However, I believe that it is now possible to augment focus group tests by using a pilot survey and even to take greater advantage of laboratory experiments. Development of a standard set of field instruments in this regard would be worth pursuing.

Tournaments and certification in particular depend on good preplay public relations and postplay dissemination of results. How does one prepare the public to collaborate? How does one introduce the tournament concept into a particular cultural environment? What forums does one convene to bring together disparate interest groups within a jurisdiction in order to stimulate team formation? What scope is there to use the Internet and remote education technologies to reduce the cost of providing commonly needed reform technical assistance during a tournament, and what does experience say about the suggestions in this regard offered in appendix C? There are many methods as well as media to choose from. The field of strategic communication is certainly growing, and it would be useful to have more research on its application to the design of reputational awards for maximum incentive effect in tournaments and certification. Part of the success of the PROPER project in Indonesia owes to its clever use of communication. Mastery of these issues may also help in developing techniques to overcome the problem of political reticence to being measured (see section 7.2.4).

In a different context, Kanbur (2001) raises some interesting collateral issues that have a bearing on PIJCs. He asks how to increase donor accountability and how to apportion credit and blame when an intervention has mixed-team players, for example, as in his original case, a joint partnership. He also worries about such issues when dealing with vested interests and when donor, government, and team member contributions may be subject to fungibility of funds. He rightfully suggests that one must pay more attention to overall impacts rather than individual contributions. Ironically, vis à vis the donor this is much more of a problem for conventional project designs, where the donor takes on a much more direct role in guiding outcomes and in decisionmaking. With the types of incentive mechanisms presented in this book, the donor is "only" responsible—and, therefore, only blameworthy—for designing and setting the parameters of the game, being forced to take a hands-off approach once these are established. Regarding apportioning blame and praise when the player comprises separate local entities, teamwork is what matters, and team members themselves will know whom to blame or praise. Moreover, each party's agreement to play on the team presupposes its acceptance of the risks and rewards.

The analysis of incentive mechanism effectiveness often identified shortcomings in the incentives facing aid sponsors, both internal to their organizations as well as imposed by their funding sources. Concrete proposals to change the organizational incentives facing donors so as to encourage them to become more ambitious and innovative, however, are outside the scope of this book and have been treated elsewhere.[34] Nonetheless, beyond their aversion to innovation, sponsors also may avoid PIJCs due to certain characteristics specific to this class of mechanism. Finding out what these are and testing out design enhancements to deal with them would be valuable. One could start by asking why sponsors have not been more proactive in replicating those PIJCs they have already demonstrated to be successful.[35]

Finally, though I have perhaps given insufficient attention in this book to the use of PIJCs in the service of performance-based revenue transfers in a regularized, fiscally decentralized system, further research would be welcome on which local budgetary expenditures are amenable to tournament mechanisms and on practical implementation guidelines for matching instruments to SNG administrative capacity and other pertinent local initial conditions.

Randomized Evaluation Considerations

The literature on randomized impact evaluation is already large, and this is not the place to review where its areas of current research are. This literature, however, typically examines the issues related to random assignment for a series of variations of a single treatment. It thus seems more suited to embedding randomized trials

34. See Collier (2002); Kremer (2003); and William Easterly "Tired Old Mantras at Monterey," op-ed, *Wall Street Journal,* March 18, 2002.

35. In fairness, some of the cases presented here have been replicated. According to Lynnette Wood of ARD (Burlington, Vt.), the firm has now implemented for USAID in Jordan a mechanism similar to their mancomunidades design (though I do not know whether the apparent incentive weaknesses identified in this book have been addressed). The PROPER initiative has been widely copied in Asia, and the Galing Pook report card has inspired many copycat applications.

into a standard, bilateral, contracted activity. Conducting randomized impact evaluation across jurisdictions under a certification or a tournament, in which each jurisdiction may be applying its own "treatment" to achieve performance, presents challenges for evaluation design.

A central question for project designers is whether to integrate a randomized evaluation into a PIJC in the first place. How much more does it complicate the intervention, and how much more capacity does it demand from the local PIJC participants? The earlier discussion on PIJC simplification is relevant here. Clearly there is a tradeoff between allocating project resources and participant effort in the pursuit of current output objectives, on the one hand, and deriving lessons for future applications, on the other.

It is not unusual to hear a donor that is favorably disposed to M&E—but put off by the added time it has historically required at the end of the project—make the plea that evaluation results should be available in real time to be relevant to operations. This is exactly the motivation behind the proposal in this book for donors to design their interventions within the framework of *prospective* randomized evaluation, since this embeds the monitoring and evaluation technology directly into the project. However, it poses the challenge of how to get the right information to the right potential users at the right time, which will require that evaluators develop better communication strategies. My guess is that once donors recognize that *prospective* randomized evaluation can mean real-time feedback on project developments, they will become much more receptive to M&E. Moreover, this approach would greatly reduce the tensions between implementer and evaluator so common historically on retrospective donor project evaluations (though it does create a new source of tension between evaluator and project designer).[36]

Both the incentive-compatible mechanisms presented in this book as well as randomized evaluation require interacting with a much larger number of direct recipients than donors have generally experienced before. One wonders, therefore, as the demand for evaluation continues to grow, will this have an impact on donor receptivity to PIJCs?

Finally, from my own experience I can confirm that there is a tendency, when given the chance, for evaluators to request and collect information beyond the point where its marginal benefit equals its marginal cost of collection. In short, a final research challenge, whether or not a randomized evaluation is included within one's PIJC, is how to set priorities when faced with unlimited information demands?

---

36. My experience in designing MCC evaluations has borne this out. Projects are designed at the MCC by sector experts who, despite their intellectual acceptance of M&E, only accept input from the M&E department at the margins—and often once the design is far along. Overall, there is tremendous pressure to field the projects, and anything that slows down implementation is highly frowned upon in practice.

Empirical Research Strategies

As is generally appropriate for a first step in a research program on a new subject, this book has taken the middle ground in analysis and investigated a broad range of PIJC applications. However, since the appropriate parameters defining the universe of PIJC application was not known in advance, case study selection was necessarily nonrandom. As a second step in a research program, therefore, one could envision empirical strategies at opposite extremes of the analysis spectrum. On the one hand, one could conduct more in-depth nonstatistical analysis of a small number of applications to examine both the underlying political process of undertaking the PIJC as well as the factors that actually impeded or facilitated its outcomes and sustainability. On the other hand, one could carry out a more exhaustive search for PIJCs (some of which are found in appendix A) to create a database of existing applications. Using the database, one could draw a random sample to code in detail, using the frameworks presented in this book. This would allow the investigator to revisit many of the tentative conclusions reached here using a true random sample and armed with sufficient degrees of freedom for more sophisticated multivariate analysis. These two analytic extremes could be enriched by exploring how to include interventions based on standard bilateral contracts into the analysis.[37]

Looking to the Future

Sponsors are now interested in leveraging their assistance by becoming "advocates for change." PIJC offers a potentially powerful way for them to do so. The survey of sponsor interventions presented here suggests that there is much room to expand both the scope and the scale of PIJC applications. As this book has made clear, fresh ideas are abundant, though additional practical experience with them is still necessary, and there is a risk that ambitions might run ahead of absorptive capacity. What is needed, therefore, are more initiatives to encourage incorporation of these incentive mechanisms into aid products and more research into practical, minimally obtrusively methods to extract rigorous lessons from them. One of the goals of this book has been to develop a set of frameworks and guidelines to help focus design and testing of such initiatives. In this way—as with microfinance over the last decade—today's experimentation can yield tomorrow's successful implementation models.

---

37. The inclusion into the sample of non-PIJC applications that nonetheless could have been treated using PIJC approaches is not as straightforward methodologically as it might appear. This is due to "selection bias," which makes it statistically difficult to disentangle the direction and source of causality. For example, was an outcome due to the incentive design chosen or to characteristics of the application itself, which influenced both its outcome as well as the sponsor's choice of incentive design?

A

Inventory of Projects

Project A: Output-Based Aid to Increase Coverage of Paraguay's Aguateros

Contact: Franz Drees, Jordan Schwartz, and Alexander Bakalian, the World Bank's Latin America and the Caribbean Regional Office

Description: Given the constraints of the state water utility and the traditional water users' association model, Paraguayan officials concluded that private providers would be the best means of reaching unserved communities and rapidly expanding rural coverage. The rural water agency, SENASA, agreed to implement a pilot output-based aid program to attract *aguateros* (small, informal, private water companies) and local construction companies to small towns, large villages, and periurban communities. To meet the minimum requirements for safe, reliable service, private operators were contracted to build water networks (a borehole, disinfection, storage tank, and a distribution system with household connections). Meters were installed at the discretion of the operator unless a customer requested one. Water standards and hours of service were set out in a contract between the community and the operator. Perhaps most important, the operators were required to connect any household within the defined service area that requested a connection and paid the fee. Private operators were awarded the contracts by bidding on the fee they would charge users up front to connect to their system. Once selected, operators could charge users for the connection fee in installments at a defined interest rate. Operators would recover their costs from the connection subsidy (paid by

SENASA) and the connection charge and tariff (both paid by users). Each town had the right to reject the winning bid if it considered the connection fee too high.

PIJC mechanism: The bidder that was both responsive to the technical requirements and offered the lowest connection fee would be declared the winner.

Source: Drees, Schwartz, and Bakalian (2004).

Project B: IDA Conditional Grants Based on Tracking of Heavily Indebted Poor Countries (HIPC)

Contact: Danny Leipziger, vice president and head of the Poverty Reduction and Economic Management Network, World Bank

Description: Sixteen public expenditure management indicators are used to evaluate progress on HIPC areas, and grants by IDA depend on such progress.

PIJC mechanism: Pecuniary certification

Source: International Monetary Fund and World Bank, "Update on the Assessments and Implementation of Action Plans to Strengthen Capacity of HIPCs to Track Poverty-Reducing Public Spending," April 12, 2005 (www.imf.org/external/np/pp/eng/2005/041205a.pdf).

Project C: Olympic Games Host City Selection

Contact: International Olympic Committee (IOC)

Description: The candidate cities were selected after a working group of IOC administration members and external experts studied their applications. An assessment was made of each applicant city's ability to stage high-level, international, multisport events and to organize quality Olympic Winter Games in 2010, based on eleven technical assessment criteria: government support and public opinion, general infrastructure, sports venues, Olympic village, environmental conditions and impact, accommodation, transport, security, experience from past sports events, finance, and general concept.

PIJC mechanism: Cities compete for the right to host the Olympic Games. After applications are submitted, the IOC makes the decision. The cities that are nominated to the international competition to host the games also have to win the nomination of their respective National Olympic Committee (NOC). (NOCs also supervise the preliminary selection of potential bid cities. Before a candidate city can compete against those in other countries, it first must win the selection process by the NOC in its own country. The NOC can then name that city to the IOC as a candidate to host the Olympic Games.)

Note: The host city for the World Cup is also chosen in a similar manner. The only difference is that the Fédération Internationale de Football Association

(FIFA) decides (via a rotation system) which continent is going to host the World Cup, and then only countries in that region of the world can bid to host it.

Source: Candidature Acceptance Working Group (2006); also available at http://multimedia.olympic.org/pdf/en_report_1073.pdf.

Project D: Clean City Program (ADIPURA), Indonesia

Contact: Good Governance Institute, Indonesia

Description: This is a locally implemented, public disclosure program at the local government level with the aim of encouraging good governance, sustainable development institutions, and sound environmental management, as well as meeting the Millennium Development Goals.

PIJC mechanism: Measurable and comparable indicators were developed for leadership, capacity of local government, promotion of civil society, delivery of basic services, economic development, sustainable development, and equity. The performance of local governments was then compared, and the results were made public to use "blame and praise" to stimulate improvements along the seven dimensions of the program.

Source: Makarim (2006).

Project E: The Buenos Aires Concession

Contact: Lorena Alcazar, Manuel A. Abdala, and Mary M. Shirley, World Bank

Description: "Water distribution and sewage collection are natural monopolies, so the scope for direct market competition is limited to minor activities, such as billing and revenue collection. In the Buenos Aires concession, competition was introduced through the bidding process. This process, which plays a critical role in drawing out enough information to ensure that a concession is awarded successfully, generally worked well."

PIJC mechanism: "The rules required potential bidders to prequalify to limit the bidding to firms with strong technical and financial capabilities and to ensure that any foreign bidders would be the very top operators. The call for bids went out in June 1992, requesting two envelopes. The first, which determined whether a bidder qualified, held technical offers (including legal features of the bidder, a mission statement, operational plans, proposed regulations for users, and a US$3 million guarantee of commitment to the offer). The second envelope, opened if a bidder qualified, held financial and economic offers, including adjustments to the current tariff rate, indicators of financial strength and commitment, and an explanation of how the bidder would operate with the new tariff. The contract would go to the bidder offering the largest discount to the public tariffs. The rest of the information to be provided was essentially intended to demonstrate

that the discount proposed would allow revenues consistent with the level and timing of expenditure commitments."
Source: Crampes and Estache (1996); also available at http://rru.worldbank.org/Documents/PublicPolicyJournal/091crampes.pdf.

Project F: Innovations in American Government Award

Contact: Ash Institute for Democratic Governance and Innovation, Harvard Kennedy School

Description: The Innovations in American Government Program, in operation for more than twenty years, is a significant force in recognizing and promoting excellence and creativity in the public sector. Through its annual awards competition, the program provides concrete evidence that government can work to improve the quality of life for citizens and that it deserves greater public trust. Many award-winning programs have been replicated across jurisdictions and policy areas, and some have served as harbingers of today's reform strategies or as forerunners to state and federal legislation. By highlighting exemplary models of government's innovative performance, the program serves as a catalyst for continued progress in addressing the nation's most pressing public concerns.

PIJC mechanism: In the first round of competition, experts—both practitioners and scholars—screen all received applications. Applicants who advance beyond the first round submit a substantive, supplementary application (approximately 8,000 words). The second round of competition takes place in the fall and involves experts who evaluate the supplementary applications and select fifty programs from the applicant pool to advance in the competition. Each of the fifty programs receives extensive press coverage marking their achievement. The third round of competition takes place during the winter and results in the selection of finalist programs to advance in the competition. The fourth round of competition consists of a site visit. Innovations evaluators visit each of the finalist programs to conduct a two-day assessment. After the completion of a successful site visit, each of the finalist programs is officially named an Innovations Award Finalist and receives further press coverage. The fifth and final round of competition takes place in late spring and involves representatives from the fifteen selected Finalist programs making presentations before the members of the Innovations National Selection Committee, who then select the winners of the award. Each of the winners is then eligible to receive a grant of $100,000 to be directed toward replication and dissemination activities.

The winners of the Innovations Award are announced in conjunction with the annual Excellence in Government Conference, which typically takes place in July.
Source: Available online at http://ashinstitute.harvard.edu/corporate_site/innovations#446 and at http://innovationsaward.harvard.edu/Awards_Cycle.cfm.

Project G: Managed Competition in Indianapolis: The Case of Fleet Services

Contact: School of International and Public Affairs, Columbia University
Description: "The City of Indianapolis has been widely touted as a success story for managed competition. Faced with a fiscal crisis, its mayor, Stephen Goldsmith, introduced competitive bidding to redefine the roles of local government and the private sector in providing public services. The results generated greater efficiency, windfalls in savings for the city, as well as in-house units that were able to effectively compete with their private counterparts."

The contracting experience of Indianapolis was not unique in the United States. Managed competition and, especially, privatization gained momentum in the 1980s and 1990s as an anti–big government, pro–free-market ideology swept the nation. Beyond ideology, however, there are a number of pragmatic reasons for government managers to consider managed competition. First and foremost, competition is seen as a way to lower costs, an important consideration for elected officials who are either unwilling or unable (by law) to raise taxes. Government managers can also use competition to improve the quality of service they provide. Opening service provision to competition "brings unconscious managers to consciousness and makes recalcitrant workers cooperative," in the words of Linda Morrison, former director of competitive contracting under Philadelphia mayor Ed Rendell. It also allows government to draw on the best expertise available, whether in the existing organization or in the private sector. Governments are asked by their citizens to carry out an extremely wide range of tasks, from "writing traffic tickets to giving tennis lessons, from printing documents to paving streets. No organization could do so many tasks well," argue William Eggers and John O'Leary, prominent advocates of privatization. Stephen Goldsmith notes that private bidders "have technologies we don't have, research we don't have, scale we don't have. It's not that our employees are bad, but our technology and research and scale are limited."
PIJC mechanism: Public agencies and private agencies bid or compete to win government service contracts.
Source: Chang and others (2005); also available at www.innovations.harvard.edu/cache/documents/11043.pdf.

Project H: Poland and Czech Republic Compete for Toyota Plant

Contact: None available
Description: The Czech Republic competed with Poland for acquisition of a Toyota–PSA Peugeot Citroën plant. The result was attributable to differences in the incentive packages provided by the Czech and Polish governments, a stable Czech economy, and greater proximity to European Union markets.

PIJC mechanism: FDI competition
Source: See http://search.epnet.com/login.aspx?direct=true&db=buh&an=5889966.

Project I: Community Development and Livelihood Improvement "Gemi Diriya" Project

Contact: Karen Sirker, social development specialist
Donor: World Bank
Description: "The development objective of the proposed 12-year program for the Community Development and Livelihood Improvement 'Gemi Diriya' Project for Sri Lanka is to enable the rural poor to improve their livelihood and quality of life. The objective of the proposed first four-year phase of the program would be to enable the communities of Uva and Southern provinces to build accountable and self-governing local institutions and to manage sustainable investments by: (i) devolving decision-making power and resources to community organizations; (ii) strengthening selected local governments which demonstrate responsiveness and accountability to rural communities; and (iii) working with federations of village organizations, the private sector and non-governmental organizations (NGOs) on economic empowerment to increase the size and diversity of livelihood options. The project comprises the following five components: Component 1, Village Development, strengthens village organizations (VOs) and funds priority sub- projects. Component 2, Institutional Strengthening, builds the capacity of local and national agencies and supports organizations to respond to community demands. Component 3, Innovation Seed Fund, pilots innovative ideas that need experimentation, learning and incubation. Component 4, Project Management, facilitates overall coordination, implementation, and management of the project. (v) Component 5, Village Self-Help Learning Initiative Pilot, completes implementation of the ongoing pilot in Polonnaruwa district."
Competition Mechanism: The program uses community scorecards and the media to implement change.
Source: See World Bank, "Sri Lanka: Community Development and Livelihood Improvement 'Gemi Diriya' Project" (www.worldbank.lk/external/default/main?pagePK=64027221&piPK=64027220&theSitePK=233047&menuPK=287062&Projectid=P074872).

Project J: Corporate Governance Scores

Author: Standard and Poor's
Description: The corporate governance score (CGS) scale runs from CGS-1 (lowest) to CGS-10 (highest). The scores reflect Standard and Poor's assessment of a company's corporate governance practices and policies and the extent to which these serve the interests of the company's financial stakeholders, with an emphasis on shareholders' interests.

PIJC mechanism: The CGS triggers strategic behavior by the players (companies) because they want to get a high rating to attract investors (Note: The CGS is determined with the cooperation of the companies being rated.) Company credit ratings may also be an example.

Source: See their website at www2.standardandpoors.com.

Project K: Bosnia and Herzegovina: Citizen-Driven Decisionmaking

Contact: Slobadanka Dukic, Fesjal Kirlic, and Maniza Naqvi

Description: In Bosnia and Herzegovina, where years of authoritarian rule had left citizens unaccustomed to a high degree of participation in governance, the Community Development Project (CDP) has helped citizens gain a voice in shaping municipal financing priorities for investments in water supply networks, central heating systems in schools, school playgrounds, sewage systems, youth centers, local roads, bus shelters, radio stations, and ambulatory facilities.

In addition to restoring important social services and infrastructure, the project's success has deepened the institutional development of municipalities and strengthened ties between local governments and citizens of all ethnicities. It also has built interethnic and interentity alliances at the citizens' level by creating conditions for joint decisionmaking, dialogue, and negotiations within communities.

CDP financing has a ceiling of $50,000 per project. Based on their performance, municipalities can be eligible for additional financing. Each grant can either finance one investment or support several for which funding has been mobilized but is insufficient. The project focuses on the poorest municipalities in the country. A major goal is to continue the process of creating conditions for return by rebuilding roads and repairing infrastructure.

PIJC mechanism: Although this project does not have any explicit tournament, it does feature a number of PIJC components. By using performance grants, for example, this project may create an implicit competition among the participating communities. If community A is meeting the performance requirement to secure additional funds for improvement projects, it may create public pressure in the other communities to do even better.

Source: See http://info.worldbank.org/etools/reducingpoverty/casestudy.asp?type=case.

Project L: Nigeria—Community-Based Urban Development

Contact: World Bank, Africa Regional Office

Description: The Community-Based Urban Development Project will demonstrate inclusive and replicable approaches for the sustainable delivery of basic municipal services, in poor unserved or underserved settlements, and facilitate partnerships between poor urban communities, local, and state governments for decisionmaking related to on-site public expenditures in settlements, thereby fostering good governance. Project components will finance: upgrading of basic municipal infrastructure in seven cities within seven states; fund infrastructure subprojects in cities within thirteen states, based on criteria to improve urban poverty; capacity building and training to develop strategic infrastructure and knowledge-sharing networks; implementation support and monitoring and evaluation systems to assist in the establishment of project implementation units (PIUs) in all states; development and implementation of an appropriate AIDS education information and communication campaign in the project areas, namely, in project-supported schools and clinics, and along the solid waste collection, transport, and disposal network; and a project preparation facility (PPF) to enable project preparation for the cities under the first component, to be reimbursed from project funds once the project becomes effective.

PIJC mechanism: The project uses a form of certification to decide which communities move on to phase 2: "The seven Phase I States will become eligible for participation in Phase II as soon as they have implemented 20 percent of physical works of their first subprojects. The six additional States in Phase II will become eligible for participation as soon as they meet the [additional] eligibility criteria. . . . All States will develop viable proposals up to the preliminary engineering stage with their own resources guided by the procedures in the Project Implementation Manual (PIM)."

Possible PIJC components:
   —Tournament (certification)
   —Recipient self-selection and demand
   —Overcoming collective action problems
   —Mechanisms to increase governance
   —Participatory development

Source: World Bank, "Nigeria—Community Based Urban Development," Report PID9122 (www-wds.worldbank.org/external/default/WDSContent Server/IW3P/IB/2000/05/24/000094946_0005240537582/Rendered/PDF/multi0page.pdf).

Project M: Race to the Top

Contact: Race to the Top Secretariat, International Institute for Environment and Development

Description: "The objective of the Race to the Top (RTTT) project was to develop . . . benchmarks in partnership with a broad coalition of civil society organizations and to work with leading supermarkets to apply them. The overall aim was to promote accountability and transparency within the UK supermarket sector, [and] in doing so, [build] incentives for the major UK supermarket companies to improve and communicate their social, environmental and ethical policies and performance over a five-year period. The methodology centered on a process of engagement between supermarkets and civil society organizations with interests in a variety of social, environmental and ethical issues. The main activity was a collaborative benchmarking process, supplemented by additional research, good practice case studies and ongoing dialogue. This was all carried out within a structure that combined centralized project management and brokering, devolved responsibility for input into the benchmarking development process through seven thematic groups, and strategic guidance by an independent advisory group."

PIJC mechanism: The project creates a tournament between supermarkets by scoring their relative performance on social, environmental, and ethical policies. The scores are published, which creates public pressure and incentives for supermarkets to improve their policies.

Possible PIJC components:
—Tournament (benchmarking)
—Participatory development

Source: Fox and Vorley (2004); also available at http://racetothetop.org/documents/RTTT_final_report_full.pdf.

Project N: Government Performance Project

Contact: Campbell Public Affairs Institute

Description: Under the auspices of the Pew Charitable Trusts, the Maxwell School of Citizenship and Public Affairs of Syracuse University has, since 1996, rated the management capacity of local and state governments and selected federal agencies in the United States. The project, called the Government Performance Project (GPP), is administered by the Maxwell School's Alan K. Campbell Public Affairs Institute. The GPP evaluates the effectiveness of management systems and examines the role of leadership in government entities. In doing so, the project studies and evaluates public sector management in five management system areas and determines how well they are integrated. The GPP does not focus primarily on performance; it analyzes management capacity, which is the foundation for good results. Finally, the project aims to communicate its findings to government agencies as well as to the public.

PIJC mechanism: The project creates an implicit competition among government agencies and local and state governments by evaluating and publishing its findings. As a result, local and state governments compete for higher rankings and publicity, which may stimulate business development and bring more citizens (and therefore revenue) to the state or county.

Possible PIJC components:
—Tournament
—Public relations
Source: See http://sites.maxwell.syr.edu/gpp3.

Project O: International Council of Toy Industries (ICTI) CARE Process

Contact: ICTI CARE Foundation Secretariat; also Allan Hassenfeld, president
Description: This organization is "involved in an effort to create a global standard for the ethical manufacture of toys. Enforcing stricter standards is good business as well as good ethics, the organization claims, because it reassures customers and enables toymakers to continue outsourcing their manufacturing [to places such as] China." The organization states that approximately "1.3m workers, around one-third of those employed in Asia by the industry, are covered by the CARE Process, which is policed by toymakers and NGOs." As a result, the organization notes that for these firms "child labor is seen less and less, because firms know that if they are found employing children they immediately lose their certificate of compliance."
PIJC mechanism: Simple certification. What is particularly interesting for this certification is the use of peer monitoring to keep the cost of enforcement down. Moreover, as in microfinance, such monitoring is incentive compatible because it is in the interest of firms to identify competitors who have reduced their cost by violating the CARE Process standards.
Source: See "Face Value: Santa's Happy Helper," *The Economist,* December 20, 2008. See also "Welcome to the ICTI CARE Process" (www.icti-care.org).

Project O: Promoting Accountability in the Budget Cycle: The Public Service Accountability Monitor in South Africa

Contact: Xolisa Vitsha
Description: The Public Service Accountability Monitor (PSAM) is an independent monitoring unit dedicated to strengthening democracy in South Africa and based at Rhodes University in South Africa's Eastern Cape province. It gathers information on the management of public resources and the handling of misconduct and corruption cases by government departments. This information is collected in a rigorous, objective, and politically impartial fashion. By publishing this information, the PSAM hopes to give members of parliament, civil society organizations, and ordinary citizens the tools necessary to hold government ministers and public officials accountable for their performance and use of public resources.

PIJC mechanism: The PSAM's scorecard is designed to provide impartial answers to a series of questions about coherent planning, performance, accountability, and delivery by government departments. All questions are weighted equally and a score of 1 (for yes) or 0 (for no) is awarded to each answer. The total score is calculated as a percentage of the points scored versus the number of questions posed.

Possible PIJC components:
   —Tournament (implicit)
   —Scorecards
Source: See www.psam.org.za.

Project P: Blue Flag Project

Contact: Foundation for Environmental Education, Copenhagen, Denmark
Description: "The Blue Flag is given to beaches and marinas that meet a specific set of criteria concerning environmental information and education, water quality, safety and services and environmental management. It has become a symbol of quality recognised by tourists and tour operators and can be used for the promotion of the awarded beach or marina. The programme is designed to raise environmental awareness and increase good environmental practices among tourists, local populations and beach and marina management and staff. The programme criteria are also designed to work with the national, regional and local legislation of each country, thereby assuring that the legislation is being followed, or it can be used to set a benchmark higher than what already exists."
PIJC mechanism: The project creates an implicit tournament among beaches and their surrounding communities in order to attract tourists.
Possible PIJC components:
   —Tournament
   —Participatory development
Source: Foundation for Environmental Education (2006); also available at www.blueflag.fi/files/9/Blue_Flag_brochure.pdf.

Project Q: Green Globe

Contact: Green Globe Project
Description: Green Globe works with travel and tourism companies and communities to maintain good environmental and social practices, deliver maximum benefit to all interested parties, and provide choice for concerned consumers. Travel and tourism companies, communities, ecotourism products, and development projects participating in the Green Globe program are located in countries worldwide and represent most sectors of the travel and tourism industry. Green Globe provides benchmarking and certification under four standards: company

standard, community standard, international ecotourism standard, and the design and construct standard. A new precinct planning and development standard is currently being piloted.

PIJC mechanism: The project uses benchmarking and certification as an incentive mechanism.

Possible PIJC components:
—Tournament
—Participatory development

Source: See www.greenglobe.org.

Project R: Inter-American Development Bank Fund to Promote Dominican Youth Entrepreneurship

Contact: Peter Bate, Inter-American Development Bank

Description: "The project seeks to help young men and women with a college or technical education to overcome the hurdles entrepreneurs encounter when they try to start a business without enough training, work experience, financial support or networks of contacts. . . . Under the project, a training methodology will be developed and instructors will be trained in teaching young people how to start and run businesses. The youths will have help in preparing business plans and opportunities to gain experience through internships in established firms or mentoring provided by seasoned businesspeople. . . . The project will directly help 750 youths develop business skills and select 300 teams of young entrepreneurs with feasible ideas to start businesses. Three contests for business plans will be held to pick 50 teams that will receive cash awards of up to $1,000 to cover start-up costs as well as mentoring from business leaders."

PIJC mechanism: The project uses business plan competitions among youth to further develop their entrepreneurial skills.

Possible PIJC components:
—Tournament

Source: Inter-American Development Bank, "IDB Fund to Support Project to Promote Entrepreneurship among Dominican Youths," press release, Feb 8, 2005 (www.iadb.org/news/articledetail.cfm?language=English&artid=368&artType=PR).

Project S: Sustainable Agriculture Network

Contact: Rainforest Alliance

Description: "Since 1991, the [Sustainable Agriculture] Network has developed guidelines for the responsible management of export agriculture, certifying bananas, coffee, cocoa, citrus, and flowers and foliage according to environmental and social standards, in a process that, from the onset, has been participatory, transparent, and independent. Farms that meet the Sustainable Agriculture Network standards are 'certified' and may use the Rainforest Alliance-certified® label in marketing their products, gaining the reward of a marketplace that increasingly demands responsible farm management practices. The Rainforest Alliance has certified more than 10 million acres of forests worldwide, as well as agricultural products, and brings international recognition and credibility to the Network's certification efforts and ecolabel. Producers ranging from large agribusinesses to smallholder cooperatives have joined in this campaign to reduce environmental impact and increase community benefits of agriculture."

PIJC mechanism: Certification

Possible PIJC components:
— Actionable indicators and use of benchmarking
— Recipient selects tasks to implement
— Ensures minimum performance threshold is met
— Demand-driven targeting of technical assistance

Source: Rainforest Alliance, "The Sustainable Agriculture Network: Latin American Conservation Groups Raising the Standard for Export Agriculture" (www.rainforest-alliance.org/programs/agriculture/pdfs/san-description.pdf).

Project T: Canadian Education Freedom Index

Contact: Claudia R. Hepburn, director of education policy, Fraser Institute

Description: "The Canadian Education Freedom Index measures the freedom that parents in different provinces have to educate their children. It does this by comparing policies governing the three types of school they might choose if the public system is unsatisfactory to them: home schools, independent (or private) schools, or charter schools. It does not measure the very real differences in school choice available in different parts of the same province because, though such measurement would certainly be valuable and revealing, the work lies outside the scope and resources of this project. Rather, it measures the ease with which parents can establish the education they want for their children if what they want is not provided in the public system.

The Canadian Education Freedom Index does this by collecting a variety of objective indicators of educational freedom into one document so that anyone— parent, politician, journalist or student—can compare the policies of different provinces across the country."

PIJC mechanism: The project creates a competition among the provinces by using an index to "grade" their education policies.

Possible PIJC components:
—Tournament

Source: Hepburn and Van Belle (2003); also available at www.fraserinstitute.org/ Commerce.Web/product_files/CanadianEducationFreedomIndex.pdf.

Project U: Enhancing Municipal Service Delivery Capability (Phase II)

Contact: Bradford R. Philips, director, Regional and Sustainable Development Department, Agriculture, Natural Resources, and Social Sectors Division, Asian Development Bank

Description: "This TA aims to institutionalize the modified benchmarking and continuous improvement program for effective delivery of municipal services within the three most successful municipalities in phase 1, i.e., Bangalore, Cebu City and Colombo designated as core municipalities; and introduce these techniques to an additional nine municipalities. Specifically the TA will:

(i) build the capacity of core municipalities to drive and implement change;

(ii) use the core municipalities to mentor three other municipalities in each country on the use of benchmarking and continuous improvement techniques;

(iii) establish a mechanism for participation and feed back from the community and non-government organizations (NGOs) on the effectiveness of delivery of municipal services, and publicize the results through the media; and

(iv) expand the communication network of the municipalities to facilitate comparing performance indicators, sharing experiences and learning good practices in the delivery of municipal services."

PIJC mechanism: Benchmarking

Possible PIJC components:
—Tournament
—Participatory development

Source: ACIG International (2003); also available at www.adb.org/Projects/Benchmarking/final_report.pdf.

Project V: Michigan's School-of-Choice Program

Contact: Michigan Department of Education

Description: Michigan offers charter schools and statewide public school choice to children residing in districts that opt to participate in the state's schools-of-choice program. Eligible high school students may enroll in college courses for high school or postsecondary credit.

PIJC mechanism: Charter schools and public "schools-of-choice" are beginning to replace the "assignment system"—whereby children are assigned to a particular government school based on where they live—with school choice, where parents have the right, freedom, and ability to choose the safest and best schools for their children. Charter schools and schools-of-choice programs represent "incentive-based" education reform (competition among school districts).

Possible PIJC component:
—Tournament

Source: See Ladner and Brouillette (2000); also available at www.mackinac.org/archives/2000/s2000-04.pdf. See also Heritage Foundation, "School Choice: Michigan" (www.heritage.org/research/education/schoolchoice/Michigan.cfm).

Project W: Montgomery County CHOICE Program

Contact: Montgomery County Public Schools (Maryland)
Description: "In Grade 8, students choose a high school they would like to attend that contains a Grades 10–12 academy program in which they are interested. After admission to a high school, students will identify an academy program within the school that they are interested in attending in Grades 10–12."
PIJC mechanism: Students are given the opportunity to choose the public high school that they want to attend within the Montgomery County Public School system. This creates a competition among the high schools in the school district.
Possible PIJC component:
  —Tournament
Source: Montgomery County Public Schools, "School Assignment Process" (www.mcps.k12.md.us/schools/downcounty/choice/process.shtm).

Project X: Michigan's Universal Tuition Tax Credit (UTTC)

Contact: Mackinac Center for Public Policy
Description: "The UTTC has the following features and benefits:
  —It gradually phases in a tax credit for tuition paid to *any* Michigan elementary or secondary school—public or private. It is a direct dollar-for-dollar credit against taxes owed, not simply a deduction.
  —The tax credit may be claimed by *any* taxpayer—individual or corporate. This includes a student's parents as well as relatives, friends, neighbors or businesses. A large company, for example, could pay $2,000 tuition for each of 1,000 low-income children and receive a $2,000,000 tax credit.
  —The tax credit applies to three major state taxes: the Individual Income tax, the Single Business Tax, and the 6-mill state education property tax. These taxes represent state revenue of approximately $7.5 billion.
  —It is a per-child tax credit, allowing the full credit to be applied to each child in a family."
PIJC mechanism: This program features a competition between private and public schools for students and revenue (tuition). The tax credit gives parents the opportunity to send their children to the school of their choice.
Source: Mackinac Center for Public Policy, "Executive Summary" (www.mackinac.org/article.aspx?ID=1054).

Project Y: Commitment to Development Index

Contact: David Roodman, Center for Global Development
Description: The Commitment to Development Index ranks twenty-one of the richest nations on their performance in each of the following policy areas:
   —Quantity and quality of foreign aid
   —Openness to developing-country exports
   —Policies that influence investment
   —Migration policies
   —Environmental policies
   —Security policies
   —Support for creation and dissemination of new technologies.
PIJC mechanism: Tournament among twenty-one rich countries based on competitive comparison of indicator scores
Source: Center for Global Development, "Commitment to Development Index 2007" (www.cgdev.org/section/initiatives/_active/cdi).

Project Z: Changemakers Innovation Award

Contact: Charlie Brown, executive director, Ashoka's Changemakers
Description: "Changemakers is an initiative of Ashoka: Innovators for the Public that focuses on the rapidly growing world of social innovation. It provides solutions and resources needed to help everyone become a changemaker and presents compelling stories that explore the fundamental principles of successful social innovation around the world.

Changemakers is building the world's first global online 'open source' community that competes to surface the best social solutions, and then collaborates to refine, enrich, and implement those solutions. Changemakers begins by providing an overarching intellectual framework for collaborative competitions that bring together individual social change initiatives into a more powerful whole.

To keep the framework dynamic, the online Changemakers' community identifies and selects the best solutions and helps refine them. The result is global action frameworks, drawing on the work of social entrepreneurs, that seed collaborative action and visibility on a global scale—making a big difference, field by field.

The 'open sourcing social solutions™' model aims to challenge the traditional focus of issues like human trafficking and conflict resolution with a broader, more complete set of stakeholders. As such, each one serves as a platform for building a practitioner- and investor-engaged community that sparks new waves of innovation around problems stuck on conventional approaches."

Competitions are open to all types of organizations (charitable organizations, private companies, or public entities) from all countries. Any application is eligible to compete if it reflects the theme of the particular competition, is beyond the stage of idea, concept or research, and, at a minimum, is at the demonstration stage and has demonstrable success.

PIJC mechanism: Consider an example of a competition held in the health field. "The winners of this Changemakers Innovation Award will be those entries that best meet the following criteria:

—Innovation: The initiative introduces novel elements—in the type of health products/services provided, in the healthcare delivery model or financing mechanism, for example—that contribute to improving health for low-income and marginalized populations. It is based on leveraged points of intervention.

—Impact: The initiative addresses a major health issue for low-income and marginalized populations and has the potential to benefit a significant number of people not only in the location of origin but also at the country, regional, or global level.

—Strategy: There is a well-designed operational model to implement the initiative and reach out to beneficiaries. Additionally, there is a solid plan to expand or replicate the model beyond current beneficiary groups/locations.

—Sustainability: The initiative has demonstrated a cost-effective approach to provide health solutions. There is a strong funding base and a strategy to sustain it financially over the long-term.

—Additional criterion: Strategic Business-Social Partnerships (This is not a requirement to qualify in the competition, but will only be taken into account for the Special Award): The initiative has developed or has plans to develop a partnership that includes at least one business and one citizen sector organization in order to provide a comprehensive response to a health challenge. The partnership is strategic, central to the initiative, and leverages the core competencies of all partners involved."

Sources: See Changemakers, "About Changemakers" (www.changemakers. net/about); "Competition Guidelines: How to Improve Health for All" (www. changemakers.net/en-us/node/11525/competition/guidelines).

Project AA: Charter Schools

Contact: Mauricio Palacios, University of Maryland

Description: "One of the most popular forms of school system decentralization is charter schools. As the 2005 report by the Government Accountability Office (GAO) explains, charter schools are 'public schools that are exempt from certain state and local regulations in exchange for increased accountability for improving student achievement' (GAO 2005). Charter Schools are publicly financed. However, each school is 'autonomous and has a unique charter that states the aims, objectives, and mandate of the schools' (O'Reilly and Bosetti 2000, p. 20). Charter schools are primarily accountable to the parents and their students. However, they are also accountable to the applicable governing body, which insures that achievement standards are met and applicable laws followed (GAO 2005). In addition, charter schools are also required to renew their license every five years, a decision that is partly based on the school's performance on standardized tests."

PIJC mechanism: "Supporters of charter schools view them as a mean to revitalize and improve the effectiveness of public schools (O'Reilly and Bosetti 2000, p. 19). They argue that charter schools create incentives for traditional public schools to improve. Supporters maintain that 'market mechanisms such as various school choice plans will a) improve the effectiveness of schools through competition among schools for students [as well as funding], b) reduce inefficiency in the administration and delivery of education, and c) have the effect of improved educational outcomes' (O'Reilly and Bosetti 2000, p. 20)."

Source: Mauricio Palacios, "A Review of Charter School Experience in the United States," term paper for University of Maryland course FMST381: Poverty and Affluence, spring 2006.

Project BB: Kids Count Data Book: State Profile of Child Well-Being

Contact: William P. O'Hare

Description: The national and state-by-state study reports on the well-being of America's children and promotes discussion on ways to secure better futures for all children. The Data Book ranks states on ten key indicators and provides information on child health, education, and family economic conditions.

PIJC mechanism: This is more of an information campaign than a tournament because there are no rewards or strategic action by the participants. However, it might create an implicit tournament between states for which the reward would be publicity and political gains for government officials (governors).

Source: Annie E. Casey Foundation, "Kids Count 2008 Data Book Online" (www.aecf.org/kidscount/sld/databook.jsp).

Project CC: Cleanest and Greenest Town Award

Contact: Jesus G. Dureza, press secretary, Office of the Press Secretary, Government of the Philippines

Description: "Originally launched in 1994 as the Clean and Green Program, [it] was changed to Gawad Pangulo sa Kapaligiran (GPK) in 1999 pursuant to Executive Order 113. The search takes into consideration the Local Government Units (LGUs) performance in the following areas, namely; general cleanliness, urban space greening and support systems."

PIJC mechanism: Award competition. The town mentioned in the source received a 15,000 Philippine peso cash prize from the government of Samar Province and a citation.

Sources: Government of the Philippines, "Paranas Wins Samar 'Cleanest and Greenest Town' Award," August 19, 2005 (www.gov.ph/news/?i=12452).

Project DD: Most Business-Friendly City Award

Contact: Sussette Rosuelo or Grace Morella, Philippines Chamber of Commerce Secretariat
Description: The award, which is considered quite prestigious in the Philippines, was launched in 2001 "to recognize municipalities, cities and provinces for their efforts in instituting good governance in promoting trade and investment such as innovative and sound business licensing procedures, and efficient conduct of daily operations." The initiative was developed and is run by the Philippine Chamber of Commerce and Industry (PCCI), with the support of the German Technical Cooperation (GTZ).
PIJC mechanism: Award competition
Source: See Philippine Chamber of Commerce and Industry, "Search Is on for Most Business-Friendly LGUS" (www.philippinechamber.com/index.php?option= com_content&view=article&id=322&Itemid=66).

Project EE: "Cash on Delivery" Development Assistance

Contact: Kate Vyborny, Center for Global Development
Description: Proposed by the Center for Global Development, "under 'cash on delivery' aid, donors would commit ex ante to pay a specific amount for a specific measure of progress. In education, for example, donors could promise to pay $100 for each additional child who completes primary school and takes a standardized competency test. A credible baseline survey would be conducted, the country would publish completion numbers and test scores, and then the donor would pay for an independent audit to verify the numbers. The payment would be made upon a successful audit. Payments would be 'cash on delivery'—made only after measurable progress, only for as much as is verifiably achieved, and without prescribing the policy or means to achieve progress. The country could then choose to use the new funds for any purpose."
PIJC mechanism: Pecuniary certification
Source: Center for Global Development, "'Cash on Delivery': Progress-Based Aid for Education" (www.cgdev.org/section/initiatives/_active/codaid).

Project FF: GlobalGiving.com

Contact: Dennis Whittle, chairman and CEO, GlobalGiving
Description: "GlobalGiving connects user-giver to over 450 pre-screened grassroots charity projects around the world for an efficient, transparent way for projects to bid for donations. The causes, unique needs, and work being done for each

project are on the website. Users browse the website, research causes by topic or location, and pick the one that matches their interests. Donations are tax-deductible and allow givers to combine their giving with others contributing to the same project. The site claims that 85–90% of the donation is on the ground within 60 days and has an immediate impact. The giver gets regular updates of the results that have been achieved. If a giver is not satisfied with the impact of the donation for any reason, the GlobalGiving Guarantee provides them with their money back in the form of a voucher for the amount of the original donation." (Taken from organization's website May 5, 2007.)
PIJC mechanism: Pecuniary certification
Source: See www.globalgiving.com.

Project GG: Provincial Competitiveness Index

Contact: Vietnam Chamber of Commerce and Industry (VCCI), USAID, and the Asia Foundation
Description: The Provincial Competitiveness Index (PCI) assesses and ranks provinces for private sector development based on their regulatory environments. Both subjective perceptions and quantitative data are utilized. In 2005 the PCI covered forty-two provinces, which in total account for 89 percent of the national GDP. It is a collaborative effort of the Vietnam Competitiveness Initiative and the VCCI, funded by USAID.
PIJC mechanism: Pure tournament
Source: Malesky (2005).

Project HH: National Solidarity Program in Afghanistan

Contact: Clare Lockhart, Institute for State Effectiveness
Description: "This grant program is a massive effort by the government to reach rural communities across Afghanistan and address their needs by using a partici-patory approach. It is implemented by the Ministry of Rural Rehabilitation and Development through an extensive network of NGOs. The program was originally a component of the IDA-financed Emergency Community Empowerment and Public Works Project launched in 2002. It then became a national priority program under Afghanistan's development framework and has grown into the government's flagship rural development program. Elected village-level Community Develop-ment Councils (CDCs), in which women play a key role, reach consensus on development priorities, develop investment proposals, and use grants and local labor (provided gratis) to meet their needs."
PIJC mechanism: Mixed tournament
Sources: See Google Video, "Afghanistan National Solidarity Program" (http://video.google.co.uk/videoplay?docid=-9200451079109383164).

Project II: Business in Development (BiD) Challenge

Contact: Nils de Witte, director, Business in Development

Description: The BiD Challenge adapts to the limited access to financial and nonfinancial means for small- and medium-size enterprises (SMEs) in developing countries. By participating in the BiD Challenge, entrepreneurs can not only win prize money, but they are also exposed to an international network of investors, companies, and organizations and receive personal coaching from business experts in writing a professional business plan. The BiD Challenge is supported by thirty different partners, including the Dutch Ministry of Foreign Affairs. The annual BiD Challenge is open to start-up or established entrepreneurs with a business proposal for a new or the expansion of an existing enterprise in a developing country. The enterprise's investment need should be between €5,000 and €500,000 and should be profitable within three years. In 2007 participants could win up to €20,000, with a total of €240,000 in prize money available. In addition to a business plan competition, the BiD Challenge includes a platform for knowledge and networks, in which employees are engaged to use their knowledge in supporting entrepreneurs and in which investors get access to quality business plans. In this way the BiD Challenge not only stimulates entrepreneurship in developing countries, it also puts companies and investors in contact with poverty reduction in a unique way. Because of its success, the initiative has been rolled out in several developing countries.

PIJC mechanism: Pure tournament

Sources: "Fighting Poverty with Profit: The BiD Challenge 2007 Is Opened!" press release, April 2007 (www.peaceparks.org/news.php?mid=702&pid=15). See also www.bidnetwork.org.

Technical Exhibits for the Detailed Case Study Assessments

Appendix B1. Russian Fiscal Tournament Indicators

Objective	Criteria for measuring performance	Expected outcomes
Budget process Extend coverage of the budget and improve the clarity and methods of budget process.	Conformity of regional budget to budget code.	Regional budgets standardized along lines of legislation.
	Consolidation of extrabudgetary funds into the regional budget.	No extrabudgetary funds at the regional level.
	Separation of budget into current and capital components.	Greater transparency over capital budgeting.
	Introduction of medium-term financial planning.	Medium-term plan or forecasting for budget and macrovariables.
	Assessment of preferences, grants-in-aid, and subsidies. Move toward payment of benefits rather than granting of preferences.	Preferences, exemptions, or subsidies become transparent and are reduced, and over time are replaced by payment of benefits.
	Introduction of satisfactory treasury execution of budgets.	Improved management, execution, and transparency of the budget.

(continued)

Objective	Criteria for measuring performance	Expected outcomes
Tax policy Systematize tax policy in regions so that it is consistent with federal legislation, encourages transparency and mobilization of revenues, and discourages arrears.	Conformity of regional tax system to federal legislation.	Regional tax policy consistent with federal legislation.
	Reduction in regional tax arrears.	Tax arrears approach zero (remaining related only to insolvency issues).
	Reduction in noncash payment of taxes.	100 percent cash payment for taxes.
	Process for granting tax exemptions legalized and limited.	Process transparent, helps promote "level playing field."
	Establish basis for property tax by developing property rights registration.	Property rights are registered and protected.
Expenditure management Improve overall use, allocation, and mechanics of expenditure.	Development of spending priorities.	Improved allocation of resources.
	Reduce wage arrears to budget employees.	Wages arrears for budgetary institutions do not exceed one month's pay and are brought to zero over time.
	Methodology for evaluating efficiency and effectiveness of expenditures put in place.	Improved effectiveness of resources over time.
	Implementation of clear procurement procedures, including competitive bidding and full information on bids, and results published in mass media.	Over 70 percent of budget expenditures on goods and services are awarded through tenders; full information on competitive bidding and tenders available in mass media.
Intergovernmental system within region Improve clarity and predictability of resource flows between regions and local governments.	Legislation detailing expenditure authority between regional and local administrative levels.	Expenditure responsibilities are clear.
	Reduction in regional unfunded mandates (to local governments).	Regional unfunded mandates approach zero over time.
	Standard rates of revenue assignment (sharing) across region.	Increased predictability on revenue side.

(continued)

Objective	Criteria for measuring performance	Expected outcomes
	Clear methodology for allocating transfers.	Allocation of resources to local governments transparent and predictable.
Debt management Improve information base and management of debt.	Introduce consolidated accounting for all regional liabilities.	Quantification and transparency of all debt liabilities.
	Reduce overdue debt liabilities (and accounts payable).	Overdue debt liabilities and accounts payable reduced to less than 20 percent of budget revenues.
	Draw up consolidated schedule for debt payments.	Pay liabilities in cash on time and in full.
	Analysis of debt capacity based on anticipated revenue flows.	Clear measure of borrowing capacity established.
Information and audit Ensure adequate auditing of use of public resources.	Public dissemination of budget.	Budget published through mass media and Internet to encourage public accountability.
	Implementation of audits by independent auditors on a systematic basis; audits publicly available.	Strengthen information base and accountability concerning use of funds.

Source: World Bank (2006b).

Appendix B2. Nigerian Scorecard Assessment Calculation

1. For *interviews with communities and LGAs:* After all of the fieldwork is completed and reports are compiled for each LGA, each individual respondent's answer to each distinct set of questions (focusing on a particular issue) will be assigned a score of 0, 1, or 2, where 0 indicates a negative situation, 1 indicates a marginal or indifferent situation, and 2 indicates a positive or promising situation.

2. The average of scores on all sets of questions will be the overall score from that community.[1] The overall scores from all three communities will be averaged to yield a responsiveness to communities score, *RC:*

RC = (sum of overall scores from each community)/(number of sets of equations)

Source: This appendix is largely taken from Terfa (2005b).
1. Currently, this includes the set of questions on project performance. Alternatively, it would be possible to treat project performance separately and give it more weight.

3. For LGAs, each respondent's answers to each distinct set of questions will be assigned a score. The average of these scores will yield an overall administrative operation score, *AO*:

AO = (sum of scores on all questions) / (number of sets of questions).

The interview with the chairman is excluded from scoring.

4. *Financial and budget indicators will be rank-ordered before a point score is assigned.* In a given state, the top third will be considered acceptable, the middle third marginal, and the bottom third unacceptable. However, if LGAs tend to form clusters for any given set of indicators, then all LGAs in the top cluster will be considered acceptable, the second marginal, and so on. Average of scores on all indicators will yield a financial and budgeting score, *FB*.

5. *Information on reporting compliance* will be scored on the same scale as interview responses, based on standards of what constitutes an acceptable, marginal, or unacceptable delay. These will be sent for each individual report, based on the required frequency of reporting. Scores on each report will be average to yield a reporting score, *R*.

6. *Audit results and LGA responsiveness* to these results will be scored on the same scale as interview responses to yield an audit score, *A*.

7. State feedback from interviews conducted with appropriate senior state technical officials will yield a state feedback score, *S*.

8. The *overall scoring formula* is:

$$\text{LGA scores} = \left[(2RC + AO)/3\right] + FB + R + A + S.$$

Appendix B3. Summary of Municipality Ranking Variables, *Mancomunidades* Project, Honduras

Variable	Notes

Good governance
1. *Cabildo* meetings, *c*:
   $c = C_1 + 2C_S + E_1 + 2E_2 + E_3.$
	Purpose: Civil society participation and transparency
	   C_1 = number of cabildos that are purely informative.
	   C_S = number of cabildos that solicit citizen input, vote on measures, or are otherwise participatory.
	   E_1 = 1 if cabildo meeting minutes are available upon request, or are given to participants at the end of the cabildo meeting or at the next cabildo.

(continued)

Variable	Notes
Thresholds: Types A, B: $c \geq 8$ Types C, D: $c \geq 6$	$E_2 = 1$ if cabildo meeting minutes are posted on a municipal bulletin board, in a public library, or in some other easily accessible public location. $E_3 = 1$ if the meetings themselves are broadcast. Note: Minimum legal number of cabildo meetings is five.
2. Other civil society participation, O: $$O = \Sigma_{n=1}^{5} C_n + 2(C_6 + C_7),$$ where $n = 1$. Thresholds: Types A, B: $O \geq 3$ Types C, D: $O \geq 2$	*Purpose:* Civil society participation and transparency $C_1 = 1$ if there was at least one plebiscite held during mayor's current term. $C_2 = 1$ if a *Comité de Desarrollo Municipal* (CODEM) exists. $C_3 = 1$ if at least one meeting of the CODEM was held in last twelve months. $C_4 = 1$ if a *comisionado municipal* is assigned. $C_5 = 1$ if other general assembly meetings are held to solicit public input. $C_6 = 1$ if there is a transparency committee with a general governance (as opposed to project-specific) mandate. $C_7 = 1$ if the transparency committee meets at least quarterly.
3. Current year's budget developed, Y: $Y = H_1 + H_2 + 3H_3 + 2H_4 + 3H_5 + H_6 + H_O.$ Thresholds: Types A, B: $Y \geq 6$ Type C: $Y \geq 4$ Type D: $Y \geq 2$	*Purpose:* Technical quality and transparency H_1 = with help of financial advisers or external accountants or auditors. H_2 = with input from municipal council. H_3 = with input from community leaders. H_4 = with input from transparency committee. H_5 = with input from the general public. H_6 = with input from donors or NGOs. H_O = with input from others (specify).
Sustainability and commitment 4. Plans and priorities, F: $$F = P + \sum_{i-1}^{3} \sum_{n=1}^{4} P_{i,n}$$	*Purpose:* Commitment and political will $P = 1$ if a strategic plan, capital investment plan, or other similar plan exists.

(continued)

Variable	Notes
	For the three ($i=1,2,3$) highest priority projects:
	$p_{i,1}$ = part of the municipal budget is allocated to the project, or municipal staff are dedicated to it.
	$p_{i,2}$ = community input (for example, labor or local materials).
	$p_{i,3}$ = other community, municipal, or other donations.
	$p_{i,4}$ = other, external sources of input to the project.
5. Sustainability of completed projects, M: $$M = \sum_{i=1}^{3} \sum_{n=1}^{4} S_{i,n}$$ Threshold: All types: $M > 3$	*Purpose:* Sustainability For the three ($i=1,2,3$) most important projects completed in the last two years:
	$s_{i,1}$ = community involvement in selection, design, and implementation of original project.
	$s_{i,2}$ = community input (for example, labor or local materials) to O&M.
	$s_{i,3}$ = ongoing community social audit of project.
	$s_{i,4}$ = municipal budget allocated to O&M.
	$s_{i,5}$ = existence of a project-specific transparency committee (not a general governance transparency committee).
	$s_{i,6}$ = other (specify).
Absorptive capacity	*Purpose:* Capacity in terms of staff availability to support projects.
6. Staff available to act as counterparts, A: $A = (N*H - 40e)/(40*M)$ Threshold: $A < 0.25$	M = total number of municipal staff. N = number of staff involved as "counterparts" in projects. H = hours per week, on average, spent supporting projects by the project counterpart staff. e = 1 if a portion of the municipal budget is allocated to new positions filled if or when needed. Note: For planning purposes (that is, at the "tactical level"), USAID will need to know *which* staff are committed to what projects, and the end dates of the projects.

(continued)

Variable	Notes
7. Staff ability, S: $\quad S = \Sigma\, T_i$, $\qquad$ where $i = 1$ to 3. $\quad$ Thresholds: $\qquad$ Types A, B: $S = 3$ $\qquad$ Type C: $S \geq 2$ $\qquad$ Type D: $S \geq 1$	*Purpose:* Capacity in terms of staff ability to support projects. $\qquad T_1$ = qualifications of municipal accountant meet or exceed published minimum qualifications. $\qquad T_2$ = qualifications of head of tax administration meet or exceed published minimum qualifications. $\qquad T_3$ = qualifications of head of cadastre meet or exceed published minimum qualifications. Note: This is an optional variable that can be used to distinguish among municipalities that have published job requirements with which to make the comparison. Many municipalities do not have them.

Source: ARD (2004, annex C).

C

Anatomy of a PIJC Application

W hat would the project design of a full-fledged PIJC application look like? This appendix describes the methodology and work plan for the Morocco case study described in section 4.2.3. This text draws from a field guide prepared by IRIS, a think tank at the University Maryland, for UNIDO and was drafted for an implementation proposal for the U.S. State Department's Middle East Partnership Initiative, to which UNIDO planned to contribute substantial technical assistance in kind. The reader may therefore interpret "donor" for MEPI and UNIDO, and "implementer" for IRIS.[1]

Project Start-Up

Upon receipt of project award, the international consultant project team (referred to hereafter as the Project Team) would immediately commence the following activities.

Set Up the Project Implementation Unit

Aided by the Center for Regional Investment (CRI) and other local experts, the staff of the project implementation unit (PIU) will be recruited and trained.[2] The

---

1. Meagher and Zinnes (2004) provide a detailed step-by-step field guide, complete with focus group and other protocols, for implementing the PIJC described in this appendix.

2. PIUs now are regarded as undesirable, as illustrated by a target in the Paris Declaration agenda that specifically postulates a reduction in the number of PIUs (Linn 2008, private communication). However, this view is principally held for the case where they are free-standing entities. In the case of Morocco, the PIU was firmly within and collaborating with the rest of the investment promotion bureau (CRI) and, as such, its objective was closely aligned to that of the government agency within which it was situated.

PIU would be a small team of Moroccan professionals and support staff. It would be responsible to the Project Team for managing and ensuring implementation of all phases of the project on an ongoing basis, including supporting and working with the Project Team home office, visitors from the Project Team, the steering committee, and all participating communes. The PIU will also coordinate the work of Moroccan expert teams during focus group sessions, surveys, convocations, and technical assistance workshops. The PIU will be housed in and supported by the CRI located in Safi, which would provide office facilities as well as personnel. This is a natural partnership in that it provides the most appropriate location and support for the project while building on the strengths of the CRI, which is mandated to facilitate business start-up and operations.

Develop Detailed Project Schedule

The proposal work plan and schedule to implement the project will be further refined by the Project Team and its partners at the start of the project.

Convene Steering Committee

As the senior decisionmaking body of the project, the steering committee will be convened to approve the work plan and schedule. This committee comprises the CRI director, directors of each partner organization, the Project Team's project director, the UNIDO Investment Promotion Office director for Morocco, as well as several senior government officials. The steering committee brings together relevant leaders and experts from both government and civil society and ensures the necessary legitimacy as well as in-depth country guidance and support to the project. The steering committee would meet on a quarterly basis to review progress and would be available for consultation as needed.

Preparation for the Tournament

For tournament incentives to function properly, key issues of the design, including the choice of tournament tasks, and the nature and structure of rewards, as well as the logistical and procedural rules of the game, must be developed with care. While much of the hard design work was carried out during the UNIDO-sponsored phase of project conception, these insights need to be fine-tuned and drafted into tournament documents and implementation procedures. It is important to understand that *all* aspects and procedures of the tournament must be clearly stated to participants *in advance* to establish the right incentives and legitimacy of the enterprise.

Tournament Documents

The main document to be prepared is the tournament rule booklet. In addition to containing the steps and procedures of the "game," this document will describe the menu of tasks from which the communes may select, the types of technical assistance available during the tournament in support of the reforms they select, and the types of rewards that winners, runners up, and placers will receive. The rule booklet will also explain how to earn points by implementing tournament tasks. In short, for each task a commune will receive tournament points for completing a de jure (typically a "stroke-of-the-pen") procedural reform and, conditional on achieving the de jure threshold, will receive additional tournament points based on its de facto performance in reform implementation. Finally, the booklet will explain how a commune's Business Institutional Environment (BIE) Star rating, the set of indicators summarizing the friendliness of the commune's business-related institutional environment, is computed. The booklet will be drafted in collaboration with project partners as well as other interested donors to take full advantage of local knowledge and resources. These documents are then carefully vetted and updated as a result.

Establishing the Tournament Tasks

The principal reason for the tournament is to stimulate reforms and improvements to the local institutional environment facing business. Toward this end, concrete tasks must be identified. In the design phase of this project carried out in collaboration with UNIDO, IRIS drew on ideas flowing from economic theory and policy research in many countries and engaged in fieldwork to collect significant information to develop a "menu" of tasks from which competing communes could choose. These tasks would likely be drawn from the areas of land site development, business operational requirements, regulatory environment, administrative effectiveness (planning, service provision), communal resource mobilization and use, administrative transparency and accountability, and management and oversight of officials. During preparation of the rule booklet, these tasks will be updated and revetted to ensure that they are both aligned with MEPI pillars and in demand by local business. The number of tournament points assigned to the successful completion of each task must also be established and vetted.

Tournament Rewards

There are several types of possible rewards. These include technical assistance to communal councils on reform during the tournament; at the midway point of the tournament, incentive bonus rewards to communes that show zeal in their efforts; prizes to the winners; prizes for placing (completing a task successfully); and consolation prizes. Prize recipients will be recognized in a ceremony to be held in the capital and attended by national figures, donor representatives, and business leaders. The prizes comprise domestic and international marketing of the commune and its firms; study tours for communal council members and trade tours for local firms; certificates of recognition from the *wali,* the king's representative in the province (or, possibly, from the king himself); technical assistance to the communal administration as well as SME firms in the commune; and assistance in acquiring cofinancing for local investment.

The selection of these benefits will depend on several factors. First, winners will receive an awards budget to enable them to "spend" their reward points by selecting from a menu of benefits of varying value. Second, the choice of rewards to offer will depend on the exact nature of the demand for various types of rewards, as determined by the results of the focus groups conducted at the start of the project. Third, the Project Team will conduct some gaming experiments to determine whether communes would be more highly motivated by fewer, larger rewards or by smaller, more numerous rewards.

The project envisions three sources of prizes. First, this proposal has specifically budgeted funds for midway tournament prizes for ten communes as well as a prize for the winning commune and two runners up. Second, UNIDO has agreed to offer technical assistance presentations on investment promotion as a midway incentive reward; SME training in such areas as preparation of business plans, promotion of industrial partnerships, economic and financial evaluation of projects, and identification of financing facilities to firms in the winning (and placing) communes; and installation of and access to the UNIDO investment promotion software platform in communes that win, place, or receive points for completing one or more tasks (consolation prizes). Third, several other donors have expressed interest in this activity and are likely to provide additional rewards once the MEPI would choose to fund the activity. The Project Team has been engaged in discussions toward this end with intermediaries of the government of Italy and the World Bank. This application's budget includes some limited funding for finalizing these negotiations and having the PIU pursue opportunities for donations from local and foreign firms with an interest in the reforms contemplated.

One of the benefits of the tournament design is that it creates a second-level tournament among the provinces (Doukkala and Abda) in addition to that played at the level of participating communes. This encourages each provincial-level government to look for regulatory opportunities under its control to facilitate reforms among its communes. Therefore, the winning province will be assessed by determining the average number of points received per commune in the province. The primary reward to the winning province would be a program of international marketing through the project and extra technical assistance. This will be accomplished in collaboration with UNIDO, the project's own BIE Star indicators website, and, hopefully, by additional contributions from other donors (see previous paragraph).

Tournament Logistics

Complementary to the preparation of tournament documents are tournament logistics. Among the procedures that require detailed logistics are the communications and publicity strategy, the various all-commune convocations, the management of in-tournament technical assistance, and the system for maintaining contact with and monitoring of participating communes.

Parallel to establishing the reward structure, the project will develop a communications and advertising strategy that will be crucial for generating interest among the players and their political representatives. In addition, a marketing strategy will also be required for promoting the winners of the tournament, which is an important element of the reward structure. Both of these strategies may require a multimedia effort, for example, radio, TV, presentations to communal councils, public meetings, and newspaper announcements. Last, concrete procedures for convening the commencement of the tournament will be established, as well as for keeping the players in touch with the tournament organizers. For example, regional meetings would be held with representatives of the communes aspiring to participate in order to discuss the tournament. Finally, two all-commune meetings are planned during the tournament: one at the outset to introduce the tournament goals and rules and one at the end of the tournament in the form of an awards ceremony.

The Project Team and UNIDO would conduct six assistance workshops for each group of reform tasks on the tournament menu. The presenters will then be available online as advisers to answer participants' technical questions during the tournament. The exact logistics of this provision will be worked out at this step of the project. Depending on the number of communes that choose to compete, these workshops will be held either in one central location or in two locations.

Given the novelty of this project, good feedback systems to maintain contact with the representatives of the participating communes, as well as to monitor performance, will be important. To keep costs down—traveling periodically to eighty-nine sites is infeasible—the project will test another innovation, namely, the use of the Internet to stay in touch. While disseminating (downloading) tournament information over the Internet may not be considered unusual, the plan is to also require the participating communes to self-report progress by uploading performance status information.

Website Design

Use of the Internet will be a central part of the project. The tournament will have its own web page on the website of the Project Team's principal partner, the CRI. This is intended to be mutually reinforcing: CRI clients will learn of the tournament, and investors attracted to the BIE Star indicators and interested in the winning communes will learn of the CRI. This website will be used to advertise the tournament and generate interest in it; to keep participants up to date on tournament activities, news, and insights; as a means for participants to self-report by transmitting performance status to the project team; as the platform for the BIE Star program to generate investor interest; to provide technical assistance updates by task as well as to maintain a technical forum; and for access to the UNIDO investment promotion software.

Vetting of Materials

Working from a correct understanding of the local context and social environment is key to harnessing the power of the tournament's incentives. Thus, considerable effort is dedicated to vetting and pretesting the materials, procedures, and parameters developed during the previous tournament preparation step. All aspects of tournament planning will be critiqued and subject to local feedback. This includes the format and clarity of the rule booklet and its procedures, the appropriateness of tournament tasks and rewards, the benchmark survey instruments, and the communications and publicity strategy. The following summarizes the techniques (focus groups, mini-surveys, and gaming experiments) to be used.

Focus Groups and Information Gathering

To collect additional information and receive feedback, the project's partner associations will organize focus groups targeted at each MEPI pillar. Given the goal of fostering collective action within a locality, information will be solicited from diverse groups that include the communal councils, women's organizations, SME owners and associations, as well as other governmental and civil society groups. To confirm the conclusions of these sessions (which are necessarily based on a very small sample), the partner associations will then administer structured questionnaires to their stakeholder constituencies, whose support is necessary for creating robust tournament incentives. Both the focus group protocols and the survey instruments will be developed by IRIS, whose principals will also attend the focus groups, with input from its Moroccan collaborators.

Pretesting and Fine-Tuning the Tournament

To provide an added level of confidence and to fine-tune the transaction design, tournament parameters under consideration will be pretested in small-scale gaming exercises during the focus group sessions. Among other factors, these will help in testing the sensitivity of tournament efforts to perceived difficulty of tasks and the reward structure (the size of rewards and the number of placers to reward as "winners").

Baseline, Benchmark, and BIE Star Indicators

The final stage of preparation involves constructing a concrete, objective performance indicator for each task. These indicators will be used to construct a baseline to measure where each commune stands on each task before the tournament and then to benchmark them afterwards. These will be used to determine each commune's score for each task and, therefore, who wins. Here, use is made of advances in survey design associated with "second-generation" governance indicators (Alevy and Zinnes 2004; Esmail and others 2004). Note that to evaluate the project rigorously, it is necessary to measure ex ante baseline and ex post endline benchmarks of both participating *as well as* nonparticipating communes in the target population.

The data required for these indicators will come from several sources. First, there will be a survey of SME experience along the regulatory dimensions associated with the tasks. Second, communes will be asked to self-report performance information mostly related to administrative outcomes.[3] Third, the project partners will help track the occurrence of public participation events related to commune precommitment and task compliance. Finally, business data and government statistics will be provided by the CRI as well as the central government.

The information for these indicators can be used to create a rating system to align commune interests to those of the tournament as well as to engage in regional investment promotion later. To ensure that the public understands the meaning of such ratings, however, they must be presented in a form that can be easily understood. Toward this end, the Project Team will develop the Business Institutional Environment (BIE) Star rating system and then nationally and internationally advertise it, as a simple way to signal the quality of the business institutional environment of the communes.

Inspired by PROPER, the very successful environmental program in Indonesia (Afsah and Vincent 1997), the BIE Star system will consist of five stars that contain two pieces of important information for prospective investors. The first is the *number* of stars a commune has at the end of the tournament, *regardless of whether it chose to compete.* This indicates the *level* of quality of the governance environment for business relative to others communes, *regardless of its performance during the tournament.* Second, the BIE Star system adds a shadow around each star achieved during the tournament to indicate the seriousness of a commune to *improve* its governance environment for business. Using Morocco's national colors, the stars will be green and the shadow orange. Thus, if a four-star commune had gained one during the tournament, it would have three green stars and one green star with an orange shadow around it.

Thus the interjurisdictional competition offers two opportunities for the commune to signal to investors its amicability toward business. First, merely participating in the tournament signals a certain seriousness to improve (and, of course, placing or winning sends an even stronger signal). Second, the number of BIE stars a commune has indicates its business friendliness (whether it competed or not).

---

3. To provide the right incentives for honesty, the Project Team should have its partner associations implement a random audit strategy to check the accuracy of this reporting. IRIS will also audit all winners. This will be clearly indicated in the rule booklet.

Conducting the Tournament

The tournament proper entails several steps, which are described below.

Tournament Launch

The IJC begins with implementation of the publicity strategy developed during tournament preparation. In addition to the public announcements, information packages on rules, task options, and rewards will be distributed to all the communes in the region. The public announcements will be conducted with participation of representatives of the Moroccan government, including the region's CRI, which will have a principal on the steering committee. Communes will have time to deliberate among themselves and will be encouraged to consult with appropriate central and provincial officials and local stakeholders to evaluate the tournament proposal prior to the convocation.

Convening the Players

This marks the formal start of the tournament. All eighty-nine communal council presidents (CCPs) or their deputies in the region are invited for a one-day conference with appropriate fanfare to introduce the tournament, its rules, tasks options, and rewards menu.

Start-up of Tournament Play

At the end of the opening convention, the tournament proper begins. The communes will have ten months. First, the CCPs must discuss with their other members and constituencies as to whether to participate and which tasks to select. They then submit a formal letter to the wali indicating their intent to compete and what tasks they will select. For each selected task, the precommitment obligations must then be fulfilled, such as the holding of a public hearing as per the rule booklet. Communes may then immediately begin their reform activities (during which time the PIU, with help from the project's partners, verifies their fulfillment of precommitment obligations).

Tournament Support Activities

Implementation of project tasks is supported by several types of technical assistance to aid the communes in completing tasks and documenting their progress. First, six technical assistance workshops will be held in month 2 of the tournament portion of the project, one or two for each MEPI pillar. The project budget supports three experts while UNIDO provides three more. Second, these experts will be paid to answer questions on reform posed by the communes (via the PIU) over the course of the tournament. Third, a monthly official newsletter containing news of tournament progress and reform implementation ideas will be distributed through the Internet to each of the participating communal councils, something that should also encourage competition and, therefore, task completion and reform.

Midtournament Bonuses

Halfway through the tournament, communes that have made the quickest starts (to be precisely defined in the rule booklet) will receive award bonuses. These will be suitably publicized.

End-Tournament Benchmark

The tournament ends with the tallying of results by collecting a second set of governance indicators. As in the baseline, these come from surveys that mirror the baseline measurement. Based on these results and according to the procedures described in the rule booklet, the winning, runner-up, and placing communes are identified by IRIS and verified by the steering committee. (These measurements and additional data collected from the elicitation phases also allow for a rigorous review of the effectiveness of the IJC.)

Closing Ceremonies

Once the data are tallied and the winners established, a final CCP conference is held to announce the results of the tournament and award prizes. In addition to the wali, the Project Team hopes to enlist the participation of the U.S. ambassador to Morocco, the heads of several international donor agencies, and the press.

Posttournament Activities

Though the tournament proper is the principal activity of the project, it is but a tool for achieving a greater objective. Thus, even after the tournament is over, several activities must be pursued. These include tournament evaluation, dissemination of the BIE Star Program, rewards distribution logistics and monitoring (including winner promotion), website maintenance, and the promotion of the project concept and dissemination of results.

Tournament Evaluation

This project takes advantage of prospective randomized evaluation procedures (PREP), which incorporate into a donor activity a statistically rigorous means of evaluation. (See Kremer 2003, Azfar and Zinnes 2003, and Greenberg and Shroder 2004.) Once the tournament is over, the Project Team's econometricians will use the tournament's experimental design and benchmark information to test whether the improvements observed by participating communes could be attributable to chance, compared to the control group.

Public Diplomacy-Outreach and Network of Participants

Throughout the project, the public and stakeholders at different levels will be involved and kept informed via the project's communications and advertising strategy.[4] The network of communes, associations, and government officials resulting from the competition will continue to have access to the project website after the tournament, and through it network members will be able to use contacts formed during the competition to communicate with those in the region who share their institutional objectives (for example, women entrepreneur partnerships). Competition "graduates" can also be called upon as consultants in efforts to replicate the project elsewhere. This has obvious benefits for the sustainability of the reforms. To maximize the realization of these opportunities, the Project Team should craft an implementation plan in year 2 of the project.

BIE Star Program

Using the results of the end-of-tournament benchmark survey and other data collected, the team will compute the BIE Star indicators (see the section on "Baseline, Benchmark and BIE Star Indicators"), which will be promoted over the Internet to inform and attract business to the better-performing communes.

Rewards Logistics

Tournament rewards will likely include technical assistance, industry overseas tours, cofinancing, and marketing of the winning communes. The logistics and monitoring associated with the distribution of these rewards are part of the project's posttournament activities and administered through the Project Team's subcontract with DIS, the Moroccan logistics firm.

Website Maintenance

To ensure that the project's outputs remain widely available, the project's web pages on the CRI website should be maintained. Among the outputs requiring the web are the BIE Star Indicators Program, the marketing components of tournament rewards, and the dissemination of the project concept and outcomes.

Other Project Activities

A few other miscellaneous activities are part of running a PIJC. One is *reporting*; the Project Team would submit to the donor quarterly reports on the status of the various project activities. Likewise, it would issue monthly Internet bulletins to tournament participants and stakeholders, the latter including civil society and

---

4. The "public diplomacy" referred to in the heading consists mainly of the project's continuous efforts throughout the project to solicit stakeholders' ideas and feedback to keep competition tasks in line with local sensitivities, while also explaining the benefits of the reforms to be accomplished.

other interested parties. A second activity is *document drafting*. The majority of report drafting would occur at the end of the tournament preparation step, when all the tournament materials have been finalized, and also after the posttournament benchmark, when the results have been analyzed. Other drafting periods would occur after the technical assistance workshops and in month 17, when project evaluation has been completed. The third activity is *project management*: though the PIU would manage day-to-day activities on the ground, project principals would also have a key role in the continued management of activities, especially as related to component design and techniques, experts recruitment, budgetary oversight, facilitation of partner collaboration, and contact with the donor. Finally, before the public dissemination described above, an *internal presentation* for the donor would be held to address and discuss donor-specific questions, concerns, and, potentially, follow-up.

APPENDIX

D

Mathematical Treatment of PIJC Leveraging of Sponsor Funds

W hile chapter 2—as well as common sense—argues that a tournament approach would leverage sponsor funds, the actual sources of the economies merit some fleshing out, especially under rational expectations (that is, where all players make decisions based on the actuarially correct odds). This appendix seeks to pinpoint the various potential sources of these economies.

Consider a sponsor with a budget of B faced with two alternative project designs. In the standard approach, the sponsor picks N^s recipients, who then receive funding of B/N^s.[1] In the tournament approach, the sponsor identifies a region with N^j potential jurisdictional recipients of which the top N^a win awards, with $N^a \leq N^j$. Let I^{std} and I^{trm} be the measures of recipient performance under the standard and tournament approaches, respectively, and be equal to 1 if a recipient is successful and 0 otherwise.

To begin, assume that tournament awards are salient (that is, they motivate effort). Also assume that under the standard approach, a recipient (who is picked by the sponsor) exerts sufficient effort to achieve project success with probabil-

---

1. Recall from chapter 2 that under the standard approach, the sponsor develops a one-to-one contract with each recipient and then works closely with the recipient to ensure success. For simplicity, I assume that when standard contracts are given to more than one recipient, each is the same size. Note that italics in superscripts and subscripts are used as indices to denote (usually ordinal) variables and that standard, nonitalicized fonts are used for name extensions of variables. Showing the name is pertinent only to a subgroup; hence N^s and N^a refer to the variable N (number) but only cover the subgroups of those receiving the standard and tournament approach, respectively, while N^s (which, by the way, is not used here) would refer to the sth unit's value of N.

ity P_s whereas under tournaments the probability of success for each of the top N^a is 1. Finally, assume that a proportion e of the remaining $N^j - N^a$ jurisdictions in a tournament (that is, those who do not "win") exert sufficient effort so as to succeed while the rest do not succeed.

Under these assumptions the expected value of performance under the standard approach is $E(\Sigma I^{std}) = N^s P_s$ and under the tournament approach is

(1) $$E\left(\sum I^{trm}\right) = N^a + e\left(N^j - N^a\right) = \left(1 - e\right)N^a + eN^j.$$

Which approach generates higher performance and under what conditions? Under the above assumptions, the tournament is preferred if

(2) $$E\left(\sum I^{trm}\right) > E\left(\sum I^{std}\right) \text{ or } \left(1 - e\right)N^a + eN^j > N^s P_s.$$

Let us evaluate expression 2 for the case favorable to the standard approach, namely, that $N^s = N^a$, $P_s = 1$, and $e > 0$. Here $E(\Sigma I^{trm}) > E(\Sigma I^{std})$ if $e (N^j - N^a) > 0$. This always holds, so under these conditions (and assumptions), the tournament approach generates performance superior to that of the standard approach.

So what does it take for the standard approach to be preferred? To answer this one needs to return to the assumptions, three of which turn out to be particularly strong. The first concerns e, which could be quite small. While this does not affect our interpretation of expression 2, it will become an issue below. The second is whether and under what conditions $I^{trm} \approx I^{std}$, that is, "successful" jurisdictions have the same performance under both approaches. In other words, why should one expect tournament performers (I^{trm}) to be at the level of participants who receive full sponsor attention in the standard approach (I^{std})? Here, there are two situations.

The first situation is where the equal performance assumption is for the N^s and N^a. For these players, it is not obvious which approach would provide better performance. While it is true that the N^s have been specifically selected by the sponsor and then receive greater attention, the competition ensures that the N^a are the best performers of N^j jurisdictions. For these reasons the assumption that $I^{trm} = I^{std}$ is probably fair.

The second situation to consider is the assumption that the other $e (N^j - N^a)$ jurisdictions in the tournament (that is, those who do not win but still succeed) performed as well as the N^s chosen and directly helped by the sponsor under the standard approach. To examine the importance of this assumption, I will look at the case where the $e (N^j - N^a)$ jurisdictions in a tournament perform *worse* on average than the N^s in the standard approach.

For this purpose one needs to consider an alternative specification for the performance metric of nonwinners in a tournament. Assume that while all jurisdictions have roughly identical initial conditions, nonplacer performance is $I^n \le I^{std}$.[2] Expression 2, which states the condition for the tournament to be preferred, now becomes

$$(3) \ E\left(\sum_{i \le N^j} I_i^{trm}\right) = N^a I^{trm} + e\left(N^j - N^a\right)I^n > I^{std} N^s P_s = E\left[\sum_{h \le N^s} \left(I_h^{std}\right)\right],$$

where i and h are the respective indexes of summation. If, as above, one lets $I_i^{trm} = I_h^{std}$ for the $N^s = N^a$, then expression 3 becomes

$$(4) \qquad\qquad N^a\left(1 - P_s\right)I^{std} + e\left(N_j - N^a\right)I^n > 0,$$

and once again there are still no reasonable values of the variables or parameters that would cause expression 4 to be untrue.

This leads to the conclusion that the only way for the standard approach to achieve better performance is to drop the third strong assumption and allow $I^{trm} < I^{std}$ for (at least some of) the $N^s = N^a$. In particular, let $m \equiv I^{trm}/I^{std}$ and $k \equiv I^n/I^{std}$. Then, retaining the assumption that $N^s = N^a$, expression 3 becomes

$$(3') \quad E\left(\sum I^{trm}\right) = N^s m I^{std} + e\left(N^j - N^s\right)k I^{std} > I^{std} \ N^s P_s = E\left(\sum I^{std}\right),$$

which simplifies to the condition

$$(5) \qquad\qquad N^s\left(m - P_s\right) + ek\left(N^j - N^s\right) > 0,$$

or $$\qquad\qquad \left(P_s - m\right)\big/ek < \left(N^j/N^s\right) - 1.$$

To determine how likely it is for this inequality to fail and therefore lead the standard approach to have better performance, one can insert some reasonable parameter values into expression 5. In particular, plugging $N^s = N^a = 3$, $P_s = 1$, $e = 1/6$, $m = 3/4$, $k = 1/3$ and $N^j = 18$ into expression 5 yields

$$(6) \qquad\qquad \left[1 - (3/4)\right]\big/(1/6)(1/3) = 18/4 = 4.5 < (21/3) - 1 = 6.$$

While at first this appears to be a very close outcome, with tournaments only slightly edging out the standard approach, one should note that the parameter values selected were extremely favorable to the standard approach. For "fairness" one should also consider the *minimal* case favorable to tournament, namely that $m = 1$ (the rationale of which is presented above).[3] Inspection of expression 5

---

2. Presumably, I^n depends (via its influence on degree of effort) on the probability of winning and the size of the award. Separately, note that for simplicity I still assume that all tournament winners receive the same size award.

3. I should reiterate the point raised in the text regarding competition. If competition breaks down, say, due to the presence of either collusion or too few players, then the case for $m = 1$ becomes tenuous.

shows that in this case tournament performance always dominates the performance under the standard approach.

The Player's Side

Yet another set of assumptions to examine in the quest for the conditions under which the standard approach would do better than a tournament design relates to the player's behavioral response to a given set of rewards in a tournament. Recall that in a standard contract, sponsors commit to provide funds of $B^S = B/N^s$ with certainty to each recipient whereas an award in a tournament with N^j players and $N^a = N^s$ winners would need to be $B^T = B^S N^j/N^a$ to achieve the same expected value. However, I would argue that a tournament award of this size is neither realistic—it would require huge awards (since $N^j/N^a \gg 1$)—nor would it be necessary since smaller amounts would be sufficiently salient.

To see why, one must first consider what the purpose is of the sponsor's payment. Assume that the cost of implementing the tasks agreed between the sponsor and recipient is C and that the benefits *perceived by the recipient* are V.[4] One can divide the costs into input costs of C^I, transaction costs of C_d^{Tr} and C_j^{Tr} (reflecting the cost to the sponsor, d, and to the jurisdiction, j, of overcoming problems of trust, technical knowledge, and coordination), and compensation costs of C^C to those who lose from the project.[5] Likewise, one can divide the benefits into those from the reform, V^R; those pecuniary and in kind, V^P, as provided by the sponsor; and those that are reputational (fame or shame), V^F.[6] Assume that $V \geq B^S$; if this is not the case, then the sponsor should first engage in a public education campaign or, in the case of the standard approach, perhaps seek a different recipient.[7] Note that while C^C can be significant, it must be smaller than $V - V^P - C^I$, or the project should not be done.[8]

---

4. In fact, V^{std} may be larger than V^{trm} due to the risk premium. Also, for the present discussions, I ignore the possibility that the Vs might take on different valuations ex ante and ex post.

5. Examples of where compensation might be considered would be to importers after trade liberalization; laid off, redundant civil servants; ferry operators when a bridge is built; and so on. Note, too, that C^C would only need to be credibly promised, not borne, until after reforms were actually under way.

6. I would argue that there should always be a reputational benefit to winning a tournament, otherwise the latter was poorly designed.

7. This is less of a problem with the tournament since only those who perceive the net benefits will be stimulated to pursue the sponsor's proposed tasks. Of course, if there is a general lack of appreciation of the benefits of the sponsor's initiatives, more reform per tournament would be forthcoming if preceded by an education campaign.

8. Since by assumption a reform is not undertaken unless it generates net benefits, ideally there should be some institutional conveyance to ensure that some of the net benefits are redistributed as compensation to the losers. Thus the sponsor's compensation funds primarily serve to credibly signal that such compensation will occur.

There may be several non–mutually exclusive reasons why an award having an expected value smaller than the funding received in a standard contract might be sufficient to motivate tournament play.[9] These include the cases where the sponsor helps to cover:

1. input costs of the reform where there is either limited availability of public finance or capital market failure;

2. a bribe (award) or coordination device to overcome the transaction cost of collective action (and a signaling device that the central government is pre-committed);

3. the insurance (risk) premium against reform failure (that is, costs expended exceed materialized benefits), since jurisdictions and their officials and constituencies are more risk averse than the sponsor; and

4. a fund to compensate losers in the case where the net economic benefits to the initiative are positive (that is, compensation funds must not be a bribe to convince a reluctant population to voluntarily do something that would otherwise be against its will).

Note that this list does not include having the sponsor cover a gap between the expected costs and expected benefits. This is because a sponsor should never fund a project for which $E(V^R) < E(C)$. If the sponsor believes stakeholders place too little value on V^R given its own appreciation of benefits, then the sponsor should wage an education campaign before implementing the project.

I will now look at cases 1 through 4 in more detail. In the case 1, a jurisdiction has no way to finance actuarially profitable activities. Hence any tournament would have to be based on either past activities or performance in which pecuniary costs are small. In such a situation, the award size comparison between a tournament and a standard contract becomes academic: the award in each case is the same. The difference is that under the tournament the funds go to the jurisdiction that will use them most productively.[10] Finally, if due to case 1 the sponsor covers the same costs as under a standard contract, then the problems shown in cases 2 and 3 revert to those also faced under a standard contract and should not be seen as motivations for additional sponsor funding only under the tournament approach.

Next note that with $V^R > C$ and no capital market failure, if jurisdictions actually *want* the reforms, the assistance (or bribe) needed to initiate action should not

9. In what follows, I assume that the project activity is to undertake a reform though the reader should understand reform as representing whatever objective the project entails, for example, infrastructure creation.

10. In theory a loan, being more incentive compatible, would be better than a grant. However, debt limitations in local public finance law as well as the existence of weak institutions and high collection costs might lead sponsors to favor a grant.

have to cover the full project cost.[11] Here there are two general cases to consider. First, it is possible that the jurisdiction's stakeholders do not understand the need to overcome transaction costs or to compensate losers but only recognize the project input costs. In this case the appropriate sponsor response should be to provide education to get the players to acknowledge this source of costs. Otherwise, a sponsor might need to pay C_d^{Tr} or C^C or both, though by the preceding arguments (and footnote 8, in particular) both of these would be substantially smaller than B^S.

Second, if stakeholders appreciate the need to overcome transaction costs and to compensate losers, they may be individually or collectively risk averse. In this case the sponsor need only in theory provide insurance. Since this may be institutionally challenging, another alternative is for the sponsor to offer to pay the risk premium.[12] I would argue that if properly targeted, such a subsidy would still be much smaller than B^S.

A final reason as to why under a standard contract a sponsor may be offering more than required to get the reform implemented relates to asymmetric information. In particular, the recipient almost always has more idiosyncratic information about costs than does the sponsor. Letting O^b be the beneficiary's minimum acceptable offer from a sponsor and O^d be the donor's offer, this means that any $O^d < O^b$ will be rejected while any $O^d \geq O^b$ will be accepted. Hence, it is quite likely that negotiations could end at a point where $O^d > O^b$.[13] A separate argument that arrives at the same conclusion is that without competition there is no impetus for the recipient to implement tasks cost-effectively; in fact, without competition it is unlikely that the recipient even *knows* the tasks' true costs.

In summary, I have argued that there are really three "valid" considerations for setting the amount a sponsor needs to pay. The first is as a substitute source of funding (due to demand or supply-side "failures"). Here the amount to offer could reach C. Second, the sponsor could act as an outside coordinator or referee and thereby reduce or eliminate the C^T cost component. Without a funding constraint, it would still be "valid" for the sponsor to pay the risk premium.[14] Finally, the sponsor might be able to lower or even eliminate the amount required by precommitting to fund a national (and, if appropriate, international) public relations campaign to enhance the reputation of winners and—what is at least as important—to "shame" the reputation of jurisdictions at the lower end of the tournament ranking. (As discussed in the text, it is critical that all potential jurisdictions be aware that such a campaign will occur.)

---

11. In the standard contract approach, it is not unusual for the sponsor to want the reform more than the recipient.

12. This is an interesting option that I have not seen specifically treated in the literature.

13. Recall the old adage that if your offer is accepted in the bazaar, then you offered too much!

14. See Zinnes and Alevy (2005) on how to assess risk aversion experimentally.

Before the issue is examined from the sponsor's side, some additional remarks are in order. First, note that in case 2, while by assumption $V > C$, it is possible that $C^{\mathrm{I}} < V^{\mathrm{R}} < C$, that is, that both reputational benefits and transaction costs are substantial. This insight is critical from a design perspective since it implies that it is "cheaper" for the sponsor than for the jurisdictions to reduce transaction costs (sponsors have the attention and trust of all parties) and to increase reputational benefits (sponsors enjoy economies of scale and can design the tournament around socioeconomic and cultural features that increase the reputational benefits of winning). Second and for completeness, note that the expected value of the game to jurisdiction i is approximately

$$(7) \quad \mathrm{E}[V - C] \approx \left[\left(N^{\mathrm{a}} / N^{\mathrm{j}} \right) \left(V^{\mathrm{P}} + V^{\mathrm{F}} \right) + e V^{\mathrm{R}} \right] - \left[C^{\mathrm{I}} + C^{\mathrm{C}} + C_{\mathrm{j}}^{\mathrm{Tr}} + Q \right],$$

where Q is the risk premium, costs are assumed the same for successful and unsuccessful players, and where one assumes that the expected value of the reputational impact for nonwinners is zero.[15] Finally, it now should be clear that what and how much the sponsor should pay cannot be determined without empirical investigation (calibration), such as through the use of mini-surveys, field pilots, or "lab" experiments.

The Sponsor's Side

So, from the sponsor's side, does a tournament leverage funds, that is, provide more reform for less money than the standard approach, given a sponsor's budget of B? To answer this, one first needs to look at the sponsor's cost side and pin down a metric for comparisons.

Let the sponsor's own operational costs of the standard and tournament approaches be $C^{\mathrm{opS}}(N^{\mathrm{s}}) > 0$ and $C^{\mathrm{opT}}(N^{\mathrm{a}}) > 0$, respectively, where $dC^{\mathrm{opS}}/dN^{\mathrm{s}} = c$, a constant, and $dC^{\mathrm{opT}}/dN^{\mathrm{a}} \approx 0$. "Operational costs" refer to all the costs up until project implementation—primarily project design and preparation. Project implementation costs—which were denoted by B, above—would then cover technical assistance, materials and infrastructure, rewards, M&E, as well as C^{I}, C^{C}, and Q. (For simplicity, I assume below that $C_{\mathrm{j}}^{\mathrm{Tr}} > 0$ but $C_{\mathrm{d}}^{\mathrm{Tr}} \approx 0$). Hence the total cost *to the sponsor* of the tournament and the standard approach is $B^{\mathrm{trm}} = B + C^{\mathrm{opT}}$ and $B^{\mathrm{std}} = B + C^{\mathrm{opS}}$, respectively.

Which is bigger, $C^{\mathrm{opS}}(N^{\mathrm{s}})$ or $C^{\mathrm{opT}}(N^{\mathrm{a}})$? The assumptions regarding the functions' derivatives above imply that there is a size, N^*, above (below) which

---

15. This would be the case if the value of being ranked R places below the median nonwinner is the negative of being ranked R places above the median nonwinner. Note that one of the reasons that this is an approximation is that the value of the technical assistance, except as it generates reform benefits, is missing.

$C^{\text{opS}}(N^s)$ is larger (smaller) than $C^{\text{opT}}(N^a)$. This reflects the inherent economies of tournaments—which may not be true for implementation, a later step (that by definition is not included in operational costs).

To determine whether tournaments leverage project funds, one needs to compare performance per unit cost of a tournament, L^{trm}, against that of the standard approach, L^{std}:

(8) $$L^{\text{trm}} \equiv \left[\text{E}\left(\sum I^{\text{trm}}\right)\right]\!\Big/ B^{\text{trm}} > \left[\text{E}\left(\sum I^{\text{std}}\right)\right]\!\Big/ B^{\text{std}} \equiv L^{\text{std}},$$

or

(9) $$L^{\text{trm}} = \left[N^a m I^{\text{std}} + e\left(N^j - N^a\right) k I^{\text{std}}\right]\!\Big/\!\left(B + C^{\text{opT}}\right) > [I^{\text{std}} N^a P_s]\!\Big/\!\left(B + C^{\text{opS}}\right)$$
$$= L^{\text{std}}.^{16}$$

The problem here is that one needs to know how big N^a would be in a tournament whose implementation budget is $B \equiv N^s B^s$. From equation 7 one can see that the unit implementation costs for a tournament versus a standard approach are $C^{\text{imT}} = C^I + C^C + Q$ and $C^{\text{imS}} = C^I + C^C$, respectively. Hence the total implementation cost for N^s and N^a is

(10a) $$N^a C^{\text{imT}} = N^a \left(C^I + C^C + Q\right)$$

(10b) $$N^s C^{\text{imS}} = N^s \left(C^I + C^C\right).$$

The total cost then combines the operational and implementation components:

(11a) $$C^T = C^{\text{imT}} + C^{\text{opT}} = N^a \left(C^I + C^C + Q\right) + C^{\text{opT}}\left(N^a\right)$$

(11b) $$C^S = C^{\text{imS}} + C^{\text{opS}} = N^s \left(C^I + C^C\right) + C^{\text{opS}}\left(N^s\right).$$

Hence, if $N^a = N^s$, then $C^T > C^S$ if

(12) $$N^s Q > C^{\text{opS}}\left(N^s\right) - C^{\text{opT}}\left(N^s\right).$$

This expression clearly holds if $N^s \leq N^*$. Let $N^C(N^s)$ be the function indicating the point where $C^T[N^C(N^s)] = C^S[N^C(N^s)]$, that is, the number of awards in the tournament for which the total cost is just equal to that of the total cost of standard contracts negotiated with N^s jurisdictions. Note that $N^C(N^s) > N^*$.

16. Note that alternative metrics would be $[\text{E}(\sum I^{\text{trm}})]/N^a$ and $[\text{E}(\sum I^{\text{std}})]/N^s$ or even $[\text{E}(\sum I)]/N$.

Next, one can use equation 5 to also find the function $N^P(N^j,P_s,m,k,e)$, indicating the point where the number of awards in the tournament is such that the total performance of the standard and tournament approaches is the same. This occurs at

(13) $$N^P\left(N^j,P_s,m,k,e\right) = N^j \big/ \left\{\left[(P_s - m)\big/ek\right]+1\right\}.$$

By applying the parameter values used to evaluate equation 5, one can see that equation 13 does not place constraints on N^P for an approach to be preferred other than the definitional limits of $0 \le N^P \le N^j$.

The conclusions of equations 12 and 13 lead to six nonoverlapping zones for N^s, as summarized in table D-1 and illustrated in figure D-1. *In theory* there are two unambiguous sets of conditions (zones 1 and 4) where the contract (standard) approach is both a better performer *and* less expensive than the tournament approach, and two unambiguous sets of conditions (zones 3 and 6) where the opposite is true, namely, that the tournament approach is both a better performer *and* less expensive than the contract approach. Hence even the favorable conditions identified in equation 5, where the standard approach was preferred from the performance side, are now potentially inconclusive, since for some cost conditions (zone 5) the standard approach would be more expensive than the tournament approach.

Table D-1. *Conditions for an Approach to be Preferred, Given $N^a = N^s$*

	Relative size of cost and performance critical conditions	
	$N^C < N^P$ ($N^P = N_1^P$ *in figure D-1*)	$N^C > N^P$ ($N^P = N_2^P$ *in figure D-1*)
	Zone 1: $N^s < N^C < N^P$ $\Rightarrow I^{std} > I^{trm}$, $C^{std} < C^{trm}$ $\Rightarrow$ Contract preferred	Zone 4: $N^s < N^P < N^C$ $\Rightarrow I^{std} > I^{trm}$, $C^{std} < C^{trm}$ $\Rightarrow$ Contract preferred
Relative position of N^s	Zone 2: $N^C < N^s < N^P$ $\Rightarrow I^{std} > I^{trm}$, $C^{std} > C^{trm}$ $\Rightarrow$ Inconclusive	Zone 5: $N^P < N^s < N^C$ $\Rightarrow I^{std} < I^{trm}$, $C^{std} < C^{trm}$ $\Rightarrow$ Inconclusive
	Zone 3: $N^C < N^P < N^s$ $\Rightarrow I^{std} < I^{trm}$, $C^{std} > C^{trm}$ $\Rightarrow$ Tournament preferred	Zone 6: $N^P < N^C < N^s$ $\Rightarrow I^{std} < I^{trm}$, $C^{std} > C^{trm}$ $\Rightarrow$ Tournament preferred

Source: Author's calculations.

Figure D-1. *Derivation of When Tournaments Are Preferred to the Standard Contract*

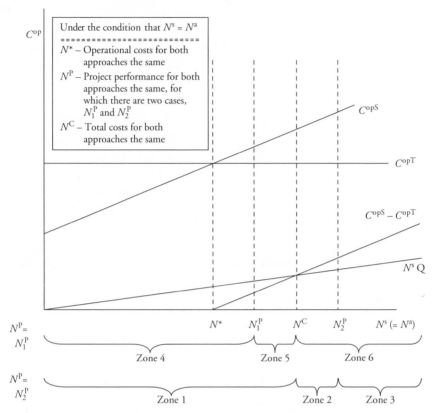

Source: Author's calculations.

References

ACIG International. 2003. "Final Report for Enhancing Municipal Service Delivery Capability (Phase II)." TA 5959 REG. Manila: Asian Development Bank.

Afonso, José R., and Sérgio Guimarães. 2008. "Commentary on Clifford Zinnes, 'Increasing the Effectiveness of Public Service Delivery: A Tournament Approach.'" In *Fiscal Decentralization and Land Policies,* edited by Gregory K. Ingram and Yu-Hung Hong, pp. 395–397. Cambridge, Mass.: Lincoln Institute of Land Policy.

Afsah, Shakeb, and Jeffrey R. Vincent. 1997. "Putting Pressure on Polluters: Indonesia's PROPER Program." Case study. Harvard Institute for International Development (March).

Ahmad, Junaid, and others. 2005. "Decentralization and Service Delivery." Policy Research Working Paper 3603. Washington: World Bank (May).

Alesina, Alberto, and David Dollar. 2000. "Who Gives Aid to Whom and Why?" *Journal of Economic Growth* 5, no. 1: 33–63.

Alevy, Jonathan E., and Clifford Zinnes. 2004. "Survey Methods for Eliciting Confidential Information with an Application to the Informal Sector in Mongolia." Paper presented at the 2005 Public Choice Society Meetings. New Orleans, March 18–20.

_____. 2005. *The Size and Character of the Informal Sector and Its Shadow Economy in Mongolia.* Ulanbaator, Mongolia: Mongolian Open Society Foundation.

ARD, Inc. 2004. *Rating System and Analysis of Pilot Application in Municipalities and Mancomunidades. Final Report for Transition Year Technical Assistance for Municipal Development in Honduras (II).* Burlington, Vt.

Arndt, Christiane, and Charles Oman. 2006. *Uses and Abuses of Governance Indicators.* Paris: OECD.

Azfar, Omar. 2003. "Introduction to the New Institutional Economics." IRIS Forums Discussion Paper F1-1. College Park, Md.: Center for Institutional Reform and the Informal Sector.

Azfar, Omar, and Clifford Zinnes. 2003. "Improving the Effectiveness of Technical Assistance through the Use of Prospective Evaluation Procedures." Forum Series on the Role of Institutions in Promoting Growth. Task Order 7, SEGIR/LIR PCE-I-00-97-00042-00. USAID (February).

347

_____. 2005. "Which Incentives Work? An Experimental Analysis of Incentives for Trainers." IRIS Discussion Paper 05-01. College Park, Md.: Center for Institutional Reform and the Informal Sector.

Bahl, Roy, and Johannes Linn. 1992. *Urban Public Finance in Developing Countries.* Oxford University Press.

Barder, Owen, and Nancy Birdsall. 2006. "Payments for Progress: A Hands-Off Approach to Foreign Aid." Working Paper 102. Washington: Center for Global Development.

Bertrand, Marianne, Esther Duflo, and Sendhil Mullainathan. 2004. "How Much Should We Trust Differences-in-Differences Estimates?" *Quarterly Journal of Economics* 119, no.1: 249–75.

Bhatnagar, Subhash, and Arsala Deane. 2004. "Building Blocks of e-Government: Lessons from Developing Countries." *PREMnotes* (World Bank newsletter), no. 91 (August).

Blackman, Alan, Shakeb Afsah, and Damayanti Ratunanda. 2004. "How Do Public Disclosure Pollution Control Programs Work? Evidence from Indonesia." *Human Ecology Review* 11, no. 3: 235–46.

Boone, Peter, and Jean-Paul Faguet. 2002. "Multilateral Aid, Politics, and Poverty." In *The Global Crisis in Foreign Aid,* edited by Richard Grant and Jan Nijman, chap. 2. Syracuse University Press.

Brinkerhoff, Derek W. 2002. *Managing Policy Reforms: Concepts and Tools for Decision-Makers in Developing and Transitioning Countries.* Sterling, Va.: Kumarian Press.

Brook, Penelope, and Murray Petrie. 2001. "Output-Based Aid: Precedents, Promises and Challenges." In *Contracting for Public Services: Output-Based Aid and Its Applications,* edited by Penelope Brook and Suzanne Smith, pp. 3–11. Washington: World Bank.

Cadwell, Charles. 2005. "Bangladesh Local Government Accountability Project Protecting the Rights of Persons Vulnerable to Trafficking." Grant proposal to the U.S. Department of State, Bureau of Democracy, Human Rights, and Labor (March 22).

Candidature Acceptance Working Group. 2006. *XXII Olympic Winter Games in 2014.* Lausanne, Switzerland: International Olympic Committee.

Center for Democracy and Governance (CDG). 1998. *Handbook of Democracy and Governance Program Indicators.* Technical Publications Series PN-ACC-390. USAID.

Center for Institutional Reform and the Informal Sector (IRIS). 2005. "Local Governance and the Business Environment in Morocco: Harnessing the Power of Incentives." Grant proposal to the U.S. Department of State, Middle East Partnership Initiative (January).

Chang, Hai-Chiao, and others. 2005. "Managed Competition in Indianapolis: The Case of Indianapolis Fleet Services." Columbia University, School of International and Public Affairs.

Clapp-Wincek, Cynthia, and Richard Blue. 2001. "Evaluation of Recent USAID Evaluation Experience." Working Paper 320. USAID, Center for Development Information and Evaluation (June).

Clement, Cindy, and Albie Ashbrook. 2001. "A Local Government Competition to Improve the Business Environment in Romanian Counties." Mimeo. USAID.

Collier, Paul. 2002. "Making Aid Smart: Institutional Incentives Facing Donor Organizations and their Implications for Aid Effectiveness." IRIS Institutions and Development Discussion Paper 02-08. College Park, Md.: Center for Institutional Reform and the Informal Sector.

Collier, Paul, and others. 1997. "Redesigning Conditionality." *World Development* 25, no. 9: 1399–1407.

Cook, Thomas D., and Monique R. Payne. 2001. "Objecting to the Objections to Using Random Assignment in Educational Research." In *Evidence Matters,* edited by Frederick Mosteller and Robert Boruch, pp.150–78. Brookings.

Cowen, Tyler. 2007. *Discover Your Inner Economist: Use Incentives to Fall in Love, Survive Your Next Meeting, and Motivate Your Dentist.* London: Dutton Adult.

Crampes, Claude, and Antonio Estache. 1996. "Regulating Water Concessions: Lessons from the Buenos Aires Concession." *Public Policy for the Private Sector* (World Bank newsletter), note 91 (September).

Dasgupta, Partha, and Ismail Serageldin, eds. 2000. *Social Capital: A Multifaceted Perspective.* Washington: World Bank.

Dollar, David, and others. 2004. *Improving City Competitiveness through the Investment Climate: Ranking 23 Chinese Cities.* Beijing: China Finance and Economics Publishing House.

Drees, Franz, Jordan Schwartz, and Alexander Bakalian. 2004. "Output-Based Aid in Water: Lessons in Implementation from a Pilot in Paraguay." *Public Policy for the Private Sector* (World Bank newsletter), note 270 (April).

Druchel, Kate, Malcolm Russell-Einhorn, and Clifford Zinnes. 2005. "Democracy, Human Rights, and the Rule of Law in the People's Republic of China." Grant proposal solicitation (State-GRANTS-010405-001). U.S. Department of State, Bureau of Democracy, Human Rights, and Labor.

Duflo, Esther. 2003. "Scaling Up and Evaluation." Paper prepared for the World Bank Annual Conference on Development Economics (ABCDE). Bangalore, India, May 21–22.

———. 2005. "Field Experiments in Development Economics." Mimeo. MIT, Department of Economics and Abdul Latif Jameel Poverty Action Lab (December).

Duflo, Esther, and Michael Kremer. 2005. "Use of Randomization in the Evaluation of Development Effectiveness." In *Evaluating Development Effectiveness: World Bank Series on Evaluation and Development,* vol. 7, edited by George K. Pitman, Osvaldo N. Feinstein, and Gregory K. Ingram, pp. 205–32. New Brunswick, N.J.: Transaction Publishers.

Easterly, William. 2006a. "The Big Push Déjà Vu: A Review of Jeffrey Sachs's *The End of Poverty: Economic Possibilities for Our Time.*" *Journal of Economic Literature* 44, no. 1: 118–27.

———. 2006b. *The White Man's Burden: Why the West's Efforts to Aid the Rest Have Done So Much Ill and So Little Good.* London: Penguin Press.

EdInvest. n.d. *Public-Private Partnership Toolkit.* CD-ROM. Washington: International Finance Corporation.

Esmail, Talib, and others. 2004. "Bottom-Up Administrative Reform: Designing Indicators for a Local Governance Scorecard in Nigeria." Africa Region Working Paper 68. Washington: World Bank (June).

Espina, Carlos, and Clifford Zinnes. 2003. "Institutional Incentives within USAID: How Do They Affect Project Outcomes?" IRIS Forums Discussion Paper F5-1. College Park, Md.: Center for Institutional Reform and the Informal Sector.

European Bank for Reconstruction and Development. Various years. *Transition Report.* London.

Faguet, Jean-Paul. 2000. "Does Decentralization Increase Government Responsiveness to Local Needs? Decentralization and Public Investment in Bolivia." Discussion Paper 999. London: Center for Economic Performance (January).

Fielding Smith, James. 1999. "The Benefits and Threats of PBB: An Assessment of Modern Reform." *Public Budgeting and Finance* 19, no. 3: 3–15.

Foundation for Environmental Education. 2006. *The Blue Flag: Eco-Label for Beaches and Marinas.* Copenhagen.

Fox, Tom, and Bill Vorley. 2004. "Stakeholder Accountability in the UK Supermarket Sector." Final report of the Race to the Top project. London: International Institute for Environment and Development.

Frey, Bruno, and Reiner Eichenberger. 1999. *The New Democratic Federalism for Europe: Functional Overlapping and Competing Jurisdictions.* Northampton, Mass.: Edward Elgar.

Furubotn, Erik, and Rudolf Richter 1999. *Institutions and Economic Theory: The Contribution of the New Institutional Economics.* University of Michigan Press.

Galing Pook Foundation. 2005. *Gawad Galing Pook 2005: A Tribute to Innovation and Excellence in Local Governance.* Quezon City, Philippines.

Gariba, Sulley. 2005. "Trends in the Evaluation of Efforts to Reduce Poverty." In *Evaluating Development Effectiveness: World Bank Series on Evaluation and Development,* vol. 7, edited by George K. Pitman, Osvaldo N. Feinstein, and Gregory K. Ingram, pp. 331–35. New Brunswick, N.J.: Transaction Publishers.

General Accounting Office (GAO). 1996. "Foreign Assistance: Status of USAID's Reforms." NSIAD-96-241BR (September).

Glewwe, Paul, Nauman Ilias, and Michael Kremer. 2003. "Teacher Incentives." Mimeo. Harvard University, Department of Economics.

Government Accountability Office. 2005. "D.C. Charter Schools: Strengthening Monitoring and Process When Schools Close Could Improve Accountability and Ease Student Transitions." GAO-06-73 (November).

Green, Jerry R., and Nancy L. Stokey. 1983. "A Comparison of Tournaments and Contracts." *Journal of Political Economy* 91, no. 3: 349–64.

Greenberg, David H., and Mark Shroder. 2004. *The Digest of Social Experiments.* 3d ed. Washington: Urban Institute.

Greene, Katrina. 1999. "Narrative Summary of FY97. Evaluations." USAID, Research and Reference Services (January).

Grootaert, Christiaan, and Thierry van Bastelaer, eds. 2002. *The Role of Social Capital in Development.* Cambridge University Press.

Harford, Tim, and Michael Klein. 2005a. "Aid and the Resource Curse." *Public Policy for the Private Sector* (World Bank newsletter), no. 291 (April).

_____. 2005b. "The Market for Aid." *Public Policy for the Private Sector* (World Bank newsletter), no. 293 (April).

Hartmann, Arntraud, and Johannes Linn. 2008. "An Assessment and Prognosis for Scaling Up Projects: A Review of Experience and Recommendations for the Future." Brookings Institution, Wolfensohn Center for International Development.

Hepburn, Claudia R., and Robert Van Belle. 2003. "The Canadian Education Freedom Index." Studies in Education Policy. Vancouver, Canada: Frasier Institute.

Kagel, John H., and Alvin E. Roth, eds. 1995. *The Handbook of Experimental Economics.* Princeton University Press.

Kanbur, Ravi. 2001. "Economic Policy, Distribution and Poverty: The Nature of the Disagreements." *World Development* 29, no. 6: 1083–94.

Kecamatan Development Program (KDP). 2005. "Kecamatan Development Program: Information Package 2005." Jakarta: Government of Indonesia, Ministry of Home Affairs (October).

Klitgaard, Robert, Ronald MacLean-Abaroa, and H. Lindsay Parris. 1998. "A Practical Approach to Dealing with Municipal Malfeasance." Paper presented at the Mediterranean Development Forum Workshop. Marrakech, September 3–6.

Knack, Steve, Mark Kugler, and Nick Manning. 2001. "Second-Generation Indicators." Preliminary report. London: U.K. Department of International Development (August).

Kremer, Michael. 2003. "Institutions, Aid and Development Assistance." IRIS Institutions and Development Discussion Paper 03-6. College Park, Md.: Center for Institutional Reform and the Informal Sector.

Kusek, Jody, and Ray Rist. 2004. "Assessing Country Readiness for Results-Based Monitoring and Evaluation Systems." *PREMnotes* (World Bank newsletter), no. 87 (June).

Ladner, Matthew, and Matthew J. Brouillette. 2000. "The Impact of Limited School Choice on Public School Districts." Midland, Michigan: Mackinac Center for Public Policy.

Laffont, Jean- Jacques, and Jean Tirole. 1993. *A Theory of Incentives in Procurement and Regulation.* MIT Press.

Lazear, Edward, and Steve Rosen. 1981. "Rank-Order Tournaments as Optimum Labor Contracts." *Journal of Political Economy* 89, no. 5: 841–64.

Makarim, Nabiel. 2006. "Implementing Effective Public Disclosure Programs for Environmental Management." Mimeo. Jakarta: Good Environmental Governance Program (May).

Malesky, Edmund. 2005. "The Provincial Competitiveness Index on the Business Environment in Vietnam." Mimeo. USAID, Vietnam Competitiveness Initiative.

Martens, Bertin. 2005. "Why Do Aid Agencies Exist?" *Development Policy Review* 23, no. 6: 643–63.

Martens, Bertin, and others. 2002. *The Institutional Economics of Foreign Aid.* Cambridge University Press.

Martinez-Vazquez, Jorge, and Jameson Boex. 1999. "Fiscal Decentralization in the Russian Federation during Transition." International Studies Program Working Paper 99-3. Georgia State University, Andrew Young School of Policy Studies.

Meagher, Patrick, and Clifford Zinnes. 2004. "The Use of Inter-Jurisdictional Competition to Strengthen the Investment Climate: A Field Guide and Application to Morocco." Final report for the UNIDO Investment Promotion Office. College Park, Md.: Center for Institutional Reform and the Informal Sector.

Mendel, Toby. 2004. "Legislation on Freedom of Information: Trends and Standards." *PREMnotes* (World Bank newsletter), no. 93 (October).

Millennium Challenge Corporation (MCC). 2005. "Impact Evaluation Services Request for Proposal." Solicitation MCC-05-RFP-0029.

————. 2006. *Budget Justification, 2007.*

Mookherjee, Dilip. 2006. "Decentralization, Hierarchies, and Incentives: A Mechanism Design Perspective." *Journal of Economic Literature* 44, no. 2: 367–90.

Moynihan, Donald P. 2003. "Performance-Based Budgeting: Beyond Rhetoric." *PREMnotes* (World Bank newsletter), no. 78 (February).

Murphy, Kevin, Andrei Shleifer, and Robert W. Vishny. 1989. "Industrialization and the Big Push." *Journal of Political Economy* 97, no. 5: 1003–26.

Murrell, Peter. 2002. "The Interaction of Donors, Contractors, and Recipients in Implementing Aid for Institutional Reform." In *The Institutional Economics of Foreign Aid,* edited by Bertin Martens, Uwe Mummert, and Peter Murrell, pp. 69–111. Cambridge University Press.

Nalebuff, Barry J., and Joseph E. Stiglitz. 1983. "Prizes and Incentives: Towards a General Theory of Compensation and Competition." *Bell Journal of Economics* 14, no. 1: 21–43.

Narayan, Deepa. 2002. "Applying Empowerment Principles." *Empowerment and Poverty Reduction: A Sourcebook.* Washington: World Bank.

Niskanen, William A. 1971. *Bureaucracy and Representative Government.* Chicago: Aldine-Atherton.

Nordtveit, Bjorn H. 2004a. "Managing Public-Private Partnership: Literacy Education in Senegal." Africa Region Human Development Working Paper 72. Washington: World Bank.

————. 2004b. "When Governments Get Creative: Adult Literacy in Senegal." Education Notes policy brief. Washington: World Bank (July).

————. 2005. "The Role of Civil Society Organizations in Developing Countries: A Case Study of Public-Private Partnerships in Senegal." PhD dissertation. University of Maryland, Department of Education Policy and Leadership.

————. 2008. "Producing Literacy and Civil Society: The Case of Senegal." *Comparative Education Review* 52, no. 2: 175–98.

Oates, Wallace E. 2002. "Fiscal and Regulatory Competition: Theory and Evidence." *Perspektiven der Wirtschaftspolitik* 3, no. 4: 377–90.

Olson, Mancur. 1965. *The Logic of Collective Action.* Harvard University Press.

O'Reilly, Robert, and Lynn Bosetti. 2000. "Charter Schools: The Search for Community." *Peabody Journal of Education* 75, no. 4: 19–36.

Organization for Economic Cooperation and Development (OECD). 1999. "Performance Contracting: Lessons from Performance Contracting Case Studies and a Framework for Public Sector Performance Contracting." PUMA/PAC (99)2. Paris.

————. 2004. "Public Sector Modernization: Governing for Performance." Policy brief (October).

Ostrom, Elinor. 2000. "Collective Action and the Evolution of Social Norms." *Journal of Economic Perspectives* 14, no. 3: 137–58.

Ostrom, Elinor, and others. 2002. *Aid, Incentives, and Sustainability: An Institutional Analysis of Development Cooperation.* Stockholm: Swedish International Development Cooperation Agency.

Picciotto, Robert. 2005. "Use of Evaluation Findings to Improve Development Effectiveness." In *Evaluating Development Effectiveness: World Bank Series on Evaluation and Development,* vol. 7, edited by George K. Pitman, Osvaldo N. Feinstein, and Gregory K. Ingram, pp. 347–54. New Brunswick, N.J.: Transaction Publishers.

Platteau, Jean-Philippe. 2005. "Institutional and Distributional Aspects of Sustainability in Community-Driven Development." In *Evaluating Development Effectiveness: World Bank Series on Evaluation and Development,* vol. 7, edited by George K. Pitman, Osvaldo N. Feinstein, and Gregory K. Ingram, pp. 275–98. New Brunswick, N.J.: Transaction Publishers.

Polishchuk, Leonid, and Ann Brown 2002. "Grants Manual: Improvement of Economic Policy through Think-Tanks Partnership Projects." Mimeo. USAID, Regional Think-Tank Partnership Program.

Pritchett, Lance. 2002. "It Pays to Be Ignorant: A Simple Political Economy of Rigorous Program Evaluation." *Journal of Policy Reform* 5, no. 4: 251–69.

Public Affairs Foundation (PAF). 2004. "Benchmarking Public Service Delivery at the Forest Fringes in Jharkhand, India: A Pilot Citizen Report Card." Discussion paper. Bangalore (October).

Sachs, Jeffrey D. 2005. *The End of Poverty: Economic Possibilities for Our Time.* New York: Penguin Press.

Shah, Anwar. 1997. "Balance, Accountability, and Responsiveness: Lessons about Decentralization." Paper prepared for the World Bank Conference on Evaluation and Development. Washington, April 1–2.

Shleifer, Andrei. 1985. "A Theory of Yardstick Competition." *Rand Journal of Economics* 16, no. 3: 319–27.

Smith, W. 2001. "Designing Output-Based Aid Schemes: A Checklist." In *Contracting for Public Services: Output-Based Aid and Its Applications,* edited by Penelope Brook and Suzanne Smith, pp. 91–117. Washington: World Bank.

Smoke, Paul. 2008. "Local Revenues under Fiscal Decentralization in Developing Countries: Linking Policy Reform, Governance and Capacity." In *Fiscal Decentralization and Land Policies,* edited by Yu-Hung Hong and Gregory K. Ingram, pp. 38–68. Cambridge, Mass.: Lincoln Institute of Land Policy.

Steffensen, Jesper. 2007. "Performance Based Grant Systems: Using Grants as Incentives— Concept and Lessons Learned." PowerPoint presentation. Taastrup, Denmark: Nordic Consulting Group (May).

Svensson, Jakob. 2003. "Why Conditional Aid Does Not Work and What Can Be Done about It?" *Journal of Development Economics* 70, no. 2: 381–402.

Terfa, Inc. 2005a. *Final Report of Rural Local Governments Scorecard Assessment Report,* vol. 1. Report for the World Bank. Ontario (October).

_____. 2005b. *Final Report of Rural Local Governments Scorecard Assessment Report,* vol. 2. Report for the World Bank. Ontario (October).

Thampi, Gopakumar. 2007. "Holding a Mirror to the Government: Experience with Citizen Report Cards." PowerPoint presentation. Bangalore: Public Affairs Foundation.

Thiel, Markus. 2004. "The Conditionality of US and EU Development Aid upon Democratization: A Comparison." *E-Working Papers* 2, no. 1: 1–22.

Tiebout, Charles. 1956. "A Pure Theory of Local Expenditures." *Journal of Political Economy* 64, no. 5 (October): 416–26.

Tietenberg, Thomas. 2000. "Disclosure Strategies for Pollution Control." In *The Market and the Environment,* edited by Thomas Sterner, pp. 14–49. Northampton, Mass.: Edward Elgar Press.

U.S. Agency for International Development (USAID). 2005. "Fragile States Strategy." PD-ACA-999 (January).

_____. 2006. "Support to Democratic Systems and Governance in a Changing Environment in Bolivia." RFTOP 511-06-029 (July).

Watkins, Sharon. 2004. "Senegal: Education Pilot in Support of Female Literacy." *Findings Infobrief: Africa Region* (World Bank newsletter), no. 99 (April).

Weingast, Barry. 1995. "The Economic Role of Political Institutions: Market-Preserving Federalism and Economic Development." *Journal of Law, Economics, and Organization* 11, no.1: 1–31.

Williams, Adley and Company. 2002. "Report on Agreed-Upon Procedures Related to Performance Monitoring for Indicators Appearing in the FY2003 Results Review and Resource Request Report for Selected Missions." Report 9-000-02-001-S. USAID (July).

Williams, Vera, and Inna Kushnarova. 2004. "The Public Sector Governance Reform Cycle: Available Diagnostic Tools." *PREMnotes* (World Bank newsletter), no. 88 (July).

Williamson, Oliver. 1975. *Markets and Hierarchies: Analysis and Antitrust Implications.* New York: Free Press.

_____. 2003. "Institutions and Development." IRIS Forums Discussion Paper F1-3. College Park, Md.: Center for Institutional Reform and the Informal Sector.

Wood, Robert C., and Gary Hamel. 2002. "The World Bank's Innovation Market." *Harvard Business Review,* November, pp. 104–12.

World Bank. 1998. *Assessing Aid: What Works, What Doesn't, and Why.* Oxford University Press.

_____. 2001a. "Comprehensive Development Framework: Meeting the Promise? Early Experience and Emerging Issues." Washington (September).

_____. 2001b. "Report and Recommendation of the President of the International Bank for Reconstruction and Development to the Executive Directors on a Fiscal Federalism and Regional Fiscal Reform Loan in the Amount of $US120 Million to the Russian Federation." Report P7504-RU. Washington (December).

_____. 2001c. *World Development Report 2000/2001: Attacking Poverty.* Oxford University Press.

_____. 2002. "State and Local Government in Nigeria." Report 24477-UNI. Washington (July).

_____. 2005a. "Social Accountability in Development Policy Lending." *Social Accountability: Strengthening the Demand Side of Governance and Service Delivery.* CD-ROM. Washington.

_____. 2005b. *The World Development Report 2004: Making Services Work for Poor People.* Oxford University Press.

_____. 2006a. "Implementation Completion Report on a Loan in the Amount of US$120 Million to the Russian Federation for a Fiscal Federalism and Regional Fiscal Reform Project." Report 34693. Poverty Reduction and Economic Management Network, Europe and Central Asia Region. Washington (January).

_____. 2006b. "Report and Recommendation of the President of the International Bank for Reconstruction and Development to the Executive Directors on a Fiscal Federalism and Regional Fiscal Reform Loan in the Amount of $US120 Million to the Russian Federation." Report P7504-RU. Washington (July).

_____. 2006c. "Stengthening the Performance of International Financial Institutions." In *Global Monitoring Report 2006,* chap. 4. Washington.

_____. Various years. *Doing Business.* Oxford University Press.

World Economic Forum. Various years. *Global Competitiveness Report.* Geneva.

Young, Peyton. 1998. *Individual Strategy and Social Structure: An Evolutionary Theory of Institutions.* Princeton University Press.

Zinnes, Clifford. 2004. "Implementing a Formal Inter-Jurisdictional Competition to Improve Governance: An Application to Morocco." Paper presented to the Middle East and North Africa Economics Associations, annual meeting of the Allied Social Science Association. San Diego, Calif., January.

_____. 2006. "Harnessing Inter-Jurisdictional Competition to Increase Donor Effectiveness." Paper presented at Wolfensohn Center seminar. Washington, January 11.

Zinnes, Clifford, and Jonathan Alevy. 2005. "IRIS Center Proposal in Response to the MCC's 'Impact Evaluation Services Request for Proposal.'" Solicitation MCC-05-RFP-0029. College Park, Md.: Center for Institutional Reform and the Informal Sector.

Zinnes, Clifford, and Aruna Bolaky. 2002. "Harnessing the Power of Incentives: An NIE Framework for Increasing Aid Effectiveness." Task Order 7, SEGIR/LIR PCE-I-00-97-00042-00. USAID (February).

Zinnes, Clifford, Yair Eilat, and Jeffrey Sachs. 2001. "Benchmarking International Competitiveness in Transition Economies." *Economics of Transition* 9, no. 2: 315–53.

Zinnes, Clifford, Jim Hansen, and Ray Miller. 2005. "Harnessing Local Initiatives to Stimulate the Growth of Free-Market Agriculture in Uzbekistan." Proposal submitted to the Foreign Advisory Service of the U.S. Department of Agriculture. University of Maryland College of Agriculture and Natural Resources and the IRIS Center (February).

Zinnes, Clifford, Patrick Meagher, and Stefano Giovannelli. 2006. "Come promuovere cambiamenti istituzionali a livello locale." In *Le Nazioni Unite e lo sviluppo industriale,* edited by Marco Di Tommaso and Stefano Giovannelli, pp. 269–91. Milan: Franco Angeli.

Index